DRUGS
IN SOCIETY
Causes, Concepts and Control

Michael D. Lyman
Columbia College

Gary W. Potter
Eastern Kentucky University

anderson publishing co.
2035 reading road
cincinnati, ohio 45202
(513) 421-4142

since 1887

DRUGS IN SOCIETY
Causes, Concepts and Control

Copyright © 1991 by Anderson Publishing Co., Cincinnati, OH

ISBN 0-87084-548-9
Library of Congress Catalog Number 90-84732

Kelly Humble *Managing Editor*

Cover Design by John H. Walker

FOREWORD

The literature of drugs and crime control is considerable and expanding in near quantum fashion since the senseless, highly publicized drug-related deaths of John Belushi, Len Bias, and Don Rogers, prominent American figures in entertainment and professional athletics in the 1980s. When one reviews the literature, writings prepared by a variety of individuals can be found. Such authors include attorneys, legislators, physicians, sociologists, psychiatrists, coaches, addicts, corporate tycoons, athletic franchise owners, psychologists, students, parents, social workers, former hippies, gang members, and an endless array of others. Ironically, everyone writes as an expert, professing to present inside information. A conclusion commonly drawn in these writings is that not many people seem to understand the totality of the drug scene and its massive societal implications. Consequently, the field begs for a suitably descriptive reference book, one that would be recognized as preeminent in today's literature.

Professors Lyman and Potter, in their book *Drugs In Society: Causes, Concepts and Control*, fill this immense void and do so in terms that lay people can readily understand. The book is well written, and it spares the reader from the long words, technical terms, academic jargon, endless statistics and legalese about the current state of today's drug abuse situation, and about how the drug problem interfaces with the American system of criminal justice.

Refreshingly well organized, the book is comprised of three parts. In Part I, titled "Understanding the Problem," the reader is provided with information that illustrates the nature of the drug problem itself. Here the authors present an historical and comprehensive look at drug abuse and an in-depth look at drug identification and pharmacology. Thought provoking social theories of drug abuse and criminality are also discussed along with backgrounds of source-country involvement in the drug business. Part I also includes a discussion of the evolving political roles of source countries as well as the problems of police corruption and money laundering.

Part II, "Gangs and Drugs," offers three particularly insightful chapters, beginning with the study of the relationship between the drug trade and organized crime. The specific characteristics of organized crime and drug cartels are first discussed. Having laid this foundation, the authors provide a detailed analysis of both the international and domestic drug trade, with specific focus on the roles of both traditional and newly emerging gangs.

Part III is titled "Fighting Back." This important section sets out detailed information on ways with which America is dealing with the drug dilemma. Specifically, there is a chapter on various drug control initiatives that takes the reader through the history of U.S. drug control policy. The chapter also examines drug laws, the specific roles of drug enforcement agencies and a host of current suppression tactics. The chapter titled "Critical Issues in Drug Control" then discusses some unconventional approaches and their place in combating the drug menace. Such issues include drug courier profiling, reverse stings, the use of electronic surveillance, needle exchange programs, drug testing and the use of drugs in sports.

Concluding chapters of Part III voice both the pros and cons of legalizing drugs. This discussion is enhanced by the inclusion of a comparative look at legalization in Amsterdam, decriminalization in the state of Alaska, and the British heroin experiment. The last chapter gives the reader a thorough look at drug treatment and prevention programs. These chapters are not just timely and relevant to understanding the drug problem and what can be done about it; they address urgent concerns.

This text is a comprehensive sourcebook which provides reliable information about the illicit business of drugs, drug trafficking, drug control policy, and enforcement practices. It is a no-nonsense book which confronts issues in a clandestine business where factual and reliable information is fragmented and sometimes difficult to find. The content of *Drugs In Society* has been meticulously culled over the years from a vast array of information which has been presented in technical papers, staff reports and memoranda, news magazines, newspapers, technical and academic journals, police reports, intelligence documents, and in reports from the U.S. Bureau of Justice Statistics, the U.S. Department of Justice, the U.S. Drug Enforcement Administration, and numerous other investigative and informational resource agencies.

The authors have drawn upon information acquired from both practical experience and exhaustive research in the field of drug control and enforcement. They write with insightful understanding.

In conclusion, the most potent weapon against illicit drugs is intelligent prevention. In order to prevent a problem, the issue relevant to that problem must first be understood. *Drugs In Society* is an extraordinary book which will allow its readers to understand the drug problem, its scope, and the strategies that may be implemented to control the problem. This book deserves acclaim as a significant contribution to the literature. May it be widely circulated and read.

Samuel G. Chapman
University of Oklahoma

PREFACE

The preparation of a book of this nature is a tremendous task. This is because drug abuse is a diverse subject that encompasses numerous disciplines such as sociology, politics, medicine, psychology, criminal justice, public policy, and law. Many social, political, and public policy changes have set the stage for this text. While *Drugs In Society: Causes, Concepts and Control* is designed to give the reader a comprehensive look at the breadth of drug trafficking, drug control policy, and enforcement measures, it should be acknowledged that no text will adequately exhaust all pertinent issues.

Drugs In Society is a book about the many aspects of the most ominous business in American history: drug trafficking. It is a book about drugs, drug addiction, drug dealers, corrupt officials, the "narcs," the courts, personal and public values, public policy, the laws, the killing, the cheating, and the rising numbers of ruined communities and lives in the United States and across the world.

Discussions of drug control typically generate the political volatility of other heated social issues such as abortion, gun control, and capital punishment. It is therefore a primary goal of the authors to address this subject in a realistic fashion with equitable consideration given to both liberal and conservative viewpoints.

The book, designed to offer information in a logical flow, is prepared in three parts: Understanding the Problem, Gangs and Drugs, and Fighting Back. Each part contains chapters that focus on the many critical areas of America's drug problem and give the reader a foundation for rational decision making within this complex, multidisciplinary field.

We would like to extend an overall "thank you" to the many individuals who assisted in the preparation of this project, as clearly there are too many to mention. Specifically, thanks is most deserved for the many friends and associates in the drug enforcement profession, our colleagues in criminal justice and higher education, and the always helpful people at the National Institute of Justice, the National Center for Drugs and Crime Control, the Drug Enforcement Administration, and the Bureau of Justice Statistics.

Michael D. Lyman
Columbia College

Gary Potter
Eastern Kentucky University

Contents

PART II
GANGS AND DRUGS   165

PART III
FIGHTING BACK   253

INTRODUCTION

For many Americans, the drug problem is a remote one occurring somewhere else: heroin is abused by the poor in far away ghettos, cocaine is snorted by the very rich, other drugs are consumed by fast-trackers in the entertainment industry. Even the local drug busts feature characters from some other neighborhood. However, we can no longer afford to view drug abuse as someone else's problem. For one thing, most of us are too well acquainted with the most abused drug in the country: alcohol. The fatal consequences of alcohol abuse outweigh those associated with any other drug. Secondly, the networks of people involved with the illicit drug trade—from members of organized crime groups to casual dealers—often have little respect for our laws and legitimate forms of commerce.

As the drug industry begins to command more loyalty from some parts of our population than does the Constitution, our own civil government slowly erodes. Already in some South American countries (as well as many urban neighborhoods in the United States) the drug industry has, practically speaking, replaced civil government. In 1989, drug lords in Colombia, South America retaliated against that government's drug crackdown by facilitating over 50 bombings throughout the country. One such bombing resulted in the killing of 52 innocent people at the secret police headquarters in Colombia. Earlier that year traffickers claimed responsibility for the bombing of a Colombian airliner, tragically killing 107 people. So the drugs and violence continue. *Drugs In Society: Causes, Concepts and Control* addresses these and many other issues associated with drug abuse in the United States.

Perhaps accepting the problem—that is, facing it and not running away from it—is the first step in readying any workable solutions. This is the primary concern of Part I: Understanding the Problem. This section addresses the history of drug use, drug pharmacology, drug abuse ideology, and drug trafficking from source countries through both discreet and nondiscreet markets. Part I also focuses on drug crimes, which include official corruption and money laundering.

Organized crime gangs attracted to the lucrative drug trade are not only rooted in major U.S. cities but are spreading throughout the country to communities of all sizes. Not only are traditional organized crime groups like the Mafia involved in drug trafficking, but violent youth gangs such as the Crips and the Bloods, which are imitated by other youth gangs on a more modest level, have also become associated with the drug trade.

The Jamaican posses strive for control of neighborhood sales of crack cocaine and use violence to maintain that control. Outlaw motorcycle gangs such as the Hell's Angels have added the drug trade to other criminal endeavors. Part II of this book, called Gangs and Drugs, addresses the problem of organized crime involvement in the drug trade. Specifically, the most significant drug trafficking organizations, such as the Colombian cartels, La Cosa Nostra, outlaw motorcycle gangs, California youth gangs, Jamaican posses, and prison gangs are discussed.

As Americans accept the dimensions of drug abuse here and abroad, we are faced with many questions: What went wrong? What do we do now? Does the problem lie in the area of public health, culture, sociology, education, or criminal justice? While each of these areas claims some legitimate explanations, the criminal justice view is featured in Part III, Fighting Back.

Part III looks at what is being done about the problem and considers the role of the federal drug enforcement organizations, drug laws, and local drug enforcement initiatives. Additionally, critical issues such as drug courier profile enforcement initiatives, needle exchange programs, drug testing in the workplace, legalizing drugs, and drug abuse in sports are all discussed.

Today, drugs in our society pose and perpetuate a myriad of social problems. They threaten our standard of living. Drug abuse has accounted for many ruined and lost lives, including the innocent victims of drug abuse, the victims of AIDS, victims of drug-related diseases and accidents, and the lives of many police and drug enforcement officials. Still more horrifying are the deliberate killings associated with drug trafficking. In recognizing the significant social consequences of drug abuse, President Ronald Reagan signed a national decree in 1986 proclaiming drugs a threat to national security. Limited as any initiative is, overwhelming as the socioeconomics of the drug industry are, pervasive as social acceptance of drugs is, and dangerous as the big-time professional traffickers are, we can only hope that we can rise as a nation to meet this challenge.

PART I

UNDERSTANDING THE PROBLEM

Drug abuse and trafficking exist at the center of a multitude of problems in public health, social, and political arenas. It seems that almost everyone has formed an opinion on what the drug problem is and what to do about it. Many opinions on the drug problem, however, are based on fragmented or unsubstantiated information. This section will attempt to piece together the many foundational segments of the drug abuse puzzle to present a complete picture.

This section will also set the stage for the remainder of the book by discussing such topics as the history of drug abuse, the nature of the drug problem, and the pharmacology of the most widely abused drugs.

CHAPTER 1

THE DRUG ABUSE LEGACY

Because of the notoriety of drug abuse during the 1960s, many people assume that this decade was most responsible for our nation's current drug problem. Indeed, as we will see, the 1960s played a significant role in the development and propagation of certain drugs of abuse, but the roots of the problem go back much further in history.

History Repeats Itself

The drug abuse legacy of civilized man began thousands of years ago in such diverse areas as China, Egypt, India, the Middle East, and the Americas, where cannabis, ephedra, and opium were used for medicinal purposes and as general health tonics. In many cases, the medicinal use of these plants turned to recreational use, creating a pattern of use to abuse that has continued to the present.

Seven thousand years ago, the Sumerians left records of a "joy plant," presumably the highly addictive opium poppy (papaver somniferum). The euphoric effects of medicinal use led to recreational abuse of opium in Sumerian society.

The Chinese discovered alkaloid ephedrine (Ephedra sinica), an inhalant, as far back as 3000 B.C., and marijuana (cannabis sativa) by 2000 B.C., Chinese emperors in the third millennium B.C. ate or brewed cannabis in tea. The custom of drying and smoking cannabis was imported later from India.

Within a few centuries, alcohol abuse in Babylonia was a significant enough problem to inspire legal controls. In 1700 B.C., the Code of Hammurabi included censure of public intoxication.

Likewise, opium abuse in ancient Egypt increased to such an extent that, by 1500 B.C., Egyptian scriptures had censured the practice. Again, opium use,

3

which had medicinal origins as a pain reliever in surgery, had become opium abuse.

In South America, the Incas were chewing the coca leaf, the plant from which cocaine is derived. By 1000 B.C., the Incas believed that the coca leaf (Erthroxylon coca) aided in the digestion of food and the suppression of their appetites. So highly valued was the coca leaf that it was used instead of gold or silver to barter for food and clothing. Coca chewing is even reflected in the art of that period. For example, a ceramic statue, now housed in a museum in Ecuador, portrays an Indian with the characteristic chewer's bulge in the cheek.

Greek literature in the first millennium B.C. records an awareness of both opium and alcohol. The hero of Homer's epic tale *The Odyssey* had to forbid his sailors from eating the lotus flowers when visiting the African land of the Lotuseaters. This imaginative tale about the lotus eating dreamers suggests Homer's familiarity with opium use among North African cultures. Later, in 400 B.C., Hippocrates, the father of modern medicine for whom the Hippocratic Oath is named, recommended drinking the juice of the white poppy mixed with the seed of nettle. While massive wine festivals were an important part of Greek culture, there were nonetheless laws restricting the excessive use of alcohol.

In still another culture, hallucinogens were commonly used. Around 100 B.C., the Aztec Indians of North America were using dried peyote cactus buttons in religious ceremonies. Tribesmen believed that they would get closer to the gods and nature if they consumed this magical plant. Magic mushrooms (psilocybin) and morning glory seeds (ololiuqui) were other organic hallucinogens commonly used by the Indians.

Ancient cultures all around the world, then, established customs of drug use quite independently. However, with improved ships, more extensive sea travel, and political and military expansion, one culture began to influence another. For instance, the Roman conquest of the eastern Mediterranean in the first century A.D. contributed to the spread of opium use. Whether the drugs were imported or indigenous to a culture, drug use continued to flourish.

Drug use was so established in India, both for recreational and commercial purposes, that the Susruta treatise of 400 A.D. catalogued with unprecedented detail various types of cannabis preferred by the Indians. For example, Bhang, a strain generally considered weak in potency, was brewed into tea. Ganja, a more potent type of cannabis, was usually smoked. The high-grade charas, similar to hashish or Sinsemilla, was commonly eaten by affluent Indians.

Four hundred years later, in the ninth century, Arab traders introduced opium to China. Within a few more centuries, opium smoking in China ("chasing the dragon") would become a major public health threat.

Drugs even entered military rituals in several parts of the world. Some eleventh century Persian warriors smoked hashish to prepare for battle and for their fate as martyrs. Al-Hassan-ibn-al Sabbah (The Old Man of the Mountains) led such a band of Shiite Moslem warriors. Indeed, the word *assassin*, which later evolved through European use to mean the murderer of a political figure, comes from Hassan's name. On the other side of the world, Incan warriors commonly chewed coca leaves. Some historians partially attribute Pizarro's defeat of the Incan empire in 1532 to the fact that many Incan warriors were so inebriated that they were mentally and physically unable to fight.

In North America, the American Indians have a long tradition of smoking tobacco, a custom which was eventually introduced to European sailors. Magellan took tobacco to parts of Africa, while the Portuguese carried it to Polynesia. In the 1600s, Sir Walter Raleigh introduced pipe smoking to England. Jacques Nicot, who first took tobacco to France, claimed that tobacco had great medicinal properties. In fact, the stimulant that is the most dangerous chemical in tobacco, nicotine, is named after him. The popularity of tobacco spread so rapidly in many Asian and European countries that some countries began to censure it. Japan, for example, prohibited smoking in the mid-1650s, and at about the same time, smoking tobacco was punished by disfigurement or death in parts of Europe.

The age of exploration contributed greatly to the spread of culture, colonialism, commerce—and drugs. Whether mildly stimulating or dangerously addictive, drugs and the drug trade flourished. Explorers introduced some African cultures to tobacco and borrowed from them other drugs. In 1621, the Ethiopian coffee bean was introduced in England, and by the 1650s, coffee houses were well established in London and elsewhere.

HEROIN'S LEGACY

1874 Heroin is isolated from morphine.

1898 The Bayer Company of Germany commercially produces heorin, which is later found to be more potent than morphine.

1900 Heroin is determined to be highly addictive even though it was originally believed to be a cure for opium addiction.

1914 The Harrison Narcotics Act is passed, which restricts the manufacture, importation, and distribution of heroin.

1824 Heroin becomes readily available on the black market, as its manufacture is prohibited.

1930 The French Connection becomes the primary international supplier of heroin to the United States.

1964 The controversial methadone maintenance program is launched to treat opiate addicts.

1970 Heroin is classified as a Schedule I Narcotic by the Controlled Substances Act.

1985 U.S. government estimates that there are 500,000 to 750,000 heroin addicts in the United States.

As indicated earlier, opium addiction had established itself as a major health threat in China. During the 1800s, the Manchu dynasty tried to restrict opium use through legislation that focused on trade. The main target of such legislation was the East India Company of Great Britain, which supplied China with opium from India, then a colony of the British Empire. In fact, the British forced their colonial subjects into a widespread system of opium production that gave the British a virtual monopoly on the opium trade. Today's opium cultivators in Southeast and Southwest Asia are the descendants of farmers that were forced to participate in the British opium trade. In spite of legal controls, the opium problem in China became so great that Great Britain and China were on the brink of war.

In the early 1800s, the Manchu government passed a standing order for its army to detain and search any British vessel suspected of carrying opium. This led to the first of two great opium wars between China and Britain (1839-1842). The first war resulted in the defeat of China. The victorious British quickly claimed that opium consumption was harmless, encouraged its use, and reaped the profits from its trade. Consequently, Chinese officials continued their objections and a second war (1856-1860) broke out. The Anglo-French War, a joint offensive by Britain and France, resulted in the second defeat of China. Presumably, profit from the opium trade was more important than Chinese welfare to those countries (France, Britain, Russia and the United States) that imposed the Tienstsin Treaty (1858) on China. China at first refused to ratify the treaty, but by 1860, the defeated nation was forced to agree to key provisions: the legalization of opium and the opening of eleven more ports.

Opium use had also spread to Great Britain and continental Europe. Aiding in the perpetuation of the addiction cycle in Britain was the manufacture of many opium-based, over-the-counter preparations with harmless sounding names such as Mother Bailey's Quieting Syrup and Munn's Elixir. Laudanum, an opium-based painkiller, was also commonly used during the 1800s.

Throughout the eighteenth and nineteenth centuries, derivatives from opium and new chemical preparations resulted from advances in chemistry. German chemists developed anodyne, a liquid form of ether, in 1730. The British chemist Joseph Priestly, best known for his discovery of oxygen, held laughing gas parties in his home after he invented nitrous oxide (N_2O) in 1776. During the early 1800s, chloroform gained popularity as an anesthetic. Meanwhile, a German pharmacist named F.W.A. Serturner developed the opium derivative morphine, which he named after Morpheus, the Greek god of dreams and sleep. Morphine use in surgery led to the invention of the hypodermic needle in 1853. Doctors at that time believed that patient addiction to morphine could be avoided if the drug were injected rather than swallowed. Another opium derivative, codeine, first manufactured in 1832, was used as a cough suppressant.

In the 1860s, the American Civil War triggered a drug epidemic resulting in hundreds of thousands of morphine addicts, 400,000 of which were in the Union Army alone. The indiscriminate use of morphine and of commercially available opium-based drugs prevailed on the battlefields, in prisons, and even on the home front. Self-medication for grief and pain often resulted in high dosages and, eventually, addiction. Meanwhile, opium use increased on the west coast. Many of the Chinese lured to California with the promise of work on the railroads brought with them the practice of smoking opium. Opium dens were so commonplace in San Francisco that the city passed an ordinance in 1875 to curtail opium use. This was considered the first anti-drug law in the United States.

In the next decade, more newly discovered drugs contributed to the use-to-abuse pattern. Around 1870, Oscar Liebreich developed chloral hydrate, one of the first sedative hypnotics. In combination with alcohol, chloral hydrate was commonly abused as a recreational drug and for nefarious mixtures, such as the "Mickey Finn," a knockout cocktail used by muggers and robbers. Meanwhile, in 1878 cocaine was first isolated in an alkaloid form in an attempt to cure many of the postwar morphine addicts in the United States. The "cure" was soon used recreationally on a widespread basis. By 1886, Atlanta-born John Styth Pemberton introduced the soft drink Coca-Cola, which had a cocaine base for the next twenty years.

Although cocaine had failed as a cure for morphine addiction, it was erroneously hailed as a cure for other problems. One report in 1883 explained how Bavarian soldiers given cocaine had renewed energy for combat.

Sigmund Freud, inspired by American and German medical literature, first used cocaine as an aid in therapy in the 1880s. He used the "magical substance" in the treatment of depression and believed it to be a good treatment for asthma and certain stomach disorders. Freud's professional use led to a secret personal habit that was known only to a few personal friends and associates during the later years of his life.

As medicinal cocaine use spread throughout Europe, so did its commercial and recreational appeal. A popular European elixir called Vin Mariani (named after its inventor Angelo Mariani) surfaced in Paris and consisted of red wine and Peruvian coca leaf extracts. In the 1880s, it was thought that Vin Mariani was probably the most widely used medical prescription in the world; the elixir was even used by popes, kings, queens, and other rulers.

Cocaine had failed as a cure for morphine addiction, so it was with great pride that the Bayer Company in Germany announced a "wonder drug" designed to cure morphine and cocaine addictions. The new drug, heroin, also a derivative of opium, was soon found to be at least three times as addictive as the morphine it was supposed to remedy.

Meanwhile, the Aztec custom of using peyote had spread northward in the Americas. The Comanche Indians first incorporated peyote into their religious ceremonies in the 1870s. This religious practice continues and is protected by United States law. Less than twenty years later, the drug mescaline was isolated as the hallucinogenic ingredient in peyote. (Many decades later, mescaline was thought by many to be a "risk-free" recreational drug.)

At the turn of the century, alcohol abuse was spreading throughout society to all social classes and racial groups. Epidemic alcohol addiction in the United States finally led to the controversial eighteenth amendment and the era of prohibition. Prohibition only limited the legal consumption of alcohol; illegal markets thrived. Alcohol and marijuana, which served as an inexpensive substitute for costly black market alcohol, were easily available in, among other places, underground bars called "speakeasies."

The beginning of the twentieth century also saw the introduction of many new drugs as a result of medical research. It was in 1903 that barbiturates were first manufactured in Germany, and in 1912 that amphetamines were mass produced as a medication for asthma. Benzedrine inhalers were introduced for the first time in 1932, for treatment of respiratory conditions. In 1938, the painkiller Demerol, which is presently a highly prized substitute for heroin on the streets, was first synthesized and placed on the market.

MARIJUANA'S LEGACY

c.2000	Reference to marijuana found in India.	
1545	Hemp is introduced to Chile.	
1611	Hemp is cultivated by early settlers in Virginia.	
1856	Putnam's Magazine publishes an account of FitzHugh Ludlow's marijuana consuming experiences.	
1875	"Hashish houses" appear and are modeled after Chinese opium dens.	
1920	Marijuana use for recreational purposes increases during prohibition.	
1933	Marijuana linked to the "crime wave" of the 1930s.	

1937	The Marijuana Tax Act is passed and outlaws untaxed possession or distribution of marijuana.
1950-60	Recreational marijuana use spreads on college campuses and high schools.
1970	The Controlled Substances Act lists marijuana as a Schedule I hallucinogen and defines penalties for possession and distribution.
1970-85	Marijuana use continues to spread to most segments of society. An estimated 57% of American youth have used it.

We have seen that drug abuse in the early twentieth century was nothing new or unusual. What was relatively new was the *variety* of drugs abused and the *extent* to which each decade since 1900 can be characterized by the popularity of a particular drug, especially in the United States.

The Roaring Twenties set the stage for widespread abuse of alcohol and marijuana in the United States. Marijuana became even more popular during the 1930s. Due to widespread misinformation about the effects of marijuana, some newspaper accounts postulated that the "crime wave" of the 1930s—that is, the era marked by Pretty Boy Floyd, Bonnie and Clyde, and Machine Gun Kelly—resulted in part because of the dramatic increase in marijuana use.

Amphetamines, originally prescribed to curb obesity and depression, became popular among students, professionals, and even housewives who sought the euphoric effects of the drugs. The popularity of amphetamines continued through World War II, partly because they were so easily obtained with a doctor's prescription. As soon as the user market for amphetamines surpassed the legitimate sources of supply, an illicit market was created to meet the demand.

LSD (lysergic acid diethylamide) was popularized during the 1940s and 1950s in certain communities. It was initially discovered in 1938 by Drs. Albert Hoffman and W.A. Stoll, Swiss chemists who were experimenting with a parasitic fungus that grows on rye (ergot fungus). The use of LSD for mental disorders was widely researched in the 1940s and was praised by the psychiatric community in the 1950s. As the 1950s gave way to the 1960s, many members of the psychiatric community used LSD for both therapy and recreation. In 1962, Harvard professor Dr. Timothy Leary and his protegé Richard Alpert began treatment of inmates with LSD at the Massachusetts Correctional Institute. One year later, under a cloud of scandal, they were relieved of their positions at Harvard. LSD was also tested by the Central Intelligence Agency (CIA) as part of its efforts to find the ultimate "truth serum," and then later in an attempt to find a "mind control," drug. In fact, the CIA administered LSD to unsuspecting, nonconsenting victims, at least one of whom committed suicide.

Use of LSD through most of this time was restricted to a small part of the U.S. population. More common in the 1950s was the use of marijuana, tranquilizers, and various combinations of drugs. The coffee house frequented by members of the 1950's "Beat Generation" often served as clearinghouses for these drugs as much as for coffee. Tranquilizers, ranging from the minor benzodiazepines to more dangerous barbiturates, can produce an intoxication similar to that produced by alcohol. Again, the easy availability of tranquilizers via prescriptions contributed to its abuse. (The two most widely abused depressants today are Valium and Librium.) Like many amphetamines, tranquilizers have been available through both legitimate and illicit markets. Mixed drug use or *poly-drug* use, such as taking "uppers" in the morning for energy and "downers" at night to induce sleep, also became more commonplace during the 1950s and

1960s. Some adolescents at this time experimented with such drug trends as glue and paint sniffing, occasionally with lethal consequences.

A Closer Look: The Age of Aquarius Grows Up

"It was a mistake," said Supreme Court nominee Douglas Ginsburg of his marijuana smoking in the 1960s and 1970s. Of course, it wasn't a mistake at all, at the time, but Ginsburg didn't know then that he was going to get sandbagged by history. His first encounter with smoking marijuana was in the 1960s, when it was a prerequisite to joining hip circles of students, radicals, Bohemians, civil rights activists, war protesters, and all the heroes of the counterculture.

How could he have foreseen an age when Nancy Reagan would adopt the tone of a Maoist commissar advocating the extermination of flies when she proclaimed in USA Today: "Each of us has a responsibility to be intolerant of drug use anywhere, anytime, by anybody. Every one of us has an obligation to force the drug issue to the point it may make others uncomfortable and ourselves unpopular....Be unyielding, and inflexible, and outspoken in your opposition to drugs."

Marijuana was so fashionable for a while that even conservative pillar William F. Buckley would sail offshore to smoke it in international waters and then flaunt it in a newspaper column. Ginsburg's fall was more than a political matter. It was a collision among conflicting strains of the modern U.S. culture—in this case, the reality of widespread drug use versus our Puritan, often-hypocritical moralism. Ginsburg is another victim of this year's public fixation with private lives.

He was the point man for a generation of Americans who are reaching the age when they will be asked to run society's institutions. It is the '60s generation, whose common experiences were rock music and dope and the subculture—a subculture dedicated to the proposition you could never trust anyone older than 30, in Abbie Hoffman's memorable formulation. "Folks are going to have to get used to this," said Robert Beckel, 38, who ran Walter Mondale's presidential campaign in 1984. "This is the age of Aquarius growing up."

"There is a certain irony here," in the words of a prominent Republican, age 43, who was close to the Reagan White House. Ginsburg "is too modern. He's been married twice, his wives don't take his name, he smoked a little pot, he ran a computerized dating service—he sounds like a modern American. Are we ready for a modern American on the Supreme Court?"

Said David Musto, a professor of psychiatry and the history of medicine at Yale: "Goal-oriented people saw drugs as helping them in the late '60s and early '70s. The irony is that people never get more upset about drug use as it rises, they get more upset as it goes down. They become more intolerant. Now they see exercise, abstinence and healthy food as helping us be all we can be. The Reagan administration has thrived on this. Now its nominee to the Supreme Court has become a victim of it."

According to reports, Ginsburg last smoked marijuana in 1979. This was one year after marijuana hit a peak in use among high school students, according to Musto, and a year after the peak numbers of the U.S. public told pollsters that marijuana should be legalized.

In 1973, 18 percent of the general public agreed with legalization, according to data compiled by the Bureau of Justice Statistics. By 1978, it was 30 percent and by 1986, it was back to 18 percent. It was a different 18 percent as well. In 1973, legalization was approved by 32 percent of U.S. citizens with a college education, 15 percent with a high school education and 6 percent with a grade school education. By 1986, only 22 percent of the collegians approved, while the numbers of high- and grade-schoolers that favored legalization had increased slightly.

Furthermore, youth, the great hope of 1973, had abandoned marijuana when a new generation came on the scene in 1986. While 42 percent of people aged 18 to 20 approved of legalization in 1973, only 16 percent did in 1986. Between 1980 and 1986, the percentage of college students reporting use of marijuana within the last 30 days fell from 34.3 to 23.6 percent.

Source: Allen, H. and R. Kaiser (1987). "The Age of Aquarius Grows Up," *Columbia Daily Tribune*. November:16.

The Age of Aquarius—the 1960s—is notorious for the celebration of drug abuse among the youth. Never before had drug abuse reached such a large, youthful audience. Widespread antiwar (Vietnam) sentiment contributed to a larger student distrust of authority and of government policies. This antiestablishment sentiment among many youth, combined with the drug habits that many U.S. veterans brought home from Southeast Asia, created an unprecedented positive climate for drug experimentation by adolescent users. Other cultural threads, such as the lyrics of rock music and the creation of psychedelic art, reinforced a drug-oriented youth culture.

American soldiers who served in Vietnam became addicts by the thousands, as had their counterparts in the Civil War. Heroin, marijuana, and hashish were widely available to the servicemen, many of whom became addicts and then drug traffickers. Since the Vietnam War, recreational use of heroin has escalated in the United States, especially in the economically depressed inner city. Consequently, as of 1989, the Drug Enforcement Administration estimates that there are roughly 500,000 to 750,000 heroin addicts in the United States. Controversial methadone clinics opened in 1964 to treat opiate addicts. Although methadone is effective, it is itself a highly addictive narcotic drug (see Chapter 14).

In the 1960s, cocaine was slowly gaining impetus as a recreational drug, but it was only affordable to the affluent consumers. Other drugs popular during this time were amphetamines (speed) and psychoactive drugs such as LSD, MDA, STP, and DMA that offered the user altered sensory perceptions and even hallucinations.

In spite of the end of the Vietnam conflict in the early 1970s and subsequent calming of the social and political waters, drug abuse failed to wane. The use of already popular phencyclidine (PCP) increased during this time along with the newly developed depressant Quaalude (methaqualone). Cocaine was still growing in popularity to the point at which small gold cocaine spoons on necklaces were the rage in some social circles. In fact, during the 1970s, New York's exclusive discothèque Studio 54 displayed a dance floor that was decorated by a huge cocaine spoon. Supposedly, preferred clientele were furnished free samples of the drug. By the end of the 1970s, use of cocaine and its close cousin, methamphetamine, were still gaining momentum. Methamphetamine and other domestic drugs, such as PCP and LSD, were illegally produced around the United States in an increasing number of clandestine laboratories.

THE LEGACY OF LSD

1938 LSD is first produced in Basel, Switzerland.

1943 Dr. Albert Hoffman accidentally ingests a lysergic acid compound and experiences "fantastic visions." Hoffman later takes LSD purposely to study the effects.

1949-53 LSD is researched for treatment in mental disorders, alcoholism, and epilepsy.

1956 Recreational use of LSD by members of the psychiatric community.

1962 Drs. Timothy Leary and Richard Alpert of the Harvard Center for Research in Human Personality use LSD on inmates at the Massachusetts Correctional Institute.

1963 The federal government investigates Leary and Alpert, who are relieved of their positions at Harvard.
The illicit market for LSD begins, and different types of LSD appear across the country.

1965 New York is the first state to outlaw LSD.

1967 LSD is reported to damage white blood cells in laboratory studies.

1968 Negative effects of LSD, such as flashbacks and "bad trips," are reported across the nation.
The popularity of LSD peaks and stabilizes in the late 1960s.

1970-85 Different forms of LSD, such as blotter, micro-dot and window pane acid, appear on the illicit market.
Recreational use of LSD experiences phases of popularity and disinterest every 3 to 5 years.

Hallmarks of the drug abuse story in the 1980s include the synthesis of drugs and the lifestyles of some music and sports celebrities. "Designer drugs" are deadly synthetic substances similar to opiates and hallucinogens. However, in some areas, they are technically legal since they can be produced without certain illegal chemical analogs. Crack, developed in the 1980s as a freebase form of cocaine, provided an inexpensive but potent alternative to cocaine. The crack and methamphetamine markets of the 1980s spawned an upsurge in organized crime. Newcomers to the drug trade included such Los Angeles-based youth gangs as the Crips and Bloods as well as Jamaican gangs known as posses. Many cities across the United States are now terrorized by the drug-related violence of such gangs. This, in turn, provided a basis for much media and entertainment industry attention. One example is the 1988 film *Colors*, which portrays the violence of inner-city youth gangs involved in the drug trade.

Meanwhile, many top athletes were turning to anabolic steroids, a muscle builder, to maintain a competitive edge. Mass disqualifications of athletes dominated the coverage of the Pan Am games in Caracas, Venezuela, in 1983. In 1988, Canadian athlete Ben Johnson gained notoriety and lost an Olympic gold medal due to his use of steroids.

Drugs also ruined the lives of other celebrities. Comedian John Belushi died as a result of respiratory complications from the use of cocaine mixed with heroin (an "upper" and a "downer") known as a "speedball" in 1982. The deaths of two athletes in June 1985 helped bring home the tragedy of cocaine abuse. Len Bias had been drafted out of the University of Maryland by the Boston Celtics; he celebrated with cocaine and died of cardiac arrest. Cleveland Browns football player Don Rogers also died that month from cocaine poisoning.

As drug use increased among American youth, so did drug education programs aimed at curbing the problem. Former First Lady Nancy Reagan's "Just Say No" campaign was subject to ridicule by those who accused it of being simplistic and unrealistic, while supporters defended it as a common-sense prevention strategy that focused on potential first-time users rather than hard-core street addicts. Despite lukewarm support for programs such as "Just Say No," the public became more intolerant of drug-related tragedies. This outrage finally resulted in the controversial drug testing of air traffic controllers, train engineers, bus drivers, and other employees whose jobs were associated with public safety.

Additionally, the medical cover story of the decade, AIDS (Acquired Immune Deficiency Syndrome), helped clarify the association between drug use and public safety. Those among the high-risk groups for AIDS, a lethal, infectious disease for which there is no cure, are intravenous drug users such as heroin addicts. Because of the nature of heroin abuse, such activity commonly takes place in secluded settings such as urban "shooting galleries," where the sharing of hypodermic syringes (also illegal in most jurisdictions) has become commonplace. American recreational drug use has thrived in the 1980s, but not as a result of ignorance about the drugs themselves. Indeed, no society has been more aware of the tragic price paid for substance abuse.

THE LEGACY OF PCP	
1959 PCP was first developed as a dissociative annesthetic for use in surgery. **1960** Medical use of PCP on human patients was discontinued because of violent side effects. Veterinary medicine adopts the use of PCP as animal tranquilizer. **1965** Recreational use of PCP spreads because of illicit production of the drug.	**1965-70** PCP is sold as THC and cannabinol on the streets becasue people were beginning to associate the effects of PCP with negative experiences. **1978** President Carter enacts specific legislation against PCP. **1980-90s** Clandestine laboratory technology spreads in the manufacture of PCP.

Looking Ahead

It is difficult to speculate about the future of recreational drug use in our society because of the ever-changing social climate. As history has proven, the basis for social acceptance of some drugs and not others is not rational or consistent. Should certain drugs be authorized by law for recreational use? If lawfully sanctioned, under what circumstances should drug use be permitted? Given the high incidence of drug-related crime and drug-related health problems, can we responsibly consider the legalization of any dangerous substance? Or have the health problems associated with drug abuse and the ancillary crime associated with drug trafficking in the illicit market become so dangerous that a post-prohibition approach is required?

It appears that customary use of such drugs as coffee, tobacco, and certain over-the-counter drugs will continue throughout the 1990s. Alcohol use will undoubtedly continue despite initiatives on community, state, and national levels for curbing many of the dysfunctional aspects of alcohol abuse.

Illicit consumption of substances such as marijuana and cocaine will most likely continue, but to what extent is uncertain. Perhaps public education and prevention programs in the future will meet the challenge of informing drug users and prospective drug users of the dangers of these substances. In addition, it is likely that continued research will spread insight into the psychological and physiological effects of these drugs. Based on the advancements in chemical technology, clandestine drug manufacturers will probably conceive of new ways to increase the potency of drugs and reduce the retail price.

Responsibility for combating the drug problem in the future rests with governmental functions such as law enforcement, treatment and prevention programs, and the court and correctional systems. Additionally, others who must share in this responsibility include parents, teachers, and clergymen. Only through this multidisciplinary approach can the incidence of drug abuse and drug-related crime be reduced and ultimately abolished.

Summary

Of all the social phenomena affecting public health and safety, it is clear that drug abuse has superseded all other forms of widespread social deviance. There is much agreement that drugs can cause severe social problems and that some drugs are less harmful than others. However, there is little agreement as to which drugs are less harmful and to what extent they should be tolerated.

Cannabis and the opium poppy have been generally accepted as the oldest mind-altering drugs of abuse, as historic records of their use date back some 7,000 years. Further, these two drugs have been associated with both medical treatment and recreational uses. The regional origins for these drugs include South America for the coca plant, North America for alcohol and peyote, and Mexico, Southeast Asia, Southwest Asia, and China for opium and cannabis.

During and after the Civil War, morphine was widely used and abused as a pain killer. Toward the end of the nineteenth century, "cures" for morphine addiction were developed. For example, cocaine (first produced in 1878) and heroin (1898), both thought to be non-addicting antidotes for morphine addiction, were synthesized during the last quarter of the century. Other drugs, such as barbiturates and amphetamines, were also developed around the turn of the century, and have proven to be some of the most widely abused drugs in history.

The early 1900s paved the way for federal drug control measures such as the 1914 Harrison Narcotic Act. This comprehensive act exemplified the national concern over the abuse of coca- and opiate-based drugs. While Prohibition (1920-1933) was designed to reduce alcohol consumption, it resulted in an increase of marijuana use. In addition to the increase of marijuana consumption during this era, there was an increase in the abuse of other drugs such as cocaine and heroin.

It was the late 1950s that saw the synthesis of PCP, which proved to be harmful to human patients but was successful as a general anesthetic for animals. Shortly thereafter, LSD, originally developed in 1938, was studied by Harvard Professor Timothy Leary and became one of the first widely used, recreational "psychedelic" drugs.

Much social and political unrest with civil rights protests, race riots, the women's liberation movement, and demonstrations against United States involvement in Vietnam marked the era of the 1960s. Abuse of drugs such as co-caine, marijuana, amphetamines, LSD, and PCP, also continued to flourish dur-ing this period.

As the 1970s approached, the harmful effects of illicit drugs were down-played by the media and entertainment industry, as certain drugs such as cocaine achieved an elevated status among drug users. To supply the growing numbers of drug users, many entrepreneurial drug chemists began to cook their own batches of drugs such as methamphetamine and PCP. By the early 1980s, there was a significant increase in clandestine laboratory technology, which continues to spread across the United States.

Designer drugs such as "china white" heroin and "ecstasy" are illicit drugs that became popular during the 1980s. Each of these also represents innovative clandestine laboratory advances by domestic criminals desiring a piece of the il-licit drug market.

The 1980s also saw the genesis of crack, which is a potent, freebase form of cocaine. The popularity of crack created a great profit margin which lured many new organized crime groups into the drug trade. Competition over cities and neighborhoods as sales turf by organized crime has become the primary concern of policy makers in the early 1990s.

DISCUSSION QUESTIONS

1. Discuss some of the most common historical uses of drugs. Include medicinal, religious, and recreational uses.

2. Discuss China's role in global drug abuse and how that country attempted to deal with its own problem of opium addiction.

3. What were some of the early commercial uses of cannabis?

4 How has the historical use of opium in China affected drug abuse in the United States today?

5. Discuss the Civil War's unique association with the drug morphine. Was the use of morphine during the Civil War a benefit or detriment to the American society?

6. Discuss the first antidrug law passed in the United States and the circumstances surrounding it.

7. Compare the drug abuse climate in the United States before and after the passing of Prohibition in 1920.

8. List the social elements of the so-called "Age of Aquarius" that possibly accelerated drug use during the 1960s and early 1970s.

9. What social and political elements of drug abuse 100 years ago can be identified and compared with our drug abuse problem of today?

CHAPTER 2

UNDERSTANDING DRUGS

The literature on drug identification and pharmacology is rich with varying opinions. In this chapter, we will examine those drugs that are particularly prevalent and hazardous in society today. We will also study legal distinctions and categories of drugs, as well as the pharmacology of each.

Defining Drugs

To establish a basis for understanding drug abuse, perhaps we should begin by considering the question: why do people use drugs? Today the term "drug" seems to serve as a catchall term for just about any medicinal or chemical substance. In fact, it refers both to dangerous substances such as heroin or LSD, which are illegal to possess and have no medicinal value and to more benign substances such as over-the-counter drugs like aspirin and certain nonprescription cold remedies. Webster defines the word *drug* in a general sense as "a substance used by itself or a mixture in the treatment or diagnosis of disease."

The above definition, however, fails to recognize the use of drugs for applications other than the treatment of disease. Therefore, at the risk of oversimplifying the term, a more practical definition might be as follows:

any substance that causes or creates significant psychological and/or physiological changes in the body.

It is here where we may first identify a primary misunderstanding about the term as the traditional definition fails to recognize *"recreational"* or nonmedical use of certain substances. Although most drug use for the treatment of a legitimate medical problem is not only lawful but appropriate, the term "drug" actually encompasses a much broader scope of definition.

Webster's definition excludes consideration of the recreational category of drugs. Certain ordinary substances such as sugar and caffeine do not meet Webster's definition either, but they do alter the user's physical well-being and mental awareness and are, of course, lawful to possess. We should, therefore, recognize that a drug is actually any substance that alters the user's physiological and/or psychological state, whether for medical or nonmedical use. In an attempt to understand reasons for drug use, let us take a closer look at the rationales for wanting to alter one's physical or mental state.

Reasons for Drug Use

Are there are only one or two motivations for drug use, or is it more likely that a multitude of reasons and complex interactions must be considered to understand the problem? Indeed, many reasons exist that drug users offer as justifications for dangerous drug consumption. Some reasons are obvious and others are more enigmatic.

The Natural High

Endogenous

The term "natural high" refers to a desired euphoric feeling naturally produced by the body. A multitude of studies by experts in social behavior suggest that people naturally desire to alter their state of consciousness at certain times throughout their lives. For example, children may help illustrate the innate desire to alter one's consciousness by the very manner in which they play. For all their innocence, children sometimes spin themselves into dizziness or desire to ride on the merry-go-round at the local amusement park to achieve a thrill and the corresponding physical exhilaration.

Many adults also enjoy riding the ferris wheel or roller coaster for the mere excitement of the experience. Such an indulgence, in and of itself, may raise or distort perceptions of reality while generating endocrine drug reactions such as the production of adrenaline and noradrenaline.

Endogenous drugs are chemicals naturally produced in the body; they change our moods and actions.

The endocrine-producing glands in our bodies don't always produce chemicals such as "uppers" like adrenaline. The body also manufactures its own "downers," such as serotonin and gamma-amion-butyric acid (GABA) . These "highs" are particularly appealing, as they are produced naturally, without the interference of external chemical stimuli.

Chemicals like those mentioned are called "*endogenous*," that is, because they are produced in the body. Endogenous chemicals produced by the brain and various glands change our moods and actions. These chemicals resemble some drugs taken by people for recreational purposes. For example, a group of endogenous chemicals called *endorphins*, discovered in 1975, closely resemble heroin or morphine, but they are naturally produced by the human body and act to relieve pain. The release of endorphins has been well documented by runners, for example, who seem to generate these drugs to cope with pain and to provide energy while running (the "runner's high").

Happy Hour

As with the term "natural high," the term "happy hour" does not refer to a reason why people become intoxicated but rather to a social forum where ritualistic recreational chemical use occurs in groups. Millions of people look forward to the traditional "happy hour" after a long day's or week's work. The altering of one's mental state (or "*attitude adjustment*") through alcohol consumption is lawful, socially acceptable, and even commonplace.

Such indulgence, however, is regulated through each state's criminal code because of the potential for accidents or criminal behavior if drinkers become intoxicated. Although it is legal, alcohol is a drug that can drastically change one's psychological and physiological condition.

Most states have established limits for alcohol consumption in ways such as: 1) restricting where liquor can be purchased; 2) increasing penalties for driving while under the influence (alcohol and illicit drugs alike); 3) establishing special criminal provisions for crimes committed while intoxicated; 4) criminalizing the transportation of liquor out of bars in "go-cups;" and 5) regulating open liquor containers in motor vehicles.

Medical Use

Ingesting "harder" and more dangerous drugs, under certain circumstances, is lawful if prescribed by a medical practitioner that has identified a physical or psychological requirement for such medication. Morphine, for example, is a dangerous and highly addictive narcotic drug, but when taken under a doctor's supervision, it can be an extremely effective pain killer both during surgery and recovery.

The lawful distribution of dangerous drugs mandates the legal manufacturing of them by legitimate pharmaceutical companies. The highly controlled circumstances in the manufacturing, distribution, and storage of dangerous substances will be discussed in greater length later in this text.

Religious Use

Although some modern-day religions incorporate mind-altering substances such as wine in their ceremonies, few religions condone using enough of the substance for participants to become intoxicated. Exceptions to this, however, exist in certain cultures. For example, since the 1700s, North American Indian cultures have used peyote cactus, which produces a psychoactive drug, in religious ceremonies. Eating or smoking peyote was embraced in elaborate ancient ceremonies as a means to gain "oneness" with the spirits and with nature.

Today, members of the Church of the Native American Indian are authorized in most states to use peyote in their religious ceremonies. Use of the drug, however, outside of a religious ceremony or by non-Indian participants is prohibited under law. Ironically, those Indian cultures that embrace the use of peyote in their religious practices at the same time consider alcohol a curse. In a similar vein, followers of traditional Coptic Christianity, whose most recognizable U.S. denomination are the Rastafarians who use marijuana in their religious observations in much the same way other churches use wine (see Chapter 4).

To Alter Moods and Metabolism

When people are depressed, anxious, or bored, it is reasonable for them to desire a change in their mental state. Drugs are sometimes used both legally and illegally to create a shift in personalities, attitudes, and to improve our moods. Such measures might include the consumption of stimulants (uppers), depressants (downers), or even psychoactive drugs (hallucinogens that are either organic or clandestinely manufactured).

In those cases in which the undesirable mood is due to a natural physiological chemical imbalance, certain drugs may be lawfully prescribed by physicians to help offset the body's chemical deficiencies. Excessive use of Valium and Librium, for example, was common in the 1950s to uplift depressed feelings.

These drugs were commonly prescribed because most doctors believed that they were safe. In reality, not only can the drugs be dangerous by themselves, but they can be particularly dangerous if combined with other drugs. Today "*poly-drug use*" is common where many drug users ingest amphetamines in the morning as a "pick-me-up" and then take barbiturates in the evening to help "wind down." This, of course, creates a classic abuse cycle in which one type of drug is required to counteract another. Another common example of poly-drug use, particularly among those taking downers for medical purposes, is combining barbiturates and tranquilizers with alcohol, a combination that heightens inebriation and is potentially deadly.

To Inspire Creativity

Through the years, musicians, poets, and novelists have hailed the effects of certain drugs that supposedly promote creativity. Many such artists have believed that drugs (often belonging to the hallucinogen family) can release inhibitions and unleash a creative thought process. Such individuals include poet Edgar Allen Poe (1809-1849), who had a weakness for laudanum (tincture of opium); British literary writer Aldous Huxley (1894-1963), who experimented extensively with mescaline in the 1950s (and was quoted as stating "pharmacology antedated agriculture"); the nineteenth-century poet Oliver Wendell Holmes (1809-1894), who indulged in ether; and popular comedian Lenny Bruce, whose physical addiction to heroin ultimately cost him his life.

In this crusade, let us not forget who we are. Drug abuse is a repudiation of everything America is. The destructiveness and human wreckage mock our heritage."

President Ronald Reagan, 1987

Drug Definitions and Categories

When addressing the task of understanding the many different drugs that are currently abused on the street, perhaps we should first consider certain clinical terms and the definitions that are commonly associated with drugs and drug use. These terms define certain predominant effects of drugs and are generally associated with the most dangerous drugs of abuse.

To begin, we should consider that drug abuse can be described in many different ways. Generally, however, the pathological use of substances that affect the central nervous system fall into two main categories: substance depencence and substance abuse. *The Diagnostic and Statistical Manual* (DSM III-R, 1987) endorsed by the American Psychological Association defines psychoactive drug dependence as the presence of three of the following nine symptoms for at least one month:

1. The person uses more of the substance or uses it for a longer period than intended.

2. The person recognized excessive use of the substance: may have tried to reduce it but has been unable to do so.

3. Much of the person's time is spent in efforts to obtain the substance or recover from its effects.

4. The person is intoxicated or suffering from withdrawal symptoms at times when responsibilities need to be fulfilled.

5. Many activities (work, recreation, socializing) are given up or reduced in frequency because of the use of the substance.

6. Problems in health, social relationships, and psychological functioning occur (e.g., excessive use of alcohol is often linked to depression).

7. Tolerance (discussed below) develops, requiring larger doses (at least a 50 percent increase) of the substance to produce the desired effect.

8. Withdrawal symptoms (discussed below) develop when the person stops taking the substance or reduces the amount.

9. The person uses the substance to relieve the withdrawal symptoms (e.g., smoking crack cocaine because feelings of paranoia and physical discomfort begin to develop).

The term psychoactive substance abuse is also defined by DSM III-R as a less severe version of dependence. It is diagnosed when the person's use of a substance is maladaptive but not severe enough to meet the diagnostic criteria for dependence.

To understand the various types of drugs and their effects, a system of categories has been established. Each of these six categories (stimulants, depressants, hallucinogens, narcotics, cannabis and inhalants) may contain both legal and controlled substances. Each substance possesses unique characteristics and will be discussed next.

- *Physical dependence.* Physiological (or physical) dependence on a drug refers to an alteration of the normal body functions that necessitates the continued presence of a drug in order to prevent the withdrawal (or abstinence) syndrome, which is characteristic of each class of addictive drug.

- *Psychological dependence.* Psychological dependence is a term that generally means the craving or continuation of the use of a drug because it provides the user with a feeling of well-being and satisfaction.

- *Tolerance.* Tolerance* is a situation in which the user continues regular use of a drug and must administer progressively larger doses to attain the desired effect, thereby reinforcing the compulsive behavior known as drug dependence.

- *The withdrawal syndrome.* Withdrawal* is the physical reaction of bodily functions that, when deprived of an addictive drug, causes increased excitability of those same bodily functions that have been depressed by the drug's habitual use.

The Stimulant Family

Stimulants are a category of drugs that literally stimulate or excite the user's central nervous system. The two most common stimulants are nicotine, from tobacco products, and caffeine, commonly used in soft drinks and coffee. These substances are an accepted part of our culture and are, therefore, widely used. Generally speaking, these products are consumed not only for recreation, but when used in moderation, they may be taken to relieve minor fatigue.

Although health problems are commonly associated with the use of both nicotine and caffeine, other stimulants produce more powerful physical and psychological dependence. Stimulants are popular because they make the user feel stronger, more alert, and decisive. As mentioned, excessive use of stimulants (or "uppers") may evolve into a pattern where they are taken regularly and countered in the evening with depressants (or "downers").

---

* *Tolerance* and *withdrawal* at one time were used to define the term *addiction*, implying that addiction was a physiological process rather than a psychological dependency. This distinction is not made clear by DSM III-R. In addition, addictions with obvious tolerance and withdrawal symptoms are not always disabling, as when a patient becomes addicted to prescribed pain medication.

Stimulants are commonly used by dieters, people involved in boring, rote, repetitive work, or by those working extra jobs and in need of additional energy for a longer period of time than the average workday. Accompanying a temporary sense of exhilaration is irritability and a loss of appetite. When the effects of the stimulant wear off, the body experiences a "crashing" or a sudden exhaustion. The "crash" is sometimes experienced in tandem with chest pains, headaches, and even paranoia.

The Seduction of Cocaine

From the 1960s era of the "flower children," cocaine has now advanced in popularity to become one of the most commonly abused drugs in the United States. Cocaine, considered the most potent natural stimulant, is extracted from the South American coca plant. In the late 1980s and early 1990s, cocaine has grown to be an illicit drug of great popularity on the streets and one that generates considerable wealth for criminal organizations in the United States and South America. In fact, cocaine and its freebase form, "crack," have grown into a multibillion-dollar industry, which sustains the emerging entrepreneurial drug gangs such as the Crips, the Bloods, and Jamaican Posses, as well as a number of already well-established criminal organizations such as "La Cosa Nostra" (discussed in Chapter 8).

As discussed in Chapter 1, cocaine was hailed in the nineteenth century as a wonder drug for addiction and other ailments. Like the opiates, it was controlled by such legislation as the 1914 Harrison Narcotics Act. Now, because it is one of the most available and inexpensive drugs on the black market, there is an increasing demand for the drug.

Cocaine, a white crystalline powder, is commonly diluted through the use of other white powders such as baking soda, lactose, mannitol, and even some local anesthetics such as lidocaine. It traditionally has been snorted and then absorbed through the linings of the nose into the brain. Since the mid-1980s, smokeable "freebase" cocaine called "crack" has become popular in many American cities.

Cocaine's limited but legitimate use is in nose and eye surgery. It is considered invaluable because of its ability to anesthetize tissue while simultaneously constricting blood vessels and limiting the amount of bleeding. Most other applications of cocaine have become obsolete due to the synthesis of other drugs that have similar characteristics.

For many years, cocaine was thought of as being relatively safe, unlike other drugs such as LSD and PCP. Studies and research have shown, however, that side effects from cocaine use are common. Side effects include: anxiety, restlessness, extreme irritability, paranoia, and formication. In the early 1970s, studies of cocaine-related deaths indicated that, between 1971 and 1976, only 111 deaths had been reported. But with the advent of freebasing, those statistics increased markedly, with the number of cocaine-related deaths quadrupling between 1979 and 1981.

DEFINITIONS OF COCA AND COCAINE

COCA. A member of the plant genus *erthroxylon*, which contains as many as 250 species. Coca contains at least 14 different alkaloids, which constitute between 0.25 percent and 2.25 percent of the leaf weight. These alkaloids are a combination of ecgonines, tropeines, and hygrines. The principal alkaloid of psychopharmacologic interest is cocaine, which represents an average of 86 percent of the total alkaloid content of coca.

COCA PASTE. A crude extract of the coca leaf that contains 40 to 85 percent cocaine base, along with companion coca alkaloids and varying quantities of benzoic acid, methanol, and kerosene.

COCAINE. Also known as 2-beta-carbomethoxy-3-beta-benzoxytropane. It is also known as the benzoyl ester of methylecgonine, cocaine alkaloid, cocaine base, cocaine free base, base, or free base. Pharmaceutical cocaine is 100 percent pure. Street preparations of cocaine free base average 95 percent pure with varying amounts of diluents and adulterants (commonly lidocaine).

COCAINE HYDROCHLORIDE (HCl). The acid salt of cocaine formed with hydrochloric acid, also known as cocaine muriate or street cocaine. Pharmaceutical cocaine hydrochloride is 100 percent pure. Street preparations average 55 percent pure with varying amounts of diluents and adulterants.

Source: *Journal of Psychoactive Drugs*, Vol. (14)4 Oct.-Dec. 1982.

Current estimates are that only 10 percent of cocaine users inject or freebase the substance (as opposed to snorting it), but those that do inject or freebase account for 76 to 92 percent of all cocaine-related deaths (NIDA, 1989). In any case, the risk of death exists in the form of heart attack or stroke from excessive use and, particularly, from freebasing.

Because of its pleasurable effects, cocaine has the potential for psychological dependence. Recurrent users may resort to larger doses at shorter intervals in order to maintain their highs. The danger of psychological dependence is directly related to the amount and frequency of use. For years it appeared that the high cost of cocaine would serve to limit the use and control many of the dysfunctional attributes of the drug. However, with the advent of crack cocaine, the drug has become more affordable and more commonly available.

The cycle of cocaine use roughly approximates the following phases:

Phase 1   *Experimental* — Those that fall into this category do not use the drug consistently enough to become addicted but may easily fall into regular use due to peer pressure.

Phase 2   *Occasional* — The user in this phase maintains a consistency of cocaine use that falls short of compulsive (discussed next). Occasional use, however, may tend to build tolerance.

Phase 3   *Compulsive* — The cocaine user in the compulsive phase will not pass up an opportunity to take cocaine. By the time he or she has reached this phase, a strong psychological dependence has taken effect.

Phase 4   *Dependent* — Once having reached this phase, the user has little control over choices to do the drug. He or she will experience severe states of depression, and financial hardship, and will commonly deal cocaine to friends in order to support his or her own habit.

The intensity of psychological effects of cocaine, as with many psychoactive drugs, depends on the rate of entry into the blood. Intravenous injection or freebasing produces an almost immediate and intense high. Conversion of cocaine hydrochloride into cocaine base yields a substance that becomes volatile when heated and produces crack, which is discussed below.

Excessive doses of cocaine may cause seizures and even death from respiratory failure, stroke, cerebral hemorrhage, or heart failure. The untimely deaths of young athletes Len Bias and Don Rogers during the mid-1980s help to illustrate the dangerousness and unpredictability of the drug. Studies have revealed that there is no specific treatment for cocaine overdose. So, in the event that a user thinks that a tolerance to the drug could develop, he or she might be mistaken. In fact, it is thought by some that repeated use lowers the dose at which toxicity occurs, so that there is no known *safe* dose.

We're at an important crossroads in our nation—the awareness that drug abuse is now epidemic and at the same time that an even deadlier drug is now available for consumption. That drug is crack, and it's sweeping across our country like a tidal wave. It's inexpensive and highly depressive, our young people are using it in all of our metropolitan areas, and our police and law enforcement people are asking us what we are doing about educating our young people about the dangers of this deadly new drug.

Source: Rangel, Charles (1986). *The Crack Cocaine Crisis.* Committee on Narcotics Abuse and Control, 99th Congress, Joint Hearing.

How Cocaine Works

The exact effects of cocaine on the human body aren't quite clear. According to an article appearing in the January 1989 issue of *National Geographic*, the physical cyclical effects of cocaine are as follows:

Upon ingestion, cocaine first enhances then later interferes with the transmission of the pleasure signals of the brain. A message is carried across the synapse between the long axon of one nerve cell and the body of another by chemicals called neurotransmitters.

Of the neurotransmitters released by cocaine, the most important is *dopamine*. Dopamine fills receptors on the body of the next cell and sparks a continuation of the message.

Normally, pumps reclaim the dopamine but, according to a leading theory, cocaine blocks this. Dopamine remains in the receptors, sending an enhanced message before breaking down. Prolonged cocaine use may also deplete dopamine, rendering the sensation of pleasure impossible for the user (White, 1988).

THE DOPAMINE SYSTEM

The pleasure sensation of taking drugs (such as heroin or cocaine) is, in part, mediated through the body's dopamine system. The dopamine transmitter system is thought to mediate the satisfaction people obtain from performing life's tasks: eating, to sex, to a job well done. Drugs such as heroin and cocaine are pernicious because they short-circuit the dopamine system, giving a person an overdose of pleasure in the absence of achievement.

Source: Henningfield, J.E. (1989). *Insight Magazine*, (May 9):53.

Crack

Since the mid-1980s, however, the practice of smoking, or *"freebasing,"* cocaine has become increasingly popular. Freebasing can be accomplished either through traditional methods or through the smoking of *"crack"* cocaine. Traditional freebasing, the method used before the advent of crack, is accomplished by mixing cocaine HCl with ether or some other volatile liquid, adding water, and then heating it. The fumes are then inhaled and the drug is absorbed by the linings of the lungs and delivered within 15 seconds to the brain.

Crack use appears to cross all racial, social, and economic boundaries. But because of its low cost and easy availability, it has hit young people in the inner cities particularly hard. Many have turned to crime and prostitution to support their habits. Others have become accomplices in the crack epidemic, running what are known as "crack houses" for the sale and dispensing of the drug. A police detective in Los Angeles—which is a center for crack use—observed that the crack business has become the largest single employer of inner city youth.

Source: Testimony from Joint Hearing before the Select Committee on Narcotics Abuse and Control, 1986.

The method of smoking crack is less complicated than the traditional freebase method discussed above. It is also safer from a logistical point of view because crack is not a volatile material. All the user has to do is heat a chunk of crack with the use of a small glass pipe. The crack vaporizes and the fumes are inhaled. The freebase high only lasts from 8 to 11 minutes, requiring the user to smoke more and more of the drug to prolong its effects.

Crack, a retail form of freebase cocaine, gained popularity during the early 1980s. Crack, or cocaine base is available in the form of chips, chunks, or rocks, sells for as little as $5 per rock, and provides the user with an almost immediate euphoric feeling.

Crack is made from a cocaine hydrochloride solution that is heated in a pan together with baking soda. This yields a solid chunk of cocaine product, which is then cut up into hundreds of tiny chunks resembling soap chips. The chips are then placed into small vials or plastic packets and sold anywhere from $5 to $50 per container.

COCAINE: How It Hurts

Daily or "binge" users characteristically undergo profound personality changes. They become "coked out." They are confused, anxious,
and depressed. They are short-tempered and grow suspicious of
friends, loved ones, and co-workers. Their thinking is impaired; they
have difficulty concentrating and remembering things. Their work and
other responsibilities fall to neglect. They lose interest in food and sex.
Some become aggressive; some experience panic attacks. The more
they use the drug, the more pronounced their symptoms become.
Over time, cocaine begins to exact a toll on the user's body as well as
his mind.

Those that sniff the drug regularly experience a running nose,
sore throat, hoarseness, and sores on the nasal membranes
(sometimes to the point of perforating the septum). Many experience
shortness of breath, cold sweats, and uncontrollable tremors as their
consumption increases. Long-term use may damage the liver.

Because cocaine kills the appetite, many habitual users suffer
from malnutrition and lose significant amounts of weight. Poor diet results in nutritional deficiencies and a host of other problems, many of
which are compounded by a lack of sleep and a deterioration of personal hygiene.

Intravenous users risk hepatitis, AIDS, and other infections from
contaminated needles. Freebase smokers risk harm to the lungs.

Because adolescents are growing and therefore more vulnerable
to the effects of drugs, cocaine can be even more harmful.

Source: Bell, R. (1987). Toward a Drug Free America. *Challenge Newsletter*. National
Drug Policy Board (March).

Amphetamines

The amphetamine family of stimulants (dextroamphetamine, methamphetamine, and amphetamine, also referred to on the street as "speed") represents yet another popular but dangerous stimulant drug. Shortly after the introduction of amphetamine into the medical community, its prescribed uses increased. For example, the use of amphetamines in over-the-counter medicines,
such as inhalers, was common for a while. Soon after, many dangerous side effects were documented and the medical use of amphetamines was greatly reduced. Actually, medical use of amphetamines is strictly limited to conditions
such as narcolepsy, attention deficit disorders in children, and some cases of
obesity.

The illicit use of amphetamines closely parallels that of cocaine with regard to its short- and long-term effects. As such, amphetamines are often used as a cheaper substitute for costly cocaine. In many areas of the country, the clandestine manufacture of amphetamines is common, as users desire the high but do not want to pay the high price of cocaine. With this illicit production of the drug, organized crime groups such as outlaw motorcycle gangs provide an estimated 40 percent of the illicit amphetamine and methamphetamine consumed on the street.

Ice

The 1980s also saw the emergence of yet another "conversion" drug, resulting from the transformation of one substance to another. The new drug, "Ice," sells on the street for about $50 per gram. It was developed by traffickers out of reconstructed methamphetamine, a once-popular recreational stimulant. Ice, whose popularity has impacted particularly hard in Japan, is also called *shabu* or *hiroppon* in the Orient. It consists of tiny icelike crystals designed to be smoked (freebased) by the user. The expected high reported by the typical ice user is anywhere from eight to sixteen hours, compared to the eight- to ten-minute high offered by its close cousin, crack, which is also a stimulant.

Side effects of Ice include fatal lung and kidney disorders, in addition to long-lasting psychological damage. As mentioned, Ice is not a new drug but a converted drug, as crack was converted from cocaine. It has appealed to both recreational users as well as those that desire a super-charged type of speed for alertness and physical steadfastness.

The emergence of Ice in the United States is also distinguishable from the mid-1980s emergence of crack, in that Ice's host drug, methamphetamine, can easily be manufactured domestically. This is obviously an advantage for local traffickers that are proficient in the manufacturing and distribution of methamphetamine powder.

The popularity of Ice in the United States began in Hawaii in the mid-1980s. During a brief four-year period, police estimate that it surpassed the popularity of marijuana and cocaine there. The genesis of Ice in Hawaii goes back to Korea, which, along with Taiwan, leads the world in manufacture and export of the drug. Koreans learned of the drug methamphetamine from the Japanese, who had developed it in 1873.

The Depressant Family

Contrary to the effects of stimulants are the depressant category of drugs. Drugs falling into this category also have a potential for abuse due to their physical and psychological characteristics. Like many dangerous substances, if taken under the supervision of a physician, drugs in this category may be beneficial in treating conditions such as anxiety, irritability, tension, and insomnia. When abused, depressants produce a state of intoxication closely resembling that of alcohol.

Drugs falling in the depressant category are not all controlled or unlawful. That is, even compounds that can be purchased over the counter can also have dangerous effects on the user. One such substance is alcohol, which, when taken in moderation, will produce a mild sedation. The name "depressant" does not literally mean that the user becomes depressed, but refers to depression of his or her central nervous system. Initially, in heavier doses, some depressants may give the user an uplifting feeling similar to that produced by stimulants. After prolonged use, the user tends to become sluggish, with impaired judgment, slurred speech, and a loss of motor coordination.

Tolerance with depressants (as with stimulants and narcotics) develops rapidly with regular use, which adds to the likelihood of an overdose or even death. Those that use depressants and that fail to follow their physician's recommendations for use may find that their daily doses will increase 10 to 20 times the recommended therapeutic dose.

As mentioned earlier, many stimulant users will frequently use a depressant to help them calm down at the end of the day. The level of danger rises, however, when the user chooses to mix depressants with alcohol, creating a *synergistic* effect. This occurs when two or more drugs are taken together and the combined action increases the normal effect of each drug. Because of this action, a drug that can normally be taken safely can have a devastating effect if taken with a drug that acts synergistically with it.

Perhaps one of the most important dangers of depressant use is the abrupt cessation of high-dose depressant intake, which will result in the characteristic *withdrawal syndrome* (discussed above). Such a condition becomes manifest by feelings of anxiety, vomiting, loss of appetite, increased heart rate, profuse sweating, and even convulsions similar to those occurring in grand mal epilepsy. The latter symptom will usually peak in approximately the third to seventh day of abstinence, depending on the type of depressant used, and is considered to be life threatening unless conducted under medical supervision.

Barbiturates

The most frequently prescribed depressants are barbiturates, which are commonly prescribed to induce sleep. About 15 derivatives of barbituric acid are currently in medical use. These are used to induce sleep or calm nervousness and will usually take about one hour to take effect.

Barbiturates are classified as ultra-short, short, intermediate, and long lasting, with the duration of effect lasting from 6 to 16 hours respectively. These include such drugs as hexobarbital (Sombulex), pentobarbital (Nembutal), secobarbital (Seconal), and phenobarbital (Luminal).

Quaaludes

A widely abused depressant of the late 1970s and early 1980s was the Quaalude, or methaqualone. Although now outlawed, the Quaalude (in counterfeit version) is still manufactured clandestinely in foreign markets, smuggled into the country, and sold on American streets. The Quaalude is chemically unrelated to the barbiturate but has been responsible for many cases of poisoning and overdoses. It is sold in a tablet form, is ingested through the gastrointestinal tract, and is commonly stamped with the names "Lemon 714" or "Rorer 714." In large doses, it can cause coma and convulsions. Other than Quaalude, methaqualone has been marketed under other names such as Parest, Mequin, Optimil, Somnafac, and Sopor.

The Hallucinogen Family

Although hallucinogens have been in existence in one form or another for hundreds of years, they first gained widespread, popular appeal during the 1960s. Hallucinogenic drugs are both natural (organic) and synthetic (man-made) and act on the central nervous system by distorting auditory, tactile, and visual perceptions of reality. Although the use of some hallucinogens has been known to uplift the user's senses, many experiences with hallucinogens, particularly when "coming down," are of a negative and depressive nature. Tolerance is another trait of hallucinogen use. Users frequently find themselves requiring more and more of the drug to feel the original effects.

According to many, hallucinogen users experience the ability to "hear sights" and "see sounds." Colors are amplified into a kaleidoscopic prism within the mind. Occasionally, depression accompanies a negative or "*bad trip*," and will manifest itself in the form of suicidal tendencies in the user. Another negative side to the use of hallucinogens is the possibility of "*flashbacks*," which are fragmentary or recurring hallucinations that may occur many months or even years after the last dose of the drug has been taken.

LSD (LSD-25, lysergic acid diethylamide)

LSD is produced from lysergic acid and is a clear, odorless liquid substance derived from the ergot fungus that grows on rye (see Chapter 1). Because of the extremely high potency of LSD and its structural relationship to a chemical already found in the human brain, its effects were originally studied as treatment for some types of mental illness.

LSD is clandestinely manufactured and comes in several street forms:

1. Window Pane—This form consists of thin squares of gelatin, each containing approximately one drop of LSD.

2. Blotter Acid—This form of LSD is impregnated on paper, often with numerous miniature cartoons printed in rows. Each cartoon contains approximately one drop of LSD.

3. Micro Dot—These are tiny multicolored tablets which are so small that they can be concealed under one's thumbnail. They are called such names as Purple Haze, Orange Barrels, and Strawberry Sunshine.

The average effective oral dose is from 30 to 50 micrograms, but the amount per dose varies greatly. The effects of higher doses will persist for 10 to 12 hours.

PCP (Phencyclidine)

PCP is an hallucinogen that was originally developed in 1959 as a general anesthetic. Because of negative side effects such as convulsions and delirium, its use for human patients was rapidly discontinued. In the 1960s, PCP became commercially available for use as a veterinary medicine under the trade name Sernylan. In 1978, PCP was transferred from a Schedule III to a Schedule II drug under the Controlled Substances Act. Because of this legislation, most (if not all) of the PCP encountered on the street is manufactured in clandestine laboratories rather than diverted from legal channels.

PCP has been sold under numerous other names that reflect its bizarre and unpredictable effects: Jet Fuel, Angel Dust, Supergrass, Rocket Fuel, or THC. Other names include Wack, Water, Shirms, Dips, and Shirm Sticks (names for liquid PCP or cigarettes dipped in liquid PCP).

As indicated, PCP is available in two distinct forms: powder and liquid. The powdered form achieved most of its popularity during the early 1970s and through the mid-1980s, but has been replaced in many areas with liquid PCP.

The liquid form of the drug is yellowish-tan in color, much easier to manufacture than the powdered form, and able to retain a high volatility due to a higher concentration of ether present in its chemical makeup.

PHENCYCLIDINE OR PCP

Physical and Psychological Damage

PCP affects motor and autonomic nervous system functions as well as sensory perceptions and behavior. Physical effects include stroke, brain hemorrhage, hyperthermia (with body temperatures as high as 108 degrees) increased heart rate, shortness of breath, sweating, increased salivation, increased secretions from the lungs, urinary retention, wheezing, and severe bronchial spasms. Bizarre movement disorders, such as tremors, writhing, and jerky movements, may occur, and grand mal convulsive seizures—prolonged seizures may follow high doses. Death can occur from respiratory depression, seizures, or cardiovascular collapse.

The psychological effects of PCP are unpredictable. Users report a range of effects, including a sense of euphoria and well-being, excitement, exhilaration, sedation, drunkenness, and slow or speeding thoughts. Outwardly, users may be disoriented and confused and their speech may be slurred.

The most significant, observable change is in the personality of the user. Mood fluctuations, distortions in thinking, deterioration of attitudes, lack of personal responsibility, and impaired judgment regularly accompany PCP use.

Higher doses of PCP have produced violent psychosis with psychotic reactions that can last for weeks. These reactions include auditory and visual hallucinations, delusions, and paranoia. While these symptoms are most common in higher doses, they can occur at any level of use and may distort perceptions to the point that the user commits suicide or acts violently against others. The question of permanent brain damage from the use of PCP has not been settled.

Source: Miller, N. (1988). Toward a Drug Free America. The National Drug Policy Board (March).

Along with the rescheduling of the drug in 1978, the respective penalties for manufacture, sale, and possession were also increased to serve as a deterrent. Since the early 1980s, however, the proliferation of clandestine PCP laboratories has become evident in numerous states across the country.

Peyote and Mescaline

While PCP is a synthetic hallucinogen, the peyote cactus and its psychoactive ingredient mescaline are of an organic origin. This drug is derived from the so-called "buttons" of the peyote cactus. As mentioned in Chapter 1, the use of the peyote cactus by Indians in northern Mexico has been common since the earliest recorded history. The religious use of peyote by the Native American Church has been exempted from certain provisions of the 1970 Controlled Substances Act. Peyote is usually removed from the cactus, allowed to dry, ground up into a powder, and is taken orally.

Psilocybin Mushrooms

Yet another organic hallucinogen is the psilocybin or "*magic mushroom*" (also called "shrooms"), which has seen some traditional use by Native Americans and is also relatively popular among recreational hallucinogen users. Mescaline affects the user much like LSD. As mentioned, the active ingredient is psilocybin, which can also be manufactured synthetically.

When taken orally, psilocybin is one of the most rapidly acting hallucinogens. Its effects can usually be felt in 10 to 15 minutes, and reactions will last for about 90 minutes to four hours. Physical effects include dilated pupils, an increased heart rate, and a rise in the user's blood pressure. Psychological effects include difficulty in thinking, mental relaxation, detachment from surroundings, and feelings of anxiety. Tolerance to psilocybin has been well documented over the years.

MDMA (3,4 Methylenedioxymethamphetamine)

Adding to the laundry list of popular hallucinogens is the relatively new drug MDMA, which is also known on the street as Ecstasy, XTC, Eve, and Essence. This drug, which gained much popularity during the mid-1980s, had the misleading reputation of creating a strong euphoria for the user while being a relatively harmless drug.

MDMA had its origin in 1914, when it was developed by the German pharmaceutical company Merck as a diet pill but was never commercially manufactured. In spite of this fact, its possession or use was not prohibited until 1985. The popularity of the drug saw a brief upsurge during the 1970s as a substitute for the popular hallucinogen MDA, which was illegal. Nevertheless, its popularity was overshadowed by the prevalent recreational use of LSD.

As mentioned, MDMA was finally outlawed in 1985 and classified as a Schedule I drug. Strong opposition to this measure came from the psychiatric community, which claimed that the drug was beneficial in therapy. Just prior to that time, MDMA was especially popular in college towns and urban areas; it was thought by some to be an aphrodisiac. The popularity of MDMA during this period was fueled by many newspapers and television stations that carried stories about it. Even the popular comic strip Doonesbury featured the drug on occasion.

MDMA is taken orally and commonly packaged as a white powder contained within a gelatin capsule or as an off-white tablet. Street prices range from $8 to $20 per dosage unit throughout the country. Chemically, MDMA is similar to mescaline and possesses both hallucinogenic and stimulant properties. At low levels, it is mildly intoxicating, rarely produces hallucinations commonly associated with other more common hallucinogens, and the effects last about 30 minutes.

Although much research is needed on MDMA, the National Institute of Drug Abuse (NIDA) reported in 1989 that MDMA can temporarily destroy brain-cell nerve endings in animals and may be capable of inflicting permanent brain damage in the long term. Because research findings have been inconclusive about MDMA's impact on humans and because there is some indication of therapeutic benefits, MDMA remains a controversial drug.

The Narcotics Family

The term "narcotics" signifies a legal category of drugs that refers to opium and opium derivatives or their synthetic substitutes. Generally speaking, drugs falling into this category are painkillers that are indispensable in medical treatment, but are also very potent and extremely addictive.

The initial effects of the drugs may be unpleasant for the user and may include such feelings as nausea, vomiting, drowsiness, apathy, decreased physical activity, and constipation. Strong doses can lead to respiratory depression, loss of motor coordination, and slurred speech. Users that desire the brief euphoric effects of narcotic drugs may develop tolerance and increase their doses of the drug. Repeated use of narcotics will almost certainly manifest itself in both physical and psychological addiction.

Usually, narcotics are administered either orally or by injection. Intravenous drug users will commonly use one of two methods of injection:

1. *Skin popping*—Injecting the drug just under the skin and into the muscle.

2. *Mainlining*—This is where the drug is injected directly into the veins of the user.

In the event that the physically addicted user is deprived of the drug, the first withdrawal signs are usually noticed shortly before the time of the next desired dose, which is anywhere from 36 to 72 hours after the last dose. Other symptoms, however, such as watery eyes, runny nose, yawning, and perspiration will appear about 8 to 12 hours after the last dose. As the abstinence syndrome progresses, the user will experience loss of appetite, irritability, insomnia, "goose flesh," and tremors accompanied by severe sneezing. When the symptoms reach their peak, the user becomes weak and vomits while experiencing stomach cramps, diarrhea, and an increase in heart rate. These symptoms linger for five to seven days and then disappear.

Narcotics are of both natural and synthetic origins. Of the natural-origin narcotics, the most common are opium, heroin, and morphine. All of these drugs are derived from the opium poppy plant, known as the papaver somniferum. This plant only grows in certain parts of the world and is most commonly found today in Southeast and Southwest Asia, as well as in Mexico.

The opium poppy produces a seed pod that, when unripe, is traditionally lanced with a knife by farmers to obtain a milky liquid that oozes out of the incision. A more modern method, however, is the industrial poppy straw process of extracting alkaloids from the mature dried plant (see Chapter 4). Through this legal method of poppy harvesting, more than 400 tons of opium or its equivalent in poppy straw is imported annually into the United States.

The U.S. Drug Enforcement Administration estimates that at least 25 alkaloids can be extracted from raw opium. These fall into two categories:

1. The *phenanthrene alkaloids*, which principally produce morphine and codeine and are used as analgesics and cough suppressants.

2. The *isoquinoline alkaloids*, which are used in the production of intestinal relaxants and cough suppressants. (This category has no effect on the central nervous system and, therefore, is not regulated under the Controlled Substances Act.)

Heroin

Heroin (diacetylmorphine), a narcotic originally synthesized from morphine in 1874, was initially thought to be a cure for morphine addiction. It is a central nervous system depressant that will also relieve pain in the user.

Heroin was first controlled by the Harrison Narcotic Act of 1914, which was a law born out of international concerns about opium use and an increasing problem of addiction among middle-class women that used many over-the-counter remedies. In spite of legal controls, it took some 20 years before existing stocks of heroin were ultimately removed from store shelves.

Heroin is now considered the most widely abused of the narcotic family of drugs and is produced exclusively on a clandestine or illegal basis. In fact, it is considered a top choice of drugs to be trafficked by traditional Italian organized crime groups, as well as by African-American organized crime groups and international Chinese drug cartels.

Pure Asian heroin is white (brown heroin comes from Mexico) and has a bitter taste. The differences in brown and white heroin are attributed to the methods of manufacturing, which make use of various refining methods, which leave different impurities. In fact, pure heroin is rarely sold on the street. Street heroin is usually only two to three percent pure and may be diluted with lactose, starch, quinine, or even strychnine, the latter of which accounts for many heroin overdoses (see Chapter 3).

As mentioned, heroin is usually administered through intravenous injection, but occasional users may choose to inject the drug under the skin or even smoke heroin on the tip of a cigarette. It has also been administered orally or by snorting. Because of the physically addictive nature of the drug, addicts may require several injections (or "fixes") daily.

As mentioned, heroin depresses the central nervous system but also acts as a pain reliever. Because of the depressant nature of heroin, it tends to reduce severely the potential for aggressive behavior in users. Accompanying effects include a feeling of euphoria or "floating" and a sensation described as orgasmic. In addition, effects include constipation and suppression of the coughing reflex, followed by sleep or "nodding off."

"Black Tar" Heroin

A crude form of heroin that appeared on the drug scene during the early 1980s is "black tar" heroin. By most accounts, this type of heroin is thought to be manufactured by Mexican traffickers in the Sonora, Durango, Sinaloa, and Guerrero states of Mexico, smuggled to the United States by illegal aliens and migrant workers, and distributed through extended family connections in the United States. In 1987, according to DEA, law enforcement authorities found black tar in at least 27 states, with most of the use concentrated in established Mexican-American communities.

Black tar is crudely processed heroin that may appear to be dark brown in color. It is either sticky like roofing tar or hard like coal. It is known by such street names as "tootsie roll" and "goma," and its growing acceptance in the street stems from its high purity, low price, and widespread availability. Black tar is typically injected by the user. The purity levels for black tar have been documented to be as high as 93 percent, with 60 to 70 percent considered common. Because of its high purity, there has been a sharp increase in reported heroin-related injuries since its emergence in the early 1980s.

Hydromorphone

A commonly abused synthetic narcotic is hydromorphone, which is also known as Dilaudid.® Marketed in both injectable and tablet form, it is faster acting and has a greater sedating effect than morphine, and its potency is anywhere from two to eight times as great. Dilaudid is commonly obtained through theft in drug stores, fraudulent prescriptions, and diversion from legitimate manufacturers. Tablet form is normally a stronger form than liquid. The tablet is frequently dissolved and injected by the drug user.

Methadone

German scientists synthesized methadone during World War II because of a shortage of morphine. It is chemically unlike morphine but retains the same effects as morphine. The methadone maintenance program, introduced in 1964, was designed as a treatment for heroin addicts.

Methadone is administered in both oral and injectable form and has a longer duration of effect than morphine or heroin. In fact, its effects may last up to 24 hours, thus rendering the drug as a valuable aid in the treatment of heroin addiction (see Chapter 14).

"Designer" Drugs

"Designer" drugs have risen out of a new technology adopted by illicit drug manufacturers. That is, manufacturers produce potent drugs that are not yet covered by criminal codes and therefore are designed to be legal to possess. This process is attempted through resynthesizing already existing drugs to the point where they have the same basic effects on the user, but the chemical-molecular structure of the drugs has been altered so that they cannot be defined under the law as illegal. Most states today have adopted laws dealing with this problem; many of them have subsequently outlawed the analogs (basic chemicals) with which designer drugs are made.

One of the most dangerous of the designer drugs that emerged during the mid-1980s is "china white" heroin. Designer china white should not be confused with the China White that was common during the operation of the French

Connection and that was actually an opiate derivative. Designer china white is a totally synthetic, white powder that has the same general characteristics of heroin but is estimated to be at least 1,000 times more potent.

Designer china white heroin is actually a compound known as fentanyl (3-methyl fentanyl or 3-alpha fentanyl). Users of this drug have reported danger-ous side effects such as Parkinson's disease, which cripples part or all of the af-flicted person's body.

The Cannabis Family (marijuana)

Although indexed in this text as a substance in a category all its own, cannabis is classified by the Controlled Substances Act as a Schedule I drug—a mild hallucinogen. Cannabis sativa, or the hemp plant, grows wild throughout most areas of the world and has long been cultivated for its use in manufacturing rope, textile materials, certain feed mixtures, and even as an ingredient in paint.

MARIJUANA: A PROFILE

When ingested, marijuana stays in the body for a long period of time. It is soluble in oil and fat, but totally insoluble in water. The ratio is 600 to 1, so that once it gets inside the cell, it has difficulty getting back into the bloodstream the way that other drugs do. Alcohol, for example, is completely soluble in water and also in the bloodstream. So, as fast as it is consumed, it circulates in the bloodstream, is burned up, and leaves the body within 24 hours. Marijuana or its lipid-soluble cannabinoid molecules just stay in the body. A marijuana smoker, therefore, will usually smoke several joints just to get high and refortify his system before the existing marijuana has a chance to leave.

Tests have revealed that marijuana is stored in the brain, which consists of about one third fat tissue. The impairment of brain cells disrupts primary chemi-cal functions, resulting in the alteration of perception, memory, intelligence, and personality. Even long after the user feels high, he may not realize it, but he is still under the influence of the drug as long it remains in his system.

Marijuana is claimed to be nonaddictive because physical withdrawal symptoms are almost nonexistent. The reason for this absence, however, is because marijuana cannot be withdrawn rapidly. The body of the user has its own supply of the drug. It is estimated that it takes one week for the stored marijuana to drop to one half, two weeks to drop to one fourth, three weeks to drop to one eighth, etc.

Source: John B. Macdonald, et al., Addiction Research Foundation, Toronto, Canada (1986).

In spite of a lengthy history of both use and abuse, marijuana (also spelled marihuana) was outlawed by the 1937 Marijuana Tax Act (see Chapters 1 and 10), and by 1941, it had been deleted from the *U.S. Pharmacopoeia* and the *National Formulary*, the official compendia of drugs.

Marijuana, both a domestic and a foreign money maker for drug traffickers, is produced in large quantities in countries such as Colombia, Mexico, Jamaica, and Panama, as well as in the states of Hawaii, Kentucky, Oregon, and California. Most commercial marijuana ranges from 3 to 4 percent THC content.

Advances, however, in the chemistry and horticulture of marijuana cultivation have increased the potency of the plant over the years. Clandestine growers are constantly striving to increase the *THC (delta-9-tetrahydrocannabinol)* content of the plant, for it is the THC content that gives the user the desired high and reflects a corresponding market price for the drug. A rarer strain of marijuana considered to be the most potent is *sinsemilla* (a Spanish word meaning without seeds). Sinsemilla is a hybrid strain of marijuana that is prepared from the unpollinated female cannabis plant and may produce a yield of over 12 percent THC content.

SUMMARIZING MARIJUANA'S HARMFUL EFFECTS

1. Marijuana is fat soluble and is stored for months in the fatty tissues of the body. The lipid-soluble cannabinoid molecules (THC) become embedded in cell membranes and eventually saturate them. Once the cell membrane becomes saturated with THC, the vital nutrients can no longer be transported into and out of the cell, resulting in the loss of cell energy and ultimate cell death.

2. World renowned brain researcher Dr. Robert Heath of Tulane Medical School concluded from experiments on monkeys that the greatest damage occurs in the area of the brain that affects one's motivation.

3. Marijuana users claim that the drug is harmless because it is not physically addictive. The reason for this, however, is because it cannot be withdrawn rapidly. The body builds up its own supply. It takes one week for the stored marijuana to drop to one half, two weeks to drop to fourth, three weeks to drop to one eighth, etc.

4. Over 8,000 scientific research studies were published in the book *Marijuana: An Annotated Bibliography* (University of Mississippi Research Institute). These studies concluded that marijuana is harmful to the mind and body alike.

Source: Committee on Substance Abuse and Habitual Behavior. Commission on Behavioral and Social Sciences and Education. National Research Council, Washington D.C., (1982).

MARIJUANA ON TRIAL: ANOTHER VIEW OF ITS DANGERS

Powerful support for fundamental revisions in our attitudes and policies toward marijuana was contained in an historic decision in September 1988 by Francis L. Young, the chief administrative law judge of the United States Drug Enforcement Administration. For the first time in history...there had been a full review of the evidence about marijuana in medicine before an impartial judicial tribunal. The federal government and reform organizations, including the Drug Policy Foundation, presented documents and expert witnesses on all sides of the issue over a period of many months....There was vigorous cross-examination and the submission of extensive briefs. After presiding over this exhaustive inquiry, the DEA official recommended that marijuana be rescheduled so that it could be used by doctors in medicine.

In reaching that decision, Judge Young reviewed the massive body of evidence and came to conclusions that, while focussed on the issue of medical use, destroy many of the fundamental ideas at the base of the drug war:

*   "There is no record in the extensive medical literature describing a proven, documented cannabis-related fatality."

*   "[T]he record on marijuana encompasses 5,000 years of human experience....Yet, despite the long history of use and extraordinarily high number of social smokers, there are no credible medical reports to suggest that consuming marijuana has caused a single death."

*   "In strict medical terms, marijuana is far safer than many foods we commonly consume."

*   "Marijuana, in its natural form, is one of the safest therapeutically active substances known to man."

*   "The evidence in this record clearly shows that marijuana has been accepted as capable of relieving the distress of great numbers of very ill people, and doing so with safety under medical supervision. It would be unreasonable, arbitrary, and capricious for DEA to continue to stand between those sufferers and the benefits of this substance in light of the evidence...."

Source: Testimony of Arnold S. Trebach at the public hearing on drug control held before the Interior Committee of the Deutsche Bundestag, the parliament of the Federal Republic of Germany, Bonn, March 13, 1989.

Cannabis products are usually smoked by the user. The high from the drug is felt in minutes and usually lasts for two to three hours. The effects of the drug vary from one user to the next but in mild doses generally include feelings of restlessness, well-being, relaxation, and a craving for sweets. Stronger doses will illicit stronger reactions such as subtle alterations in thought formation, changes in perceptions, rapidly fluctuating emotions, an altered sense of self-identity, and impaired memory.

Research into the medicinal benefits of cannabis during the last 20 years has focused on the development of a cannabis product that will not produce negative side effects. Probably the most active research being performed on cannabis is the treatment of nausea and vomiting caused by chemotherapeutic agents in the treatment of certain types of cancer. In addition, research continues on the use of marijuana in the treatment of glaucoma.

Marijuana's potential dangers are subject to intense debate, and the issue is far from resolved, as can be seen from the two summaries, which reach diametrically opposed conclusions.

In addition to marijuana, another potent cannabis product is hashish or "hash." Most of the hashish encountered on American streets originates in the Middle East, where large plantations of the plant flourish. Basically, hashish (and its close cousin "hashish oil") is made by a boiling process in which all but the THC resins of the plant are extracted. Hash, although usually smoked, can be eaten as well and contains about 20 percent THC content.

The Inhalant Family

Inhalants are a diverse group of chemicals that produce psychoactive or mind-altering vapors. They include such common household products as aerosols, gasoline, glue, solvents, and butyl nitrates marketed as "room odorizers." Sniffing even moderate amounts of inhalants for even a short period of time can disturb vision, impair judgement, and reduce muscle and reflex control. Death from sniffing inhalants occurs suddenly and without warning as a result of suffocation, respiratory collapse, or heart failure.

Inhalants are widely available to drug abusers of all age groups. Because of this fact and because of their deadly side effects, inhalants are considered one of the most dangerous drugs available.

Summary

Perhaps one of the greatest reasons for drug abuse is a misunderstanding about the effects of drugs and their general pharmacology. Frequently, drug users listen to other drug users about the effects of a particular drug; such information is commonly incorrect. Drugs can be virtually anything that alters the user's physical or psychological makeup. Therefore, the word "drug" could rightfully refer to such compounds as heroin, LSD, and marijuana, along with sugar, salt, and caffeine.

Why do people use drugs? The reasons are many. Some people desire a stimulation of the endocrine chemicals within the body. These internal chemicals tend to emulate the effects of morphine and give a feeling of euphoria. Other people use drugs to alter their moods in the traditional "happy hour" forum, and still others use certain drugs for treatment of physical or mental medical conditions.

All drugs, whether or not they are controlled, fall into one of six categories: stimulants, depressants, hallucinogens, narcotics, cannabis, and inhalants. Drugs in the stimulant category literally stimulate the central nervous system and make the user feel more alert. The most commonly abused illicit drugs in this category are cocaine (including crack), amphetamines, and methamphetamines.

The depressant category represents drugs that have a different effect on the user. Although early stages of ingestion of depressants may create a feeling of exhilaration for the user, these drugs actually depress the central nervous system. Alcohol is a lawfully obtainable depressant, while depressants such as barbiturates and sedative hyponotics are usually physically addicting and pose the greatest physical dangers to the drug abuser.

Hallucinogens are a unique category of drug, as they are not physically addicting and their use is not as common as other categories of drugs. Hallucinogens such as LSD, PCP, and MDMA (Ecstasy) are considered dangerous drugs for other reasons. For example, users of LSD encounter the possibility of "bad trips" or "flashbacks" resulting from the use of the drug. PCP users frequently become completely detached from reality while experiencing violent hallucinations. Those that use PCP can injure themselves (even breaking bones) unwittingly because PCP also acts as an anesthetic.

The narcotic category refers to drugs such as heroin, morphine, opium, and Dilaudid, which are physically addicting and which emulate the effects of opium. All drugs within this category are controlled, and possession of lawfully manufactured narcotics is permitted only pursuant to a lawful prescription.

Marijuana or cannabis is discussed as an individual category of drug, but, according to the Drug Enforcement Administration, it is considered a mild hallucinogen. Although cannabis had a legitimate use during the early history of the United States, it is outlawed, to one extent or another, in all states. Its beneficial use in medicine is still under study, and some medical professionals claim that the THC content of the drug tends to aid in the remission of cancer of the iris.

At last, the use of inhalants has become popular for many, especially adolescents. Breathing the fumes of such household products as glue, paint, and gasoline may pose more risk of physiological damage to the user's brain than any other dangerous substance.

DISCUSSION QUESTIONS

1. What are endorphins and how do they relate to drug abuse?

2. Discuss some of the specific health risks of drug abuse.

3. Define the terms psychological and physiological dependence.

4. Discuss the definition of the term "drug."

5. List and discuss the nine criteria for drug dependence as outlined by the DSM III-R.

6. How does the previous criteria for drug dependence differ from DSM III-R's definition of drug abuse?

7. List the historical and traditional justifications to explain drug use over the years. Your discussion should include both medicinal and recreational drug use.

8. Discuss the different categories of drugs, and give examples of each.

9. Discuss the drug cocaine and its effects (both negative and positive) on the human body.

10. List the reasons why people desire the effects of marijuana, and discuss the adverse psychological and physiological effects of the drug.

11. What are the various ways heroin users ingest the drug?

12. Describe the differences between "black tar" heroin and powdered heroin.

13. List and discuss some widely used synthetic narcotic drugs.

14. What are designer drugs and how do they effect the drug user?

15. Discuss the similarities between the street drugs ice and crack.

CHAPTER 3

THE NATURE OF THE DRUG PROBLEM

Despite decades of governmental efforts to thwart the use of illicit drugs in the United States, it is clear that in the 1990s, drug abuse will continue to be a major social problem. The varying reasons for this conclusion will be discussed throughout this text, but one thing is increasingly clear: there will be no "quick fixes" or easy solutions to the existing problem.

Dilemmas in searching out solutions to our country's drug problem are illustrated, in part, by arguments over which drugs are good or bad for the user. In addition, a considerable degree of debate exists over which drugs pose the greatest threat to public health and safety. Additionally, controversy centers on the issue of legalization of certain drugs that according to some, are relatively harmless to the casual user, and, when controlled and legally proscribed, create a series of different problems.

The use of the term "*drug abuse*" illustrates, in part, the confusion surrounding the drug issue. To some people, any use of an *illicit* drug is drug abuse, while to others, using a drug to the extent that it compromises his or her physical or psychological well-being is a more accurate interpretation of the term. The latter definition would infer that one can take drugs and use them responsibly (a premise that itself is controversial).

The current state of affairs involving drug use clearly indicates that pervasive use of dangerous substances is widespread. In 1988, for example, the White House Conference for a Drug Free America (WHCDFA) reported that approximately 37 million people used an illegal drug in the last year and that one in every ten Americans used an illicit drug during the past month.

Adding to the physical dangers of substance abuse is the reality that drugs alter a person's behavior. Psychoactive drugs alter a person's mood, perception, attitudes, and emotions. As a result, concern is often expressed about the impact of drug use on work and familial and social relations. In addition, there is

growing concern about the relationship between mind- and mood-altering substances and violent crime in society at large.

---

*Probably the most fundamental value or interest of our nation is sur-
vival of the American people as a free and prosperous society. This
ideological premise is the hallmark of every official action undertaken
by our government and is manifested, for example, in:*

    *1)   the maintenance of strong military forces to deter attack
         from foreign adversaries;*

    *2)   the sending of food to less fortunate foreign countries,
         and*

    3)   in educating our young in public school systems.

Source: White House Conference for a Drug Free America, 1988

    There can be no doubt that drug abusers account for a disproportionate
amount of both violent and property crime. Although the precise relationship
between drugs and crime is still dubious, there are several manifestations of this
relationship that deserve close attention. The first is the relationship between
crime and addiction. Heroin addicts (and those addicted to other drugs) require
money in order to maintain their habit. Drug addicts frequently find that the
cost of their habit exceeds their ability to pay for the drugs, especially in light of
the fact that illegal drugs are often priced at 40 to 50 times over the clandestine
cost of manufacturing them. If the addict cannot finance his or her habit, he or
she will commonly turn to other sources of income, such as prostitution, burglary, and robbery, rather than seek treatment. The alternative is to become
physically ill from the symptoms of withdrawal.

    In addition to the problem of paying for a drug habit, drug users face the
additional problem of acquiring their drugs in an underground marketplace,
which brings them into contact with a wide variety of criminal actors. Although
many addicts are accustomed to criminal lifestyles, those that are not are susceptible to victimization. Their habit brings them into contact with the criminal
underworld, thereby creating opportunities for them to become involved in
criminal activities that they might not ordinarily have considered.

    Finally, drugs are both an intuitive escape and a natural occupational re-
course for many inner-city youth. Drugs provide a quick, although illusory, escape from the problems of poverty, unemployment, and underemployment, poor
education, and a myriad of other social problems faced by inner-city youth. In
addition, drugs provide a quick route to material success and accumulation of
wealth for others, as discussed later in this chapter. It has become an attractive
occupational alternative, that is, an "easy" way out. After all, the drug-using

population is already out there, cash revenues are tax free, and the potential income can make millionaires out of children barely in their twenties.

When trying to identify the antecedents of the "drug problem," we should
realize that there is no single drug abuse problem, but rather a series of overlapping problems. For instance, because of chemical differences in each person's
physical make-up, even the most common illicit drugs have very different effects on each user. These effects range from mild euphoria to deep depression,
from relaxation to psychotic behavior, and from the "munchies" to drug-induced
death by overdose.

In addition, there are many different types of users, from the "yuppie" professional that uses drugs "occasionally," to the physically addicted user in the
poverty-stricken inner city. Those that traffic drugs also present a prism of different types, from the small-time free-lancer in schools and on street corners, to
the leaders of vast international cartels.

Figure 3.1

Overview of the Drug Crisis

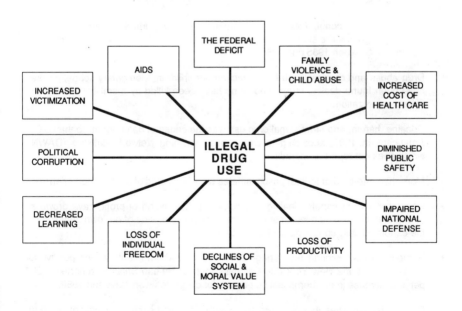

SOURCE: The White House Conference for a Drug-Free America, 1988.

VICTIMS OF DRUG ABUSE

- In 1987, 16 passengers died in an Amtrak train that collided with another train whose conductor had been smoking marijuana.

- Automobile drivers under the influence of mind-altering substances have killed and maimed thousands of victims.

- Children and spouses have been beaten and even murdered by those under the influence of drugs.

- Children are born addicted and are abandoned at birth by drug-using mothers.

- A 1988 survey of American households by the National Institute for Drug Abuse indicates that 37 percent of all Americans over 12 years old (that is, more than 70 million people) have tried an illegal drug and that 12 percent of the same population are thought to have used an illegal drug in the past month.

- In 1987, an estimated one-half of all high school seniors report having tried marijuana, 36 percent said that they had tried it in the past year, and 21 percent replied that they had used it in the past month.

- Americans waste billions of dollars on illegal drugs each year.

- The Bureau of Alcohol, Tobacco, and Firearms (ATF) reports that Jamaican criminal drug organizations are suspected in more than 800 drug-related murders that occurred nationwide between 1985 and 1988.

- Drug abuse and drug violence have reached our children; elementary school children have been found dealing drugs, and some have been killed by members of drug trafficking organizations.

- Cocaine, heroin, and other illegal drug use was the cause of death for more than 3,000 Americans in 1987, according to Drug Abuse Warning Network statistics (DAWN), which does not report all mortalities.

- More than one-third of federal prison inmates were convicted of drug-related offenses.

- International drug cartels, dealing in billions of dollars worth of profit, have grown so strong that they threaten legitimate governments in some parts of our own hemisphere; the cartels actually control parts of some countries.

- Some inner-city hospitals report huge increases in newborn infants testing positive for drugs. In fact, the New York City Commissioner for Human Services reported a 284 percent increase in newborns testing positive for drugs between 1986 and 1988.

- Drug abuse tarnishes American prestige worldwide, and it casts a shadow over the future of our children.

Source: WHCDFA, 1988

The social effects of drug trafficking are accentuated and reinforced by their direct and indirect economic impact. The sums spent on drugs represent resources lost to legitimate productive enterprises. The money that is laundered by drug traffickers seems to corrupt all that come into contact with it. Consequently, drug traffickers that purchase legitimate businesses have learned that it is easy to integrate dealers into society. Drug traffickers that make use of existing legitimate businesses have learned that, where such vast sums of money are involved, even respectable citizens can be induced to overlook the source of the money (see Chapter 6). In addition, the economic effect carries over into the work place, where drug-using workers increase costs of production, raise levels of absenteeism, and raise the incidence of accidents on the job, all of which impel employers to implement expensive anti-drug-abuse programs.

Severe health problems are also created when drug abuse prevails. These include drug overdoses, poisonings from "street" drugs as well as from improperly consumed pharmaceutical drugs. Even marijuana can have devastating long-term effects. Not only is marijuana the drug with which many users begin, but marijuana cigarettes have many times the tar and carcinogens that tobacco cigarettes have.

Additional problems include addicted mothers that give birth to addicted babies and the spreading of diseases such as hepatitis and AIDS through the sharing of contaminated needles by drug users. The proliferation of the crack house has given rise to the spreading of the AIDS virus. In many crack houses, prostitution flourishes as sex-for-drugs is a common transaction.

The AIDS Story in America Since June 1, 1981:

TOTAL CASES:	104,210
TOTAL DEATHS:	61,655
Infection from homosexual/bisexual contact:	60,983
Cases attributed to IV drug use:	18,298
Cases among those age 13-29:	22,141
Total number infected:	1.5 million (est.)
Number infected age 13-29:	220,000 (est.)

Source: Center for Disease Control, 1989

THERE'S MORE BEHIND DRUG ABUSE THAN BOREDOM

Ask the 16-year-old drug abuser from any class, race, or ethnic division why he or she abuses drugs or alcohol, and you'll get a mumbled explanation about having "nothing to do" and living in a situation where "everybody else is doing it."

Deep down on the demand side of the problem of drug abuse in America lie three causal considerations. First is the desire—known to very normal, healthy persons—to experience the exhilaration of a "high." Drug-induced highs, however, bring with them a dependency on drugs.   Highs resulting from athletic, academic, artistic, or other achievements are, of course, unaccompanied by damaging and eventually destructive dependencies. But such highs do not come easily.

The second causal consideration on the demand side for drugs is the desire to avoid pain—physical or psychological pain. In a culture that cannot tolerate the thought of pain—physical or psychological—it isn't surprising that avoidance of all pain, at all times, by all means, should become something of a supreme value. Our cultural denigration of pain, disappointment, discouragement and monotony encourages escape at any price.

Our collective passivity resulting from a growing preference to have everything ready-made, available on demand and without delay, has left us holding the bag of boredom. "There's nothing to do!" We wait impatiently to be "turned on" and thus render ourselves vulnerable to drug-induced flights not just from humdrum reality, but from the human challenge of transforming reality by the exercise of human creativity. And creativity, even when inborn, does not develop easily.

The third causal consideration in examining the "why" of the human demand for drugs is biological. Babies born of addicted mothers are themselves addicts, right from the start. Other biological predispositions to addiction are possible, but they will not become addictions if addictive substances are never used. The determination to refuse does not come easily, especially when "everyone's doing it." It is not easy to resist peer pressure, to swim against the everyone-is-doing-it tide.

There are reasons, of course, why apparently normal people—young people for the most part—will turn to drugs for the experience of a high. Some like to take risks. Risk-takers often fail to measure carefully the consequences. And where addictive substances are involved, risk-takers rarely recognize that one experience can lead to the captivity of addiction—not cause it immediately but lead inevitably to it. Risk-taking is as easy as ignorance, and no less damaging. It is not easy to avoid destructive dependencies.

There are also reasons why normal young people want to avoid pain. Most are obvious. Less obvious is the fact that commercial advertisements have instructed them to take pills for the elimination of heartburn long before they knew what these maladies were.

Pain has no redemptive value in the value system of a secular society. And the "no pain, no gain" equation applies only to weightlifters and athletic overachievers, not to normal folks. Pain, in any case, is never easy to bear.

Psychological pain is more often felt than understood by the young. Typically, it is just left unattended and unanalyzed. To the adolescent eye, everyone else is happy, except me. All others feel good about life and about themselves; I'm the only one with the problem.

Adolescents appear to take strange delight, we know, in making classmates and other peers feel uncomfortable. They project upon others, more often than not, their own unease, insecurity and self-deprecation. If only they would open up and talk about the dark view they have of themselves. But it is not easy to open up and drop the mask. It is not easy to admit to one's self-doubt or deficit of self-esteem. Besides, who would want to listen?

Who's around to listen or to care? So adolescents are vulnerable to the easy exit, to the seduction of drug-related escapes from psychological pain.

What might be done about all this? How can parents, helping professionals, or just friends, put themselves between potentially troubled adolescents and their problems?

Just about everyone has a healthy appetite for the highs this life has to offer through legitimate pleasure and honest achievement in balanced and what Edward Bennett Williams used to call "contest living." The contest confronts us every day. The balance is between matter and spirit, soul and body, faith and reason. The contest is never an easy victory, nor is the balance ever easy to achieve.

To the young we should be saying simply this: Do not be taken in by the big lie our culture of consumerism perpetuates. Do not believe that to have is to be, that to have more is to be more fully human and, the worst lie of all, that to live easily is to live happily.

If they can say yes—and really mean it—to that simple lesson, the young will be able to say no to drugs. If enough of them do, the bottom will fall out on the demand side of the market for drugs. In the face of no demand, the supply we seem to be unable to control will no longer be the problem we seem to be unable to solve.

Source: Byron, W.J. (1989). "There's More Behind Drug Abuse Than Boredom." *The Kansas City Star* (June 4):G6.

Drug abuse also has the ability to affect society on a much greater level—national security. Many larger drug organizations, particularly the South American and southeast Asian cartels, have already become so powerful that they wield as much power as many Latin and Central American governments. Drug money from these organizations has corrupted government officials, many of whom are charged themselves with the responsibility of drug control. In fact, the immense power and financial reserves of some of the largest drug trafficking organizations have made them attractive partners in intelligence operations (such as those conducted during the Vietnam War and in Central America), thereby rendering U.S. policy confused and contradictory at times. Other drug source countries that are hostile to the United States view drugs as a weapon to use against American society.

Drug production and abuse is clearly an international problem. As of the preparation of this text, fifteen countries are listed by the U.S. State Department as major drug source countries. Four of these, Afghanistan, Burma, Iran, and Laos (all opium producers) have been decertified for United States assistance under the provisions of the Foreign Assistance Act. Two other countries, Panama and Syria, have been decertified for failure to control drug trafficking and money laundering. Colombia, the largest exporter of marijuana and cocaine to the United States, still receives U.S. assistance partly to encourage the Colombian government in its internal battle with the drug traffickers and insurgent groups. In defense of this posture, the U.S. State Department issued this official statement:

A much needed infusion of government military capability had handsome results in 1988: over 23 tons of cocaine seized, more than 800 labs destroyed including 29 major complexes, and more than 600,000 gallons of precursor chemicals seized. In January and February (1988), Colombia continued to take the initiative in a series of raids on major cocaine-producing facilities that yielded the largest seizure ever of precursor chemicals. The strong actions against cocaine refining were particularly welcome as a test of Colombia's continuing courage to resist the violence of well-armed traffickers and insurgent groups.

The aerial spray program has succeeded in eliminating about 90 percent of traditional cannabis cultivation; however, new growth in other regions pushed Colombia back into position as the number one exporter of marijuana to the U.S. Strategies are being revised to meet this challenge, and the U.S. has confidence in the cannabis spraying program....As much as has been done, Colombia must do more, not just to eradicate crops but to overcome corruption and intimidation. Colombia fights a two-front war against the traffickers and insurgents, too often in league with one another. We will continue to assist in meeting that challenge.

Attitudes About Drugs

Perhaps the varying attitudes people harbor about drug abuse and control lay the foundation for confusion about the issue. Many positions are no longer "clear-cut" about substance abuse or control. Some drug users and former drug users have spoken out forcefully against drugs, while others have urged a reconsideration of prohibition. Many parents, while strongly antidrug themselves, have ambivalent feelings about the drug laws when their sons or daughters are drug users. Drug use, which in the past has been more neatly confined to particular groups in society, now has taken root in all social strata. This means that virtually all of us have friends, relatives, and associates that are or have been drug users.

Although social drug control policy is discussed in Chapter 13, it might be significant to review the basis of certain attitudes behind drug use and control. From earliest recorded time, society has exhibited social conflict over such heated issues as religion and politics, the latter of which is afforded greater attention in this book.

One's willingness to criticize or accept public consensus frequently hinges on one's political attitudes. Such attitudes will most likely lean toward the conservative (right) or the liberal (left) view. Those of the former persuasion tend to be more traditional and opposed to change, while those that hold liberal views seem to be more open-minded and willing to try the untried. Excesses in either of these convictions tend to foster unrealistic views and attitudes.

The issues of drug use and control have blurred even these traditional political distinctions. While most conservatives, for example, favor tough laws, more police, and refined due process procedures for accused criminals, some leading conservatives are actually arguing for repeal of the drug laws. They base their positions on two fundamental conservative tenets: first, the belief that the free market is self-regulating and will reduce drug abuse if allowed to operate, and second, the traditional conservative position put forward by John Stuart Mill that government should interfere as little as possible with individual freedoms.

Liberals, on the other hand, have traditionally stressed due process rights, non-law-enforcement approaches to crime, and the belief that crime is rooted in a myriad of social problems. Yet, it is the leading liberal legislators, such as Representative Charles Rangel and Senator Edward Kennedy, who are the strongest supporters of unyielding antidrug efforts.

Who Uses Drugs?

Although drugs are used by every strata of society, recent data seems to indicate differences in use levels, modalities of use, and substances preferred among social classes. In 1988, the National Institute of Drug Abuse (NIDA) reported that cocaine consumption by the middle class is steadily declining. Accordingly, public perceptions of cocaine abuse have shifted from that of a glamorous drug mainly used by the rich and famous to its current perception of cocaine as a drug that in many forms poses a threat throughout society.

Print and electronic media alike seem to send the same message to the general populace: cocaine use is widespread and cocaine abuse can kill. Studies have revealed that perhaps the messages are being positively received by the American public. During the late 1980s, for example, the Gordon B. Black Corporation of Rochester, New York surveyed 1,461 college students and found that only 6 percent acknowledged "occasional" use of cocaine in 1988. This figure is down from its 1987 figure of 11 percent.

In addition, the survey revealed that those who said that they had friends that occasionally used cocaine dropped from 36 percent to 31 percent. The prevailing consensus, as reported by the *Washington Post*, was that the "use of cocaine and marijuana among many segments of the population, particularly middle-class professionals and college students, has declined sharply" (January 3, 1989, p. A3).

Drug abuse studies in the inner cities, however, tell a different story, as the use of crack cocaine in such places is soaring. As recently as 1986, crack was sold predominantly in larger cities such as Los Angeles, Washington, D.C., and New York City. As of the writing of this book, the drug is readily available in mid-sized cities such as Denver, Dallas, and Kansas City. Mark Gold, M.D., founder of the Cocaine Hotline, reported to the *Washington Post* that when his telephone referral and counseling service was first initiated in 1983, callers were whites with college degrees and high salaries. In 1989, however, half of the callers were unemployed and only 16 percent were college educated.

In 1989, the issue was further clarified by results from yet another survey conducted by the National Parents' Resource Institute for Drug Education (PRIDE). The survey basically debunked the myth that school-aged drug abuse in the inner city is a problem confined to blacks.

In the survey, 296,180 white students and 59,898 black students at 958 schools in 38 states were polled during the 1988-89 school year. Cities where the information was gathered included Atlanta, Chicago, Dallas, Houston, New York, and Washington. The results showed that alcohol is the leading problem among the sample youths and that boys of both races are more likely to abuse drugs and alcohol than girls. Additionally, drug and alcohol abuse tend to increase as the students progress through school.

David Musto, a Professor of psychiatry at Yale University, has written that we are quickly moving to a "two-tier system" of drug consumption, marked by declining use among middle-class whites and increasing use among poor minorities. In his book, *The American Disease: Origins of Narcotic Control*, he stated that the American society is repeating an earlier cycle of drug use. Musto pointed out that, at the turn of the century, drugs were readily available and widely tolerated. As the incidence of abuse gained momentum, consumption dropped off and social attitudes became sterner.

Figure 3.2

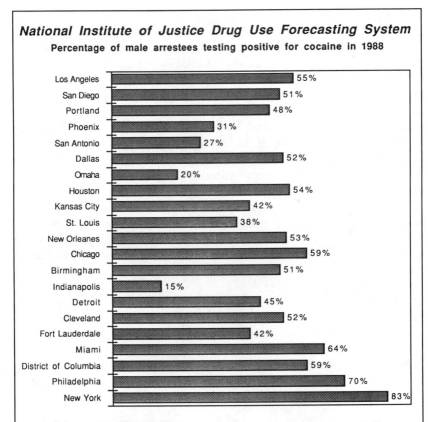

National Institute of Justice Drug Use Forecasting System
Percentage of male arrestees testing positive for cocaine in 1988

City	Percentage
Los Angeles	55%
San Diego	51%
Portland	48%
Phoenix	31%
San Antonio	27%
Dallas	52%
Omaha	20%
Houston	54%
Kansas City	42%
St. Louis	38%
New Orleanes	53%
Chicago	59%
Birmingham	51%
Indianapolis	15%
Detroit	45%
Cleveland	52%
Fort Lauderdale	42%
Miami	64%
District of Columbia	59%
Philadelphia	70%
New York	83%

NIJ's Drug Use Forecasting System measures drug use among persons arrested for serious crime in 21 major U.S. cities. The program obtains voluntary, confidential urinalysis specimens from a new sample of arrestees each quarter. From 54 to 90 percent of male arrestees tested during April-June 1988 used drugs such as cocaine, PCP, heroin, marijuana, or amphetamines. The chart above shows the prevalence of cocaine use during the most recent quarter in 1988 for which data were available.

SOURCE: National Institute of Justice, 1989.

Musto further stated that, as the two-tier effect becomes more pronounced and minorities become more and more associated with drug abuse, public support for treatment may begin to wane. The result could be increased public support for more police, more prisons, and harsher sentences, which Musto feels would be futile measures. "My concern is that as drug use declines among middle-class Americans, they will refuse to invest in the long-term needs of the inner city, like education and jobs. A primary task facing Drug Control Policy Director William Bennett is harnessing the current anti-drug energy and making it productive."

The Social Costs of Drug Use

As indicated earlier, law enforcement initiatives against drug abuse and trafficking are a financially exhausting undertaking. Drug abuse also costs society billions of dollars in many other ways. Such costs are built into the increasing need for drug treatment and prevention programs, lost productivity on the job caused by impaired drug users, and the cost of federal programs. For example, in 1988 the federal antidrug budget was almost $5 billion, compared to President Bush's 1991 proposal, which called for a budget exceeding $10 billion. The 1991 figure does not include the costs of individual state and local law enforcement initiatives (see Chapter 10).

In addition to the financial burden imposed on Americans by drug abuse, there is yet a greater price to pay: the effects of drugs on our youth. Studies have revealed that most drug users began to use drugs as adolescents or even as grade school children. The reasons commonly offered are peer pressure, few legitimate means of income, and broken homes, among others. Adolescent drug abuse also impairs the learning capabilities of children and, in some cases, can even cause severe emotional problems.

Additionally, one should remember that drug abuse is an illegal activity, and when drugs are indiscriminately used around children, a discrete message is sent to them that gives legitimacy to this activity, particularly when parents themselves are the drug users. The National Drug Policy Board reported in 1988: "In New York City an alarming number of child abuse incidents directly attributed to drug abuse were documented. Specifically, from 2,627 to 8,521 in two years."

COSTS TO SOCIETY

Crime Costs—Victimization of innocent individuals is the most obvious cost to society. Although theft is the usual crime of the drug user, drug-related assaults and muggings are often committed also. And of course, drug consumers themselves are often placed in positions where they are susceptible to victimization. While marijuana users engage in violent crime to a lesser extent than cocaine users, the overall crime rates among marijuana users nationally were found to be three times higher than that of non-users of marijuana or that of alcohol users.

Judicial and Penal System Costs—A related cost of drug use is that imposed on the law enforcement, judicial, and correctional systems. Depending upon judicial level, the average cost per jail/prison bed ranges from $20,000 to $40,000 per year and the number of inmates grows approximately 6 percent per year. It is estimated that the national expenditures for corrections will exceed $21 billion in 1990. The total cost of drug abuse to the criminal justice system includes not only corrections but also police, legal, and court costs.

Corruption Costs—Corruption of police and judicial officials is an additional cost placed on society. Some researchers estimate that cocaine trafficking is the principle source of financing for drug-related corruption and that over one-half of income collected by organized crime is generated by cocaine (see Chapters 6, 7, and 9).

Transfer of Illegal Income Costs—Much of the illegal drug money is subsequently transferred from the criminal to the legitimate economy, providing both a base for private influence on enforcement and judicial agencies and a cover for those funds unreported to tax agencies by criminal individuals and organizations. The coercion of organized crime implies higher prices for all consumers, with as much as a two percent increase in some industries. Even more troubling is the fact that this infusion of capital into the legitimate economy from the drug black market further integrates the underworld and the "upperworld," making it even more difficult for law enforcement agencies to deal with the problem of organized crime.

Medical and Social Costs—Society must meet the medical and welfare expenses for treatment of both drug users and those affected by their actions, both purposeful and unintended. These include: the expenses for facilities and staff for drug-specific programs, emergency room and generic hospital care for drug abusers that have overdosed or that have been injured while intoxicated, and hospital costs for victims of drug users, including those that are the victims of violent crime or that have themselves been injured through accidents attributable to another's impairment. Communicable diseases such as hepatitis and AIDS are more readily passed on due to the methods and environment of the drug user. Welfare assistance places an indirect burden on society due to the transfer cost required for minimal substance maintenance.

Productivity Costs—Drug abuse leads to absenteeism and inefficiency on the job. Initial research indicates a high level of unemployment associated with heavy alcohol use. In addition, heavy use of a drug like cocaine increases the probability of illegal activity, such as drug dealing, within the employer's firm. A study of household income effects of marijuana usage indicated a drop of as much as 40 percent in income for those employed persons who reported any history of daily use (Research Triangle Institute, 1984, p. a-22; Dembo, 1986; Davis, 1982). Productivity losses amounted to $8.7 billion as a result of addict criminal behavior (Research Triangle Institute, 1984, E-6).

Family Costs—Family costs include the reduced income to the family, increased tension and violence, the associated increase in the probability of child abuse (or, at a minimum, improper care), the possibility that the children will themselves become users, the limitation of opportunities for the child if he becomes a user, and the effects on the fetus of drug use by the mother.

Source: U.S. Department of the Treasury, August 1987.

The Violence

In August 1989, drug traffickers exploded a bomb alongside Secretary of State George Schultz's motorcade during his visit to Bolivia. The purpose of Schultz's visit was to deliver a speech supporting a Bolivian crackdown on the cocaine trade. This incident is not an unusual one for source countries such as Bolivia, as there have been many reports of Latin American traffickers that have offered large cash bounties for the assassinations of certain U.S. government officials that oppose the illicit drug trade.

The proliferation of drug-trafficking groups operating in the United States has also increased. For example, in October 1988, the Treasury's Bureau of Alcohol, Tobacco, and Firearms conducted what was dubbed as "Operation Rum Punch." In this operation, numerous members of cocaine- and crack-dealing Jamaican posses were arrested throughout the country. Violence exhibited by this group between 1987 and 1989 is thought to have resulted in the murders of an estimated 1,400 people.

[S]peak the truth: that drugs are evil, that they ruin and end young lives...that drug dealers are murderers and should be treated as such.

President George Bush, 1989

With the propagation of drug gangs interested in their share of the drug pie, drug-related crime has also spread to ancillary areas where profit motive outweighs the motivation of the addict to stay "well." Self-styled drug gangs such as the Los Angeles-based Crips and Bloods wage turf wars and calculated acts of revenge over the control of our neighborhoods. These gangs also recruit members as young as eight years old to deal drugs or act as spotters in this vicious and violent business.

The pursuit of higher education and legitimate work is no longer considered by many of these individuals to be the best way to get ahead in life. The allure of gold chains, fast cars, status, and parties has stifled the growing process for many gang members. Indeed, drugs represent a set of already stifling environmental factors that create a social gauntlet between the children and their education, and legitimate employment.

Indeed, the violence associated with the drug problem poses one of the paramount concerns of this illicit business. A 1988 "Americans Talk Security" poll of registered voters disclosed that 86 percent considered drug trafficking to be a major concern to national security and that 41 percent deemed combating international trafficking to be one of the most important goals in maintaining national security. The survey also revealed that 50 percent of those polled admitted that they knew someone who used illicit drugs.

Addicted Babies

As indicated earlier in this chapter, health problems arising out of drug abuse are one of the principal concerns in drug control efforts. One such issue is the problem of cocaine-addicted babies. In a 1988 study, Ira Chasnoff, president of the National Association for Parental Addiction Research and Education, estimated that 11 percent of all births, or 375,000 babies, are born to addicted mothers every year. This figure represents a threefold increase in such births since 1985.

Detection of cocaine use by pregnant mothers can only be discovered within 24 to 48 hours after use, so even such a high estimate may be extremely conservative. Problems exist because symptoms of a pregnant women who suffers from cocaine addiction may not always be apparent to hospital officials. In many cases, pregnant addicts may not even visit hospitals until they are in labor and are ready to deliver.

Much attention was focused on the issue of cocaine-addicted babies during the late 1980s because of the serious health-related risks facing unborn children. Such hazards include strokes while babies are still in the womb, physical malformations, and increased risk of death during infancy. In addition, because of the earlier mentioned practice of "sex-for-crack" by some pregnant woman, many babies are born with ancillary health problems that include sexually transmitted diseases.

Dr. Gordon B. Avery of Children's National Medical Center in Washington, D.C. stated that it is typical for cocaine babies to be born prematurely. He added, "In addition to the medical complications facing otherwise normal premature babies, cocaine babies face special hardships such as hydrocephaly (water on the brain), poor brain growth, kidney problems and apnea (an unforeseen stoppage of breathing)" (Kantrowitz, 1990).

Confusion in this area of drug abuse is partly attributable to the fact that as recently as 1982 there were still medical textbooks on high-risk obstetrics which stated that cocaine had no harmful effects on the fetus. A fetus is particularly vulnerable to cocaine for several reasons:

1. Although the placenta does shield the womb from many large, complex molecules (particularly those that can't defuse across fatty cell membranes), it is an open door to cocaine. This occurs because cocaine is attracted to fatty compounds, and once the drug enters the blood and tissues of the fetus, it remains there longer than it does in an adult.

2. The effects of cocaine on the mother-to-be also pose some threat
    to the fetus. That is, when a woman addicted to crack gets preg-
    nant, the well-being of the fetus and of her own body are not her
    primary concerns.

3. An estimated 40 to 50 percent of cocaine-addicted pregnant
    woman have been exposed to the AIDS virus.

4. Among cocaine-addicted babies, the average birth weight is ap-
    proximately 21 ounces lower than normal, while the average
    head circumference is about three quarters of an inch smaller
    than the average among normal babies. These differences lead to
    future learning difficulties and an increased risk of infant mortal-
    ity.

Demographically, the problem of cocaine-addicted babies extends beyond
the inner city and across the national social spectrum. In many larger cities such
as New York, hospitals report that their obstetric and pediatric wards are overburdened and that drug-related costs contribute greatly to the overall cost of
health care (Revkin, 1989).

Fueling the problem of cocaine-addicted babies is the emerging problem of
older children that are born as cocaine-addicted babies but who survive to three
to six years of age. "They operate on an institutional level—they eat and sleep,
and eat and sleep. Something has been left out" (Kantrowitz, 1990). Social
workers and hospital professionals claim that these "cocaine children" may even
have difficulty playing or relating with other children, as they display symptoms
of paranoia and distrust toward others. It has become a sobering reality that
even if drug abuse were halted today, society would be forced to deal with its effects in one way or another for the next 50 to 75 years.

The New Consumerism

The clandestine methamphetamine/crack market has created a new type of
consumerism (for lack of a better term) that accompanies trafficking ventures.
The new consumerism can be viewed from two angles: the drug user consumerism and the drug dealer consumerism.

Because of drug user consumerism, many supermarkets have noticed increased sales of items such as scouring pads, cough syrup, and inhalers of Pri-
matene Mist. The sales of these and similar items illustrate their greater worth
in a clandestine market than in a legitimate market. Scouring pads and steel
wool, for example, are used for cleaning drug pipes and holding crack at the

bottom of the bowl. Grain alcohol is commonly used to ignite crack, and the inhalers give drug users an added euphoric feeling or "rush" while under the influence of stimulants.

Stolen goods are a common means for drug users to get money for drugs. Studies have shown that "T-tops" from the roofs of sport cars are commonly bartered or sold for drugs. Other favorites are virtually anything electronic, such as video cassette recorders, microwave ovens (also used to make crack), stereos, and video games.

At the opposite end of the consumerism spectrum is the drug dealing side. Items such as cellular phones, pagers, personalized license plates, jewelry, firearms, and automobiles have actually boosted the legitimate market. Cellular phones and pagers are commonly used to arrange drug transactions, deliver supplies, and arrange for money pickups.

Personalized license plates have emerged as a type of status symbol. Variations of "boof" and "sling," for example, may refer to smoking and selling crack. Expensive rings and gold chains and watches are commonly used for bartering for drugs. This is because such items are easily carried into crack houses, and many dealers covet the items as status symbols.

Figure 3.3

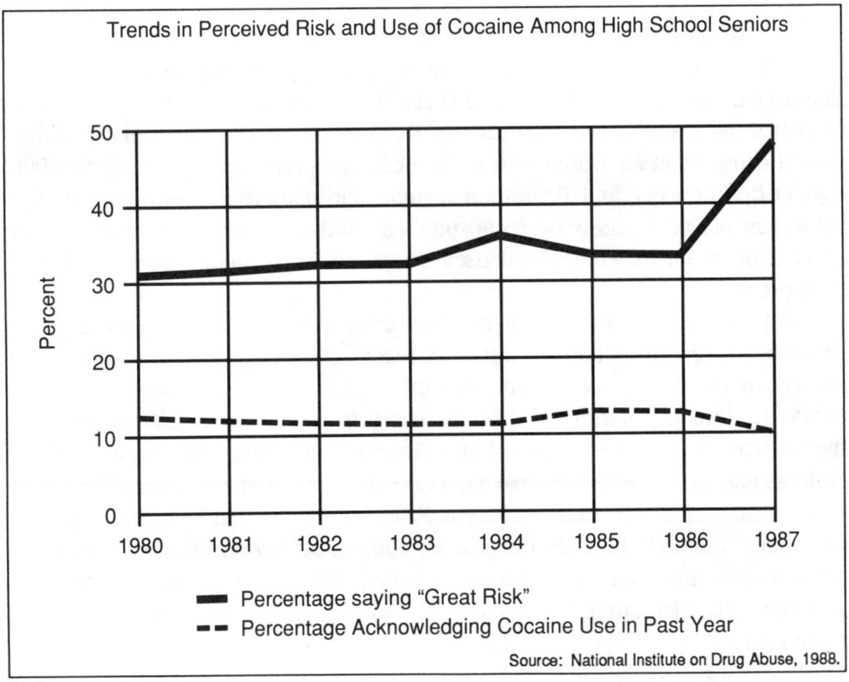
Trends in Perceived Risk and Use of Cocaine Among High School Seniors
Percent
50
40
30
20
10
0
1980
1981
1982
1983
1984
1985
1986
1987
Percentage saying "Great Risk"
Percentage Acknowledging Cocaine Use in Past Year
Source: National Institute on Drug Abuse, 1988.

Weapons such as the 9-millimeter semi-automatic have achieved a certain popularity with many drug dealers. The 9-millimeter, commonly referred to as a "muscle gun," is compact and has an intimidating appearance. Automobiles are also one of the most sought after of the drug dealer's status symbols. Vehicles such as Mercedes Benzes, and Rolls Royces have been seized by law enforcement agents after the vehicles have been purchased with cash earned from illicit sources.

The buying trends discussed above pose serious ethical, moral, and legal dilemmas for retail merchants that may be suspicious of some customers but may not have firm grounds for refusing business from those customers. Problems are presented when customers present merchants with large sums of cash in exchange for goods. Specifically, merchants should not morally judge a person because he possesses large amounts of cash or because he is from a certain side of town. Still, such merchants may find that the money that they receive from any transaction may ultimately be subject to forfeiture under federal law if the customer turns out to be a drug dealer.

Supply and Demand

The demand for drugs in the United States has created an industry that generates, according to conservative estimates by the Justice Department, $100 billion a year. Of course, the demand fuels the supply side of the drug problem. Statistics from the National Institute of Drug Abuse in 1989 show the distribution of drug use at an estimated 6 million cocaine users, approximately 500,000 regular heroin users, and 19 million regular marijuana users. Further statistics show that out of a survey of 36 hospitals around the country, an estimated 11 percent of pregnant women had used drugs, most commonly cocaine, during their pregnancy.

An estimated 80 percent of the illicit drugs consumed in the United States originate in foreign countries, although recent estimates indicate that over 50 percent of the marijuana consumed in the U.S. is now domestically produced. While the foreign countries will be discussed in greater detail later in this text, the primary foreign sources are Latin America, including Mexico, Colombia, Bolivia, and Peru; the opium-growing regions of southeast Asia, including Laos, Burma, and Thailand; and southwest Asia, including Iran, Afghanistan, and Pakistan. Although these are the primary sources of illicit drug supply, traffickers in many other areas of the world are involved in processing, transporting, and generally facilitating the marketing of drugs such as cocaine, heroin, and marijuana.

CLOSE UP: CHILDREN DRUG DEALERS

During the summer of 1989, a 10-year-old boy arrested for selling cocaine was led away in tears and in handcuffs to a children's shelter, where he was ordered held for failure to appear in court on two previous arrest warrants. During a 30-minute hearing, Suffolk County (New York) family court Judge Donald Auperin ordered the boy detained despite his mother's assurances that she would make sure that he showed up at the next hearing, scheduled for later that week. The mother also had been subpoenaed at the boy's two previous court dates.

The child, believed to be the youngest suspect ever arrested on Long Island on drug selling charges, remained silent and showed no emotion until he apparently realized that he would not be released. Then he began to cry. His mother left the courtroom sobbing after watching her son, wearing sneakers and blue jeans with a rolled-up comic book in his back pocket, being led away. He was taken to the Nassau County Children's Shelter in Westbury.

The boy's attorney entered a not guilty plea on the youth's behalf. A 14-year-old accomplice, arrested with the 10-year-old, was released in his mother's custody after his attorney argued that the boy posed no danger to society. Both youths were arrested after police saw them allegedly dealing crack cocaine on a street corner. As the youths tried to flee on a bike, the 10-year-old dropped a bag containing three $20 crack vials. One of the youths also had $226 in cash.

Source: Associated Press, January 13, 1990.

The Etiology of Drug Abuse and Crime

The search for solutions for reducing drug abuse and crime has baffled law enforcement authorities, social scientists, and criminal justice academicians alike. Although many proposed solutions to the problem will be discussed throughout this book, several widely accepted social theories exist that explain why people use drugs and under what circumstances they become lured into criminal lifestyles. Although these theories will be examined later in this chapter, perhaps it would be appropriate to discuss first the concepts of vice and of victimless crime, terms commonly associated with drug crimes and drug abuse.

Vice and the Victimless Crime

While "vice" in normal parlance refers to any bad habit or evil conduct, it specifically refers in legal jargon to the supplying of any illicit good or service.

For example, smoking cigarettes may be a vice in the ordinary sense, but only those activities that have been specifically outlawed are generally considered "vice crimes," which include drug trafficking, loansharking, gambling, and prostitution.

Some vice crimes are actually legal under carefully regulated circumstances. Gambling, for instance, is legal in some states under some circumstances. Nonetheless, illegal gambling activity thrives on the skirts of controlled gambling institutions. Through uncontrolled illegal organizations, profits may exceed those that can be realized through legitimate channels.

"Vice" is the supplying of illicit goods or services, such as prostitution, gambling, loansharking, and drugs.

Enforcement techniques, especially for vice crimes like drug trafficking, can be controversial because a police officer's professional code of conduct and the letter of the law with regard to criminal investigations are sometimes violated in order to obtain information. Enforcement is particularly difficult in these cases because there is usually no complainant or victim as there is in more traditional criminal violations. Therefore, law enforcement officers must rely on a high degree of surreptitiousness and ingenuity to make arrests. This can be illustrated, for example, by the drug investigator that is tolerant of a certain amount of drug use on the part of his or her informant, while other people are under investigation for drug use activity similar to that of the informer.

In a study of drug law enforcement, Peter K. Manning and Lawrence John Redlinger listed the questionable and corrupt practices that have been associated with narcotics agents. The list included taking bribes, using drugs, buying and selling drugs, arrogation of stolen property, illegal searches and seizures, protection of informants and their drug trafficking activities, and violence. Drug enforcement professionals, while willing to admit that there is a certain degree of corruption in all law enforcement agencies, defend their profession by pointing to several factors. First, because of the accessibility of federal grant money in the early 1990s, professional training is more readily available to drug enforcement officials than ever before. Second, the adoption of a field training officer program (FTO) for drug enforcement personnel in larger departments has helped weed out individuals during their probationary period that are not considered competent for the job. Third, because of an increase in drug testing programs within law enforcement agencies, administrators have a new tool to check officers for drug abuse.

As to the term "victimless crime," another distinction must be made. A crime is usually characterized by an act that hurts someone or something or by the potential for the act to hurt someone or something. An exception is in the case of drug abuse, as the primary victim, the drug abuser himself, is a willing participant in the activity. In addition, there are generally no complainants in vice crimes, for the reasons previously discussed. So, when charges are filed in vice cases, the state (or government) is the complainant. Hence the term "victimless crime" came into use. This does not preclude the fact, of course, that innocent people are also commonly victimized by drug abuse.

Victimless crimes are those where all participants are willing participants.

So why do people choose drug abuse as a social lifestyle? What fuels one's ambition to become involved in a criminal drug trafficking organization or in a behavior that is considered criminal? These questions will be addressed next in the context of sociological theories that attempt to explain the social nature of the drug problem.

Anomie

In 1938, Robert Merton introduced the concept of anomie to explain an individual's motive for involvement in deviant social behavior or crime. In this theory, the ends become more important than the means, and an individual will resort to deviant means if no legitimate means are available. The cultural goal of financial success, for example, is highly valued by the individual. But if that individual finds: (1) that less value is attached by society to how that success is achieved and (2) that legitimate routes to financial success are blocked, he or she may opt for illegal means to achieve that particular end. For example, owning a home is generally considered one of the "Great American Dreams," but for many low- or fixed-income families, this dream cannot be obtained through legitimate means. As a result, people from these families often "become estranged from a society that promises them in principle what they are deprived of in reality" (Merton, 1964: 218).

In particular, to illustrate his theory, Merton cited a preoccupation with material success (or "pathological materialism") endemic in American culture. A legitimate profit motive may be channeled through deviant means (drug dealing, for example) when there are social barriers to legitimate channels such as good schooling, good jobs, and higher income. The result may be the creation of a criminal, a person willing to break the law to reach his or her goals.

Merton further explains that there are five modes of individual adaptation to the contradiction between promised goals and available means. These modes of adaptation are conformity, ritualism, rebellion, retreatism, and innovation.

Anomie occurs when a society or group of people are deprived of in reality what they are promised in principle.

It is of course the first and third modes, conformity and rebellion respectively, that may offer the most intelligible explanation of society's involvement in drug use. The fifth mode, innovation, creates one of the fundamental social infrastructures for involvement in organized crime.

The crime phenomenon of the California youth gangs, for example, that spread to many major cities in the mid-1980s, suggests that Merton's philosophy has contemporary validity. Such gangs represent thousands of inner-city youth from the Los Angeles area that have become extremely organized and that target large cities as the base from which hundreds of thousands of dollars of drug money is realized (see Chapter 8).

Cultural Transmission

A study first published in the early 1940s by researchers Clifford R. Shaw and Henry D. McKay (University of Chicago) developed the theory of cultural transmission. The research for this study focused on criminality, particularly among young people, in Chicago during the 1920s and 1930s. The researchers examined certain neighborhoods that were consistently "high crime" neighborhoods over several decades. Specifically, research revealed that, although the ethnic composition of these neighborhoods changed over time, the level of criminality remained the same.

As a result of this study, it has been suggested that the attitudes, values, and norms of these areas are not only conducive to crime but are transferred, over time, from one ethnic group to another. According to this theory, children become indoctrinated into a life of crime at an early age. This occurs particularly in males that associate regularly with criminals and look to them as role models.

Cultural transmission is the transmission of values, attitudes, and norms from one generation to another over a given period of time.

Differential Association

Some theorists embrace the concept of differential association in attempting to understand an individual's involvement in criminal activity. This theory, formulated by Edwin Sutherland, says that a principle part of learning criminal behavior occurs within intimate groups. This occurs in two ways. First, individuals, particularly those living in economically depressed areas, tend to identify with the financially successful role models in their communities, (drug dealers, pimps, and gamblers). Second, certain individuals are exposed to the lifestyle and techniques of criminal behavior in their communities. The specifics of what is learned is based on the frequency of contacts and duration of each association. According to Sutherland, the individual learns specifics of criminality such as specialized techniques, attitudes, justifications, and rationalization. It is through the learning of these traits that a favorable predisposition to criminal lifestyles is developed. Sutherland offered nine basics of differential association, which are as follows:

1. Criminal behavior is learned.

2. The fundamental basis of learning criminal behavior is formed in intimate personal groups (e.g., gangs).

3. Criminal behavior is acquired through interaction with other persons in the process of communication.

4. The learning process includes the techniques of committing the crime and specific rationalizations and attitudes for criminal activity.

5. General attitudes regarding respect (or lack of respect) for the law is reflected in attitudes toward criminal behavior.

6. A person becomes delinquent or criminal because of an excess of definitions favorable to violation of the law over definitions unfavorable to violation of the law.

7. Differential association may differ in duration, frequency, and intensity.

8. The processes for learning criminal behavior parallel those of any other learning process.

9. Criminal behavior is an expression of general needs and values (as with noncriminal behavior), but it is not explained by those needs and values.

Differential association is the learning of criminal behavior through intimate personal groups.

Differential Opportunity

Differential opportunity is another popular theory that parallels Merton's theory of anomie and one that attempts to explain criminality and preoccupation with material success. Richard A. Cloward and Lloyd E. Ohlin (1960) wrote that many male adolescents experience extreme deprivation of opportunity. Therefore, many feel that their position within society is somewhat fixed and unchangeable and that there are few legitimate ladders to success. It is this theory that holds that when conditions of severe deprivation prevail, delinquent behavior results. Cloward and Ohlin have identified three types of delinquent subcultures:

1. The retreatist subculture (where drug use is the primary focus).
2. The conflict subculture (where gang activities are dedicated to destruction and violence as a way of gaining status).
3. The criminal rackets subculture (where gang activity is devoted to utilitarian, or profit-motivated, criminal pursuits).

Differential opportunity occurs when severe deprivation along with extremely limited legitimate ladders of success result in delinquent behavior.

Summary

Today's drug situation is a result of complex social interactions affecting many different people, places, and things. It is referred to in a number of different ways by public speakers, politicians, the media, and private citizens. Terms used to describe the situation include the drug crisis, the drug problem, the drug dilemma, the drug epidemic, and the "war on drugs."

However people choose to refer to them, drugs have re-molded the social fabric of communities, the work environment of businesses, the learning environment of schools, the criminal justice system, and the drug treatment industry, just to name a few. From all indications, drug abuse, in one form or another, is here to stay.

There is no single drug abuse problem. The current drug situation poses numerous problems, and each seems to require a specific antidote. Drug problems present themselves as related to both health and public safety, and much controversy exists around the best solution for the problem. The existence of drugs in our communities poses a considerable financial burden for society. Costs include: the cost of crime itself, criminal justice system costs, medical costs for victims, and the loss of productivity in the work place. Other hidden costs include the moral cost of corrupt public officials and family strife for drug users and their loved ones.

The very nature of the drug problem creates an element of criminality and the accompanying violence commonly associated with that element. New organized crime groups such as the Jamaican posses and the California-based Crips and Bloods have emerged since the "drug culture" itself materialized, and their presence has become well known in many communities throughout the nation. Long-established crime organizations have also flourished since the drug epidemic gained momentum.

Drug trafficking and related drug activity is referred to by many as a "vice" crime. Additionally, many tend to refer to this type of behavior as "victimless" because all participants are willing to engage in the act. Because of this observation, many feel that the enforcement of such crimes is the equivalent of government attempting to police morals and personal values, and that such crimes should not be considered crimes at all, but should be regulated and taxed.

Explaining the criminal behavior that commonly accompanies drug abuse are several social theories. Included are theories of anomie, cultural transmission, differential association, and differential opportunity. Each of these theories explains the basis for either drug abuse or criminality and can be applied to the study of modern-day criminal behavior.

DISCUSSION QUESTIONS

1. The term "drug abuse" is a diverse one, meaning many things to many people. Discuss its meaning to you and why there exists so much difference in the ways in which people view this problem.

2. Other than drug users themselves, who are the victims of drug abuse in our society?

3. Public opinion polls have indicated that drug abuse is the number one social problem in the United States. Discuss some of the reasons why the drug problem is considered a major social problem by so many.

4. Discuss some of the health-related problems inherent in drug abuse.

5. What are some social theories that help explain why some people turn to drug abuse?

6. What are the distinctions between the terms vice and victimless crime?

7. Is there truly such a thing as a victimless crime? Discuss your response.

8. List the ways that cocaine addiction in pregnant females affects their unborn children.

9. Discuss the social and health-related ramifications experienced by children born of addicted mothers.

10. Discuss the "new consumerism" of drug trafficking and its effects on the ethics and morals of legitimate business enterprises.

11. Discuss Robert Merton's traditional social theory of anomie and how it relates to drug abuse in the 1990s.

12. Discuss the differences in differential association and differential opportunity, and how these interact with the phenomenon of drug abuse.

CLASS PROJECTS

1. Discuss with fellow classmates or friends their perceptions of the country's drug problem and what can be done to solve it.

2. Locate newspaper or magazine articles that discuss different perceptions of the country's drug problem.

CHAPTER 4

THE INTERNATIONAL DRUG TRADE

The enormous profits to be realized in the American drug market have intrigued both domestic and foreign traffickers. Although many dangerous drugs such as methamphetamine, LSD, and phencyclidine (PCP) are produced domestically, and a rapidly increasing proportion of the marijuana consumed in the United States is grown domestically, foreign traffickers supply an estimated 80 percent of illicit substances consumed in the United States (DEA, 1988).

Cocaine is a primary example of a drug imported by foreign drug networks. America's cocaine supply, as mentioned in Chapter 2, originates almost exclusively in South America. The coca plant is cultivated principally in Peru, Bolivia, Colombia, and Ecuador, and processing laboratories have been seized in Colombia, Brazil, and Venezuela. In 1989, new markets in these foreign countries have emerged for *bauzco*, a form of crack cocaine. Other South American and Caribbean countries have also served as transshipment centers for drugs.

An increase in the production of cocaine has resulted in a glut that has reduced its wholesale price and increased street purity. For example, in Miami, Florida, the price of a pound of cocaine in 1984 ranged from $18,000 to $23,000, but in 1989, the same quantity was selling for approximately $9,000. Accordingly, the purity of cocaine was about 35 percent in 1984, and in 1989, that figure was up to 70 percent (OCDETF, 1990).

Other drugs frequently smuggled into the United States from foreign countries are marijuana and hashish, both products of the hemp or cannabis plant. Mexico supplies an estimated 30 percent of cannabis to the United States, while Colombia supplies an estimated 33 percent, although (as indicated above) these percentages have been consistently declining due to increases in domestic production in the United States. Other foreign countries contributing to the U.S. marijuana market are the Caribbean island of Jamaica and Belize in Central America.

Opium poppies, used to manufacture heroin, are predominantly grown in Pakistan, Afghanistan, Burma, Thailand, Laos, and Mexico. The milk-like liquid is first dried, then processed into morphine, and later converted into heroin. When smuggled into the United States, heroin is usually diluted with substances such as milk, sugar, or baking soda.

Often, source countries create mutual alliances, sharing resources in order to maximize their profits. This chapter will examine some of the most active drug source countries, the drugs that they produce, and methods of trafficking drugs.

Mexico

In October 1984, a round of gunshots was fired into an automobile parked in front of the home of a U.S. Drug Enforcement Administration agent stationed in Guadalajara. This violent incident was the first of several initiated by traffickers to deter drug enforcement officials from continuing their probe into Mexican drug trafficking.

The following month in the State of Chihuahua, 10,000 tons of marijuana were seized and burned after a raid by Mexican police. These incidents became the first of many that led to a greater awareness of drug trafficking between Mexico and the United States (see Chapter 9). Mexico's participation in global drug trafficking centers around two illicit drugs: marijuana and heroin ("Mexican brown").

Mexico's extensive involvement in the drug trade has proven to be one of the most serious impediments to domestic drug enforcement initiatives in the United States. According to the Drug Enforcement Administration, Mexico has supplied an estimated one third of the heroin entering the United States since the late 1970s.

Mexico is our third largest trading partner for legal commodities...with a volume of some $30 billion annually.

In addition, in 1987, Mexico ranked second in the world in the production of high-potency marijuana. This could be attributed to the fact that there have been recent eradication efforts in Colombia, Brazil, and other South American countries that are major producers of marijuana. Today, marijuana cultivation occurs in every state of Mexico, with the heaviest concentration in the northern and western states of Sonora, Sinaloa, Chihuahua, Oaxaca, and Cuerra. Enforcement efforts have proven to be costly; in the ten year period between 1975 and 1985, over $115 million of American money was spent in the cooperative efforts between the two countries. In previous years, Mexican president Miguel de la Madrid Hurtado had referred to the problem as "a cancer in both our societies."

During the 1960s, the focus of American-Mexican drug enforcement efforts was the reduction of marijuana production and interdiction efforts along the entire 1,933-mile Mexican border. By 1975, the scope of drug enforcement in Mexico had widened to include opium poppies, which also grow in abundance throughout the country. Joint eradication initiatives between American and Mexican authorities ended in 1978 with the relinquishing of all such responsibilities to the Mexican government. In spite of successes such as the Chihuahua raid, questions slowly emerged regarding suspected criminal involvement of Mexican officials in the illicit drug trade.

Some Mexicans still assert that if the demand for drugs in the United States were eliminated, the black market drug trade in Mexico would disappear. This proclamation, common to many drug source countries, addresses the historical and global dilemma of supply versus demand. It is becoming more clear, however, that drug trafficking in Mexico is no longer a problem for the United States only. Mexican drug abuse is soaring, particularly among youths.

In 1985, the DEA reported that a survey of more than 11,000 Mexican students between the ages of 15 and 20 in 246 schools, found that 15 percent of these young people reported that they had used drugs. The drug of choice was marijuana, but other drugs named were such inhalants as glue and paint. In the late 1980s, Mexican television stations aired special reports during prime time to illustrate the devastating effects of drugs on the youth of Mexico.

Mexican Drug Smuggling

Over the years, marijuana and heroin have been the most commonly exported drugs originating in Mexico. Much cocaine, however, has also been intercepted in Mexico, which has served as a major transshipment point between Colombia and the United States. The U.S. Drug Enforcement Administration reports that overland smuggling is the most prevalent method of moving illicit drugs from the Mexican interior to the United States. Texas, California, Arizona, and New Mexico all share the Mexican border with seven ports of entry (POE).

For those who have been to the Mexican border, it is quite obvious that there is no wall, fence, or barricade separating the two countries. Moreover, U.S. Border Patrol officers assigned to watch for illegal aliens and drug smugglers find themselves undermanned and lacking much of the necessary equipment and resources to do an effective job. The remoteness of much of the border area and the great distances to be covered make patrolling an almost insurmountable responsibility. In fact, drug smugglers literally walk over the Mexican border to meet fellow traffickers on the American side, and they often do this with no United States government interference.

In a 1988 Rand Corporation Study, project director Peter Reuter asserted that the Mexican government, unlike governments in Colombia, Bolivia, and Peru, does not incur any major political threats by cracking down on the drug trade.

In fact, there is increasing willingness on the part of the Mexican government to do just that. This is due in part to the large numbers of Mexican police that have died in drug enforcement efforts. Indeed, with the number of Mexican police that have died while serving U.S. interests, it is likely that more Mexican than American police have been killed while attempting to enforce U.S. drug policies.

Ground smuggling techniques for marijuana and heroin have become quite ingenious over the years. Such methods include drugs concealed in false gas tanks, inside the backs of seats, and inside dashboards and spare tires. The movement of drugs through the use of general aviation aircraft and vessels also accounts for much Mexican drug smuggling activity.

According to the DEA, there have been more than 2,000 clandestine airstrips identified in Mexico. The strips are grouped into 10 different clusters. The number of these strips indicates the extent of the air smuggling problem and illustrates Mexico's tremendous capacity for illicit drug production. It has been estimated that one third of the airstrips are located around opium poppy growing regions, while the remainder are used for marijuana smuggling.

Almost any type of aircraft can utilize these airstrips. Types range from small single-engine aircraft, such as the Cessna 172 and 182, to larger transport aircraft. The proximity of the Yucatan Peninsula to the United States also makes an ideal transit point for drug smuggling flights, particularly for those originating in the Guajira region of Colombia. In 1986, there were some 70 clandestine airstrips identified in the Yucatan Peninsula alone.

Perhaps it is naive to hope that Mexican officials could eliminate all transshipment efforts by Mexican traffickers, but a closer working relationship between the two countires is desirable. For example, as of the preparation of this text, there is no Mexican-American provision for U.S. authorities to chase smugglers in "hot pursuit" across the border. Indeed, when U.S. chase planes approach the Mexican border, they are required, under law, to retreat.

The Mexican Heroin Trade

Mexico first emerged as a major heroin supplier during the early 1970s. This occurred just after the collapse of the "French Connection," a massive heroin trafficking operation between Marseilles and New York. Mexico experiences an opium harvest season that takes place between September and April. This includes two harvests, which peak in November and March. After the opium harvest, raw opium gum is transported from the growing fields to nearby villages by pack mules, pedestrian couriers, or vehicles. Because of the vast number of back roads and footpaths in Mexico, interdiction at this stage is almost impossible.

The opium reaches the heroin processing laboratories by means of gatherers (acaparadors). Their job is to purchase designated amounts of opium gum from the cultivators and deliver it, usually by general aviation aircraft, back to the processors that placed the order.

The conversion process (raw opium to powdered heroin) takes about three days and yields brown heroin with a wholesale purity of 65 to 85 percent. In contrast, white powdered heroin manufactured in the Middle East (discussed next) yields an average purity of 85 to 99 percent, which allows a much greater profit margin for traffickers. Most conversion laboratories are located in remote regions of the country, but some have been discovered in large cities such as Mexico City, Nuevo Laredo, and Tijuana.

Figure 4.1
Mexico
Opium Poppy and Marijuana Cultivation Areas

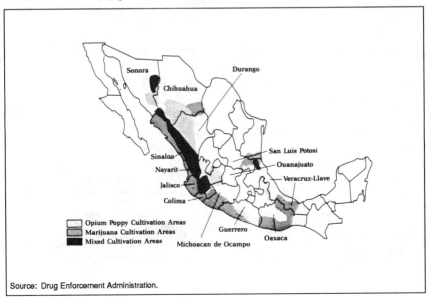

Source: Drug Enforcement Administration.

Once the complicated laboratory processing is completed by an experienced chemist, the traffickers transport the heroin to principal population areas and prepare it for clandestine shipment to the United States. Once in the United States, the principal market areas for Mexican heroin are in the southwest region, contributing an estimated 80 to 90 percent of the market there; and in the west, contributing about 50 percent of its market (DEA, 1988). While areas such as Chicago still account for a significant percentage of the market, Mexican heroin is virtually unavailable in the northeast and southeast United States.

Figure 4.2

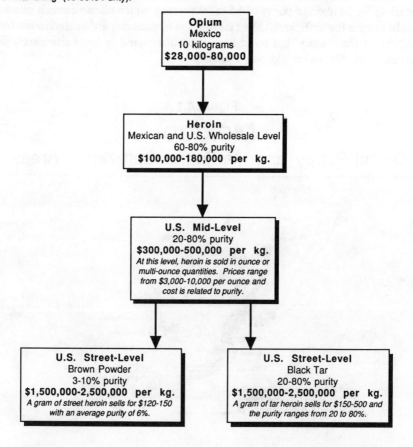

Mexican Heroin

Selling Prices for the Equivalent of One Kilogram of Mexican Heroin at Successive Stages of Trafficking (60-80% Purity).

Opium
Mexico
10 kilograms
$28,000-80,000

Heroin
Mexican and U.S. Wholesale Level
60-80% purity
$100,000-180,000 per kg.

U.S. Mid-Level
20-80% purity
$300,000-500,000 per kg.
At this level, heroin is sold in ounce or multi-ounce quantities. Prices range from $3,000-10,000 per ounce and cost is related to purity.

U.S. Street-Level
Brown Powder
3-10% purity
$1,500,000-2,500,000 per kg.
A gram of street heroin sells for $120-150 with an average purity of 6%.

U.S. Street-Level
Black Tar
20-80% purity
$1,500,000-2,500,000 per kg.
A gram of tar heroin sells for $150-500 and the purity ranges from 20 to 80%.

SOURCE: DEA, 1987

Drug Enforcement in Mexico

The primary authority for drug enforcement in Mexico is vested in the nation's chief law enforcement officer, the Attorney General. It is the Attorney General that dictates who will be prosecuted and for what drug offense. The responsibility for apprehension of drug offenders rests with the Mexican Federal Judicial Police (MFJP), which investigates all federal crimes, including drug offenses.

Drug regulatory functions are the responsibility of the Department of Narcotics under the Secretary of Health and Welfare, and of the Director of Food, Beverages, and Drugs. The Department of Narcotics is responsible for enforcing drug violations in the Mexico City area and surrounding areas.

In her book *Desperadoes*, *Time* magazine correspondent Elaine Shannon exposes the circumstances surrounding the 1985 abduction and murder of DEA agent Enrique "Kiki" Camarena in Guadalajara (see Chapter 6). According to Shannon, certain Mexican officials not only helped to plan the abduction and murder but also created an elaborate cover-up, one that continues as of the writing of this text. From Shannon's account, the Mexican government's involvement in narcotics is second only to that of the government in Panama (1988).

EVENTS OF THE CAMARENA MURDER

- November, 1984. Camarena assists in a raid on a huge Mexican marijuana plantation owned by drug lord Rafael Caro Quintero

- February, 1985. Camarena is kidnapped in Guadalajara, tortured, and murdered

- December, 1989. Caro Quintero and Ernesto Fonseca Carrillo, another drug kingpin, are convicted of the murder in Mexico City

- January, 1990. A Los Angeles grand jury indicts six more Mexicans, including Humberto Alvarez Machain

- April, 1990. Dr. Alvarez is abducted in Guadalajara and delivered to DEA agents in Texas

---

Colombia

Colombia has the dubious distinction of being the world's most active illicit-drug-producing country. During the 1980s, an estimated 80 percent of the refined cocaine and 60 percent of the marijuana available in the U.S. market originated in Colombia. Traffickers in Colombia have earned the reputation of being true entrepreneurs in the drug trade by becoming involved in virtually all aspects of the illicit drug business. Colombian traffickers have masterminded the financing of drug plantations and laboratories as well as sophisticated smuggling and money laundering operations in the United States, Canada, and Europe.

Colombia is a country of contradictions. On one hand, it ranks as one of the most economically prosperous countries in Latin America. Its economy grew by 5.5 percent in 1987 and again by 4.5 percent in 1988 (Bagley, 71). In spite of a $15.7 billion foreign debt, Colombia has never fallen behind on debt service payments. On the other hand, its enormous economic success is offset by the fact that is remains one of the most violent and corrupt countries in South America and, possibly, in the world.

The Colombian involvement in U.S. cocaine trafficking can be traced back to the influx of Cuban refugees to South Florida in the 1960s after the Castro revolution. In Florida, many immigrant Cubans formed ethnic communities that served as the economic base of continued operation for the so-called "Cuban Mafia." The Cuban Mafia is a particularly pernicious organized crime group for two reasons. First, many of its leaders developed their illicit entrepreneurial skills under the tutelage of Meyer Lansky and Santo Trafficante when they ran massive gambling and drug smuggling operations in pre-revolutionary Cuba. Second, after the Cuban revolution, many of these future organized criminals were trained in the techniques of violence, smuggling, and other clandestine activities by the Central Intelligence Agency as part of its efforts to raise and train an anti-Castro army. Once it was established in the United States, the Cuban Mafia became the major distribution organization for Colombian cocaine.

At first the south Florida Cuban Mafia organizations, in using their long-established Colombian cocaine connections, brought just enough cocaine to the United States for distribution in their own communities. But gradually they began to import larger and larger quantities of cocaine for expanding markets in the United States. By the mid-1960s, the Cuban networks expanded their distribution systems nationwide and relied on Colombian traffickers for nearly 100 percent of the cocaine distributed by the Cubans. The arrangement was simple: Colombians manufactured the drug and the Cubans trafficked it in the United States.

Gradually, however, the Colombians came to want more control of the operation, and by the 1970s, they had expanded their own trafficking role in the United States. By 1978, the Colombians had severed most ties with the Cubans and assumed the dominant role that they now play in providing cocaine to the United States. It was also during the 1970s that the incidence of violence increased as a result of several localized cocaine-trafficking gang wars and gave rise to the Colombian trafficking cartel's notoriety (see Chapter 9).

In 1981 an extradition treaty between Colombia and the United States was ratified, and for a time, traffickers were fearful of losing their immunity to U.S. criminal prosecution. If they were brought to the United States to face drug charges, they might not be able to bribe their way out, as they had done with relative ease in Colombia.

In 1982, Belisario Betancur Cuartas became president of Colombia. Although Betancur was strongly and openly opposed to drug trafficking, he also believed that the extradition treaty violated Colombia's sovereignty and said that he would not approve any extraditions during his four-year term. Rodrico Lara Bonilla was then appointed as minister of justice by Betancur. In 1984 Bonilla organized a raid on Tranquilandia, the location of the Medellin Cartel's largest cocaine laboratory, capable of producing over three metric tons of cocaine a month. As a result of the raid, the police seized a total of 13.8 metric tons of cocaine worth an estimated $1.2 billion, along with firearms, aircraft, and chemicals necessary in the production of cocaine hydrochloride. During the month following the raid, Lara Bonilla was assassinated by an unknown gunman.

In November 1985, M-19 guerrillas (see Chapter 9) stormed Colombia's Palace of Justice, murdered 11 Supreme Court Justices, and destroyed the extradition files. The siege resulted in the murders of 95 persons. It is widely believed that the Medellin Cartel had hired the M-19, as the destroyed extradition case files concerned Medellin Cartel members.

In June 1987, the Colombian Supreme Court overturned the extradition treaty with the United States. A total of 15 traffickers had been extradited since 1984. During the week of August 14, 1989, three more government officials were murdered. One of the victims was presidential contender Luis Carlos Galan, who was shot and killed by seven gunmen during a political rally near Bogota. The Galan murder prompted an enraged President Virgilio Barco Vargas to enact "summary extradition" for use in fighting the traffickers. This permits the extradition of drug criminals from Colombia to the United States while circumventing the Colombian court system.

Now, the fight is with blood....We do want peace. We have screamed for it, but we will not beg for it."

Signed "The Extraditables."
(the Medellin Cartel)

Source: *The Bogota Daily La Prensa*, 1989

In considering Colombia's extensive role as a source country, we should also consider the reasons that have enabled Colombia to maintain consistent

Kings of Cocaine Book

control of the cocaine market and much of the marijuana market for such a long period of time. A number of significant reasons can be cited for this:

1. Geographically, Colombia is well positioned to both receive coca from Peru and Bolivia and to export, by air or sea, processed cocaine to the United States.

2. The country's vast central forests are effective in concealing hidden processing laboratories and air strips.

3. Colombians have gained much experience over the years as an early pioneer in the cocaine trade. Consequently, the drug organizations have progressed from small fragmented groups of criminals to sophisticated and professional criminal cartels that are quite proficient at their trade.

Colombia, in spite of its many problems, is one of Latin America's richer countries. Its economy grows by three and one-half percent a year, and its foreign debt is only $18 billion. Investors are attracted to Colombia by its coal and oil.

The cocaine business endures in Colombia largely due to its high profitability and the excellent business practices initiated by the traffickers. Coca bushes grow best along the Andean mountain chain, mainly in Bolivia and Peru. Colombians import the semi-processed coca paste, run the laboratories that convert the paste into cocaine powder, and skillfully control the trade northward to the United States through Caribbean and Atlantic coast shipping routes.

Drug Enforcement Administration officials estimate that Colombian traffickers, over the last ten years, have increased tenfold the supply of cocaine to the United States. With the resultant market glut in the United States, traffickers are turning their attention to Europe by way of Spain, where cocaine brings four times the retail price that it does in Miami.

As previously mentioned, marijuana is also one of Colombia's primary illicit drug exports. According to findings in 1986 by the President's Commission on Organized Crime (hereinafter referred to as PCOC), Colombia supplied 42 percent of the marijuana consumed in the United States in 1984. The major percentage of this traffic was controlled by large Colombian organizations, such as the Medellin Cartel (see Chapter 7).

Marijuana is cultivated in several regions throughout Colombia, but the largest of these is along the Guajira Peninsula. Members of large Colombian trafficking organizations purchase marijuana from growers and provide protection and financial incentives to them. Marijuana is harvested twice each year, with the largest harvest occurring in the fall. The predictable harvest pattern closely parallels the level of availability of Colombian ("Colombo" or "Bo") marijuana in the United States.

The United States government estimates that almost 90 percent of culti-vated Colombian marijuana is shipped to the United States by sea, with the rest being shipped by air through the use of general aviation aircraft. The ships used are commonly referred to as "mother ships" and are usually large fishing vessels or freighters that can hold 50 tons for a 100-foot mother ship and 100 tons for a 400-foot mother ship.

CLOSE-UP: WAR-TORN COLOMBIA

On August 18, 1989, Colombia's Virgilio Barco astonished the world by declaring a "state of siege" in Colombia. This was done by the suspending of the normal operation of criminal and civil law and giving himself arbitrary powers that enabled him to prosecute drug or-ganizations. As a result, about 11,000 suspects were initially detained along with the seizure of the following goods: 678 firearms, 3,303 rounds of ammunition, 1,161 cars and trucks, 62 fixed-wing aircraft, 18 helicopters, 141 houses and ranches (one of which had its own private zoo), 30 yachts, 13 motorcycles, four tons of coca paste and 242 pounds of cocaine.

Several incidents had led up to the 1989 extradition revival. For example: on August 17, 1989, a judge investigating the murder of a leading newspaper editor was himself murdered; next, the governor of Antiquoia province (whose capital is Medellin) and the police chief of the National Security Police subsequently resigned; next, all of the country's 27,000 judges and court officials declared that they would stop work unless they were given adequate protection; then, a gunman emerged from under the platform where Carlos Galan was to address a political party in Bogota. He was fatally shot.

By the end of 1989, the U.S. Justice Department had listed 89 Colombian nationals as wanted in the United States for drug trafficking violations. All but one of these suspects, Carlos Lehder, who was ar-rested and convicted in the United States during 1987, are believed to reside in Colombia. It was in 1987 that a 1979 extradition treaty was declared unconstitutional by the Colombian Supreme Court.

Officials in Medellin estimate that there is, on the average, one killing every two hours. In 1988, about 3,000 political assassinations occurred in Colombia. Police reports estimate that one fifth of the mur-ders are not reported to authorities, and of those reported, only an es-timated three percent go to court.

Source: Associated Press, February 9, 1990.

Typically, these ships await their cargo while remaining at sea or stationed at selected Colombian ports. Once the shipment is ready for transportation to the United States, the ship travels to a selected beach site that is predetermined by the traffickers. An estimated 100 loading sites dot Colombia's north coast from Barranquilla to Portete, and all of these are linked by trails and airstrips to the major growing areas. When preparations are complete, the mother ship moves to a prearranged location about one half to 3 miles off shore. Small boats then ferry loads of marijuana from the shore to the mother ship. This is usually done during the night to avoid detection.

Marijuana traffickers commonly use the same trafficking routes established by cocaine traffickers. It is from these routes that American ports along the Gulf of Mexico and the east coast are most accessible to smugglers. These routes are as follows:

1.   The Windward Passage - between Cuba and Haiti

2.   The Yucatan Channel - between Mexico and Cuba

3.   The Mona Passage - bordered by the Dominican Republic and Puerto Rico

In May 1990, national elections were held to elect a new president of Colombia, as former president Virgilio Barco was prohibited by the Colombian constitution from seeking a second term. During the campaign, the drug issue overshadowed all other issues and resulted in the bloodiest election in the country's 180 years of independence. Reminiscent of gangland-style voter intimidation of the 1930s, the violence during the nine months preceding the Colombian election included the assassinations of three presidential candidates, 262 police officers, 93 soldiers, three judges, 15 news media employees, and an estimated 1,700 Colombian civilians. During the two weeks prior to the election, nine bombs exploded at schools, churches, shopping centers, and supermarkets killing 320 persons. One bomb destroyed a Colombian airliner, killing all 107 persons aboard.

The office of president was sought by some twelve candidates. Of these twelve, Cesar Gaviria, the Liberal Party's candidate, and Alvaro Gomez emerged as leading contenders. Gaviria's platform was basically the same as Barco's—he advocated a hard line against traffickers. Gomez, however, urged for the legalization of cocaine in the major drug-consuming countries and maintained that the only way to put the traffickers out of business was to deprive them of profits. Gaviria overwhelmingly won the election and assumed his duties on August 7, 1990.*

---

*   [The conflict between Colombian traffickers and segments of the Colombian government over the issue of extradition is an ongoing ordeal. The writings in this book are intended to reflect the prevailing posture of the Colombian government (as of the preparation of the text) and are subject to change with the tide of violence and the political and social climate within that country.]

Figure 4.3

Foreign Source Marijuana

Selling Prices for one pound of Marijuana at Successive Levels of Trafficking.

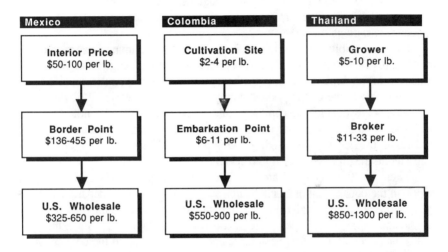

Mexico	Colombia	Thailand
Interior Price $50-100 per lb.	**Cultivation Site** $2-4 per lb.	**Grower** $5-10 per lb.
Border Point $136-455 per lb.	**Embarkation Point** $6-11 per lb.	**Broker** $11-33 per lb.
U.S. Wholesale $325-650 per lb.	**U.S. Wholesale** $550-900 per lb.	**U.S. Wholesale** $850-1300 per lb.

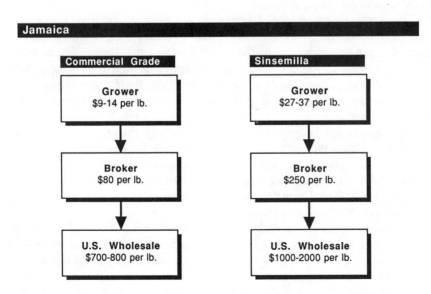

Jamaica

Commercial Grade	Sinsemilla
Grower $9-14 per lb.	**Grower** $27-37 per lb.
Broker $80 per lb.	**Broker** $250 per lb.
U.S. Wholesale $700-800 per lb.	**U.S. Wholesale** $1000-2000 per lb.

SOURCE: DEA, 1987

Bolivia

Bolivia, a South American country that straddles the Central Andes Mountain range, encompasses an area roughly equivalent to the combined size of Arizona, Colorado, Utah, and New Mexico. It is bordered to the north by Brazil, the southeast by Paraguay, and on the west by Chile and Peru. Bolivia consists of three primary topographical regions known as the Altiplano. The regions are distinguished by wide variations of rainfall as well as by local structural variations.

Bolivia exhibits wide variations in geography and climate. Its range of sea level, from 300 to 21,000 feet, and its climatic conditions range from the continuous heat of the Amazon basin to the heavy snowfall of the Andes.

Considered one of the poorest countries in South America, Bolivia has an estimated $570 annual per capita income (O'Brien, 1984). Its notoriety as a drug source country is similar to Peru's as a coca leaf producing country for international traffickers. Although growing the coca leaf plant in Bolivia is perfectly legal, the processing of it into cocaine is against the law.

There are two principal areas of coca cultivation in Bolivia: the Chapare region in the department of Cochabamba and the Yungis in the department of La Paz. Bolivia's traditional role in international drug trafficking has revolved around the supplying of coca paste to traffickers in Colombia. Since the mid-1980s, however, Bolivia has been more and more involved in the conversion of coca paste to cocaine hydrochloride. Cocaine laboratories have been discovered in the departments of the Beni and Santa Cruz.

Ironically, the emergence of Santa Cruz as a cocaine processing center was intimately connected to the pro-United States military dictatorship of Garcia Luis Meza. It was under this regime that Roberto Suarez-Gomez, Sr., the head of Bolivia's premier cocaine trafficking family, consolidated his hold on the market with the assistance of Nazi war criminal Klaus Barbie, who helped reorganize both the security systems of the Suarez organization and Bolivia's internal security police.

The Suarez family operation is one of the primary sources of cocaine paste in Bolivia. Under the former leadership of Roberto Sr., also known as "little father," son Roberto Jr. and nephew Renato Roca Suarez produce an estimated 40,000 tons of coca paste per year and earn an estimated $600,000 per year. Roberto Sr. was forced to yield control of the organization in 1988 after his addiction to cocaine resulted in his arrest.

A large portion of the Bolivian coca regions consist of only flat, marshy lowlands that are virtually isolated from the outside world. Traffickers in Bolivia, therefore, primarily rely on general aviation aircraft for transporting drugs.

Bolivia has averaged more than one government per year since 1825, so diplomatic efforts to establish eradication programs have been difficult

(O'Brien, 1984). Since the mid-1980s, however, the government of Bolivia has recognized the extent to which drug traffickers have used their tremendous financial resources to gain control over many political factions and financial institutions within the country. This has resulted in increased pressure from the government against traffickers.

In 1986, the Bolivian and United States governments joined forces in "Operation Stop Prop" to locate clandestine growing regions and manufacturing laboratories. To implement the operation, Attorney General Edwin Meese and Secretary of Defense Casper Weinberger issued a joint emergency declaration under the provisions of the Posse Comitatus Act, allowing the use of United States military resources to assist United States law enforcement agencies. Under this plan, Blackhawk helicopters were used to transport United States agents and Bolivian police to remote cocaine laboratories in Bolivia.

Ninety-five police raids resulted in the seizure or destruction of 21 cocaine laboratories, 24 transshipment storage locations, and hundreds of pounds of refined and unrefined cocaine. Authorities estimated that the labs were capable of employing and housing up to 50 workers, who were able to produce 1,000 to 1,500 kilograms of powdered cocaine per week.

Figure 4.4

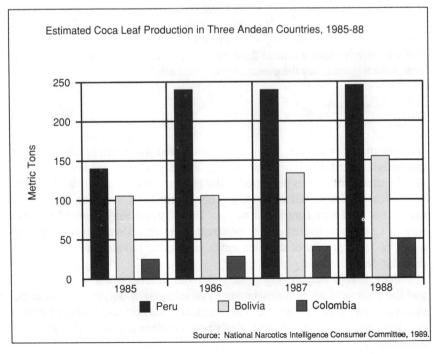

Estimated Coca Leaf Production in Three Andean Countries, 1985-88

Source: National Narcotics Intelligence Consumer Committee, 1989.

Because of such crackdowns in Bolivia, many traffickers have abandoned their laboratories, often leaving equipment and supplies intact. This resulted in a severe reduction in the demand for coca paste and a significant decline in the price of coca leaves. Between June and September 1986, the price of coca leaves fell from $125 per hundredweight to an all time low of $15. Since then, however, the Bolivian government has reported that coca production was back up from 90,000 acres in 1986 to 119,000 acres in 1989 (DEA, 1987).

After a 1989 summit between the heads of the main coca-producing countries in South America, the option of crop substitution was discussed as an alternative to the coca trade. Although it can be asserted that no legitimate crop will bring as high a financial yield as cocaine (an estimated $500 per acre), many experts believe that crop substitution combined with tougher law enforcement may place a considerable dent in coca production.

The cocaine business in Bolivia is less institutionalized than in Colombia and Peru, due to the organized crime influence of such groups as the Medellin Cartel and the Shining Path (see Chapter 9). Indeed, much of the farming in Bolivia is done by out-of-work miners that left the highlands when tin markets collapsed in the early 1980s.

In 1988, Bolivia outlawed the growing of coca for export, and government has initiated a plan in which loans are offered to the estimated 37,000 farmers that are willing to switch crops. In other initiatives, Bolivia has torched over 9,000 acres of coca since 1987 and has reduced its five-digit inflation rate to about 10 percent, which is the lowest in Latin America. Still, experts estimate that a farmer working a typical 2.5-acre coca plot can earn as much as $5,000 a year, which is ten times the average annual income.

Peru

For over 2,000 years, Peruvians have chewed the leaves of the coca plant primarily to counteract the effects of high altitude and as an aid to digestion. A certain amount of coca is permitted under law for domestic use as well as pharmaceutical purposes. Although Peru is not considered a source country for cocaine, it is a primary contributor of coca leaves, which are cultivated and then sold to Colombian traffickers for processing. In fact, Peru cultivates an estimated 60 to 70 percent of the coca leaves used in the production of cocaine hydrochloride.

Peru, like its neighboring country Bolivia, suffers from a weak economy, and the cocaine trade provides hundreds of millions of dollars in income that otherwise would not be realized. The coca leaf is the principal source of income for thousands of Peruvian farmers that find it far more profitable than coffee or other crops.

Figure 4.5

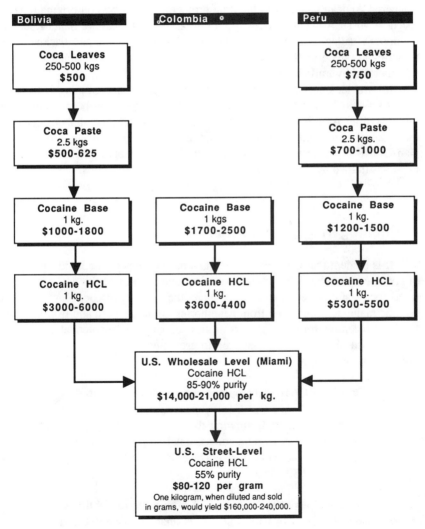

Cocaine

Selling Prices for the Equivalent of One Kilogram of Cocaine at Successive Stages of
Trafficking.

Bolivia

| Coca Leaves |
| 250-500 kgs |
| **$500** |

↓

| Coca Paste |
| 2.5 kgs |
| **$500-625** |

↓

| Cocaine Base |
| 1 kg. |
| **$1000-1800** |

↓

| Cocaine HCL |
| 1 kg. |
| **$3000-6000** |

Colombia

| Cocaine Base |
| 1 kgs |
| **$1700-2500** |

↓

| Cocaine HCL |
| 1 kg. |
| **$3600-4400** |

Peru

| Coca Leaves |
| 250-500 kgs |
| **$750** |

↓

| Coca Paste |
| 2.5 kgs. |
| **$700-1000** |

↓

| Cocaine Base |
| 1 kg. |
| **$1200-1500** |

↓

| Cocaine HCL |
| 1 kg. |
| **$5300-5500** |

↓

U.S. Wholesale Level (Miami)
Cocaine HCL
85-90% purity
$14,000-21,000 per kg.

↓

U.S. Street-Level
Cocaine HCL
55% purity
$80-120 per gram
One kilogram, when diluted and sold
in grams, would yield $160,000-240,000.

SOURCE: DEA, 1987

It is the runaway inflation experienced by Peru, as well as the internal political threat of the Sendero Luminoso ("The Shining Path"), a guerrilla group
closely affiliated with peasant and farming interests, that most concern governmental leaders in Peru (see Chapter 9).

To understand the conflict between the Peruvian government and members
of the Shining Path, "Operation Snowcap" should be considered. Operation
Snowcap, originating in 1987, began as an initiative to help residents of the be-
leaguered Andean nation with the drug problem. The operation originally consisted of 30 DEA agents assigned to a military-style firebase at Santa Lucia in
the upper Huallaga Valley. The agent's function was to serve as a backup force
to Peruvian police with a focus on attacking clandestine airstrips and laboratories operated by traffickers.

In two incidents during April 1990, members of the Shining Path fired
rocket-propelled grenades for over two hours at the base and burned down the
mission of an American priest, Father Mariono Gannon. The attacks came in
the wake of an extended interdiction and eradication program by a joint Peru-
vian-United States team. As of the preparation of this book, the United States
DEA has trained over 600 Peruvian police in drug control tactics.

Trafficking Trends in South America

It is evident that Colombia is maintaining its status as the largest producer
of cocaine hydrochloride in South America (and the rest of the world). While
some coca leaf cultivation takes place there, the majority of coca leaves used in
cocaine manufacturing come from neighboring countries Peru and Bolivia. The
financial incentive for coca growers in these countries is augmented by the fact
that the coca plant is a far easier crop to grow and harvest than other conventional crops. This is evident for three reasons:

1.   Coca is a deep-rooted crop with a life span of about thirty years.

2.   Income earned from growing the coca plant is many times the
     daily wage of growing a conventional crop. For example, farm-
     ers growing coffee will average $520 per acre annually, com-
     pared to $1,030 per acre for coca.

3.   The coca plant can be harvested from three to six times a year
     and will grow in poor soil that is unable to support traditional
     crops.

Figure 4.6

GULF OF MEXICO

VENEZUELA
COLOMBIA
BRITISH GUIANA
SURINAM
FRENCH GUIANA

EQUADOR

PERU

BRAZIL

BOLIVIA

PACIFIC OCEAN

PARAGUAY

CHILE

ATLANTIC OCEAN

URAGUAY

ARGENTINA

SOUTH AMERICA

The Colombian government's 1984 restrictions on the importation of ether and acetone, which are used in the cocaine conversion process, temporarily helped to disrupt cocaine production but has not accounted for a major decrease in its production. This is because laboratory operators found chemical substitutes for these solvents and have also devised ways to smuggle essential chemicals into the country.

Bolivia's involvement in the cocaine trade has remained somewhat consistent through the late 1980s. As mentioned, it is here that much of the required coca pasta is manufactured for later production into cocaine. In addition, due to the tremendous profit margin, Bolivian traffickers are becoming more and more involved with the total conversion process of coca past into cocaine Hydrochloride. According to a 1988 DEA report, this involvement does not yet rival that of the Colombians, although it is growing and certainly takes up the slack for any diminution in the Colombian trade.

Brazil's growing role in the South American drug trade is primarily that of a transshipment country, but it, too, may emerge as yet another source country for the finished cocaine hydrochloride product. This was evidenced by the 1987 seizures of six cocaine hydrochloride laboratories in various locations throughout the country. One of these laboratories, according to authorities, had been in operation for five months and was producing an estimated 2,000 kilograms per week.

One irony in the drug trade is that while many Americans claim drug abuse as the nation's number one priority, American chemical companies furnish an estimated 90 percent of the ethyl ether, acetone, and other processing agents required to make cocaine in South American jungle laboratories. Only in the late 1980s has there been any type of governmental focus on this problem. For example, the Federal Chemical Diversion and Trafficking Act was implemented to require chemical firms to maintain strict records on sales and equipment. Although this law is designed to deter criminal diversion of chemicals to traffickers, DEA reports that many phony "front" companies operating in the United States and Mexico have made tracking chemicals difficult. In addition, cocaine processors have successfully purchased precursor chemicals from German sources, that either produced the chemicals themselves or purchased them from American companies.

There has been some evidence of cocaine trafficking in some of the other South American countries. This includes Ecuador, where some small cocaine labs have been seized; Paraguay, where traffickers have easy access to Bolivia and where there is evidence that cocaine processing was encouraged by General Stroessner's right-wing dictatorship; and in Uruguay, where some laboratory activity was detected in late 1988 and early 1989.

In February 1990, President Bush traveled to Barranquilla, Colombia and met with the presidents of Colombia, Peru, and Bolivia. The purpose of the meeting was to promote drug control harmony and governmental coordination between the countries. Although many criticized the meeting as just another futile effort in the drug war, it was the first time such a meeting had ever taken place.

As a result of the meeting, crop substitution of coffee and flowers was discussed as a possible farming alternative for coca farmers. President Bush agreed to furnish the necessary training for Andean farmers to switch from coca to other crops, to encourage additional United States investments in Andean countries, and to consider removing the United States embargo on flower shipments from South America. The other presidents agreed to open up information channels between their governments, restrict the use of the military in each country to their own country, and hold follow-up meetings in the future.

Figure 4.7

CARIBBEAN ROUTES USED IN MARITIME DRUG TRAFFICKING

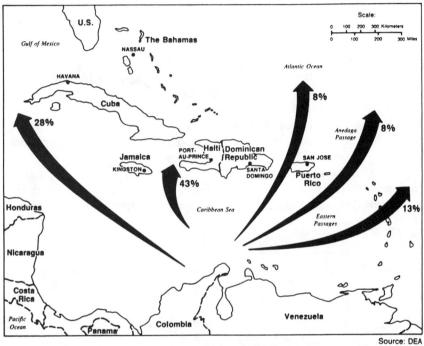

Source: DEA

The Caribbean Basin: Jamaica

Smuggling and drug trafficking by Jamaican nationals is nothing new. However, it was only in 1985 that widespread media coverage of Jamaican gangs (or *"posses"*) raised the public's awareness of the major role of Jamaican gangs in the global drug trade. While the presence of Jamaican posses in the United States will be discussed in greater detail in Chapter 8, this part of the text examines the larger role of the country of Jamaica and its contribution to international drug trafficking.

Jamaica and the Drug Trade

Jamaica's involvement in the international drug trade has always centered around two primary drug commodities: marijuana and cocaine. Although marijuana trafficking has a longer history than does cocaine trafficking, both drugs are a major financial contributor to Jamaica's organized crime element.

High-grade marijuana has been cultivated in Jamaica for over 100 years and is believed to have been introduced to Jamaica by laborers from India in the mid-1800s. Today, its use has spread to literally all segments of society, and it is estimated that between 60 and 70 percent of the islands population regularly consume marijuana (O'Brien, 1984). In spite of its years of cultivation, marijuana has been illegal since 1913. Indeed, marijuana is such big business in Jamaica and it is smoked with such frequency that the law cannot be adequately enforced.

In recent years, Jamaica's role in international drug trafficking has increased dramatically. Considered a consistent supplier of high-grade marijuana to the United States, Jamaican cultivators supply an estimated 17 to 20 percent of the American "pot" market.

Jamaica supplied an estimated 1800 metric tons of marijuana, as well as smaller amounts of sinsemilla and hashish oil, to the United States in 1984. Source: DEA, 1987

Get Cocaine from Colombia

Although Jamaican traffickers cultivate marijuana, they do not grow coca leaves or manufacture cocaine Hydrochloride. Indeed, their involvement with cocaine is that of retail distributor. Jamaican posses have reaped great profits through the sale of crack in the United States.

More and more traffickers are considering the coastal areas of Jamaica as a kind of "pit stop" for loads of illicit drugs in transit from other source countries. Northern fishing ports such as Kingston are particularly popular for transshipment methods of smuggling.

Jamaica's Political History

A turbulent political climate in Jamaica has resulted from lengthy colonial control, poor economic conditions, and violent gangs. Once Jamaica gained complete independence from Britain in 1962, the government attempted to provide adequate housing and jobs for Jamaicans. During this period, the primary political parties in Jamaica were formed. The major labor unions dominating Jamaican industrial relations are the *Bustamante Industrial Trade Union*, the

National Workers Union of Jamaica, and the *Trades Union Congress of Jamaica.*
Currently, the two dominant political parties in Jamaica are the socialist *Peoples National Party* (PNP), headed by Michael Manley, and the conservative *Jamaican Labor Party* (JLP), headed by Edward Seaga. Both of these parties alternate in the control of the country. In 1989, Michael Manley and the Peoples National Party once again gained political control of the Jamaican government through elections that year. The elections were considerably less violent than those in 1980 when extreme political differences between the two parties resulted in the deaths of an estimated 800 people and charges of CIA intervention on behalf of Seaga (who is known in Jamaica as CIA-ga).

Neighborhoods in Jamaica are politically assigned, resulting in both political and geographic associations. Originating in the social and political unrest in Jamaica, violent subgroups known as posses soon emerged; their members adopted the word they had learned from American western movies. Some of the more violent gangs hail from the streets of Kingston, Jamaica's capital, and name themselves after the very neighborhoods from which they hail. For example, the Raetown Boys and the Untouchables are linked to the Peoples National Party, while the Federal Gang, widely identified as Jamaica's premier drug trafficking organization, has associations with the Jamaican Labor Party.

Much of the turmoil in Jamaica can be traced to problems with public housing projects in the country. Probably the most significant event that precipitated drastic social changes began with the Tivoli Gardens housing project. Tivoli Gardens was the first public housing project built in Jamaica. Conceived in the 1960s, the project was an effort to provide jobs and housing to the Kingston ghetto of Trench Town. Edward Seaga, one of the leaders of the Jamaican Labor Party, provided Tivoli Gardens construction jobs and subsequent housing to JLP supporters. This created an atmosphere of "political affiliatory survival," in which one's political associations were directly related to his or her ability to secure good jobs or adequate housing.

Gangs in Jamaica existed for years before the current volatile political atmosphere existed, but with the building of the projects, the gangs have become politicized. Tivoli Gardens then became a power base and the home of one of the JLP's largest and most dangerous posses, the Shower Posse (nicknamed after a machine gun's "shower" of bullets).

The housing projects conceived by Seaga continued in operation even after 1972, when the socialist PNP came into power and Michael Manley became prime minister. In spite of many sweeping social reforms, Manley was unable to undo the damage resulting from the housing scheme initiated by Seaga and the JLP. A sister program called Arnett Gardens was soon initiated by the PNP and patterned after Seaga's Tivoli Gardens. As with Seaga and the Tivoli Gar-

dens project, Manley awarded his supporters with jobs and housing for the Arnett project, which soon became the power base for the Spangler Posse.

By the time of the 1977 election, most of the neighborhoods were politicized, and the posses had become so violent that Manley declared a state of
emergency and placed the gang leaders and their top gunmen under arrest. This
control effort failed to stop the wave of violence in Jamaica. Manley won the
1977 election, but the Jamaican economy failed to improve.

Just prior to the 1980 election, Seaga called on his JLP supporters in Miami
to send hundreds of guns to Kingston. Once winning that election, he made attempts to consolidate the posses that his own JLP party, in fact, had helped create. Some top gunmen were paid off and others were hired to assassinate rival
gunmen. Seaga also sent other gunmen to the United States to engage in two
traditional criminal practices of Jamaican posses: selling marijuana and selling
cocaine.

The Rastafarians

Ganja, a term used to describe potent Jamaican marijuana, is particularly
important to the Rastafarians and their way of life (also see Chapter 2). To understand the Rastafarian religion, which is not well documented, and its relationship to illicit drugs, it is necessary to look at its history. It was the objective
of some Jamaicans, as well as other African descendants, to separate white and
black cultures and revitalize their African heritage. In the 1930s, a black religious group appeared in Jamaica that recognized Haile Selassie (the emperor of
Ethiopia) as their messiah. Prior to taking the name Haile Selassie, he had been
known as Ras Tafari. Hence, his followers called themselves Rastafarians.

Orthodox followers commonly grow "dreadlocks," long locks of hair
formed by washing the hair and allowing it to dry without being combed. Another religious practice is that of smoking ganja. It is considered a magical herb
important to spiritual, mental, and physical health. Reggae singers, such as the
late Bob Marley, sang of the effects of the "mystical herb," and brought worldwide attention to the Rastafarians.

It is important to note that although Rastafarians do recognize marijuana as
an important characteristic of their religion, not all Rastafarians are criminals.
Conversely, even though some Jamaican posse members may be members of the
Rastafarian religion, the religion should not be arbitrarily associated with those
Jamaicans that are involved with criminal activity.

As we will discuss later, the Jamaican youth posses strangely parallel youth
gangs in the United States, especially the Los Angeles gangs. In both cases, a
generation of youth have been exposed to much street violence and illegal drug
trafficking.

CASE STUDY: OPERATION BEACON

Mickie Munday and Jim Coley formed the core of the Beacon group. Now in their forties, they had been friends since high school. They got their start in the smuggling business in 1978. Their method then was unsophisticated. They made direct flights from Colombia in general aviation aircraft loaded, at first, with marijuana and, later, with cocaine. They would land on remote roads and canal banks in South Florida and unload their cargo. In December 1981, Coley and a copilot flew across Cuba too high and too fast. The U.S. Air Force scrambled F-4s to intercept what they thought was a possible MiG and encountered Coley. Coley and his copilot dumped their load of cocaine, but they were met and questioned by U.S. Customs when they landed. Coley disappeared before charges were brought, but Harold Johns, the less cautious copilot, was arrested and convicted. Coley became a fugitive.

By October 1982, Coley and Munday were ready to resume smuggling. They joined with Phil Cardilli and Danny Simms to launch a combined boat/aircraft smuggling venture. Coley headed up air operations. Like other weekend vacationers, on Fridays he would fly a private plane from Boca Raton or Fort Lauderdale to Rum Cay or Long Island in the Bahamas. The plane would transport women passengers, referred to in the organization as "cover girls," and return to the United States with the passengers on Sunday or Monday. The intent was to avoid suspicion by appearing to be engaged in a vacationer's charter or a corporate outing. To this end, Coley and his copilot would wear "uniforms" of dark trousers, white shirt, dark tie, and epaulets.

Instead of spending the weekend in the Bahamas, Coley would fly to Colombia, pick up a load of cocaine, and fly to a group of uninhabited rocks in the Bahamas, named Scrub Cay, where the narcotics were dropped into two boats operated by Cardilli and Simms. Coley would return to Rum Cay or Long Island, where he would wipe down the aircraft, wash off the tires, and replace the remaining Colombian aviation gas with Bahamian gas to remove any physical connection between the aircraft and its secret immediate stop. The aircraft would return to the United States with only the cover girls as cargo.

Cardilli and Simms would proceed from Scrub Cay to Nassau in two very different boats to wait for the organization's amphibian airplane to fly as cover for their return to the United States. They would clear Bahamian Customs and run across the Gulf Stream to Florida on a Sunday afternoon, where the boats were only two among hundreds of boats returning from the weekend. One of the boats was a classic narcotics smuggler's profile, a "go-fast" that was all horsepower. The other boat was an open fisherman that was 40 feet long with no cabin to hide in and not enough power to run away. In fact, the open fisherman was built around a hidden drug compartment accessed by a complicated hydraulic system. If Bahamian or American Coast Guard patrols were encountered, the "go-fast" would speed away as if attempting to escape and would draw law enforcement off the real target.

The open fisherman would enter the United States through Haulover Cut in northern Dade County and proceed up the intracoastal waterway to a marina with dry storage in a warehouse structure, where it would be unloaded at a quieter time.

Munday's role was to monitor law enforcement. He operated out of a sophisticated radio room in his Miami residence. His monitors were linked to the aircraft, the boats, and to an observation post located in an 11th floor apartment overlooking the ocean, the intracoastal waterway, and Haulover Cut. Here Munday, Coley, or a confederate could watch the Cardilli/Simms boats return under the watchful eye of the amphibian as each million-dollar smuggling venture drew to a successful conclusion.

Munday had a falling out with Cardilli and Simms. In May 1985, Munday and Coley returned to their original mode, which was direct smuggling flights to the United States. Ironically, they had already been introduced, by Cardilli and Simms, to the informant that eventually did them in.

Before they resumed air operations, Munday and Coley flew many missions into the Florida Keys to test the effectiveness and range of the first aerostate radar balloon detection system deployed by law enforcement. Based on their studies, they decided to return from Colombia around the western side of Cuba and to approach Florida from the southwest. The aircraft would head for the Venice airport south of the Sarasota-Tampa metropolitan area in predawn darkness, with lights and transponder off. They would approach the beachfront airport, flying 50 feet above the waves. Once over the runway, they would switch on lights and transponder, gain altitude, and immediately log on with Tampa air traffic control. The system accepted them as an aircraft that had just taken off from Venice, which had no tower to report arrivals or departures. They would fly to their ranch in Lakeland, Florida and land on the strip there. The cocaine would be loaded in the trunk of a car, and the car would be hooked to a tow truck and towed to the delivery point in Miami. In the event of an encounter with law enforcement, the tow truck operator could plausibly deny knowledge of the contents of the trunk of the car.

Operation Beacon was begun in October 1984 as an Organized Crime Drug Enforcement Task Force (OCDETF) investigation led by Special Agents of U.S. Customs and the FBI, with cooperation of the DEA and the Florida Joint Task Group. The probe was built around the cooperation of a citizen that had been used by Cardilli and Simms as a source of sophisticated electronics equipment. He had supplied the night vision goggles used by the group to electronically enhance night vision of boat and air crews, and also supplied forward-looking infrared radar (FLIR) of the type used by the military to see darkened targets in the night.

Ultimately, this citizen was asked to build a radio beacon (hence the operation's name) that would be activated by immersion and would signal the location of an air-dropped narcotics load. Cardilli and Simms had introduced this person to Munday and Coley. The citizen, now cooperating with authorities, rose in the Munday/Coley ranks and was able to disclose, in advance, major narcotics shipments.

Other than that, Munday hadn't made a mistake. Even now, if alive, he is a wealthy fugitive unlike his lifelong pal, Coley, who is doing 20 years in federal prison.

It has been estimated that the Beacon group cleared more than $27 million in profits from the 20,000 pounds of cocaine that it was charged with smuggling. Real estate valued at $2.4 million was seized along with seven aircraft, 28 vessels, and 13 vehicles. Cash seizures included $106,000 found in Coley's home, $526,000 from the trunk of his Cadillac, and $1.4 million found buried in the ground at the Lakeland ranch.

Thanks to well-coordinated enforcement efforts, the Beacon group may have reimbursed the taxpayers for its own investigation. The social damage and human suffering inflicted by the Beacon producers can never be recouped.

Source: OCDETF, 1988

The Golden Triangle

The opium poppy from which heroin comes thrives in the bright sun and cold nights of the Golden Triangle, a remote mountainous region in southeast Asia, consisting of parts of Burma, Laos, and Thailand. By 1976, the Golden Triangle supplied more than one third of the heroin consumed in the United States. It continues to produce anywhere from four to five metric tons of opium annually.

Although the opium trade in this region has been well documented since the 1930s, the Golden Triangle first gained widespread notoriety during the Vietnam war. It was here that drugs, especially opium and heroin, were readily available, cheap, and considerably purer than Mexican heroin.

Today, poppy farmers in this region may realize anywhere from $50 to $500 U.S. dollars per day, depending on the size of their fields and the crop yield. The Golden Triangle today is responsible for much of the world's heroin supply. In fact, DEA estimates that "it furnishes approximately 50 percent of the heroin entering Canada and possibly 40 percent of that entering the U.S. market."

A kilogram of 90 percent pure heroin (referred to by traffickers as "Double Globe" and "Red Lion") is easily worth $6,000 in United States currency in growing areas such as northern Burma. The same kilogram, however, is worth between $175,000 and $225,000 after it arrives in the United States, and by the time it reaches the streets, it is only 2 to 5 percent pure, inflating the value of that same kilo to a street worth of $7 to $10 million.

To help illustrate the magnitude of opium production in the Golden Triangle, it was estimated that in 1983, the opium harvest in Burma produced 600 tons, Thailand 40 tons, and Laos 50 tons (see Chapter 7). With huge harvests and profits on the one hand, economic deprivation, persistent political instability, and military strife on the other, international efforts to control the southeast Asian drug traffic have not been successful.

The primitive technologies employed by drug traffickers in the Golden Triangle still result in massive opium production. Horse and donkey caravans haul the opium from Burma to numerous refineries in Laos and along the Thailand-Burma border. An estimated 80 to 85 percent of the finished heroin is transported over jungle trails and mountains into Thailand. The heroin crosses the border far away from Thai police inspectors. The remainder is smuggled to the United States through China, Hong Kong, and India.

Figure 4.8

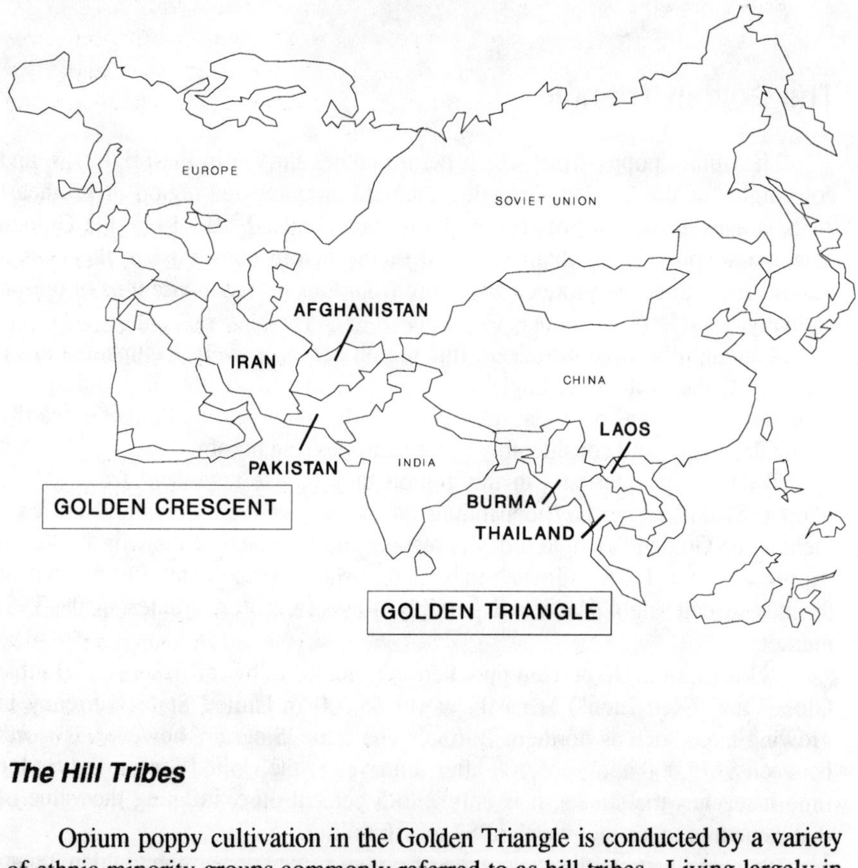

The Hill Tribes

Opium poppy cultivation in the Golden Triangle is conducted by a variety of ethnic minority groups commonly referred to as hill tribes. Living largely in inaccessible, economically underdeveloped areas, these tribal groups have sought to maintain their traditional cultures and to resist integration into the lowland political-economic systems that dominate southeast Asia. Hill tribe separateness has been reinforced by decades of neglect and discrimination on the part of the dominant lowland societies.

Hill tribe people are largely farmers, and for many of them, opium is an ideal agricultural cash crop because soil and climate are both well suited for opium poppy cultivation. Furthermore, opium resists spoilage, is compact, and has a high unit value, making it ideal for more primitive means of cultivation and transport. Middlemen are also readily available to make loans to tribesmen for future harvests or to purchase the opium crop with cash, a scarce highland commodity. Growing the opium poppy in this area is done through traditional methods of slash-and-burn farming without the use of artificial fertilizer. Local laborers cultivate and harvest the crops. Unlike many legal crops that spoil easily, opium can easily endure primitive farming and marketing conditions.

To the hill tribes, opium poppy cultivation has been a socially acceptable pursuit since it was introduced by the British generations ago (see Chapter 1). Unless the tribesmen are shown an attractive alternative, they have little reason to cease the activity.

In the 300 opium-producing villages in Thailand, for example, five hill tribes have been uniquely associated with the cultivation of opium. Of these five, the Hmong and the Karen are the undisputed leaders. The Hmong left China over 100 years ago and upon coming to Thailand, introduced their practice of growing the opium poppy. The Hmong are an independent people that live in the uppermost regions of the mountains of Thailand. So independent are the Hmong that governmental programs for health, farming, and education have failed miserably.

Unlike many legal crops that spoil easily, opium can endure primitive farming and marketing conditions.

During the Vietnam war, the Hmong made up the bulk of a secret, mercenary army fighting in Laos against North Vietnamese and Pathet Lao forces. They were provided with United States assistance, logistical support, and CIA advisers. Alfred McCoy, in his book *The Politics of Heroin in Southeast Asia*, along with many others, contended that the CIA assisted various opium-producing client forces in Laos, Thailand, and the Shan States in transporting their opium during the war, thereby, at least indirectly, creating the massive infusion of heroin into American society during the late 1960s.

Officially, the government of Thailand realizes that the Hmong's involvement in the opium trade poses social problems for the entire country, but the hill tribes' opium trade is tolerated as an economic necessity. Opium produced by Hmong tribesmen is used to trade or barter for such necessities as clothing and food.

The Karen add considerably to the volume of Hmong-produced opium. It was the Karen who were originally brought to the hills by the Hmong to assist them in their opium harvesting. Before long the Karen also realized the benefits of the opium crop and began cultivating their own. Many Karen soon became physically addicted to the opium.

In fact, the Karen used opium so freely for recreational purposes that the addiction rate in the tribe was alarming (an estimated 80 percent in 1985). Opium also served as the main pain killer for disease and other medical problems experienced by the tribe. Treatment for these addicts was therefore difficult. It has been estimated that there are approximately 35,000 addicts among the hill tribes in Thailand.

Thailand

Thailand is a southeast Asian country bordered on the west by Burma, on the east by Laos, on the southeast by Cambodia, and by Malaysia on the south. As mentioned, much of the raw opium that is eventually converted to heroin and shipped to the United States is farmed by the people of northern Thailand's hill tribes. The opium harvesting process in Thailand is basically as follows:

> In January, after a brief flowering of two or three days, the pod of the opium poppy stands exposed and is the sign of the beginning of another year's harvest. The opium harvest usually takes anywhere from a few days to several weeks. Normally, field workers equip themselves with a small curved knife, which is used to lance the side of each pod, allowing the raw opium gum to seep through. The opium gum then remains on the pod for a few hours so that the warmth of the sun can dry it. The farmers then return to the fields to collect it by scraping it off of the pod and into a pail. It is then sold to traffickers, usually during the nighttime hours. Once the traffickers have purchased the opium gum, it is transported deep into the hills to hidden refineries for processing into heroin powder.

In 1976, Thailand's Ministry of Public Health, with the assistance of the World Health Organization, established an opium treatment center near the city of Chiang Mai, in the opium-growing regions of the Golden Triangle. Treatment begins with a balanced diet to build strength and includes immunizations and family planning. Because of the remoteness of the treatment center, many addicts were unable to take advantage of treatment. As a result, a "barefoot doctor" program was adopted to take medical help to the villages.

Ironically, the opium harvest poses some unique hardships for the hill tribes. Opium is a plant requiring a high altitude for a successful yield. The cultivation season begins during January, and temperatures in the mountains during this time sometimes drop to 5 degrees, making opium cultivation an even more difficult and unpleasant task.

Figure 4.9

DRUG TRAFFICKING ROUTES: SOUTHEAST ASIA

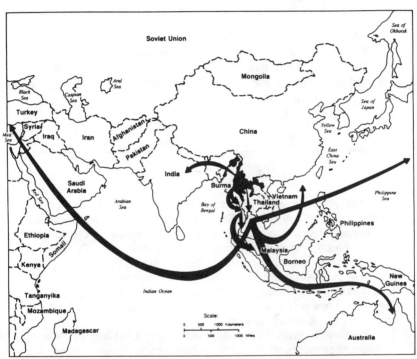

As mentioned earlier, the Thai government has attempted crop substitution with crops such as coffee, kidney beans, and potatoes. These programs have met with only marginal success. This is because the inclement weather favorable for growing opium poses dramatically inferior growing conditions for other crops, killing the trees and rotting the beans before harvest.

Considering the marginal success of the many programs that have been considered to deal with the opium-producing tribes in Thailand, four alternatives remain:

1. *Destroying the opium poppy crop.* Although theoretically considered an alternative, this has not been done for humanitarian reasons. Such an action might invite war or necessitate a major relief program.

2. *Move the tribes out of the hills.* This option would probably be unworkable because of the cultural differences between the hill tribes and the Thai people in the lowlands.

3. *Preemptive buying.* It has also been suggested that the opium could be bought by the government, but problems arise in this strategy due to the remoteness of the tribes and the fact that there would likely still be a lucrative black market for the drug.

4. *Crop substitution.* This has been generally considered the most logical alternative for destroying the opium production in Thailand, but it is one that would take an enormous amount of time and resources. Estimates of the time this would take range as high as 20 years.

CLOSE-UP: THE OPIUM WARS

DOI LANG, Thailand - Serenely perched on the hilltop overlooking Muang Teung village sits the Doi Chedi, or Mountain Pagoda, where the words "May this place remain peaceful forever" are inscribed. Around the pagoda, however, men have dug in for war. Doi Lang, a mountain range straddling the Thai-Burmese border about a mile and a half from the Mae Ai district of Chiang Mai province in northern Thailand, has long been a major conduit for opium grown in the Golden Triangle. The opium is eventually smuggled, as heroin, into Thailand and from there to the rest of the world.

Whoever controls the rugged, mountainous Doi Lang area stands to make huge profits off the lucrative narcotics trade, whose roots are the poppy field in the tri-border area that includes parts of Burma, Laos, and Thailand. Known as the Golden Triangle, the area produces an estimated 600 tons of opium each year.

Three years ago, the Shan United Army, headed by notorious drug kingpin Khun Sa, overran Doi Lang and expelled Musa soldiers and other Burmese minority groups from the area. "Back in 1982 there were about six heroin refineries here, operated by the Musa and other minorities. Now there are none," said Sai Lat, 39, a commander in Khun Sa's army.

In 1988, Sai Lat and 600 of Khun Sa's troops, now called the Shan State Army after an alliance with two other Shan rebel groups in 1985, were busy fortifying Muang Teung and their outposts at Doi Lang for a pincer attack. On September 12, 1988, a Shan State Army outpost was attacked and captured. Thai border patrol police said five of its soldiers were killed and at least four wounded. The Shan State Army claimed that it was a joint force of the Burma Communist Party and the Wa National Army that attacked their outpost and is currently preparing to launch an assault on their Muang Teung stronghold.

According to Shan State Army estimates, about 900 Burma Communist Party troops have come to the border area, bringing with them more than 2,000 pounds of morphine. At today's prices such an amount of morphine would fetch a fortune. Anti-narcotics officials estimate that one kilogram, about 2.2 pounds, of No. 4 heroin now sells for $5,000 to $6,000 on the border, compared with $2,500 last year. The higher price is attributed to crop eradication programs and tougher crackdowns on drug traffickers by Thai anti-narcotics authorities.

According to Colonel Vichit Vechasat of the Thai border patrol police, whose camp is stationed just across the border from Khun Sa's Muang Teung stronghold, the Burma Communist Party and the Wa National Army forces are trying to oust Khun Sa from the Doi Lang area in order to wrest control of the lucrative narcotics route.

The Shan State Army, since it joined forces with two other Shan rebel groups last year to form the Thai Revolutionary Council, has supposedly turned over a new leaf from its drug-dealing past. Despite the Shan State Army's new heroin-free image, antinarcotics officials in Bangkok estimate that Khun Sa still controls about 80 percent of the narcotics trade in the Golden Triangle. But judging by the fortifications being built at Muang Teung, where the Shan State Army is sparing no expense to build bunkers and erect barbed-wire fences (especially around the high ground at Doi Chedi) pushing Khun Sa out of the drug trade, which he has lorded over since the mid-1970s, will be no easy business.

Source: Associated Press, March 27, 1989.

The Golden Crescent

Following a decrease in illicit opium production in the 1970s in the Golden Triangle, three countries emerged as formidable producers of raw opium and heroin. These southwest Asian countries, Iran, Pakistan, and Afghanistan, have been dubbed the Golden Crescent because of the rich opium poppy growing regions in each country.

"Southwestern Asia is responsible for an estimated 60% of the world's heroin" (DEA, 1986). Ironically, in spite of flagrant trafficking activities in this region, opium producers there have generally looked on the abuse of heroin as an "American problem." As of the preparation of this text, however, the heroin addicts in southwest Asia outnumber American addicts almost two to one.

Opium use in the Middle East dates back thousands of years. But it was not until a few decades ago that the Middle Eastern countries that make up the Golden Crescent became politically organized.

While Iran was ruled by the Shah, the countries of southwest Asia formed an opium system that had little impact on the west. This was because much of the opium produced in the border regions of Afghanistan and Pakistan was smuggled to Iran to serve that country's immense addict population, which consists of one million addicts out of a total population of 40 million. There the opium was eaten or smoked by older, rural dwellers, although with Iranian modernization came an increasing number of heroin abusers among the urban middle classes.

In 1955, the Shah imposed a ban on domestic opium production in an attempt to suppress drug abuse. He did permit some legal production, however, to meet the requirements of registered addicts. As the Shah's dictatorship weakened and law and order in Iran became less prevalent, the farmers began to ignore the opium ban.

Before the collapse of the Shah's regime in 1979, Iran served as a "sponge" for Afghan and Pakistani opium. After the fall of the royal family, Iran became a major producer of the drug for both its own domestic use and for exportation. Political chaos in Iran only aided traffickers in their operations.

Soon there was more than enough heroin in the Golden Crescent to supply European and North American markets. The role of Turkey as a heroin transshipment country also increased. Turkish traffickers, using the large population of Turkish guest workers in Germany as a cover, first flooded Germany, then the rest of Europe, with inexpensive southwest Asian heroin that frequently ranged into the 90 percent level in purity.

As evidence of Europe's heroin epidemic mounted, concerned United States officials suspected that it would spread to the United States In October 1979, the Department of State convened a meeting in Berlin to discuss the problem. Attending the meeting were State Department representatives and DEA narcotics coordinators from United States embassies in Europe and southwest Asia.

Other international efforts were also considered in 1979, such as exploring crop eradication operations in Iran. With the untimely seizure of the United States Embassy in Iran during November of that year, all possibilities for a constructive dialogue ceased. Additionally, the Soviet invasion of Afghanistan the following month also foreclosed close cooperation with that country. Another of the many ironies of the international drug trade is the fact that the Soviet invasion seriously disrupted heroin supplies from Afghanistan. The heroin pipelines resumed the flow of drugs, in much larger volumes than before, after aid to fundamentalist Moslem guerrillas, the Mujahedeen, began to flow from western nations. Only Pakistan (discussed later in this chapter) remained as a possible area for diplomatic endeavors in the area of drug control.

Figure 4.10

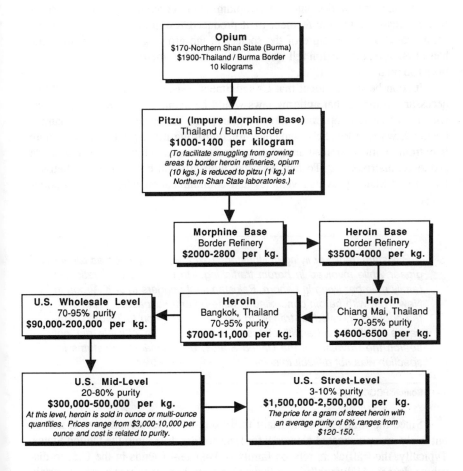

Southeast Asian Heroin

Selling Prices for the Equivalent of One Kilogram of Southeast Asian Heroin at Successive Stages of Trafficking (70-95% Purity).

Opium
$170-Northern Shan State (Burma)
$1900-Thailand / Burma Border
10 kilograms

Pitzu (Impure Morphine Base)
Thailand / Burma Border
$1000-1400 per kilogram
(To facilitate smuggling from growing areas to border heroin refineries, opium (10 kgs.) is reduced to pitzu (1 kg.) at Northern Shan State laboratories.)

Morphine Base
Border Refinery
$2000-2800 per kg.

Heroin Base
Border Refinery
$3500-4000 per kg.

U.S. Wholesale Level
70-95% purity
$90,000-200,000 per kg.

Heroin
Bangkok, Thailand
70-95% purity
$7000-11,000 per kg.

Heroin
Chiang Mai, Thailand
70-95% purity
$4600-6500 per kg.

U.S. Mid-Level
20-80% purity
$300,000-500,000 per kg.
At this level, heroin is sold in ounce or multi-ounce quantities. Prices range from $3,000-10,000 per ounce and cost is related to purity.

U.S. Street-Level
3-10% purity
$1,500,000-2,500,000 per kg.
The price for a gram of street heroin with an average purity of 6% ranges from $120-150.

SOURCE: DEA, 1987

Pakistan

Pakistan is an extremely poor country. Indeed, it is one of the poorest in the world, and funds for narcotic suppression projects are extremely limited. Nevertheless, Pakistani leaders are aware of the enormous impact on other countries of the opium produced within Pakistan's borders, as well as domestic problems that the opium trade and addiction have produced.

As an early response to the problem, the government of Pakistan issued an order banning cultivation and use of opium. This order was generally considered successful, and enforcement of it produced few problems in spite of the complicated tribal structure of the society in the growing regions. During the ban's first year, production fell from an estimated 650 metric tons in 1979 to less than 100 metric tons in 1980.

It soon became evident that United States assistance to Pakistan would be necessary to insure that antidrug laws would be maintained. The initial phase, which involved a crop eradication program, was the easiest. What remained, however, was the toughest challenge: to control the illicit production of opium in extremely impoverished areas where the farmers have few, if any, acceptable economic alternatives. To help Pakistan with difficult enforcement initiatives, the United States provided vehicles and communication gear to antinarcotics units.

A Pakistani trafficker living in Houston, Texas was employed as an engineer while involved in heroin trafficking. In the heroin operation, a family member living in Lahore, Pakistan sent couriers to JFK Airport in New York with heroin concealed in false-bottom suitcases. From JFK, the couriers traveled "in-transit" to LaGuardia, then on to Toronto. Because of their "in-transit" status, Customs Service officials did not search the travelers in the United States, and Canadian Customs inspection was not difficult to clear.

Source: PCOC, 1986

Since the mid-1970s, Pakistani traffickers have developed several unique but fairly unsophisticated networks for transporting drugs into the United States. Typically, the traffickers rely on family or Pakistani friends in the U.S. to distribute drugs. Additionally, they have also been known to make use of certain trusted black organizations in cities such as Los Angeles, Detroit, and New York. In addition, Pakistani traffickers have aligned with their Italian criminal counterparts in New York City.

Figure 4.11

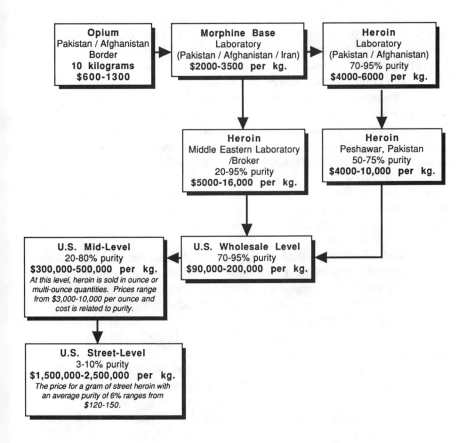

Southwest Asian Heroin

Selling Prices for the Equivalent of One Kilogram of Southwest Asian Heroin at Successive Stages of Trafficking (50-95% Purity).

Opium
Pakistan / Afghanistan
Border
10 kilograms
$600-1300

Morphine Base
Laboratory
(Pakistan / Afghanistan / Iran)
$2000-3500 per kg.

Heroin
Laboratory
(Pakistan / Afghanistan)
70-95% purity
$4000-6000 per kg.

Heroin
Middle Eastern Laboratory
/Broker
20-95% purity
$5000-16,000 per kg.

Heroin
Peshawar, Pakistan
50-75% purity
$4000-10,000 per kg.

U.S. Mid-Level
20-80% purity
$300,000-500,000 per kg.
At this level, heroin is sold in ounce or multi-ounce quantities. Prices range from $3,000-10,000 per ounce and cost is related to purity.

U.S. Wholesale Level
70-95% purity
$90,000-200,000 per kg.

U.S. Street-Level
3-10% purity
$1,500,000-2,500,000 per kg.
The price for a gram of street heroin with an average purity of 6% ranges from $120-150.

SOURCE: DEA, 1987

Afghanistan

Afghanistan is the largest producer of opium in the Golden Crescent and one of the largest producers of opium in the world (second only to Burma). With the 1988 withdrawal of Soviet military troops from the country after almost nine years of occupation, it is likely that opium production will increase.

Turkey

As a key country bordering Iran and the Golden Crescent, Turkey remains a major contributor to opium and heroin production in that region of the world. In 1987, the DEA estimated that six to seven tons of opiates, including refined heroin and morphine base, were smuggled into eastern Turkey from Iran.

Opium poppy farming has existed in Turkey for centuries and has represented a livelihood for thousands of Turkish farmers. For generations opium cultivation was conducted by private Turkish farmers, but in 1933, the Turkish government established an agency to buy the opium gum from the growers. The government then exported the opium gum to other countries, where opium alkaloids such as morphine and codeine were extracted for medicinal use. However, a considerable amount of gum was diverted and smuggled to the Middle East and France (the French Connection), where it was processed into heroin. Much of this heroin ultimately ended up in the United States. During the 1960s and early 1970s, an estimated 80 percent of the heroin on United States streets originated in Turkey.

In 1971, however, the Turkish government placed a ban on opium cultivation that became effective the following year. Because of trade losses after the 1971 ban, the Turkish government initiated the poppy straw program in 1974, in which legal opiates were produced. The poppy straw program operates under strict governmental control and allows for cultivation of the opium poppy on small licensed lots in seven provinces: Afylon (the Turkish word for opium), Isparta, Denizli, Usak, Burdur, Kutahya, and Konya.

Harvesting is done by hand after the opium has passed the green stage and has completely dried. Only the poppy heads and parts of the stalks are removed, and the result is the "poppy straw."

Between 1976 and 1980, Turkey exported an average of 8,800 tons of poppy straw per year. Today, much of the crop is purchased by the Dutch for processing in the Netherlands. India shares the market with the United States because of the "80-20 rule." This rule, supported by the United States, specifies that at least 80 percent of the raw narcotic material imported to the United States for legitimate use in medicine must originate either in Turkey or India. The remaining 20 percent can be imported from other countries.

One of the traditional opium producers in the region is the Pushtuns (also known as Pathans). This independent tribe, living on the border of Afghanistan and Pakistan, has produced great quantities of raw opium gum. The Kurds are yet another ethnic group in Iran that is heavily involved in traditional opium production.

The Kurds and Drug Trafficking

Because of the strict controls on opium cultivation, Turkey is not considered a primary source country. It does remain a major transshipment country for opiates that are produced in Afghanistan, Pakistan, and Iran (the Golden Crescent). Most of the drug dealing and trafficking in Turkey is controlled by criminal groups in Istanbul.

One such group that has a strong ethnic identity and that contributes significantly to Turkish organized crime is the Kurds. The Kurds speak Turkish and have a reputation for being fierce fighters, family oriented, independent, and devout Moslems. The Kurds have clans in both Turkey and Iran and do not recognize the border that separates the two countries. Because the Kurds frequently travel across the border, they have a convenient network for smuggling drugs.

Although many Kurdish areas lie between eastern and southern Turkey, trafficking by Kurds is by no means restricted to those areas. Many of the main heroin wholesalers in Istanbul are Kurds that first migrated from remote villages as unskilled laborers and later became wealthy in the narcotics trade.

In addition to the Kurds, many Iranians also traffic large amounts of heroin from Turkey to their Iranian contacts in the United States and western Europe. An estimated 500,000 to 1.5 million Iranians reside in Istanbul alone. Using Istanbul as a main distribution point, the Iranian traffickers smuggle both legitimate and illegitimate goods (drugs and weapons alike) to western Europe and the United States.

Drug smuggling routes in Turkey lie primarily along the eastern and southeastern areas of the country. Heroin is generally smuggled from Iran to Turkey by Turkish Kurds that travel through the mountainous border area that is not heavily patrolled by either government. The DEA estimates that, because of the harsh winters in this region, most drug smuggling into Turkey is somewhat seasonal and therefore is concentrated between May and December of each year. Authorities believe that most drug payloads arrive in the Turkish provinces of Van and Hakkiri, although some morphine base has been smuggled into Syria and Lebanon.

As mentioned, Turkey is not considered a source country for drugs *per se*, but some refining of morphine base to heroin does occur there. In 1988, several Turkish heroin refineries were seized but were found to be somewhat primitive.

These labs were set up to convert a specific amount of morphine base to heroin and were designed to be easily dismantled and moved to a different location.

As with heroin and morphine base, hashish (Turkey's biggest domestic consumer drug) is also commonly transported through Turkey from Lebanon. Other illicit commodities include firearms, which are often traded for drugs. In one specific case in 1987, the Bulgarian import/export agency Kintex was involved in a smuggling operation.

Figure 4.12

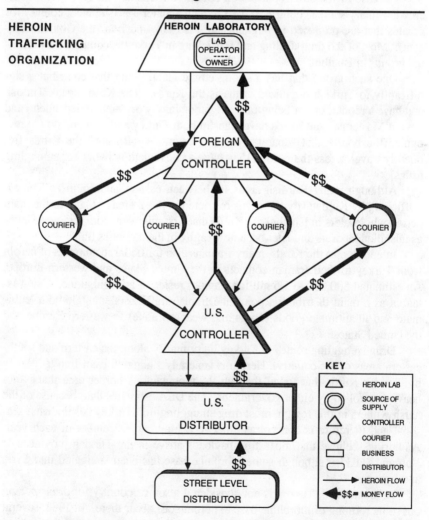

HEROIN TRAFFICKING ORGANIZATION

HEROIN LABORATORY
LAB OPERATOR

OWNER

FOREIGN CONTROLLER

COURIER   COURIER   COURIER   COURIER

U.S. CONTROLLER

U.S. DISTRIBUTOR

STREET LEVEL DISTRIBUTOR

KEY

△ HEROIN LAB
◎ SOURCE OF SUPPLY
△ CONTROLLER
○ COURIER
▭ BUSINESS
▭ DISTRIBUTOR
► HEROIN FLOW
◄-$$- MONEY FLOW

SOURCE: DEA, 1984

Hong Kong

Like the Golden Triangle and the Golden Crescent, Hong Kong also plays a significant role in international drug trafficking, particularly in money laundering and transportation. In recent years the Hong Kong Executive Council has considered new legislative proposals giving the courts more power to confiscate the assets of major traffickers.

New legal proposals would allow the court to infer that all property that the offender acquired during the six-year period prior to his or her arrest for a drug trafficking offense had been received as "payment or reward" for drug trafficking. The court would then levy a fine of an amount equivalent to the value of the property with a provision for imposing a prison term on a sliding scale up to ten years, upon default on payment of the fine.

Summary

The extent of global involvement in the illicit drug trade illustrates the magnitude of the problem, as many countries play a major role in furnishing the United States with dangerous drugs. Ironically, the U.S. is frequently blamed by these countries for providing a drug user market and nurturing an incentive for drug production in their countries.

The closest neighbor to the United States on the south is Mexico, a major producer of heroin and marijuana. Mexico's widespread involvement in the drug trade gained considerable momentum just after the collapse of the "French Connection," in the early 1970s. Efforts to thwart drug trafficking in Mexico (and some other foreign countries) have been hampered by widespread corruption within the government. Allegations of corruption among Mexico's Federal Judicial Police have been voiced for years but became more credible in 1985 with the abduction and murder of a federal DEA agent. Mexican police officers were ultimately charged with complicity in this crime.

In South America, the three Andean nations of Colombia, Peru, and Bolivia are the most active coca- and cocaine-producing countries in the world. In particular, Colombia, one of the most significant drug source countries, primarily produces cocaine hydrochloride from dried coca leaves, but also produces high-grade marijuana. Drug trafficking cartels have expanded to the point where they now threaten the democratically elected government in Colombia. Much violence prevails as a result of this, but Colombian government officials, with aid furnished by the United States, are attempting to locate, arrest, and extradite members to the United States for prosecution.

The leaves used in the production of cocaine are primarily grown in Peru and Bolivia; Peru is the primary supplier. As in Colombia, trafficking organizations also have attempted to exert control over the governments in Peru and Bolivia.

Jamaica represents a marijuana source country that has generated dangerous gangs (known as posses) that share both political and profit motivations. Governmental unrest since the 1960s has created two opposing political parties that continually strive for governmental dominance. Jamaican gangs serve the political parties in Jamaica by rallying votes for them. In the United States, the posses occupy over 18 cities and, in addition to dealing marijuana, distribute crack cocaine to generate profits that are then funnelled back to Jamaica.

The Golden Crescent is an opium growing region in southwest Asia consisting of Afghanistan, Pakistan, and Iran. It is in this region that most raw opium is produced. Opium from this region is then funnelled to other trafficking groups, where it is processed into heroin and ultimately transported to the United States for distribution. The Golden Triangle refers to Laos, Burma, and Thailand in southeast Asia. This group of countries ranks second to the Golden Crescent in raw opium production and is instrumental in trafficking much of the world's opium and heroin.

Other drug source countries in Asia include Turkey, which serves as a transshipment country for Golden Crescent opium. Turkish Kurds have been responsible for much of the trafficking in this region of Asia.

DISCUSSION QUESTIONS

1. Which areas of the world are most active in the production of raw opium and in heroin refinement?

2. Discuss the different countries that are responsible for most of the world's marijuana production.

3. Discuss the area of the world that most actively grows the coca leaf and produces illicit cocaine Hydrochloride.

4. Why are illicit drugs such as cocaine, marijuana, and heroin so difficult to control in countries like Colombia and Mexico?

5. Explain the political history of Jamaica and the illicit drugs produced there.

6. What contributions do Peru and Bolivia make to the world's illicit drug situation?

7. Discuss some of the most pressing issues in curtailing coca production in Bolivia.

8. Discuss the Rastafarian religion and how it is associated with marijuana.

9. Explain the roles of both the Golden Crescent and Golden Triangle in global drug trafficking.

10. Explain why the country of Colombia is so well suited for drug trafficking.

11. Discuss the history of Colombian cocaine traffickers.

12. What are three reasons why the coca crop is such a valuable and attractive crop for Bolivian and Peruvian farmers?

13. Discuss the volatile issue of extradition in Colombia.

14. List some of the reasons why heroin abuse has increased in recent years in southwest Asia.

15. What role do the Turkish Kurds play in the trafficking of illicit drugs?

16. Discuss the reasons why hill tribes in the Golden Triangle prefer opium as a cash crop over other legal crops.

CLASS PROJECTS

1. Locate a recent article from a newspaper or magazine that addresses the international drug problem. Discuss the trend in drug policy of foreign governments.

2. Compare drug control initiatives in various foreign countries, and discuss similarities between them. Include in your discussion the strengths and weaknesses of the programs.

CHAPTER 5

DOMESTIC DRUG TRAFFICKING

Although certain illicit drugs such as cocaine and heroin are primarily produced in foreign countries, domestic drug producers and traffickers have not passed up the opportunity to produce and cultivate illicit drugs. Marijuana, produced by both foreign and domestic traffickers, is used by some 19 million marijuana smokers in the United States. (NIDA, 1988). Other drugs, such as methamphetamine, LSD, and PCP are also produced in clandestine laboratories in the United States and foster much criminal activity in the areas of drug manufacturing and trafficking.

In addition to marijuana cultivation and clandestine laboratories, yet another source of drugs exists in the United States: pharmaceutical drug diversion. Drugs that are legally manufactured for legitimate medical treatment are sometimes diverted from the legal source of distribution and will also be discussed in this chapter.

Domestic Marijuana Cultivation

So far in this text, we have discussed several foreign cannabis sources that result in the smuggling of marijuana into the United States to meet the tremendous demand for the drug. As mentioned, marijuana is a plant that grows in almost all 50 states, so domestic cultivation contributes greatly to the overall drug problem.

Clearly, whether foreign or domestic enterprises are concerned, marijuana cultivation and trafficking has proven to be a relatively easy-entry illicit market. All that is required for a simple growing operation is seeds, a water source, land, and a willingness to enter into a criminal enterprise (that in some states can result in a prison term as long as 25 years).

Aside from the fact that domestic marijuana accounts for a conservative 50 percent of the country's retail marijuana market (although indications are that this percentage is growing rapidly [DEA, 1987]), this illicit market has spawned a relatively new type of criminal that poses unique problems for law enforcement and the community in general. These problems emanate from the fact that the marijuana grower is predominantly a rural criminal, living and operating in wooded, scarcely populated areas. The rural environment creates hidden dangers for investigators as well as many investigative challenges. It also affords the cultivator cover from easy detection by law enforcement officers and criminal "pot" poachers alike. In addition, many cultivated marijuana patches have been discovered with deadly booby traps that are difficult (if not impossible) to detect.

Figure 5.1

Domestic Marijuana

Selling Prices for one pound of Marijuana at Successive Levels of Trafficking.

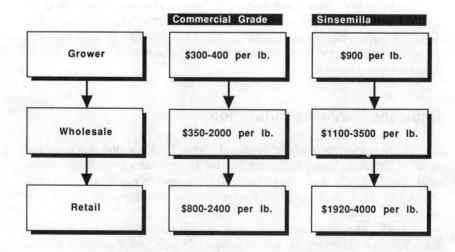

	Commercial Grade	Sinsemilla
Grower	$300-400 per lb.	$900 per lb.
Wholesale	$350-2000 per lb.	$1100-3500 per lb.
Retail	$800-2400 per lb.	$1920-4000 per lb.

SOURCE: DEA, 1987

To begin our discussion, let us first identify the types of marijuana or cannabis most commonly cultivated. As was mentioned in Chapter 2, there are several types or grades of marijuana. It is becoming increasingly clear that the marijuana cultivation business is in the throes of a horticultural revolution of sorts. That is, many growers are continuously experimenting with different techniques of producing more potent strains of marijuana for higher profits. Each cultivated grade represents different types of growing technology and results in differing degrees of potency (and prices) for the manicured retail marijuana plant.

Although state and federal drug laws do not differentiate among the grades of marijuana (they only require a showing that the drug evidence is cannabis), the grower is very interested in producing the most potent plant for greater profit margins. The DEA has identified three basic types of marijuana that grow domestically: *Indian hemp, commercial,* and *sinsemilla.*

Indian Hemp. Indian hemp (commonly referred to as ditchweed) is the most prevalent type of marijuana that grows in the United States. This is a wild growing marijuana that has little market value, and typically grows in uncultivated areas such as fields, ditch banks, fence rows, and along railroad tracks. Indian hemp grows in many types of soil and reproduces itself each year by its own seeds from the previous year's crop. These seeds can lay dormant for up to seven years.

Because Indian hemp is not cultivated from potent seeds, its THC content is quite low, averaging around 0.14 percent, as compared to other types. Because of its low potency, it will sometimes be mixed with other more potent marijuana as "filler."

Commercial Grade. Commercial grade marijuana is the most common type of marijuana sold on the street. It is produced from those cannabis plants that have been cultivated in a growing area where the male and female plants are permitted to grow at the same location and the female plants have been fertilized. As a rule, the entire marijuana plant (usually the female) is harvested, stripped of its leaves, and marketed.

The growing season usually begins around mid-April, with harvest season beginning sometime during August. At maturity, plants may reach heights of 15 feet and can be harvested up until the first frost (usually sometime in October). The THC content of the commercial marijuana plant ranges from 5 to 8 percent.

Sinsemilla Grade. Trends toward the production of higher and higher grades of marijuana have persisted since the mid-1960s. Sinsemilla, a Spanish word meaning "without seeds," is a cannabis plant that represents the most potent type of marijuana on the illicit market and the type that will bring the highest profit return for the trafficker.

Sinsemilla is produced from unfertilized female cannabis plants in a growing area where the male cannabis plants are removed prior to pollination. Marijuana plants allowed to grow in this fashion produce more flowers and resin in an attempt to attract male pollen. It is the resin and flowers that contain the highest amounts of THC, usually averaging between 8 and 12 percent potency. Frequently, it is only the female flowers (buds) that are harvested and marketed.

To produce the highest potency sinsemilla plant, many growers select high potency seeds to produce sinsemilla; in some cases, these seeds are obtained from Afghanistan, Thailand, and Mexico and will range in price from $1 to $5 each. For example, the Afghanistan strain is often chosen because it grows into a short, squatty plant that produces 1 to 2 pounds of buds per plant. These buds are high in THC content and mature in 4 to 5 months.

Many marijuana growers have also perfected indoor growing techniques that enable them to harvest plants year-round. According to the DEA, a technique developed by Oregon pot growers is one called *cloning*. In this technique, growers cultivate hybrid marijuana and select the most superior plants. A "cut" is then taken from the mother plant and soaked in a root stimulant. After the cutting develops roots, it is then planted in pots and aided by a halide lighting system.

Another technique, called *hydroponics*, is also used to grow marijuana in a greenhouse. Hydroponics is the science of growing plants in a soil-free, mineral-rich solution and is commonly used for indoor cultivation of tomatoes and cucumbers. Marijuana produced by the hydroponic method will typically produce a THC content at least twice that of marijuana produced by traditional methods. The DEA estimates that it takes only one square foot of space to grow a mature plant. Therefore, a facility with only 400 square feet of hydroponic growing area can, under optimal growing conditions, cultivate marijuana on a year-round basis and generate an estimated $5 million a year.

Marijuana cultivators and processors come from a wide range of backgrounds and operate in a variety of ways. For example, research by Ralph Weisheit has found that many west coast growers cultivate the plant for their own use and for sales to friends, but are not necessarily large traffickers. In fact, he has suggested that a considerable number of domestic cultivators are still operating within the context of a counterculture frame of reference. Weisheit's research in other areas, such as the Midwest, has generally shown marijuana cultivating and processing to be a disorganized, ancillary business that is often engaged in by otherwise law-abiding farmers. Research in Kentucky, however, has indicated that cultivation there is becoming more highly organized, with law enforcement officials warning of a "cartelization" of the trade.

In eastern Kentucky, in particular, where high grade marijuana, with THC content as high 18 percent, is grown in small plots because of the rugged topography, there is increasing evidence of sophisticated organization in the marijuana market and of the creation of incipient organized crime groups. Ironically, one of the things that appears to have stimulated the change from small, ad hoc, disorganized growing, to the creation of highly organized criminal groups, is Kentucky's federally funded law enforcement campaign against the marijuana industry. Stepped-up enforcement seems to have resulted in the creation of a more efficient and more dangerous marijuana industry.

CLOSE-UP: CITY DRUGS INFILTRATE COUNTRY LIFE

Every few months, the parcel truck would tool down the dusty road, carrying packages to the same house near the hamlet of Shellsburg, Iowa. Nothing seemed suspicious until authorities were tipped off about the contents. The goods were cocaine, an informant said. After nearly two years of watching and waiting, two men were arrested. The occupant of the house pleaded guilty to drug trafficking. A neighbor is expected to face trial this spring. Prosecutors say that in 15 months the two sold cocaine with a street value of $1.4 million.

The drug scourge is spreading to rural America. This incident is just one example. There are many. Cocaine, speed, and even crack are becoming more common in corn country. Drug labs and marijuana farms are reaping big profits in small towns, and rural police and prosecutors are seizing more dope and charging more dealers. "In small rural communities, you just don't expect to find top quality dangerous drugs available in large quantities, and that's what we're finding," said a Minnesota Bureau of Criminal Apprehension special agent. "We're making undercover purchases in towns with populations of 50." "It used to be safe in a small town," the agent said, and parents didn't have to worry because their children were far from dangerous drugs. "Now, LSD, methamphetamines, or pure cocaine are available to anyone who really looks for it."

"You're seeing it all over the country, and it's finally coming to roost here," the agent added. "This is the end of the line." That not only concerns police but also lawmakers. Senator Charles Grassley of Iowa convened a hearing in 1989 to examine the growing problem.

"What we're finding is, given the extra money a dealer can make in the state, it really behooves them to make inroads—and they are," said a spokesman for the senator. Police say that they are constantly surprised by the magnitude of the problem. One narcotics agent said that he was shocked when an informant (who had also been a dealer) recently said that he had 50 cocaine customers in a small Minnesota town and that another dealer had 100.

Experts cite numerous reasons for drug dealing in small-town U.S.A.: a depressed rural economy, a ready market with less competition than in big cities, and an ideal environment—remote settings where neighbors may be miles away, police patrols are infrequent, and law enforcement agencies often are undermanned and inexperienced. A hog farmer near Strawberry Point, Iowa was caught in 1987 trying to flee with "his overalls in one hand, a kilo of cocaine in another arm," said an assistant U.S. Attorney. The farmer was sleeping when authorities entered his house.

Sometimes, drug activity is concealed by transient populations in rural areas. In other instances, remote locales provide the perfect opportunity to avoid detection, particularly with methamphetamine labs, which emit a stench when producing a form of speed called "crank." Such labs, often run by biker gangs, have been found from Missouri to Oregon.

Authorities say that they have stepped up enforcement efforts in rural areas and have results to prove it. For example, in central Illinois, 83 persons in Peoria, Knox, and Tazewell counties were charged in 1988 in Operation Iron Eagle. Included were members of a biker group called the Satan Brothers, accused of dealing cocaine and methamphetamine. Almost all have pleaded guilty.

In South Dakota, drug sale cases rose 50 percent in 1988, said the director of the state Division of Criminal Investigation. He said that 11.3 pounds of cocaine were seized in 1987, about five times the annual amount in previous years.

In Iowa, 65 persons were indicted last October, and authorities seized 14.5 pounds of cocaine, more than 500 pounds of marijuana, and more than $300,000 in cash. Officials say that two-thirds of those indicted were Iowans. More than 55 of those charged have pleaded guilty or been convicted.

In West Virginia, 33 persons were convicted or pleaded guilty to running a crack ring out of a shopping mall in Charles Town, about 80 miles from Washington. U.S. Attorney William Kolibash said that the potent form of cocaine known as crack, supplied by Jamaican dealers, was blatantly sold until arrests in 1989. In Yakima, Washington, the Drug Enforcement Administration office, covering 11 largely rural counties, made 143 arrests during 1988.

Source: *The Kansas City Star*, August 3, 1990.

Clandestine Laboratories

As has been noted throughout this text, of the many different drugs that have become popular over the years, some are organic in nature and some are synthesized by chemists in illicit drug laboratories. It should be noted here that even though some drugs may be of an organic origin, a certain degree of chemical synthesis is necessary for the completion of the finished product. This is true, for example, with drugs such as heroin and cocaine.

Many popular drugs that have emerged over the years are synthetic in nature and originate in the *clandestine* laboratory. The most common of these drugs are methamphetamine (also known as crystal and crank), PCP, and LSD.

The spreading popularity of illicit labs is partly due to successes in federal drug interdiction efforts. Many traffickers feel safer making their own drugs domestically than they do risking detection and arrest as a result of dealing with foreign suppliers.

As with the marijuana cultivator, the clandestine lab operator commonly seeks isolation in rural settings where his or her activities will go unnoticed. For example, the largest illicit methamphetamine laboratory ever discovered in the United States was located in the mountains of rural McCreary County, Kentucky and involved participants from Kentucky, Florida, Illinois, Tennessee and other states. Often this desire for rural isolation is because of the distinctive odors emitted by "meth" and PCP labs. In an urban setting, these odors can reveal the existence of a lab.

In spite of the numerous types of drugs produced by illicit laboratories, the manufacturing process can be broken down into three distinct categories.

- *Extraction labs.* The extraction lab produces illicit substances by removing certain elements from one substance and creating another. Both hashish and methamphetamines are manufactured by using the Benzedrine inhaler method of extraction.

- *Conversion labs.* This lab converts existing illicit drugs to a different form of the same drug. Crack is an example of a drug, cocaine, which is converted into a freebase form for street sale.

- *Synthesis labs.* A synthesis lab is when a drug is transformed from one substance to another to make a different and more powerful substance. For example, the precursor P_2P is a dangerous drug that is used to manufacture methamphetamine powder. This process is different from the methamphetamine extraction method discussed above.

Investigating a clandestine lab is especially dangerous for police because of the explosive, corrosive, and hazardous materials usually associated with the drug manufacturing process and because many labs are fortified with deadly booby traps.

In many cases, even a slight spark can create a chain reaction resulting in a massive explosion of the laboratory. In some instances agents have fainted from fumes emitted from the laboratories. Because of this, investigators that raid the labs now wear protective plastic jumpsuits, rubber gloves, respirators, and air tanks. Portable showers contained in vans are sometimes used to allow agents that have become contaminated to wash off.

Crank sells wholesale for about $10,000 a pound. A successful lab operation may generate at least $250,000 worth of crank each month, that is, $1 million every four months or $3 million every year.

Criminal drug lab operators have also been documented not only mixing toxic chemicals that are deadly, but routinely dumping toxic waste down bathroom drains or in holes dug outside in the ground. These actions make some lab locations akin to hazardous waste sites.

It must also be remembered that these clandestine laboratories are usually operated by nonprofessionals. Individuals with a limited knowledge of chemistry run some of them. Other labs are run by people that have learned various processing techniques through their peers in the criminal underworld. The methamphetamine market, for example, was dominated for many years by the Pagans Motorcycle Club. The skills utilized in drug processing and the safety procedures initiated by a group like the Pagans are highly suspect.

Pharmaceutical Diversion

The DEA estimates that, because of growing popularity on the street, over 200 million dosage units of legally made drugs find their way from legitimate sources, such as hospitals and pharmacies, to the street drug abuser every year. Some are lost through drug store thefts and others through forged prescriptions. It is estimated that the greatest amount of these drugs are diverted by a handful of corrupt physicians, pharmacists, osteopaths, veterinarians, dentists, nurses, and other medical professionals.

As we have seen in earlier chapters, society foots the bill for drug abuse in terms of shoplifting, street crime, and predatory criminal acts relating to drug abuse. Society also pays the bill for drugs diverted through Medicaid and prepaid prescription plans offered by some companies and unions.

CLOSE-UP: THE METH LAB

The briefing from the California drug agent was to-the-point: "We have word that the cooker could be all screwed up from smelling this stuff and he could be violent."

The plan for the raid was simple: run into the suspected methamphetamine lab, located just east of here in a wooded and hilly area, "grab the guy and come out." It was a scenario increasingly played out in the piney woods in this part of the country. Methamphetamine labs are sprouting like mushrooms, and the illegal stimulant, also known as crank, crystal, and speed, is rivaling the popularity of cocaine for a growing army of users.

Twenty minutes after the briefing, the investigators, armed to the hilt, turned off a gravel road and drove up a secluded drive. The movement of the men seemed at odds with the gentle spring-like country afternoon. The warm afternoon sun was filtering through a thick stand of trees and was dancing off a small farm pond. The day would have otherwise seemed languid. Not today. A half dozen drug agents dressed like Ninja warriors in black chemically resistant, flame retardant hoods, shirts, and pants, charged breakneck from a van. Their target: a faded grey ranch-style house, like any other a tourist might pass if roaming these hollows and hills.

State troopers took positions to the sides of the house. Two drug agents rigidly aimed automatic pistols and shotguns into a window and door. Other agents stormed the house.

It was over in seconds. "The house is clear," a sweating federal drug agent yelled hoarsely. His chest was heaving. The agents led out a groggy man of 55 that had moved into the house last year.

The air inside the house was tested for toxic fumes. There apparently were none. The lab was in the back. It would easily rival any high school chemistry laboratory. The walls were covered with plastic sheets, and a long hose ran from a condenser to a ceiling exhaust fan, where gasses were released to the air.

Thousands of dollars of flasks, beakers, glass tubing, and large glass pots lined the walls. Two 12-liter pots containing methamphetamine oil were still cooking on two stoves under the watchful eye of a closed-circuit camera.

In cluttered rooms and hallways, and in a shed outside, agents found more evidence: 25 gallons of hydriodic acid, 25 barrels of freon, and containers of red phosphorus, a chemical that, when overcooked, can produce deadly phosphine gas, which was used as a weapon in World War I. Finally, in a back bedroom the agents struck paydirt: 29 heat-sealed baggies of white methamphetamine powder.

Source: OCDETF, 1988.

The 1970 Controlled Substances Act has authorized the DEA to regulate all aspects of the drug manufacturing and distribution process in the United States. For the more potent drugs, the DEA can even dictate the thickness of warehouse walls where they are stored (i.e., eight inches of concrete with steel rods). The DEA also controls the order form needed to purchase drugs (three carbon copies with one forwarded to DEA headquarters).

Through these mechanisms, the DEA claims that much of the diversion from warehouses and factories has been controlled. The result has been increased diversion at the retail level, marked by a sharp rise in drugstore robberies and burglaries along with increased pressure on some doctors and druggists to cross the line from "professional" to "pusher."

What is it that makes a professional registrant choose to become a law violator and "white-collar" drug dealer? Below are some motivating factors.

1. *Greed.* Pharmacists and physicians have cheap and easy access to drugs that command top dollar on the street. For example, they pay only about $50 for 500 tablets of Knoll Pharmaceutical Company's Dilaudid, a synthetic narcotic similar to morphine (see Chapter 2). On the street, Dilaudid will easily bring between $50 to $60 per tablet.

    Some corrupt professionals barter drugs or prescriptions for merchandise. Others make their living by operating "diet clinics," where they freely dispense or prescribe amphetamine tablets, even though the use of the drug for weight control is questionable.

2. *Sexual Favors.* Some investigations have revealed instances where certain physicians and pharmacists give drugs or prescriptions in return for sexual favors. There have been cases of amphetamines being given to prostitutes to help them stay awake.

3. *Salvaging a Failing Medical Practice.* Drug diversion is a particular problem in cases of failing medical practices, whether caused by incompetence, impending retirement, or location problems. Illicit activity on the part of these physicians often results from having been accustomed to high incomes that have been reduced or from being deeply in debt. An easy solution to the problem is to write illegal prescriptions or dispense pills for the easy income.

4. *Self-addiction.* The addiction to drugs is an "occupational disease" for some members of the health care community. Long hours and the easy availability of drugs make the medical profes-

sional susceptible to drug abuse. Those physicians that have become addicted may turn to diversion to finance their addiction.

5. *Senility.* Some senile doctors and pharmacists have unwittingly yielded to the demands of drug abusers. In other cases, a nurse, medical receptionist, or family member has "taken over" the practice of a senile professional and allowed dangerous drugs to be diverted.

6. *Rationalization.* Some professionals justify selling to abusers by rationalizing that they will get drugs anyway, perhaps through street crime or prostitution.

Even though pharmacists are required by law to account for every dose of dangerous drugs that they order, suspicious fires, robberies, and break-ins can destroy prescription files and cover shortages of pills. For these and many other reasons, evidence of diversion is difficult to acquire. For example, undercover agents investigating this type of criminal behavior may find that the suspect doctors claim that they were just "practicing medicine" and attempting to cure a patient by prescribing drugs for an illness. Other violations are more blatant, such as when physicians literally sell drugs to friends and associates, or barter prescriptions for merchandise.

There are other pressures on the prosecutor. He may have a social or political relationship with the registrant. And if he is in a rural county where doctor's offices are few and far between, he knows that any doctor forced out of business could leave some families without easy access to medical care. And inconvenienced voters often have good memories when the prosecutor has to stand for re-election.

Source: DEA, *Drug Enforcement Magazine*, 1977

Other problems arise in the prosecution of diversion cases. For example, prosecutors are usually anxious to file charges against drug dealers from the street, but when the drug dealer happens to be a physician in the community, charges are sometimes difficult to bring and prosecutors are often reluctant to try "respectable" citizens, who have the resources to mount an active defense against the charges. Even when charges are brought against certain physicians, prosecutors may have a difficult time convincing juries of the seriousness of the violation or it may be difficult to explain the complexities of the diversion case to the jury. In either case, and because of these considerations, a conviction may not be forthcoming in the case.

CASE STUDY: THE FIVE STAR HEALTH CLUB

The Five Star Health Club, in Fairmont, West Virginia was in reality a gambling casino. Just three days prior to a police raid that closed it forever, the club was locked up by its owners. This was not the owners' only line of work. Three of the "five stars," the Spadafore brothers, Donnie, John, and Ralph, were drug dealers. The others were their attorney and an ex-cop that was a convicted gambler.

Over a period of years beginning in 1979, the Spadafore organization smuggled multi-kilo quantities of cocaine into Fairmont, then broke it into smaller consignments for distribution in central West Virginia and in Erie, Pennsylvania. Among many other local endeavors, they owned a grocery where, on inquiry, the grocer would pour you grams of cocaine from the middle Bisquick box on the shelf.

The gang originally made their wholesale purchases in Miami but soon tired of paying stateside prices and branched out into their own version of international drug smuggling. Donnie, the leader, brought in an Erie, Pennsylvania organized crime figure, Joseph Scutelli. The organization began to specialize in complicated logistical planning in order to avoid leaving trails. A Peruvian connection was firmly established, improving certainty of supply and reducing price.

In a typical instance, three different private planes were used by the smuggling team. A ring-member pilot flew his own aircraft from Lima to Stella Maris in the Bahamas, where "the vacationers" were about to leave for Pittsburgh on a charter. "The vacationers" were a retired Erie Police Department detective and his wife, who were used repeatedly because of their ability to blend in with Caribbean tourists. Arriving in Fort Lauderdale at midnight, the couple (and the "dope") boarded another of the organization's planes, which dropped them in Pittsburgh and delivered the cocaine to an unused, unlighted runway of the Morgantown, West Virginia, airport.

At the South American end, drugs were usually packed in a pillow stuffed with llama hair. When transported by car in the United States, the drugs were wrapped in a shoe box and addressed for mailing. If challenged, the driver would report having found the box at a rest stop and say that he planned to mail it.

The Five Star attorney was versatile. At times he stored drugs or money at his home for the group. When an insurance arson was planned by the gang, this "corporate counsel" gave such advice as "put a dog and cat in the house and you'll get paid easier." According to other defendants, it was he who arranged for and delivered monthly payments to "the Charlies" to give the gang protection from law enforcement. "The Charlies," Anderson and Dodd, were the county prosecutor and the sheriff, both convicted at later dates. The lawyer also was accused of acting as lookout while the brothers broke into the police garage seeking to recover cash and cocaine that they thought was hidden in an impounded car. (Somebody else got there first.)

A fellow barrister (actually a city judge) was hired to keep police occupied inside the station next door during the break-in. The young judge was seduced into drug dealing by Donnie's offer of a trip to South America to "run some errands." He was halfway to Peru when he learned that the only errand was to pick up drugs and that he would be paid $65,000 for doing so. The temptation was too great.

The information and evidence necessary to bring down the "stars" was developed over a period of four years by agents of the FBI, IRS, West Virginia State Police, and Fairmont Police Department, under auspices of the Organized Crime Drug Enforcement Task Force. Faced with a possible life sentence in prison, the Spadafores all entered plea agreements. The mastermind, Donnie, pled guilty in the Northern District of West Virginia to charges of operating a continuing criminal enterprise, unlawful possession of an unregistered firearm, and filing a false income tax return. He was sentenced to 20 years without parole. John Spadafore's primary role in the organization had been providing the muscle; he pled guilty to RICO charges in connection with drugs and also received 20 years. Ralph's role was to provide financial services and present a legitimate front for the organization. He was the overseer of the gambling operation and was responsible for all hiring. Ralph pled guilty to violating the RICO statute in connection with gambling and was sentenced to six years. All but one of the 21 persons indicted have been convicted or have pled guilty. The last is a fugitive believed to be somewhere in South America.

One of those convicted was Carol Rae Olson, a key supplier to the Spadafore organization and a vice president of an oil company whose jet aircraft were used to move drugs. Her conviction was especially important because it severed a direct cocaine pipeline from Peru to the United States. Olson was apprehended in Hawaii with Donnie Spadafore's help and found guilty of six counts of racketeering, conspiracy, and cocaine importation. Others found guilty included Scutelli, the ring's lawyer, the city judge, two pilots, and "the vacationers."

Source: OCDETF, 1988

Summary

Although foreign traffickers make significant contributions to the drug problem in the United States, many domestic criminals also play a significant role. Domestic drug production primarily centers around three types of illicit activities: marijuana cultivation, clandestine laboratories that primarily manufacture methamphetamine and PCP, and pharmaceutical diversion.

The marijuana cultivator will produce one of two types of marijuana: commercial or sinsemilla. The commercial grade is the most common type of marijuana and is generally the easiest to grow. Sinsemilla, on the other hand, is the most potent type of marijuana and will bring twice the street price of the commercial strain. Sinsemilla is, however, a much more difficult strain to grow, as it requires more personal attention and time on the part of the cultivator. This explains why fewer marijuana growers are involved with sinsemilla farming than commercial.

The clandestine lab problem is one of growing proportions in the United States. Lab operators are the most active in the manufacturing of methamphetamine and PCP, both of which have achieved a growing popularity throughout the United States.

Finally, we examined the problem of pharmaceutical diversion by both professional patients (scammers) and registrants. The diversion of addictive and dangerous drugs is done for many reasons. Some reasons include a profit motive while other diversions are done because of a personal addiction by registrants. In either case, the problem represents a significant amount of dangerous drugs that are eventually marketed on the street for exorbitant prices.

DISCUSSION QUESTIONS

1. List the three most common types of marijuana grown in the United States.

2. How is sinsemilla grown and why is its potency so much higher than that of commercial marijuana?

3. What are the two most common methods of indoor growing of marijuana?

4. List the primary drugs manufactured by domestic clandestine laboratories.

5. Why are illicit laboratories considered so dangerous for police investigators?

6. What factors explain why a registrant might become involved in the diversion of pharmaceutical drugs?

7. Explain why the pharmaceutical drug case is usually so difficult to prosecute.

CHAPTER 6

DRUGS AND CRIME

In addition to the physiological effects and medical complications associated with drug abuse, one of the greatest public concerns is the rising spectrum of crime as it relates to the use of drugs. Clearly, a definitive but complex correlation exists between drug crimes and other types of crime, but the nature and extent of the link between drugs and crime are far from being understood. Therefore, the catch phrase "drug-related crime" remains somewhat general. Criminal justice researchers hope to clarify this category of crime in coming years in order to predict both drug trafficking patterns and non-drug criminal behavior.

To illustrate the magnitude of America's "crime" problem, the U.S. Department of Justice, Bureau of Justice Statistics (BJS) reported that in 1988, there were an estimated 12.5 million arrests, over 500,000 inmates in prison, 300,000 inmates in jail, 2.5 million individuals on probation, and an additional 325,000 on parole. In addition, BJS reports that only one half of the crimes committed are reported to law enforcement authorities, and that there are only 20 arrests for every 100 crimes. When attempting to understand what is responsible for these outrageous crime statistics (and why they are so high), one predictable common denominator is readily identified: drugs.

According to the U.S. Department of Justice, a murder occurs in the United States every 28 minutes, one rape is committed every 14 minutes, and over one dozen armed robberies take place every hour. Therefore, our prisons and jails are consistently operating at capacity, posing major problems for corrections officials. In fact, many states are now requiring the mandatory early release of many inmates solely to avoid problems of overcrowding.

This chapter will identify and discuss three critical forms of drug-related crime: street crime, official corruption, and money laundering. Each of these plays a significant role in the overall drug problem and should be confronted when considering solutions to the nation's drug dilemma.

Drugs and Crime: The "Connection"

Law enforcement officials have long been aware of the link between drugs and crime, but now research has proven what has been suspected all along, that drugs account for more crimes, arrests, persons serving time in prisons and jails, and instances of recidivism than any other variable. One of the more compelling evidentiary studies linking drugs to crime was reported in 1983 by researchers Ball, Schaffer, and Nurco in Baltimore, Maryland. The Baltimore study group analyzed long-term behavior and crime patterns for 354 heroin addicts from a sample drawn from over 7,500 known opiate users between 1952 and 1976. During a nine-year period, the sample population averaged 2,000 crime days per addict. The study revealed that when using drugs, crime rates for this group were typically four to six times higher than when not using drugs.

Another study of drug use and criminality sponsored by the National Institute of Justice in October 1984 revealed the following findings:

•   Individuals arrested who tested positive for illicit drugs (excluding marijuana) were arrested more than twice as often prior to trial than those not testing positive for drugs.

•   Arrestees identified as drug users from a positive drug test were found to miss court appearances by a rate of 50 percent higher than those who did not test positive for drugs.

In the NIJ study, all defendants participating in the study were subjected to urinalysis testing for five drugs: opiates, PCP, cocaine, methadone, and amphetamines.

More recently, a 1987 NIJ report titled "Drug Use Forecasting" articulated similar instances of drugs and crime. The following statistics were revealed in the study regarding instances of drug use and crime:

•   Between 53 percent and 79 percent of adult males arrested for serious offenses in 12 major U.S. cities tested positive for recent use of at least one drug.

•   Seventy percent of those arrested had drugs in their system at the time of post-arrest testing. Cities studied were New York, Los Angeles, Washington, D.C., Houston, Phoenix, Portland, Detroit, Indianapolis, Chicago, New Orleans, and Fort Lauderdale. The study was six months in duration and was based on both voluntary interviews concerning drug use and urine specimens obtained from over 2000 males who were arrested and charged with crimes such as burglary, larceny, and assault.

• Ninety-five percent of the arrestees agreed to be interviewed, and an estimated 80 percent provided a urine specimen. The drug tests identified marijuana, heroin, PCP, cocaine, and amphetamines as the most commonly abused substances. Poly-drug use was also common.

ADDICTS TURN TO LIFE OF CRIME TO SUPPORT DRUG HABIT

A drug addict aching for money to get high can be a one-person crime wave. "Every person we've arrested in the past two years in this unit has been a drug user," said a detective with the Kansas City, Missouri Police Department's Career Criminal Unit. "That's the reason they're stealing, doing burglaries or whatever. To support their drug habits."

Drug-motivated crimes can easily turn to violence: an elderly couple was shot to death in their south Kansas City home after being robbed of money that was to be used to purchase drugs; a firebombing killed six in a Kansas City home and was triggered by a dispute between the family and a nearby drug house.

But drug-motivated crimes are not always such headline-grabbing offenses. Addicts will do most anything for drug money: shoplifting, burglaries, check fraud, and more. Addicts use many tricks to spirit merchandise out of stores. One man who worked primarily department stores told police that he was just a small-time operator; he only averaged $15,000 a week to buy drugs.

Burglaries also go hand-in-hand with drug use. In 1989 police caught one man that they believe committed about 25 to 30 burglaries on Kansas City's west side. The burglar smashed store windows and grabbed money, stamps, and anything that could be easily carried and taken straight to a drug house. Other addicts get their courage from rock cocaine to commit robberies. Crack is the drug of choice right now, and most robberies are committed for money to buy the drug.

Homicide statistics also reflect the connection between crime and drugs. In 1987, 35 persons, or 27 percent of all homicides, were killed in drug-related violence in Kansas City. The figure jumped in 1988 to 50 victims, or 37 percent of the year's 135 homicides.

Usually both the killers and the victims are involved in the drug trade, police say. The motives range from arguments over the quality of drugs to the control of areas to sell drugs.

Similar surveys conducted by the National Institute of Justice in 11 cities found more than 50 percent of those arrested for violent crimes tested positive for drugs when they were arrested. In Phoenix, 82 percent of the men arrested for income-generating crimes such as burglary tested positive for drugs at the time. The survey found that 69 percent tested positive in Portland.

Source: Kaut, S. (1989). "Addicts Drawn to Life of Crime to Support Drug Habits." *The Kansas City Star* (February 5):A14.

Contributing to the link between drugs and crime is the influx of drugs from foreign sources. This includes an estimated 200 tons of cocaine exported from Colombia in 1989, which has resulted in soaring cocaine emergency-room admissions in the 26 largest cities in the United States. The number of persons in need of treatment totaled over 20,000 persons in 1986 and doubled in number from 1984.

Cities both large and small across the United States are now targeted by an array of drug gangs claiming turf for drug sales. According to a report by the Department of Justice, an estimated 80 percent of these individuals have already been in jail or prison, with one of every five having six or more convictions on their records. Based on these figures, it seems apparent that a more specifically defined public policy is needed in the many areas of drug abuse and a closer interaction between antidrug programs and the criminal justice system is necessary.

Official Corruption in the United States

In addition to the street crimes discussed above, there are other examples of criminal activity that are directly related to the illicit drug trade. This activity may manifest itself in numerous ways, including the corruption of public officials that taints governments and societies both domestically and abroad. Corruption, regardless of who perpetuates it, erodes communities and the governments that oversee them. That is, where official corruption exists, public service, confidence in government competency, and an overall lack of public trust and credibility result.

Official corruption also affects law enforcement and public safety in other ways. For example, it permits criminals to continue in their activities, it erodes the reputation of the department and the morale of officers, and it hampers the general effectiveness of community crime control efforts.

Corruption on the official level may take many forms. Specifically, one who has been compromised by criminal elements may take either a passive or active role in corruption. For example, in 1988, over 75 Miami police officers were under investigation at one time for possible involvement in criminal activities. Allegations included drug dealing, robbery, theft, and even murder. One investigation in particular revealed several officers who had ambushed drug dealers bringing cocaine into Miami. This investigation revealed that officers stole $13 million in cocaine from a boat anchored in the Miami River and loaded it into marked police vehicles. Duffel bags full of cocaine were reportedly "stacked to the ceilings of the patrol cars." Three of the suspects, in an effort to escape, jumped into the river and drowned.

Corruption. *The criminal manipulation of persons in influential positions or positions of public trust.*

✳ *Know for Test*

DIFFERENT FORMS OF CORRUPTION

Bribery. The receipt of cash or a "gift" in exchange for past or future assistance in avoidance of prosecution, as by a claim that the officer is unable to make a positive identification of a criminal or by being in the wrong place at a time when a crime is to occur, or by any other action that may be excused as carelessness but not offered as proof of deliberate miscarriage of justice. Distinguished from mooching by the higher value of the gift and by the mutual understanding in regard to services to be performed upon the acceptance of the gift.

Chiseling. Demanding price discounts or free admission to places of entertainment regardless of any connection with official police work.

Extortion. The practice of holding "street court," where minor traffic tickets can be avoided with a cash payment to the officer and no receipt given.

Favoritism. The practice of issuing license tabs, window stickers, or courtesy cards that exempt users from arrest or citation from traffic offenses (frequently extended to family members of officers).

Mooching. Accepting free coffee, cigarettes, meals, liquor, or groceries. Justified by being in an underpaid profession or for future acts of favoritism performed for the donor.

Perjury. Lying under oath to provide an alibi for fellow officers apprehended in unlawful activity.

Prejudice. Treatment of minority groups in a manner less than impartial, neutral, or objective, especially members of such groups that are unlikely to have "influence" in city hall that might cause trouble for the arresting officer.

Premeditated theft. Planned burglary, involving the use of tools, keys, or other devices to gain entry, or any prearranged plan to acquire property unlawfully.

Shakedown. The practice of appropriating expensive items for personal use during an investigation of a burglary or break-in and attributing their loss to criminal activity.

Shopping. Picking up small items such as cigarettes, candy bars, etc., at a store that has accidentally been left unlocked at the close of business hours.

Source: Ellwin R. Stoddard, "The Informal Code of Police Deviancy: A Group Approach to Blue-Coat Crime." *Journal of Criminal Law, Criminology, and Police Science*, 1968.

Police corruption is nothing new in America. Much official corruption in the areas of liquor and gambling was well documented during the early part of the century, when prohibition was still in effect. In many such cases, a link was established between police and politicians which favored clients who would be protected while competitors would be harassed. Various severe court actions have minimized such behavior on the part of the police, but in many cases, corruption still prevails.

The issue of police corruption poses some fundamental questions that make it difficult to define the term. Obviously blatant criminal acts by law enforcement officers pose a clear departure from accepted police conduct. However, should the acceptance of a gratuity such as a free cup of coffee also be considered a form of corruption? Herman Goldstein (1977) suggested that corruption only includes those forms of behavior that are designed to produce personal gain for the officer or for others. This definition, of course, precludes the abuse of one's official authority in areas such as police brutality when personal gain is not involved.

Perhaps one of the most highly publicized police corruption investigations was initiated by the Knapp Commission in 1970. The Commission, appointed by then Mayor John Lindsey, found police corruption to be a widespread problem throughout the New York City Police Department. Findings revealed that regular payments were made to police officers responsible for controlling gambling, narcotics, the construction industry, and prostitution operations. Amounts varied from small shakedowns of defendants to payoffs of up to $50,000.

One of the primary concerns of the Knapp Commission's findings was that even those officers who were not themselves corrupt would frequently tolerate the illegal actions of those who were. Two categories of corrupt officer were described by the Knapp Commission: "grass eaters" and "meat eaters." The distinction between the two was that "grass eaters" would accept payoffs that the job of policing happened to bring their way. "Meat eaters," however, were more aggressive and blatant in their pursuit of illicit sources of financial gain. The Commission therefore held that the "meat eaters" posed a greater threat to the integrity of the profession and the mission of the New York City Police Department.

Police officers assigned to drug investigation units have frequently become victims of corruption. This is attributed to the fact that undercover officers are required to work closely with the criminal element and even to disguise themselves as criminals in an undercover capacity. Additionally, drug investigators are frequently entrusted with large sums of money that are either issued to them by their agencies or seized as a result of an arrest. Frequently, officers are also in possession of large quantities of drugs (subsequent to an arrest or seizure) that must be transported to the police laboratory for analysis.

CLOSE-UP:
VICE OFFICERS WALK THE LINE BETWEEN CRIME AND THE LAW

The FBI investigation of alleged corruption among some Washington, D.C. narcotics officers represents a dubious coming of age for a department that has been known for decades as relatively free of taint.

Current and former Washington, D.C. police officials, as well as law enforcement experts throughout the country, say that it was only a matter of time before the District would become caught up in the same net that has led to corruption in dozens of law enforcement agencies nationwide: drugs.

Washington, D.C. Police Chief Maurice T. Turner, Jr. has said that the explosive growth in the sale and use of drugs here in the past twenty years has made it the department's top priority. Nearly one-fourth of the District's 3,380 officers are involved somehow in narcotics enforcement. Police experts provide a simple formula: the more drugs, the more potential for police corruption.

"With the increase in drugs, you're talking about an amount of money most policemen don't normally see in 10 years, and a greater opportunity and temptation," said Robert W. Klotz, a retired deputy Washington, D.C. police chief who is a consultant on law enforcement corruption.

The allegations under investigation in the District—that detectives kept drugs and money seized in raids, leaked information about a big raid to dealers, and generally became too cozy with some alleged drug dealers—closely resemble the facts outlined in several prosecutions of rogue narcotics squads around the nation, from New York to Chicago to Miami.

Indeed, the consensus among law enforcement officials is that narcotics work is the most corruptible of all because of the huge amounts of money involved, the relative discretion with which vice investigators work, and the close relationships that they often have with their drug informants. Another lesson, they say, is that improprieties in narcotics units seem to flourish in an atmosphere of loose supervision.

"My sense is that in vice work, the individual police officer is given a lot more leeway than in any other area," said W. Randolph Teslink, who until 1986 was head of the U.S. Attorney's office and had extensive dealings with Washington, D.C. police. Because narcotics work depends on an officer's initiative, many detectives generally are supervised only by their sergeants, if at all, and some officials do not provide the identities of their informers to their superiors. While detectives in robbery, for instance, keep written records of investigations in progress, narcotics officers rarely do.

Narcotics officers often get informants by pressuring drug dealers or users that they have arrested, police say. And detectives often end up using information from a drug gang to go after another drug gang. "Narcotics agents have to deal with the scum of the earth," said one veteran Washington, D.C. detective. "You have to go down into the gutter with your informant...to a vice cop, they're his bread and butter."

Source: Mintz, J. and V. Churchville (1987). "Vice Officers Walk the Line Between Crime and the Law, In Drug World Easily Eroded." *The Washington Post.*

Police administrators are cognizant of these dangers and take great care in the selection of candidates for the position of drug enforcement agent. In-depth background screening usually includes a polygraph examination and a financial investigation to determine such variables as a candidate's mental health and whether he or she is experiencing any financial hardships that might indicate a vulnerability to corruption.

When surveying the problem of official corruption in the United States, one should also consider drug abuse by public officials as yet another form of official degeneration. Historically, drug abuse by elected or appointed officials is not tolerated by most segments of our society. Many believe that such behavior epitomizes the inability or unwillingness of such individuals to lead and protect the people they serve.

One recent example of drug abuse by an elected official is the case of former Washington, D.C. Mayor Marion Barry. On January 18, 1990, Barry was arrested by police in Washington and charged with possession of cocaine. This incident, which occurred one day before he was to announce his candidacy for reelection, occurred in the aftermath of a previous indictment on drug charges. Shortly after his arrest, Barry announced that he would not seek reelection but maintained that the investigation directed toward him was racially motivated and designed to sabotage his political career. Barry was subsequently convicted of cocaine possession later that year.

Corruption in Foreign Countries

When considering the problem of official corruption in the drug trade, it is often difficult to determine whether complicity in criminal actions is on an individual basis by officials seeking their own financial enhancement or whether it is systematic and under the sanction of an entire government or official unit of that government. The corrupt official is the "*sine qua non*" of drug trafficking, and it is his or her participation, through the corruption of an official office, that protects and aids sophisticated criminals in the manufacturing, smuggling, and distribution of illicit drugs. We have briefly discussed how corruption affects law enforcement domestically; let us now examine how corruption affects drug control in illicit drug source countries.

Cuba

The United States government first suspected the Cuban government's complicity in the drug trade during the early 1960s, but many of the allegations were unfounded. Finally, in the early 1980s, many of these accusations were verified. In particular, in November 1982, the United States District Court indicted four major Cuban officials on charges of conspiring to traffic drugs.

Among those four were the Vice Admiral of the Cuban Navy and the former Cuban Ambassador to Colombia. According to the indictment, the officials were allowing Cuba to be used as a transshipment center for drug shipments destined for the United States. On one occasion, in exchange for its participation in this scheme, the Cuban government was to receive $800,000 for the sale of 10 million methaqualone tablets (Quaaludes) and 23,000 pounds of marijuana.

Other reports of official corruption have surfaced, alleging Cuban cooperation with drug smugglers who flew smuggling aircraft through Cuban airspace. According to the President's Commission on Organized Crime (1986), this was accomplished by assigning the smuggling pilots a corridor or "window" through which they could pass without any interference from the Cuban government. Recently, the Cuban government tried and convicted several high-ranking military and government officials for participating in drug trafficking.

Mexico

United States government officials have always been hesitant to make public accusations of Mexican involvement in criminal activity and in particular the drug trade. Reasons for this are that Mexico is not only one of our closest neighbors but a staunch ally and trading partner as well (see Chapter 4).

Since the early 1980s, however, evidence has surfaced to support the assertion of official corruption in both the Mexican Directorate of Security and the Mexican Judicial Police. Probably one of the most widely publicized and tragic events that illustrated the complicity of several governmental officials in the Mexican drug trade was the 1985 abduction and murder of United States Drug Enforcement Agent Enrique Camarena Salazar and his pilot Alfredo Zavala Avelar in the city of Guadalajara. As a result of the subsequent investigation into this incident, six Mexican police officials were indicted on related charges, including protection of personnel and goods, custody of drugs while in transit, and providing information. The officers cited in this investigation were reportedly receiving payoffs for official protection that ranged from $200 to $6,250 a month.

One of these six officials, the First Commandante Jorge Armando Pavon Reyes of the Mexican Judicial Police (who also headed the Camarena investigation in Mexico), accepted a bribe from drug suspect Rafael Caro Quintero in exchange for Caro's freedom.

Subsequent to the Camarena incident, Mexican President Miguel de la Madrid announced a major reorganization and consolidation of police forces. Under the reorganization, one governor dismissed an entire judicial system, including the state Attorney General and over 100 security agents (see Chapter 9).

Read through   FOREIGN CORRUPTION ALLEGATIONS
                                IN THE ILLICIT DRUG TRADE

Panama. General Manuel Antonio Noriega, the country's former military dictator, was indicted February 4, 1988, by two federal grand juries in the United States for allegedly accepting $4.6 million in bribes concerning drug trafficking activities.

Noriega allegedly provided cocaine traffickers in the Medellin Cartel, which is thought
to account for most of the cocaine that lands in the United States, with secure airstrips for
transport. He is also charged with turning Panama into a money-laundering center and a
safe haven for fugitives.

Haiti. Colonel Jean-Claude Paul, a senior military leader is suspected of aiding the flow of
cocaine into the United States. His wife was indicted on drug charges in March 1987.

Honduras. Juan Ramon Matta Ballesteros, allegedly a major dealer in the Medellin Cartel,
now lives in the Honduran capital and is a friend of senior officers and politicians. Matta is
wanted in the United States for murdering a Drug Enforcement Agent in Mexico; Honduras
refuses to extradite him.

Also, Jorge Ochoa, another alleged Medellin dealer, was arrested in November of
1987 in Colombia while driving a Porsche that belonged to the Honduran military attaché to
Colombia. This raised questions about how Ochoa borrowed the car and how the attaché
could afford it on his military salary.

Bahamas. In February 1988, a known marijuana trafficker testified in Jacksonville, Florida
that he had paid Prime Minister Lynden Pinding $400,000 to allow marijuana shipments to
pass safely through the Bahamas. In 1984, an independent commission of inquiry cleared
Mr. Pinding of drug-related crimes, with reservations. The commission linked two Bahamian cabinet ministers to drug trafficking.

Mexico. In 1985, Enrique Camarena Salazar, a U.S. DEA agent, was kidnapped and killed
in Mexico, allegedly by drug traffickers. In May, 1987, a Los Angeles grand jury indicted
two officers in Mexico's Federal Judicial Police with preventing the apprehension of the kidnappers.

Colombia. In June 1987, Colombia's Supreme Court declared its extradition treaty with the
United States unconstitutional. On December 30, a judge let Jorge Ochoa, a Medellin
Cartel dealer who is wanted for the murder of a DEA agent, walk out of prison. DEA agents
say that Colombian drug enforcement units are so infiltrated with Medellin informers that
they are unwilling to share information with their Colombian counterparts. [The tide turned
again on August 18, 1989 when former President Virgilio Barco declared a "state of siege,"
suspended the normal operations of criminal and civil law, and reinstated extradition. This
literally set off a civil war between the democratically elected government and the cocaine
traffickers.]

Turks and Calcos Islands. Norman Saunder, chief minister of these Caribbean islands,
was indicted by a U.S. grand jury in 1985 on drug charges. He later was tried in his own
country and sentenced to eight years in prison.

Surinam. Military commander Atienne Boerenveen was convicted in September 1986 by a
federal grand jury in Miami of conspiring to sell safe passage through Surinam for cocaine-
laden planes.

Source: Bradley, B. (1988). "Drug Suspicions Follow Officials in High Places." Reprinted by permission
from the Christian Science Monitor, copyright 1988 The Christian Science Publishing Society. All rights
reserved.

Ironically, the murder of Enrique Camarena, of Kiki, has had a very positive effect on the Drug Enforcement Administration....

John C. Lawn, Administrator, DEA, 1985

The Bahamas

The Bahamas and other countries in the Caribbean basin are ideally located for transshipment and refueling for drug smugglers from Mexican and South American countries. In fact, many allegations about its role in transshipments have surfaced since the early 1980s. In 1986, U.S. government intelligence reports alleged that widespread corruption had reached high government offices in the Calcos Islands where, in March 1985, the Bahamas' Chief Minister Norman Saunders was convicted of conspiracy in a drug-trafficking scheme. Witnesses in the Saunders trial testified that he received a total of $50,000 for allowing drugs from Colombia to pass freely through his country.

In yet another case, Bahamian Prime Minister Lynden Pindling was suspected in 1984 of complicity with drug traffickers when an investigation revealed that his personal bank accounts reflected deposits of $3.5 million in excess of his salary during a six-year period.

As mentioned earlier in this text, convicted drug trafficker Carlos Lehder (see Chapters 4 and 9) commonly used Saunders' cay as a refueling and transshipment point for his cocaine runs between 1978 and 1982. Subsequent to Lehder's arrest in 1987, it was learned that Lehder paid "substantial bribes" to police and customs officials to aid him in trafficking cocaine to the United States.

Panama

In the late 1980s, Panama and its leader at the time, General Manuel Antonio Noriega, a long-time United States ally, emerged in a complicated web of corruption and drug trafficking. In February 1988, Noriega was indicted by federal grand juries in Miami and Tampa, Florida on charges of drug trafficking, racketeering, and money laundering. Drug enforcement officials had been aware of Noriega's involvement in the drug trade since the early 1970s, but until December 1989, concern for maintaining stability in Panama and the Canal Zone outweighed United States concern for illicit drug activity there.

Noriega had previously worked as an informer for the Central Intelligence Agency (CIA) and allowed the agency to operate a listening post in Panama monitoring Central and South America. Lieutenant Colonel Oliver North, then a junior member of the National Security Council, and General Richard Secord also used Panama as a base for training soldiers and a place for setting up "dummy" operations to help fund Nicaraguan contras.

In 1988, DEA reports disclosed that Noriega did provide information to the United States regarding certain drug smuggling operations. During that same time, he was accepting large bribes from Colombia's Medellin Cartel for his assistance in drug-trafficking operations and for offering cartel members a safe haven in Panama to avoid prosecution. In 1985, Senator Jesse Helms of North Carolina proposed legislation cutting off aid to Panama, only to be persuaded to withdraw it later because of Noriega's assistance to the contras.

In the summer of 1987, the second-in-command of Panama's defense forces, Colonel Roberto Diaz Herrera, went public with several charges aimed at Noriega. Diaz first accused Noriega of fraud in the 1984 presidential election. He also implicated Noriega in the 1981 death of Panama's President General Omar Torrijos, which, at the time it occurred, was thought to be accidental.

In the late 1980s, it became increasingly clear that Noriega had no intention of restoring democracy to Panama, in particular in the aftermath of national elections in 1989, in which "goon squads" were dispatched by Noriega to intimidate his opposition and the voters of Panama. Political corruption of the caliber seen in Panama, Mexico, and the Bahamas is slow in development but once entrenched, difficult to purge (see the following section on cocaine money and Panama).

Finally, Noriega's reign as leader of Panama ended on December 20, 1989, as President Bush authorized "Operation Just Cause," a surprise overnight invasion in which 2,000 U.S. troops invaded Panama. Although the initiative resulted in 23 U.S. soldiers being killed and over 200 being injured, it was successful in restoring the democratically elected government to power.

The target of the invasion, Noriega, escaped during the attack, and remained on-the-run for about 48 hours. The deposed dictator then turned himself over to the Vatican Embassy on Christmas Eve, seeking political sanctuary and asylum. This sparked international diplomatic concern over the legality and appropriateness of embassies to shelter suspected international drug traffickers who are wanted by the governments of other countries.

On January 3, 1990, Noriega turned himself into authorities of the DEA outside the Vatican Embassy. He was then transported to Miami to face federal drug trafficking charges.

CLOSE-UP: NORIEGA's SURRENDER

Panama City, Panama - When Manuel Antonio Noriega finally walked out of the Vatican Embassy Wednesday night, he strode briskly, General Maxwell R. Thurman, commander of the U.S. Southern Command, said in an interview. Thurman was one of two generals near the embassy when Noriega surrendered. Their presence was one of the conditions under which Noriega said he would give himself up.

Thurman, providing some of the details of the surrender, made it clear that the Americans didn't go too far out of their way to pander to the ousted dictator. "A general was present," Thurman said, but none of the American top brass spoke to or had any contact with Noriega. "I wouldn't have spoken to him under any circumstances," Thurman said bluntly.

At Noriega's request, the Americans returned one of his captured uniforms (dark brown trousers and a tan shirt)—a going-away outfit. Asked if the United States also had provided Noriega with a pair of his favored, lucky red underwear for his flight to the United States to stand trial on drug trafficking charges, Thurman laughed.

As Thurman described the surrender, Noriega walked out of the Vatican Embassy in the company of three priests until he was met by the American soldiers who would take custody of him. The soldiers searched Noriega because the U.S. armed forces had reports that weapons were in the embassy. No weapons were found on the former general, who was briefly handcuffed until he was securely aboard an American plane bound for Homestead Air Force Base in Florida.

Thurman credited the breakthrough in Noriega's surrender to:

* Reports in local newspapers that Panamanian authorities also were about to file their own charges against him.

* A plan by the Vatican Embassy to force the issue of Noriega's departure.

* A massive demonstration by Panamanians outside Noriega's sanctuary on the afternoon of his surrender.

Source: Grimes, C. (1990). "Details Given on Noriega's Surrender." *St. Louis Post Dispatch* (January 5):A14. Copyright 1991, Pulitzer Publishing Company. Reprinted with permission.

Money Laundering

The DEA reported that during fiscal year 1989, 89 tons of cocaine were seized, exceeding cocaine seizures in 1988 by 44 percent. The wholesale value of the cocaine seized for 1989 is estimated at $28 billion. The existence of these large amounts of money illustrates the ability of large-scale drug traffickers to launder billions of dollars every year. Investigations have revealed that such laundering activities commonly utilize the services of many Fortune 500 companies.

The practice of money laundering began in Switzerland during the 1930s, as concerned Europeans began funnelling their capital beyond the clutches of Hitler's Third Reich. In time, Switzerland's well-known numbered accounts became an enormously profitable business. Today, Swiss bank secrecy laws have been relaxed due to numerous criminal cases involving money laundering. Criminals, therefore, are seeking other financial havens in which to deposit their ill-gotten gains.

The flooding of entire regions with drug money is one of the more sinister and surreptitious types of drug-related crime. The term "flooding," tracked by the regional Federal Reserve Banks, seems to describe this phenomenon with great precision. For example, every year since 1980, the Miami branch of the Federal Reserve Bank of Atlanta has reported a cash surplus in the $5 to $6 billion range. In the late 1980s, the Los Angeles Federal Reserve reported a great increase in its surplus; in 1988, the surplus was approximately $4 billion.

It is ironic that the very institutions that could do the most to stop money laundering seem to have the least incentive to do so. For example, the basic fee for recycling money of a suspicious origin averages 4 percent, while the rate for drug cash and other "hot" money may range from 7 percent to 10 percent.

Perhaps one should inquire why the investment of drug money in legitimate businesses should be a cause for concern. Considered very narrowly, the influx of large amounts of cash has provided some short-term financial benefits for Latin American debtor nations as well as domestic beneficiaries of illegal drug money. It cannot be overemphasized, however, that this flood of money is not only a consequence of the drug problem but a major problem in its own right. The money that enters the local economy is a primary cause of inflation. Even the banks that stand to gain from accommodating drug traffickers ultimately bear the costs of any losses that drug-related transactions generate.

Part of the problem the United States has with regard to money laundering activities is that American drug users are primarily consumers rather than producers of drugs. Additionally, the United States is used as a repository for large amounts of drug proceeds. As mentioned in Chapter 7, most drug profits are funneled to upper-echelon members of drug cartels rather than the low-level producers and growers. Therefore, it is because of the tremendous profits of drug trafficking organizations that new members are constantly being lured into this illicit business. Unfortunately, profits are also so large that any losses, due to forfeitures by the government, can usually be easily absorbed through future illicit dealings, making it unlikely that a drug organization will actually be put out of business.

The Los Angeles Federal Reserve has reported a great increase in its surplus; in 1988, the total increase was $4 billion.

Presumably, dealers consider that the risk of imprisonment or loss of assets is a mere risk of conducting business. Therefore, if we assume that the motivation behind the illicit drug trade is profit, then we should conclude that government action against such a lucrative class of crime must include an attack against the proceeds of that criminal act.

The success enjoyed by a drug trafficker poses somewhat of a dilemma for them: how to reduce the likelihood of detection and subsequent asset seizure by law enforcement officials. This is accomplished by a criminal technique known as money laundering, in which illegal cash proceeds are made to appear legitimate or in which the sources of illegal proceeds are disguised. As money laundering laws become more and more effective against the leaders of drug organizations, the risk of detection of such leaders is more likely. The money laundering process can take many forms, including: 1) simply merging illicit money with a legitimate cash source, which usually utilizes a business that generates large amounts of cash, and 2) using sophisticated international money laundering techniques (discussed next). The goal of the financial investigation is to reduce the rewards achieved through drug trafficking and therefore immobilize drug trafficking organizations.

Money Laundering. *A process in which illegal cash proceeds are made to appear legitimate or the sources of illegal proceeds are disguised.*

Between 1987 and 1990, both the FBI and the DEA have been actively involved in the investigation of this type of drug-related crime. In such investigations as Operation CASHWEB (FBI), Operation PISCES (DEA), and Operation C-CHASE (U.S. Customs), undercover agents infiltrated sophisticated money-laundering operations in the United States, Canada, Mexico, Panama, Colombia, the Bahamas, Aruba, and the Cayman Islands.

The principal tool utilized to detect, measure, and punish money laundering is the Bank Secrecy Act (BSA), originally passed into law in 1970. Regulations under this act, issued by the Secretary of the Treasury, provide law enforcement with four basic tools to investigate money laundering:

1. A paper trail of bank records must be maintained up to five years.

2. A Currency Transaction Report (CTR) must be filed by financial institutions whenever a currency transaction is more than $10,000. CTRs are filed with the IRS. Notably omitted from the reporting requirements are wire transfers, bank checks, bank drafts or other written orders of transfer.

3. A Currency or Monetary Instrument Report (CMIR) must be filed whenever currency or monetary instruments of more than $5,000 are taken into or out of the United States. CMIRs are filed with the Customs Service. Cashier's checks and bearer bonds made out to cash (rather than to an individual) are not covered by the reporting requirements.

4. A Foreign Bank Account Report (FBAR) is required whenever a person has an account in a foreign bank of more than $5,000 in value.

Figure 6.1

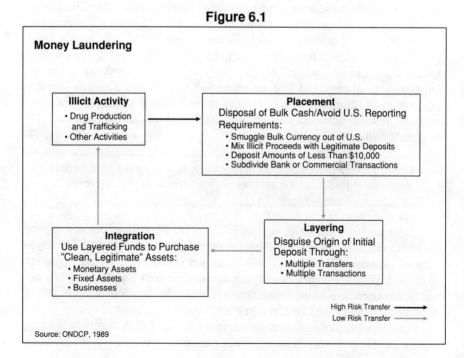

Money Laundering

Illicit Activity
- Drug Production and Trafficking
- Other Activities

Placement
Disposal of Bulk Cash/Avoid U.S. Reporting Requirements:
- Smuggle Bulk Currency out of U.S.
- Mix Illicit Proceeds with Legitimate Deposits
- Deposit Amounts of Less Than $10,000
- Subdivide Bank or Commercial Transactions

Integration
Use Layered Funds to Purchase "Clean, Legitimate" Assets:
- Monetary Assets
- Fixed Assets
- Businesses

Layering
Disguise Origin of Initial Deposit Through:
- Multiple Transfers
- Multiple Transactions

High Risk Transfer ➝
Low Risk Transfer ➝

Source: ONDCP, 1989

Money Laundering Techniques

Illegal drug transactions are usually cash transactions using large amounts of currency to pay off the different actors in each drug deal and to purchase sophisticated equipment. It is important for the trafficker to legitimize his cash proceeds in a fashion that permits him to spend it wherever and whenever he desires without attracting suspicion. Obviously, the trafficker could choose to store his cash in a strongbox or wall safe, but such methods would not be plausible for the trafficker who generates hundreds of thousands or even millions of dollars in illegal cash each year.

As mentioned, to combat this technique, the Treasury Department implemented the CTR report, which banks are required to file whenever they process cash transactions of $10,000 or more. In 1989, the U.S. government processed an estimated seven million CTRs, compared to an estimated 100,000 ten years earlier. Traffickers quickly circumvented this requirement by developing such activities as the corruption of bank employees.

CASE STUDY: PEOPLE's LIBERTY BANK OF KENTUCKY

People's Liberty Bank of Covington, Kentucky was involved in the laundering scheme of a Colombian citizen, Luis Pinto, who was involved in a cocaine ring. Pinto made large cash deposits, often close to $300,000 at a time, and made withdrawals in the form of bank drafts or cashier's checks, usually in amounts that did not require the filing of CTRs. Pinto frequently made withdrawals of $10,000 from several different branches in a single day in order to circumvent reporting requirements. Despite the suspect nature of Pinto's transactions, the bank never notified local or federal law enforcement agencies.

Source: PCOC, 1984

The many different techniques for laundering illicit proceeds are limited only by a trafficker's imagination and cunning. An entire wash cycle, to transform small denominations of currency to business, money market deposits, or real estate, may take as little as 48 hours. The chosen method used by any given trafficker will no doubt reflect his or her own situation and any unique circumstances involved. The following four money laundering techniques illustrate the ingenuity of the drug trafficker in hiding millions (and even billions) of dollars of illicitly gained revenues.

Technique 1—Bank Methods

The most common method for laundering money is one called "bank methods." In this basic technique, the trafficker takes cash to a bank and conducts a number of transactions that usually involve trading currency of small denominations for larger ones. This is done for obvious portability purposes. It is also common for cash to be exchanged for treasury bills, bank drafts, letters of credit, travelers checks, or other monetary instruments.

During the early 1980s in Miami (considered the hub of the cocaine banking business in the United States), large daily shipments of currency would arrive and be deposited in numerous accounts but they would then be immediately disbursed through the writing of checks payable to true or nominee names. Ultimately, these funds were deposited in other domestic accounts in the same or different banks or wire-transferred to offshore bank accounts in foreign countries with strict bank secrecy laws. Ironically, there is no requirement to report these transactions because the Bank Secrecy Act's reporting requirements do not pertain to interbank transfers. Therefore, the biggest problem posed to the traffickers is the initial depositing of the currency into the banks. Once funds are deposited, a trafficker can communicate with the bank through a fax machine or personal computer and literally route funds all over the world without ever coming face to face or even speaking with a banker. One method of conducting mass deposits, called "smurfing," first appeared during the mid-1980s and is discussed next.

Technique 2—Smurfing

A trafficker provides several individuals (or "smurfs") with cash from drug sales. Each smurf goes to different banks and purchases cashier's checks in denominations of less than $10,000, thus bypassing the reporting requirement. The smurfs then turn the checks over to a second individual, who facilitates the subsequent deposits into domestic banks or physically transports the checks to banks in Panama or Colombia. In some instances, the monetary instruments are pre-marked "for deposit only" making them nonnegotiable to the courier.

In transporting monetary instruments such as described above, the trafficker also circumvents yet another requirement of the Bank Secrecy Act: reporting the international transportation of currency in amounts of $10,000 or more.

Figure 6.2

Smurfing

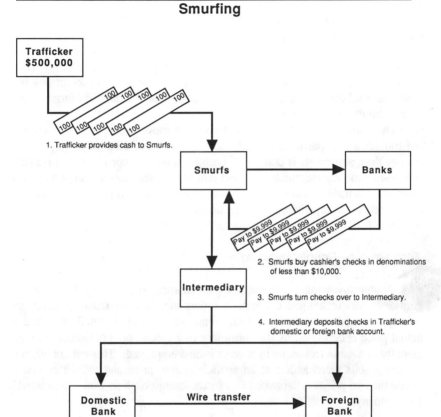

1. Trafficker provides cash to Smurfs.

2. Smurfs buy cashier's checks in denominations of less than $10,000.

3. Smurfs turn checks over to Intermediary.

4. Intermediary deposits checks in Trafficker's domestic or foreign bank account.

5. Smurfing allows Trafficker to deposit $500,000 in bank and circumvent bank reporting requirements.

SOURCE: DEA, 1987

1. Trafficker provides cash to smurfs.

2. Smurfs buy cashier's checks in denominations of $10,000 or less.

3. Smurfs turn checks over to an intermediary.

4. Intermediary deposits checks in trafficker's domestic or foreign bank account.

5. Smurfing allows trafficker to deposit $500,000 in bank and circumvent bank reporting requirements.

Technique 3—Currency Exchanges

Traffickers may also use either money exchanges or brokerage houses for facilitating the movement of their money. Foreign currency exchanges are frequently set up as store fronts that deal in large cash transactions regularly. In using the exchange, the trafficker can avoid using traditional banking institutions and, therefore, avoid risky reporting requirements. Banks traditionally deal with exchange companies and customarily will not question large transactions from these businesses.

The currency exchange business can also move money in other ways for the trafficker. In particular, money sent to other jurisdictions in payment for foreign drug shipments is common. Using a "dummy" corporation, a trafficker will sometimes contact his lawyer and request that the lawyer accept a huge deposit into his foreign account. The lawyer will then wire the money directly into the dummy account, where it remains undetected.

Technique 4—Double Invoicing

Double invoicing is yet another popular method of hiding illicit financial gains. In this technique, a company orders merchandise from a foreign subsidiary at an inflated price. The difference between the inflated price and the actual price is deposited by the subsidiary in a special offshore account. Occasionally, the same technique in reverse is also employed. This occurs when the company sells merchandise at an artificially low price and the difference between the two prices is deposited in a secret foreign bank account maintained by the company.

Technique 5—Acquisition of Financial Institutions

The fifth money-laundering method is possibly the most difficult of all to detect and simply involves acquiring a domestic or international financial institution. By controlling an entire institution, traffickers can go far beyond the immediate aim of concealing illicit earnings. They effectively take over part of the local banking system and divert it to their own needs. Such operations, which are apparent in south Florida and southern California, enable traffickers to manipulate correspondent banking relations, make overnight deposits, arrange Eurodollar loans, and abuse the so-called abuse list (those customers exempted from cash reporting requirements).

Technique 6—Wire Transfers

The wire transfer is one of the most commonly used methods for moving large amounts of money from one point to another. Its use depends on finding a United States-based financial institution willing to accept large cash deposits. One method used to accomplish this is for traffickers to bribe key bank personnel. For example, between 1980 and 1981, drug traffickers bribed a head teller, a loan officer, and the vice president of the Great American Bank in Miami. The bank then processed large amounts of cash for a fee, which was then divided among the three individuals and the bank. In exchange, the three employees agreed not to file CTRs. Instead, they issued the traffickers cashier's checks disguised as loan proceeds that were used to make wire transfers.

MONEY LAUNDERING: HOW IT WORKS

An American "businessman" approaches a banking officer of the Curacao branch of the French-owned Credit Lyonnais Nederland with an offer to deposit a six-figure cash windfall from a successful "business venture." After assuring the banker that the money is not tainted, the banker agrees to facilitate the transaction, referring to the banking arrangement as a "Dutch Sandwich."

Under this plan, the Paris bank would set up a corporation for the customer in Rotterdam, where he would deposit his cash in the bank's local branch. The American would control the newly created Dutch corporation through an Antilles trust company, but his identity as the owner would be protected by the island group's impenetrable secrecy laws. The Caribbean branch would then "lend" the American his own money held in Rotterdam.

If the American is questioned by the Internal Revenue Service or other authorities about the source of his wealth, he can point to his loan from a respected international bank.

Source: Beaty, J. and R. Hornik (1989). "A Torrent of Dirty Dollars." *Time* (December 18):50-56.

These techniques represent only a few of the ways traffickers hide their illicit revenues from drug sales. It is generally thought that traffickers, regardless of their national origin, make regular use of these techniques. The fact that so many different mechanisms exist for money laundering makes investigation of these crimes difficult and presents many unique challenges to the investigator. One great aid to law enforcement attempts was the passing of the Money Laundering Control Act of 1986, which gave investigators more latitude in investigating this type of criminal activity and in uncovering the myriad of techniques.

Financial Havens

Because of the sophistication of the international financial community, there exists a custom-made mechanism for the laundering of illegally made currency. The financial tax haven is therefore an attractive and effective mechanism for money laundering. Countries whose laws provide little or no tax on certain sources of income and, in some cases, where strict bank secrecy laws play an important role in international banking, are popular places for the trafficker to seek a tax haven. The use of an international tax haven allows the trafficker not only to achieve a tax benefit but also to effectively move money easily while insuring anonymity.

One of the first obstacles that the trafficker must overcome is convincing the financial institution to accommodate large amounts of cash on a regular basis.

Let us examine the specific reasons why traffickers may choose a particular tax haven. Several factors might contribute to this decision, in particular—ease of access and proximity to established trafficking routes. This explains why North and South American traffickers alike frequently choose havens in the Caribbean. The Cayman Islands, for example, offers secrecy to traffickers and can easily be reached by air from both continents. Certain features are generally favored by drug traffickers in their selection of financial havens and include:

- little or no tax on foreign earnings of foreign-owned corporations
- lax corporation laws
- commercial and/or bank secrecy
- attractive transportation and communications facilities
- minimal restrictions on foreign currency exchange of foreign corporations or individuals
- location near established trafficking routes
- relatively stable political climate
- availability of professional and/or business advice and assistance

One of the first obstacles that the trafficker must overcome is convincing the financial institution with access to international transfer facilities to accommodate deposits of large amounts of cash on a regular basis. The trafficker realizes that once the money is introduced into the financial system, it then becomes virtually indistinguishable from legitimate monies and can easily be moved, both quickly and confidentially, through the system. Indeed, it is the very aspects of this system, which are designed to protect legitimate confidential business dealings, that conceal the proceeds of the illegal drug trade and inhibit law enforcement efforts.

Cocaine Money and Panama

For years Panama has served the cocaine trafficking community of South America as a money laundering hub. In Panama, the Banco Nacional de Panama acts much like the Federal Reserve Bank in the United States, in that it is a clearinghouse for cash. In 1982, the U.S. Department of the Treasury examined Federal Reserve receipts of Banco Nacional de Panama to determine the amount of cocaine money accumulated in Panama. In the audit, it was determined that there was a fourfold increase in reported cash flow between 1980 and 1983. This cash flow, as it was concluded, was probably the most significant recorded flow of currency and was most likely illegal drug money. The Treasury Department, during this inquiry, estimated that more than 2.2 billion in unreported cash was transported to Panama through a variety of methods.

An example: In May, 1983, Mr. X was apprehended as he attempted to leave a Florida airstrip in his Lear jet bound for Panama. On board his plane, Customs agents found boxes containing more than $5 million in cash for which no CTRs or CMIRs had been filed. A subsequent search of Mr. X's business office revealed 30 kilograms of cocaine and an Uzi submachine gun. Information available to the DEA indicates that Mr. X had not only conducted a business of moving narcotics proceeds for various traffickers, but was also preparing fraudulent United States tax returns. According to one estimate by law enforcement authorities, Mr. X was responsible for the movement of more than $145 million in an eight-month period. He had been smuggling the money out of the United States to circumvent the filing of CMIRs.

Source: PCOC, 1984

Heroin Money and Hong Kong

In 1984, the President's Commission on Organized Crime began to evaluate the heroin trafficking networks operating in southeast Asia. It was determined that southeast Asia's share of the opium and heroin business increased by 10 percent in 1981, 14 percent in 1982, and 19 percent in 1983. In fact, in 1983, the heroin originating in southeast Asia accounted for an estimated 41 percent of the heroin seized or detected in the United States.

Hong Kong's role in laundering money from the heroin trade in Southeast Asia parallels that of Panama in the South American cocaine trade. Hong Kong's specific role has been defined by the President's Commission on Organized Crime as follows:

...Hong Kong is the major financial center for Southeast Asia's drug trafficking. Hong Kong-based trafficking organizations operate throughout the world. Longstanding ties between Hong Kong traffickers and sources of supply in Thailand allow Hong Kong organizations to operate on a very large scale. Large numbers of heroin trafficking ventures throughout the world are financed and controlled from Hong Kong. There is evidence that Hong Kong-based groups are involved in directing the smuggling of heroin into Europe and North America.

Specific information regarding the extent of Hong Kong's involvement in laundering money in southeast Asia has been difficult to acquire. This is primarily due to two factors: (1) the fact that inordinately strict bank secrecy laws there preclude foreign law enforcement agencies from obtaining required information during criminal investigations and (2) the fact that the country lacks currency exchange controls and a central bank, which makes it difficult to trace the flow of funds to and from Hong Kong.

...Responsible for moving most heroin money in Southeast Asia, it operates through gold shops, trading companies, and money changers, many of which are operated in various countries by members of the same Chinese family. Record keeping susceptible to standard audit rarely exists in this underground banking system, and coded messages, "chits," and simple telephone calls are used to transfer money from one country to another. Nonetheless, the system has the ability to transfer funds from one country to another in a matter of hours, provide complete anonymity and total security for the customer, convert gold or other items into currency, and convert one currency into that of the customer's choice.

Source: PCOC, 1986

International Cash Flow

- Some $5-15 billion of the $50-75 billion in illegal drug money earned in the United States probably moves into international channels.

- More than two thirds of the $5-15 billion is moved on behalf of foreign traffickers bringing drugs into the United States, as well as Colombians and Mexicans involved in distributing cocaine and heroin in the United States. The remainder comes from funds earned by U.S. drug dealers and distributors.

- About one third of the illegal drug money moves overseas in the form of currency, and much of the remainder is wired abroad after being deposited in the U.S. banking system.

- More than two-thirds of the $5-15 billion probably passes through Colombia or the offshore banking centers of the Caribbean basin (mainly Panama, the Bahamas, and the Cayman Islands).

Source: PCOC, 1984

Summary

When the so-called drug problem is discussed, the subject of drug-related crime is also deliberated. The very term "drug-related crime" means different things to different people because it represents many types of criminal activity. Although many consider drug crimes to be street crimes, e.g., robbery, assault, burglary, and murder, other crimes also accompany drug abuse.

Studies of the behavior of drug users have revealed that the crime rate (street-type crimes) for users may be anywhere from four to six times as high as for non-drug users. In addition to street crimes associated with drug use, other ancillary crimes such as corruption and money laundering accompany drug use.

Official corruption in the United States poses a major problem for drug control strategists and enforcement officials. Corruption is pervasive and may take any of several forms, from bribery, extortion, favoritism, and mooching to more serious types of corruption such as perjury, premeditated theft, and shakedowns of suspects.

The Knapp Commission's inquiry into police corruption first shed light on New York City's corruption within the police department. Since then, many cases of police and official corruption have surfaced around the country, making it clear that the drug trade can penetrate even the most reputable of professions.

The problem of foreign corruption parallels that experienced in the United States, with even greater repercussions. Many drug-source countries such as Colombia, Peru, and Burma are experiencing criminal forces that threaten to rival the legitimate government because of political influence gained through payoffs. Unscrupulous links have been documented between Panama's former dictator Manuel Noriega and Fidel Castro (see Chapter 9), between Colombian traffickers and Honduran officials; and between high-ranking Mexican Federal Judicial Police officials and known heroin traffickers in Mexico.

For decades, the laundering of illegally obtained currency has been a logistical problem for many organized crime organizations. The trafficker's basic concern is how to transform illegally obtained currency to currency appearing to be legitimate.

The 1970 Bank Secrecy Act has provided investigators with much-needed legal tools with which to combat this type of crime. These tools consist of specific reporting requirements for banking institutions and individuals alike. The use of these reporting requirements enable investigators to follow the path of illicitly gained currency to its source.

Money laundering techniques are sophisticated and represent considerable ingenuity on the part of the criminal. Such techniques include bank methods, "smurfing," the use of currency exchanges, and a technique called double invoicing. Laundered money is typically routed to financial institutions in foreign countries whose bank secrecy laws are much stricter than those of the United States. This gives traffickers considerable flexibility in the movement and storage of illicitly gained currency.

DISCUSSION QUESTIONS

1. List three reasons why corruption is considered a threat to public safety.

2. Discuss the different types of corruption commonly practiced by corrupt police officers.

3. Discuss the sequence of events leading to the deposing of former Panamanian dictator Manuel Noriega. What was his alleged role in the international drug trade?

4. List the sequence of events that occur during the practice of "smurfing" in a money laundering operation.

5. Explain the "bank methods" technique for money laundering.

6. What roles do Panama and Hong Kong play in global drug trafficking?

7. Discuss the use of currency exchanges in money laundering operations.

8. Discuss the Bank Secrecy Act (1970) and the use of the CTR, CMIR, and FBAR as each pertains to money laundering investigations.

9. What is the difference between corrupt officials who are termed "grass eaters" and those called "meat eaters"?

10. When considering the problem of drug-related crime, what is significant about the 1983 Ball, Schaffer, and Nurco study in Baltimore?

11. List the four basic legal tools to investigate money laundering as provided for under the Bank Secrecy Act.

12. List and discuss the six most common techniques used by traffickers to launder illicitly gained currency.

PART II

GANGS AND DRUGS

Organized crime has consistently played an important role in the perpetuation of crime. The drug problem has afforded many organized criminals increased sources of revenue with which to expand their operations and influence. Accordingly, the public safety threats to our communities by such organizations have also escalated. This section will examine the concept of organized crime, its origin and its relationship to the illicit drug trade.

PART II

GANGS AND DRUGS

Organized crime has consistently played an important role in the production of drugs. The drug problem has affected many organized crime as a dressed source of revenue, with which to expand its influence, and influence the public safety that is our communities by such organizations since their inception. This section will examine the concept of organized crime organization and its relationship to the illicit drug trade.

CHAPTER 7

ORGANIZED CRIME AND THE DRUG TRADE

Unquestionably, crime in America has been made more pernicious by two interrelated developments: drug abuse (including drug trafficking) and organized crime. For decades, so-called traditional organized crime was thought to monopolize the drug trade; but now, many new sophisticated criminal groups compete for territory and the tax-free profits offered by illicit drugs.

Indeed, for many years organized crime was nearly synonymous with one organization, La Cosa Nostra (or the Mafia). While both Sicilian criminal organizations and Italian-American syndicates are involved in the lucrative drug trade, so are many other criminal groups. The FBI reported in 1989 that the Sicilian criminal organizations alone netted an estimated $40 billion in heroin revenues. However, other crime organizations now profiting from illicit drug sales include outlaw motorcycle gangs, Jamaican posses, African-American organized crime groups, California youth gangs, and many others.

Organized crime has demonstrated an alarming degree of violence and an ability to corrupt the highest public officials. The pervasiveness of such activity either directly or indirectly threatens all businesses, neighborhoods, and people. It is a fact that large-scale drug trafficking operations, motivated by tax-free profits, require superb organization in order to avoid police detection and to compete with other criminal groups sharing similar aspirations.

To this end, such organizations can be characterized by a number of common activities. These include:

- obtaining the illicit substances (or the raw materials with which to manufacture them);

- making "connections" to acquire the illicit substances;

- arranging for the processing of drugs (either through overseas or domestic sources);

167

- developing smuggling networks with which to transport illicit materials;
- arranging for protection of the operation through corruption of public officials or the hiring of enforcers;
- locating distributors on both the wholesale and retail levels;
- developing a process whereby illegal money can be laundered or otherwise concealed from detection by law enforcement authorities.

Part II of this text will consider some of the significant actors on the criminal side of the "war on drugs." The following segment is designed to acquaint the reader with the various characteristics displayed by each gang, so that rational conclusions can be drawn regarding the role of organized crime in the American drug scene.

The Public Perception of "Organized Crime"

Organized crime is a complex criminal justice phenomenon and one for which there is no codified "legal" definition. Although no single legal definition of the term exists, many federal statutes address certain types of criminal activity typically involving organized crime. For example, statutes exist dealing with criminal conspiracies, criminal narcotics enterprises (CCE), and racketeer-influenced and corrupt organizations (RICO), but all of these are separate from and more specific than the general term "organized crime."

The very words "organized crime" imply criminal involvement by a group of individuals operating in an organized fashion. A general explanation such as this, however, fails to give adequate guidelines to criminal justice professionals, who are in need of a more precise distinction between the high-level organized drug trafficking organization and a group of two or three low-level "street-corner" drug dealers.

In 1968, Congress passed into law the first major organized crime bill, the Omnibus Crime Control and Safe Streets Act. It is the only federal statute that refers to the term organized crime:

> [Organized crime includes] the unlawful activities of members of a highly organized, disciplined association engaged in supplying illegal goods or services, including but not limited to gambling, prostitution, loansharking, narcotics, labor racketeering, and other unlawful activities....

To aid researchers in understanding the basis of what constitutes an organized crime organization, the President's Commission on Organized Crime concluded in 1986 that several variables make up an organized crime unit. These variables are the criminal group, the protectors, and specialized support. Let us now examine each of these.

1. **The Criminal Group.** A collection of individuals that are usually bound by ethnic, racial, geographic, or lingual ties. The individuals display a willingness to engage in criminal activity for profit while using violence and intimidation to protect their criminal interests and to avoid detection. Organized crime (hereinafter referred to as "OC") groups are characterized by the longevity of the group itself, which will outlast the lives of individual members. Such a group maintains rules and a code of conduct, while its management is structured in a hierarchical or pyramid-style chain of command.

   Membership in the OC group is restricted and is usually based on a common trait, talent, or need of the group. Acceptance into the criminal group is closely scrutinized by the existing members, and there is typically an initiation requirement for all recruits. Motivation for individual membership is based on the premise that the successful recruit will enjoy economic gain, protection by the group, and a certain prestige within the organization.

2. **The Protectors.** The protectors are usually associates of the criminal group that appear (at least on the surface) to be law-abiding members of the community. In fact, this group may include prominent members of the community such as corrupt politicians, bankers, attorneys, or accountants. They work to insulate the criminal group from government interference and to protect the assets of the organization.

3. **Specialized Support.** The larger the criminal group, the more it is in need of specialized support. Those individuals offering specialized support for the OC unit make up a component that possesses talent enabling the group to attain its goals and objectives. Unlike the seemingly lawful existence of the protectors, specialists include laboratory chemists, smuggling pilots, and enforcers ("hitmen") for the OC unit. Most OC specialists are overtly involved in illicit aspects of criminality.

   In addition to the specialists discussed above, the organized crime group relies on outside individuals, that is, members of the general public, for financial and other support:

   A. **User Support.** User support includes those individuals that purchase the OC group's illegal goods and services. These individuals include drug users, patrons of prostitutes, bookmakers, and those that willfully purchase stolen goods.

   B. **Social Support.** Social support includes individuals and organizations that grant power and an air of legitimacy to organized crime generally and to certain groups and their members specifically. Social support includes public officials that solicit the support of organized crime figures, business leaders that do business with organized crime figures, and those that portray the criminal group or organized crime in a favorable or glamorous light.

Source: PCOC, 1986

CASE STUDY: KEVIN RANKIN—"MOB-CONNECTED" LAWYER

Kevin Rankin was convicted for his role in an organized crime narcotics conspiracy case and was sentenced to 54 years in prison. Rankin used his status as a lawyer to suborn perjury, bribe, arrange, plan, and participate in a variety of drug trafficking schemes, and to counsel his organized crime clients on ways to conceal prospective criminal acts.

Rankin's tale as a "mob-connected" lawyer for the Philadelphia La Cosa Nostra family is loathsome. A member of that family, Raymond Martorano, together with Al Diadone, Secretary Treasurer of local 54 of the Hotel and Restaurant Employees Union, hired one Willard Moran, a "family" associate, to murder John McCullough, president of the Local 30 of the roofers union. Moran did not hesitate. As McCullough's wife looked on, Moran shot McCullough six times in the head.

Moran was charged with murder, tried, convicted, and sentenced to death. Moran acknowledged the contract nature of the killing and identified Martorano and Diadone as his employers.

Then "mob-connected" lawyer Rankin became involved as one of the lawyers representing Martorano and Diadone. The unprofessional nature of Rankin's legal services set him apart. These included obtaining and using perjured affidavits and testimony on behalf of his clients. Rankin paid Keith Pearson, a prison guard, to perjure himself. Then he drafted a perjurious affidavit concerning Moran, and Pearson signed it. This unprofessional and criminal act failed because Pearson himself was under active Federal investigation as an alleged courier in a drug deal involving Rankin and Martorano's son. When questioned by federal agents about his role as a drug courier, Pearson admitted that his perjury had been bought by Rankin. After making the admissions to federal agents, Pearson went home and killed himself.

Rankin did not stop at fabricating perjurious defenses for those accused of the contract murder. During the same time, Rankin was hosting a series of La Cosa Nostra strategy meetings involving Martorano's heroin and cocaine networks. These were designed to develop stratagems to limit Martorano's "exposure." One of the meetings involved a "mob-connected" lawyer from Miami, who was, in fact, a federal undercover agent. Rankin's meetings with this "mob-connected" lawyer were monitored. Below is a partial transcript of one such meeting where Rankin offers some advice about laundering the proceeds from narcotics transactions after the undercover agent states that he has $200,000 from a "coke deal":

Rankin: *I have a good friend down there, I'm gonna give
you his name ... his name is Jerry (last name
deleted)*

Agent: Uh huh.

Rankin: *He's an attorney ... he is schooled, that's his
business ... setting up offshore accounts...*

Agent: Uh huh.

Rankin: *... and Jerry was a very stand up guy in law
school.*

Agent: Right.

Rankin: *You call this fellow Jerry and tell him, ya know, use
my name....*

Agent: Yeah...he is a hip guy, I mean he knows...or...he
doesn't wanna know what the program is?

Rankin: *No, no, just, if you ever need any questions
answered about how...to bank your money...he'll
help you....*

Again, there was nothing subtle about Kevin Rankin's "legal advice."
As the transcript revealed, he knew that the money referred to
represented illicit profit from an illicit transaction. This did not matter.
Eagerly he gave advice to a supposed confederate to help launder dirty
money. Unlike reputable counsel, lawyer Rankin's efforts involved no
legal research, no study of case law, and no analysis of evidence.
Instead, his efforts were directed toward fabrication of evidence and
perjury: efforts that were unprofessional, illegal, and criminal.

Source PCOC, April, 1986

[See Chapter 11 section on "Forfeiture of Attorney's Fees in Drug Cases" for
further information.]

172 Part II: Gangs and Drugs

When examining organized crime organizations in the United States as well as in foreign countries, there are certain operative characteristics that we can identify. One such characteristic is the attempt by the group to compete with the functions of legitimate government. Examples of this are the following:

- *In Colombia*: cocaine cartels such as the Medellin and Cali Cartels are competing with the legitimate government in attempting to control segments of the society, offering to pay off the country's national debt, and generally acting like an alternative government.

- *In Italy*: the Sicilian Mafia has been responsible for the assassinations of many investigators and federal police that were assigned to anti-Mafia investigations. In addition, judges, mayors, union leaders, and representatives of government have been killed by organized crime members because they opposed the political or criminal activities of the Mafia.

- *In Burma*: the Shan United Army has been using force to control the Shan State since 1948, when Burma became independent from the British.

In the United States, such displays of violence against the government are not quite as blatant, but many of the same principles are still at work. In one case, for example, the Mafia in Chicago attempted to levy a "street tax" on bookmakers and pornographers. Although these activities are illicit, the function of taxing is one rightfully belonging to legitimate government.

Additionally, many cities that have experienced the influx of youth gangs have recognized that these groups have literally attempted to take control of neighborhoods for crack distribution. In many cases, witnesses that have offered to testify against certain criminal organizations have been intimidated because of the organization's reputation and encouraged not to cooperate with the government through threat of violence. Clearly, this is an absolute characteristic of the organized crime unit and one that threatens many of the fundamentals of a civilized society.

According to the U.S. Department of Justice, in order for a criminal group to be considered an organized crime group, it must have an organizational structure, it has to engage in a continuing criminal conspiracy, and its underlying goal must be the generation of profits. Such groups include both foreign and domestic organizations and will be individually discussed later in this chapter.

Drug Gangs as Organized Crime

Those criminal organizations concerned solely with drug trafficking represent organized crime models that share many of the same characteristics as traditional organized crime, but with some significant differences. These differences, as well as the evolution of "modern-day" drug trafficking organizations, will be discussed next.

It was in the early 1970s that a new kind of drug trafficking organization began to emerge. Four fundamental factors can be seen as contributing to the genesis of this new configuration of organized crime:

1. Profound social, political, and economic changes in the drug-producing and drug-consuming nations combined to accelerate and intensify the spread of drugs.

2. There was vastly increased mobility within and between consuming and producing nations, and this was aided by cheap, readily available, international transportation. There was also a huge immigration from South America and the Far East to the United States.

3. In the opium-producing countries, many peasants and urban workers had surplus time for the kinds of work needed to sustain the drug traffic.

4. In the consuming nations, old restrictions against many types of behavior, including the taking of drugs, had declined sharply. All of these factors made possible a new kind of trafficking.

When attempting to understand these organizations as a whole, we should first recognize that no one drug trafficking organization is *"typical."* Rather, there are a multiplicity of trafficking organizations that follow a few well-defined patterns. Thus, several conditions exist that seem to lend cohesiveness to the modern-day drug trafficking organization: *vertical integration, alternate sources of supply, exploiting social and political conditions,* and *insulation of leaders from the distribution network.*

1. *Vertical Integration.* Vertical integration is illustrated by the major international trafficking groups such as the Colombian cartels as well as by domestic criminal groups such as outlaw motorcycle gangs that often control both the manufacturing and

wholesale distribution of drugs. Also, city-based operations such as the California street gangs, which concentrate on domestic distribution and retail sales represent an organization with operations that are more directly linked to the end user than are the Colombian cartels or the motorcycle gangs.

2. *Alternate Sources of Supply.* Among the various types of organizational structures and operational types, most have common distribution channels and operating methods. First, most groups acquire the illicit drugs outside of the United States. Exceptions are marijuana and certain drugs made in domestic clandestine labs. Consequently, distribution channels are long and complicated. For example, there are numerous links between the coca leaves grown and harvested in the Huallaga Valley of Peru and the destination of the finished product—an American city.

    Second, many of the larger organizations acquire drugs from alternate sources of supply. Thus, the Colombian cartels can purchase either coca leaves or partially processed coca paste in any of several countries in South America. When the Turkish government clamped down on the illicit cultivation of opium poppies, drug organizations shifted their production to regions in the Golden Triangle in southeast Asia and the Golden Crescent in southwest Asia.

3. *Exploiting Social and Political Conditions.* Drug trafficking organizations today demonstrate a willingness to capitalize on vulnerable social and economic milieus. This occurs, for instance, in inner-city areas and even countries where labor markets are willing to take risks to partake of the huge profit potential offered in drug trafficking operations. Generally, most players drawn into drug trafficking are expendable, provided that the leaders remain untouched. The leaders can then choose individuals from a large pool of unskilled labor. These individuals must be willing to take personal risks and able to learn one or two menial duties in the trafficking system.

    Certain traffickers have even demonstrated that they can manipulate market conditions to make trafficking more profitable. In particular, the introduction of black tar heroin in the mid-1980s was a response to heroin shortages, while the change from cocaine HCl to crack in the mid-1980s was also an effort to offer the nonaffluent drug user affordable cocaine.

4. *Insulation of Leaders.* The organizational structure of a drug
trafficking organization can be described as a solar system with
the leaders at the center. It is only these leaders (or kingpins) that
see the organization as a whole. Trafficking leaders strive to
minimize any contact with drug buyers or the drugs themselves
as a strategic effort to insulate themselves from governmental
detection. Orbiting the leader are many different individuals that
serve various functions, e.g., money launderers, enforcers, and
attorneys, each of whom has other individuals orbiting him or
her, and the cycle continues.

Although the four preceding operational variables help explain how drug
trafficking organizations function, they fail to explain adequately the tremendous growth of such organizations. The growth of a particular organization can
partially be attributed to the fact that certain drug commodities, such as cocaine
and heroin, have highly addictive qualities. This accounts, at least in part, for a
certain degree of return business for many organizations. Here, the drug users
themselves effectively become salesmen or "ambassadors," working on behalf
of the drug trafficking organization by introducing drugs to new users. Additionally, powdered drugs such as heroin and cocaine can be much more easily
transported (smuggled) than a bulkier commodity such as marijuana.

---

*Provided that the leaders are untouched,...anyone seized by the police
or neutralized by a rival gang can easily be replaced....*

The political climate in foreign source countries also contributes to the
growth of trafficking organizations. Many such countries actually encourage
the cultivation of raw materials for drugs. Five of the most significant source
countries (Mexico, Colombia, Ecuador, Peru, and Burma) are currently experiencing serious economic and political problems reflective of their move from
conventional crops to coca, opium poppies, and marijuana; legitimate crops
simply fail to provide parallel incomes to the illicit crops.

As one can observe, the very structure of today's drug trafficking organizations poses serious tactical and investigative challenges to law enforcement officials. The volume of drugs entering the United States, the great number of trafficking organizations in existence, and the fact that methods of operation used
by these groups can change so quickly dictate that unconventional approaches to
detecting and prosecuting drug-related organized crime be considered by public
officials.

CASE STUDY: *DROZNEK/ROSA* CASE

During the course of the *Droznek/Rosa* case, two dozen defendants pled guilty, individually and in small groups, leaving only two to be tried in this four-year-long OCDETF investigation by the FBI, DEA, IRS, ATF, and the Pennsylvania Bureau of Narcotics. Among those entering agreements with the government were Marvin "Babe" Droznek and Joseph Rosa, both of whom are self-confessed soldiers in the LaRocca/Genovese LCN family of western Pennsylvania.

Having confessed to participating in a continuing criminal enterprise, Droznek made consensually recorded phone calls and "wore a wire" while pursuing business as usual—dealing cocaine. This risky activity made Droznek a devastating witness in a case noteworthy for the lack of physical evidence. There were plenty of guns but no cocaine. Droznek eventually testified against Rosa and most of the other defendants.

The prime target of Droznek's testimony was a friend that he never quite trusted, Joe Rosa. When Rosa invited him to bring $200,000 along and join him on a buying trip to Florida, Droznek set up a unique "death insurance" policy. A third party was to hold $20,000 to pay for Rosa's murder if anything happened to Droznek. Fortunately for both, the trip was canceled. When Droznek later told Rosa of his "insurance," Rosa admitted he that had indeed considered a rip-off. Droznek lived his adult life in a violent world. He admitted using threats and violence as an enforcer. He owned many guns, including submachine guns, and on occasion would fire one into the ground as a "demonstration."

Close associates of Droznek that met untimely deaths included Robert George and Mark Puzas. George was a hotel operator, drug addict, and cocaine dealer. On a Tuesday, he told Droznek that he was suspicious that a man with whom he had been dealing might be "a dirty cop." The man was, in fact, an undercover county detective. The next day, George confronted the detective with a loaded shotgun. The brave officer slapped the gun away and killed George with one shot from his .357 magnum. Mark Puzas became a confidential informant who was used by county narcotics detectives when they searched Droznek's home for marked cash after Puzas had purchased a kilogram of cocaine from him. A county grand jury recommended prosecution of Puzas during its separate investigation of Droznek. Two days after a visit from Droznek, Puzas hanged himself in jail.

Droznek worked his way up through the gambling ranks: first, as a numbers writer, then booking bets, then as a collector and loan shark, and then as a "beard," a layoff man paid a commission to keep big bookmakers from recognizing the real source of a bet. In 1984, having lost a Las Vegas sports informer that had enabled him to make some sure-thing bets, Droznek made his first "coke" deal. In the next three years, he and his associates distributed more than 200 kilos of cocaine in the Pittsburgh area.

During early 1985, Droznek was introduced, by a mutual customer, to a drug dealer and vending machine entrepreneur, William Kostrick. This customer had been a part of Kostrick's prior operation, in which Kostrick and Rosa had obtained cocaine in south Florida and utilized couriers to transport the drug to Pennsylvania. The cocaine was cut, stashed, and redistributed to various dealers. In a process that continued throughout the conspiracy, Kostrick and/or

Rosa would travel to Florida to purchase quantities of cocaine. Couriers would fly to Miami or Fort Lauderdale and rent cars for transportation back to Pittsburgh and redelivery to Kostrick, Rosa, or Droznek.

Throughout 1985 and 1986, each of the three principals developed separate sources and systems of delivery, and each would supply the others according to their needs. Kostrick, for example, developed contacts with a family from western Pennsylvania that had relocated to the west coast of Florida. This family had developed its own contacts with various Colombian and Cuban suppliers. The family members would transport cocaine in multikilogram lots to Kostrick in Pittsburgh. Rosa had developed contacts through his LCN connections. The three partners each maintained various stash houses that concealed both the cocaine and the money generated from the sale thereof. As a sideline, Droznek and Rosa, together with various other members of the conspiracy, also trafficked extensively in automatic and silenced weapons.

Each of the principals generated large amounts of cash during the operation of the enterprise. Droznek purchased a restaurant in Pittsburgh and a comfortable home in the suburbs. He also invested in certificates of deposit and utilized a number of safe deposit boxes to store his cash. Through his gambling and cocaine operations, Droznek established associations with a number of racketeers that owned and operated semilegitimate businesses. Droznek used these associates to purchase fictitious W-2 wage statements to shelter him from income tax evasion charges. One such business operated as a pollution spill cleanup business. Droznek purchased his W-2 by paying the owner, a compulsive gambler and fraud artist, a 10 percent commission for each check.

Kostrick lived relatively modestly, investing his money in the vending business, possibly stashing some of his profits with family members. Most of the locations where Kostrick's machines were placed were owned by cocaine customers or loanshark victims. Rosa spent large amounts of income for automobiles, jewelry, and entertainment. He made a number of expensive real estate purchases, which he attempted to conceal through the use of nominees. Rosa also formulated a construction and landscaping business in an attempt to generate a legitimate income in response to an extensive IRS investigation. Much of Rosa's ill-gotten gains, including $175,000 worth of jewelry Rosa had stolen from his own store in an insurance scam, were passed on to the LCN underboss.

The membership of this criminal organization included a number of past and present law enforcement officers. Robert George, a hotel owner and a major dealer for all three of the principals, had been the chief of police for a small township in the northern suburbs of Pittsburgh. George had been fired from that position in the early 1980s as a result of various acts of administrative misconduct. Kostrick and two of his convicted associates had been former North Versailles Borough police officers. Michael Monaco, who provided Droznek with gun permits, had been an Allegheny County Deputy Sheriff prior to his arrest for cocaine trafficking in 1985. Perry Perrino, convicted and sentenced to 10 years incarceration, had been an Allegheny County Assistant District Attorney during the course of the conspiracy. At Perrino's sentencing, it was alleged that he had accepted both money and cocaine from Droznek while employed as a District Attorney and that Perrino had discussed with Droznek the status of an informant in an investigation then pending against Droznek. According to Charles Sheehy, the Acting U.S. Attorney, many of the persons contacted during this investigation have abandoned their jobs, careers, or professions as a result of cocaine addiction. Almost without exception, each individual that became involved in heavy cocaine use turned to criminal activity in order to support the habit. The lure of cocaine and the wealth that can be generated from its sale were shown to have corrupted numerous public officials entrusted with the responsibility of law enforcement.

Source: Organized Crime Drug Enforcement Task Force, 1988.

Summary

To understand the many problems associated with the illicit drug trade, one must comprehend what constitutes organized crime. Defining organized crime is no easy task, as there is no "official" definition of the term. According to researchers, there are certain characteristics unique to the "criminal group" or members of the organized crime unit. Such characteristics include the provision of illicit goods or services, the arbitrary use of violence, the establishment of a code of conduct for members, the ability to corrupt public officials, and a recruitment strategy based on certain ethnic, racial, geographical, or kinship factors.

Those that belong to the criminal group are usually supported by individuals belonging to two other categories of criminals, the protectors and specialized support. The protectors are not full-fledged members but still work on behalf of the organization while appearing to be legitimate parts of society. Protectors include accountants, attorneys, and government officials. The specialized support group also consists of individuals that are not official members but possess certain talents necessary for the success of the organization. Professionals with such traits are pilots, enforcers, and chemists.

Modern-day gangs are, in part, distinguished from traditional organized crime organizations by their recent vintage. For instance, the genesis of groups such as the Jamaican Posses, the California youth gangs, and the Colombian cocaine cartels occurred around 1970, when drug abuse began to flourish in the United States. Four characteristics unique to the emerging groups are vertical integration, the use of alternate sources of supply, a propensity to exploit social conditions to further the organization, and the insulation of leaders from street-level dealers.

DISCUSSION QUESTIONS

1. Define the term "traditional organized crime," and discuss how it pertains to the illicit drug trade.

2. Discuss the three variables that make up an organized crime unit, according to the President's Commission on Organized Crime.

3. Having examined the organized crime "criminal" and "protector" groups, discuss and compare them to the players in an organized crime "support group."

4. What factors created the spawning of the new drug trafficking groups during the early 1970s?

5. Discuss some of the more successful drug trafficking organizations and how they have been able to manipulate the drug-user market to improve profits.

6. List and discuss the four conditions that lend a cohesiveness to the "modern-day" drug trafficking organization.

7. Give examples of criminal drug trafficking groups that may be considered vertically integrated.

8. List some examples of individuals that may act as "protectors" for the organized crime unit.

CLASS PROJECTS

1. Go to the library and research the historical roots of old-time organized crime organizations in the United States, and compare their emergence to the emergence of today's drug trafficking organizations.

CHAPTER 8

DOMESTIC
DRUG TRAFFICKING ORGANIZATIONS

The problem of dealing with organized crime (OC) is certainly not a new one for law enforcement agencies. The drug trade, however, has reshaped organized crime by creating new, violent, and sophisticated criminal groups. Although these groups are frequently at odds with one another, more and more are learning to work together, as they did during alcohol prohibition, to maximize profits and minimize their risk of detection. This chapter will examine some of the largest and most active domestic OC groups in the illicit drug trade.

Traditional Organized Crime (La Cosa Nostra)

In 1988, the FBI estimated that approximately 25 percent of the crime families making up La Cosa Nostra (meaning "our thing") are involved in drug trafficking. La Cosa Nostra (also referred to as the LCN or the "Mafia") has been a source of controversy in criminology and law enforcement in the United States for over 70 years. Because it had its genesis in Italy and Sicily during the mid-1800s, it could very well be discussed under the following chapter: Foreign Drug Trafficking Organizations. Due to the fact, however, that it plays such a significant role in criminality in the United States and because a great number of its members are naturalized United States citizens, La Cosa Nostra is commonly referred to as a "domestic" criminal organization.

Today, two factions of traditional organized crime operate in the United States: La Cosa Nostra (also called the Italian Mafia or Italian-American Syndicates) and the Sicilian Mafia. When considering the Cosa Nostra's role in drug trafficking, perhaps we should first consider the history of the organization itself. Because the roots of the Sicilian Mafia go back further than those of its American compatriots, that organization will be examined first.

The Mafia's History

The Sicilian Mafia has established itself in Italy as the premier criminal group. This has been accomplished through corruption, assassination, extortion, and manipulation. Its criminal influence reaches around the globe, with particular strength in western Europe, North America, and South America. The main region of influence of the Sicilian Mafia is in the southern region of Italy known as the "mezzogiorno," which is also territory claimed by two other powerful Italian organized crime groups, the Camorra and the N'Drangheta.

Both the Camorra and N'Drangheta have lengthy histories as prison groups originating in Italy. Spanish kings had ruled Naples and Sicily between the years 1504 and 1707 and again between 1738 and 1860. The Camorra was organized during the first Spanish reign, and the Sicilian Mafia, which was considered the most powerful criminal organization during the eighteenth and nineteenth centuries, was formed during the second reign. Both the Camorra and the Sicilian Mafia shared similar traits:

- each existed by selling certain criminal services to either individuals or corrupt members of the government,

- each had a formal organizational structure: the Camorra was organized into brigades or "brigata," while the Sicilian Mafia was organized into "families,"

- each had a strict code of silence or "omerta," which basically 1) dictated that family members never cooperate with government officials and 2) instituted the "vendetta," which was the code of retribution against anyone that in any way attacked or insulted a member of the "family."

The word "Mafia" appeared for the first time in public print in November 1860, when it was acknowledged that a Camorra group had established itself in the general area of Palermo, Sicily. In 1878, Giuseppe Esposito, a Sicilian Mafiosi, was the first Sicilian Mafia member to relocate, along with six others, to the United States. Upon his arrival in New York, Esposito and his men found America hostile to non-English speaking immigrants and with a criminal underworld dominated by the Irish and the Jews. Because of this, he moved to New Orleans with his Sicilian entourage, where he headed the thriving Sicilian Mafia. After being arrested in 1881 by Police Chief David Hennessey on an outstanding Italian fugitive warrant, Esposito was transported back to New York and then extradited to Italy.

Esposito was succeeded as boss by Joseph Macheca, an American-born member of the organization. Macheca soon began reinforcing the numbers of the New Orleans Mafia with new immigrants from Sicily, a practice commonly used by the American Mafia over the years. In 1890, Police Chief David Hennessey was assassinated by the Macheca crime family, a family in which ten members had been charged with murder. After a lengthy trial, all were acquitted.

The acquittals created public outrage, resulting in an angry crowd attacking Parish Prison, where 19 Sicilian prisoners were housed. The ensuing carnage included the largest lynching in history: sixteen prisoners were murdered. Some were shot but many were hanged on lamp posts. As the turn of the century approached, other Sicilian Mafia families were operating around the United States in San Francisco, St. Louis, Chicago, New York, and Boston.

The Prohibition era lasted between 1920 and 1933 and was probably the single most influential factor in providing up-and-coming Mafia families with what they needed most: enough money to infiltrate legitimate business, thereby making their illicit enterprises more difficult to detect. During this time, some of the more notorious Mafiosi arrived in the United States. Carlos Gambino, Joe Profaci, Joe Magliocco, Mike Coppola, and Salvatore Maranzano joined the likes of Joe Bonanno and Lucky Luciano.

During the 1930s, Luciano and other LCN bosses solidified their base of operation, which grew into a national organization that now occupies 25 American cities with an estimated 2,000 actual members.

The Mafia and the Drug Trade

During the 1960s and early 1970s, France became well known as a distribution point for an estimated 80 percent of the world's heroin. Marseilles became the center of heroin laboratories that processed raw opium brought in from Turkey. Heroin was then smuggled into the United States by French Corsicans as well as Sicilian and American Mafia members (the "French Connection"). In the early 1970s, the French Connection was broken up as a result of a joint investigative effort by U.S. and French authorities. Today, France is no longer considered a major producer of heroin sold on the American market.

In 1986, the President's Commission on Organized Crime stated that "heroin is the biggest money maker for the Mafia." It is thought that since the collapse of the French Connection, Italy and Sicily have assumed the role of distribution points for LCN heroin. Intelligence sources have also indicated that French chemists have assumed their traditional role of converting raw opium into heroin. The opium is transported from sources in the eastern Mediterranean countries of Syria, Lebanon, Pakistan, and Jordan.

Know for Test

LCN ORGANIZATIONAL STRUCTURE

Boss. The head of the family. He does not participate in the day-to-day activities of the organization, but is supposed to receive a cut from every income source. He usually has his own legitimate and illegitimate businesses.

Under-boss. Assists the boss. Usually he is being groomed to succeed the boss, but succession is not automatic. There is only one under-boss per family.

Consiglieri. Literally, "counselor." Assists the boss, but has no leadership authority. He is generally an older, experienced member that can advise family members. Usually only one per family.

Capo. Caporegima, or captain; supervisors of the family's day-to-day criminal operations; represents the family among the soldiers, whom the capos oversee. A capo gains his position by proving his ability as an "earner"—one that earns a great deal of profit for the family. They may have their own legitimate and illegitimate ventures and retain a part of the income paid by their soldiers before passing it on to the leadership. The number of capos in a family depends on the size of the family.

Soldier. The basic rank in the family. Sometimes known as a "wise guy," "buttonman," or "made-man;" the last term refers to any formal member of the LCN, one that has undergone the initiation ritual. To be "made," a man must be of Italian ancestry.

Associates. An informal position, yet one that is crucial to the family. An associate need not be of Italian descent; he is someone whose skills or position make him of value to the organization. Some are used as soldiers, while others are more distantly connected. The FBI has estimated that for every formal member of La Cosa Nostra there are ten criminal associates that cooperate with members and share their enterprises.

Protectors. Among any family's associates is a support network of "protectors." These are corrupt public officials, bankers, lawyers, accountants, and other professionals that protect the criminal group from governmental intervention, both civil and criminal.

Source: PCOC, April 1986

...of the 25 identified LCN families, 19 have had individual members who have been found to engage in drug violations...

The FBI reports that the Sicilian Mafia controls the transshipment of heroin through Italy to the United States from both southwest Asia (SWA) and southeast Asia (SEA) (see Chapter 4). According to the DEA, the proportion of SWA heroin to SEA heroin entering Italy is 70 percent to 30 percent, with indicators showing SWA heroin on the decrease. Methods of smuggling by the LCN have included:

- members or associates traveling by air and wearing body packs of 2 to 3 kilograms of heroin, and

- heroin secreted in toys, statues, wheels of provolone cheese, film canisters, coffee machines, dry-cell batteries, cans of baby powder, electronic appliances, mail, and clothing.

Figure 8.1

Location of American Mafia families in the continental United States

The Pizza Connection

The investigation that revealed the extent to which the Sicilian Mafia operated in the United States is popularly known as the Pizza Connection. This case, which took federal agents five years to investigate, grew out of an FBI organized crime investigation of the Joseph Bonanno Family in New York. Basically, the Pizza Connection was a massive operation involving heroin smuggling and money laundering by Sicilian Mafia members operating in the United States.

The operation ultimately led to the 1984 indictments in New York of 35 alleged members of the Sicilian Mafia. The investigation revealed that, between 1982 and 1983, the Sicilian Mafia had scheduled $1^1/_2$ tons of heroin, with an estimated wholesale value of $333 million, for importation to New York. In addition, between 1980 and 1983, the New York Sicilian Mafia was reported to have shipped in excess of $40 million in cash from New York to Sicily via Switzerland.

The breadth of the investigation expanded worldwide with Mafia members identified in such countries as Brazil, Canada, Spain, Switzerland, Italy, and the United States. So vast was the investigation that it took federal prosecutors one full year to try. Ultimately, the trial turned out to be the most costly and lengthy criminal proceeding in United States history, but proved rewarding by the securing of convictions for all but two of the defendants. Those convicted received lengthy sentences.

As a result of the information produced at this trial, some argue that not enough is being done to fight drug trafficking. Shana Alexander stated that "[the case] did not make the slightest dent in the nation's desperate drug problem. More heroin and cocaine are on the streets today than before 'Pizza' began. The trial severely overtaxed every branch of our legal system—law enforcement, bench, and bar—and taxed unfortunate jurors worst of all" (1988).

Testimony revealed that one member of the Sicilian Mafia operating in the United States, Salvatore Salamone, was entrusted with the job of changing small denomination bills to large denomination bills and transporting the money in suitcases overseas (see Chapter 6). Once the money arrived in Switzerland, several other individuals converted the bills into Swiss francs and then to Italian lira for delivery to Sicily.

The Pizza Connection illustrates a working relationship between the Sicilian and American Mafia and their "common interests" in drug trafficking and money laundering. Each organization needed the other, and the relationship was established on a basis of mutual trust and respect. In 1987, the FBI observed the following about the Sicilian and American Mafia:

1. The Sicilian Mafia operates in the United States as a separate criminal organization that specializes in heroin smuggling. The first allegiance of its members is to the "family" in Sicily.
2. Prior to initiating a major heroin smuggling operation, the Sicilian Mafia obtains the sanction of certain American Mafia families.
3. As payment for the American Mafia family granting its sanction for the operation, the Sicilian Mafia pays the American Mafia family up to $5000 per kilogram of heroin brought into the United States.

The Mafia Wars

During the early 1980s, Italy experienced an increase in violence between members of the estimated 20 Mafia families operating in and around Palermo. The violence resulted in the murders of mobsters, policemen, judges, and politicians in what was dubbed the "heroin wars." The central government of Italy has since taken initiatives toward controlling Mafia-related criminal activity. These initiatives include anti-Mafia legislation enacted on September 11, 1982. It features such measures as:

- "association" with known Mafia types is illegal, whether a crime is committed or not;

- "association" also applies to the Camorra and other "Mafia-type" groups;

- "exile" locations for convicted "Mafiosi" have been established in towns with a population of less than 10,000, and an unauthorized exit of the location shall result in imprisonment;

- property and other assets are subject to confiscation;

- telephone wiretaps are authorized on persons suspected of belonging to "Mafia-type" organizations; and

- the term "omerta" is defined in its most negative connotation as a "conduct of non-cooperation with public safety officials due to fear."

The implementation of this law resulted in the 1984 arrests of over 450 suspected Mafiosi and the subsequent trial, that has become known as the "Maxi-Processo," or maxi-trial. The arrests, which are considered the greatest Mafia crackdown since Mussolini's 1920s Mafia purge, resulted from a 40-volume, 8,632 page indictment that outlined over 90 murders, countless kidnappings, and even the use of torture chambers. Additionally, the indictment included charges of heroin smuggling and money laundering for Mafia members.

JURY CONVICTS ITALY'S TOP MAFIA BOSSES
OF MURDERS, DRUGS

ROME. A Sicilian jury convicted top Mafia bosses of murder and drug trafficking yesterday, and judges sentenced 19 of them to life in jail to climax Italy's most serious attempt in modern times to cripple the mob. Verdicts and sentencing of 452 defendants came in a bunker-like Palermo courtroom last night, 20 months after the historic Mafia trial began and 36 days after jurors and two judges began their deliberations inside an armored room. The mass trial, which was estimated to have cost at least $100 million, including $19 million for construction of the courtroom, is seen as the most severe blow against the Mafia in postwar republican Italy. Still, nobody was claiming total victory last night. "This is not the end of a repressive epoch, but the beginning of a new legality," said assistant judge Pietro Grasso after the findings were reported.

Giovanni Falcone, an examining magistrate who was instrumental in assembling the 8,636-page indictment, called the court's action "an important starting point—not the end, but the beginning." In all, the six jurors and two judges, who also weigh evidence under Italian law, convicted and sentenced 338 defendants, more than 100 of whom are still at large. Another 114 were acquitted.

With an army of police on guard outside, more than 1,300 witnesses depicted the Mafia's growth from a Sicily-centered syndicate to an international organization that made billions trafficking heroin, principally to the United States. In addition to the drug charges, prosecutors accused the defendants of 90 murders, racketeering, money laundering and other crimes, including participation in a criminal organization.

Inside the courtroom, which is connected by tunnel to Palermo's Ucciardone Prison, defendants lounged in barred, bulletproof cages as chief judge Alfonso Geordano read the court's findings, answered by scattered protests and the sobbing of relatives. During the trial, the most damning evidence came from about 30 repentant Mafia members, called "pentiti," that broke the gang's historic vow of silence and testified for the government in exchange for more lenient sentences.

In a nation that has no death penalty, prosecutors had asked for 28 life sentences and more than 5,000 years in prison. Michele "The Pope" Greco, undisputed "boss of bosses" in Palermo and chairman of the 12-man commission of Mafia Bosses that oversaw assassinations and heroin trade, was sentenced to life in prison.

As the jury began deliberating last month, the 64-year-old Greco wished the members "peace and tranquility." He was among those accused in the 1982 assassination of Italy's most respected anti-Mafia hunter, Gen. Carlo Alberto della Chiesa, and his young wife. Greco's brother, Salvatore "The Senator" Greco, got 18 years. Giuseppe "Pippo" Calo, a Mafia financial wizard and money launderer, got 23 years.

Ignazio Salvo, a millionaire businessman and one-time tax collector for the government, got seven years for criminal association. The same charge brought four years and six months for Salvatore Chiaracane, a prominent lawyer. The jury rejected the prosecution's call for 15 years for bespectacled Luciano Liggio, Mafia boss of the hill town named Corleone, which figured prominently in Mario Puzo's novel "The Godfather." He has been serving a life term since 1974, but the jury acquitted him of four murders that prosecutors charged he had masterminded from his jail cell in Sardinia.

A key prosecution witness, Tommaso Buscetta, was sentenced to three years and six months. Extradited from Brazil on drug charges in 1984, Buscetta gave investigators detailed insights on Mafia's internal structure and decision-making. A Mafia member that "turned" after six members of his family were murdered in gang warfare, Buscetta proved as credible to the Sicilian jury as he did to one in New York, which convicted 18 of 19 defendants on heroin charges following his testimony.

Montalbano, W.D. (1987). "19 Get Life Terms in Sicilian Mafia Trial." Copyright 1987, *Los Angeles Times*. Reprinted by permission.

The Mafia Controversy

While, as we have seen in the preceding discussion, there is a substantial body of opinion that argues that the Cosa Nostra or Mafia is the dominant organized crime group in the United States and plays a major role in drug trafficking, there is also considerable controversy surrounding what this organization actually is and what it actually does. Many scholars and law enforcement officials have come to doubt the view of a hegemonic Italian organized crime syndicate that is presented by the FBI and other federal agencies. They argue that the evidence in support of the existence of such a group is weak and open to other interpretations and that empirical research has failed to confirm the existence of such a dominant, complex, hierarchically organized criminal group.

Criticisms of the Mafia model fall into two distinct categories: (1) the historical evidence is sometimes weak and contradictory, and (2) empirical research conducted on organized crime fails to demonstrate the existence of the Mafia as a single, criminal conspiracy, and there are alternative models of organized crime that explain the reality of criminal entrepreneurship. To this list we will add a third—the evidence of LCN or Mafia "domination" of the drug trade is fragmentary and debatable.

Historical Controversies

Anthropological, historical, and social studies of the Sicilian Mafia, such as those conducted by Henner Hess and Anton Blok, have failed to turn up evidence of a single criminal organization. Rather, the studies point strongly to a series of localized village-based organizations, which were primarily created to protect the interests of absentee landlords and foreign invaders. These organizations formed a kind of "shadow government" in Sicily, meting out justice, controlling jobs, and providing for social control in an unstable society. While the "Mafia" may have had its origins in such a rural ruling class, it is not the same "Mafia" proposed by conspiracy theorists.

In addition, evidence relating to the importation of organized crime by Italians to the United States is open to similar questions. For example, proponents of the Mafia theory cannot tell us how it is that Italian immigration brought this criminal organization to the United States, but similar waves of Italian immigration did not bring the same organization to England, Australia, and other nations.

Supporters of the Mafia model have failed to account for the fact that organized crime existed in the United States long before the inception of Italian immigration. Further, proponents of the Mafia model must engage in considerable factual acrobatics to account for non-Italian figures that appear to have been dominant forces in the history of American organized crime, such as men like Arnold Rothstein, Meyer Lansky, Longie Zwillman, Bugsy Siegel, Bugs Moran, Dutch Schultz, Owney Madden and dozens of others.

Finally, specific historical "facts" presented by proponents of the Mafia model appear weak against close scrutiny. The Hennessey assassination is a prime example. Was the police chief of New Orleans killed by the "Mafia?" Or was the "Mafia" created, as Dwight Smith Jr. suggested, to justify the lynching of innocent immigrants? The fact is that the New Orleans grand jury failed to turn up any evidence of an Italian conspiracy, and the courts failed to convict any of the defendants. Similarly, questions have been raised about other "proofs" offered for the Mafia model.

Contemporary Research on Organized Crime

But far more significant to our discussion is the fact that empirical research on alleged LCN families has failed to substantiate the model proposed by the federal government. For example, Francis A.J. Ianni's study of an LCN family in New York suggested that the only organizational arrangement was one of an extended family. For Ianni, kinship became the prime variable in explaining how and why Italian-Americans worked together in both legal and illegal businesses. He found no evidence of an interconnected, national Italian-American crime syndicate. Joseph Albini's study of organized crime in Detroit also failed to confirm the existence of a monolithic crime structure. Albini reviewed historical documents and journalistic accounts and interviewed both law enforcement officials and participants in organized crime operations and concluded that organized crime was based on a series of loosely constructed "patron-client relations," not on a massive criminal conspiracy. Yet other studies, such as the one conducted by William Chambliss, focused on organized crime in Seattle and found a syndicate composed of local political and business leaders, leading Chambliss to argue that "organized crime" was a misnomer and that the study of official corruption would be more revealing in describing criminal syndicates. Mark Haller's study of organized crime operations in Chicago, New York, and Florida concluded that, rather than being dominated by a tightly organized criminal conspiracy, organized crime was a series of complex and often overlapping business partnerships in illicit enterprise.

Peter Reuter's exhaustive study of the gambling and loansharking industries in New York City failed to turn up either LCN domination or even widespread participation in those industries. Reuter argued that if the Mafia existed at all it "was a paper tiger" living off its popular reputation, which was fueled by journalistic and law enforcement speculation. And finally, a study of organized crime in Philadelphia revealed that not only did the Mafia not dominate organized crime in the past (at best its alleged members were functionaires of other, very large, criminal syndicates), but that the alleged Cosa Nostra family of Angelo Bruno was only one of several dozen major organized crime syndicates operating in that city. Additional studies by Alan Block, John Gardiner, Virgil Peterson, Jay Albanese, and many others have served to dispute the theory of any dominant role of the Cosa Nostra.

The Mafia and Drugs

While the views of some law enforcement officials tenaciously cling to the view of the Cosa Nostra as a single, massive criminal conspiracy, others have moved away from that position. The Pennsylvania Crime Commission, for example, has been quite active in exploring the role of other organized crime groups, particularly black crime groups and motorcycle gangs, in drug trafficking and other illicit business ventures. Potter and Jenkins, in their study of organized crime in Philadelphia, identified black gangs, Greek gangs, the K & A Gang, and motorcycle gangs as more important in drug trafficking.

There is little doubt that some individuals linked with Italian-dominated criminal organization both in the United States and Sicily have been involved in large-scale drug trafficking, as we have seen in the case of the Pizza Connection. But perhaps one should be cautious in attributing any degree of hegemony to these groups in the drug market. Drug trafficking is conducted by thousands of different criminal organizations, many of which are complex and many of which are quite large when compared to LCN groups. In spite of many successful Mafia-related drug investigations, the focus on the Mafia or Cosa Nostra has tended to distort the perception of organized crime's role in drugs. For example, it ignores the vital role played by organizations headed by Frank Matthews, Nicky Barnes, Jeff Fort, and other crime figures. It also ignores the role of non-Italians, such as Meyer Lansky and Nig Rosen, who played the major coordinating role in the infamous "French Connection." And it ignores the major role in the organization of drug trafficking played by truly pioneering organized crime figures like Arnold Rothstein, Happy Meltzer, "Dopey" Bennie Fein, and others. The role of the Mafia, although portentous, must be kept in perspective, and the roles of other major drug trafficking groups must be given appropriate attention.

Outlaw Motorcycle Gangs

Outlaw motorcycle gangs have etched an historic role in organized crime and the drug trade. Outlaw motorcycle gangs, according to the U.S. Treasury's Bureau of Alcohol, Tobacco, and Firearms (ATF), have evolved into one of the most "reprehensible" types of criminal organizations, consisting of "killers, psychotics, panderers, and social misfits."

Hunter S. Thompson, an authority on the Hell's Angels, traced the origin of outlaw motorcycle gangs back to 1947, when the POBOB or the "Pissed Off Bastards of Bloomington" (later known as the Hell's Angels), transformed an American Motorcycle Association (AMA)-sponsored hill climb in Holister, California, to a week-long brawl. Later that same year in Riverside, California, thousands attended a motorcycle run that resulted in rioting, destruction, and even two deaths. The following year, a similar motorcycle event in Riverside ended up as a riot. The police chief then blamed the outcome of the event on the visiting "outlaws," which is a term now commonly associated with members of certain motorcycle gangs.

The outlaw motorcycle phenomenon continued during the 1950s and 1960s and soon became a symbol of lawlessness and rebellion. That is to say, that for the most part, the bikers were more concerned with uninhibited good times than organized criminal endeavors. The entertainment industry portrayed these outlaw gangs in such popular films as *The Wild Ones*, *Easy Rider*, and *Angels on Wheels*.

In the late 1960s, the former president of the AMA, William Berry, became irritated over the bad publicity outlaw bikers gave to law-abiding motorcycle riders. He declared that only one percent of the motorcyclists in the United States functioned outside the spirit and intent of the law. The statement, of course, was a public relations effort on the part of the AMA to explain that only a small number of motorcycle riders represented a criminal element. The term "one percenter," however, was immediately adopted by the larger outlaw motorcycle gangs as a public affirmation of their criminal intent, and the "1%" patch is now commonly worn by gang members.

The years between 1947 and 1967 were formative ones for the early gangs such as the POBOBs. Imitators soon began to appear. In addition, larger gangs absorbed smaller ones or just muscled them out of existence. Roaming members calling themselves "nomads" traveled throughout the United States and formed alliances with other gangs. Formal organizational structures were formed and leaders were placed in charge of the various gangs or "chapters." Still, gangs in this period lacked focus and were rarely considered to be more than troublemakers by local law enforcement.

...the Hell's Angels are the largest and most sophisticated of the outlaw motorcycle gangs, boasting an international membership...

By 1970, however, outlaw motorcycle gangs were viewed differently. The gangs contributed to a monumental social change underway in the United States. This change was characterized to some degree by an explosion of drug use. First as drug users and then as dealers, motorcycle gangs were drawn into the phenomenon. As the Treasury Department proclaimed in 1988, "whatever else the 1960s changed in America, it changed outlaw motorcycle gangs."

Today, outlaw motorcycle gangs have emerged into sophisticated criminal groups that, according to the DEA, number about 850 with a membership exceeding 8,000 in the United States alone. Their criminal activities are many and varied, but include drug trafficking, contract killings, extortion, arson, fraud, embezzlement, and money laundering.

The philosophy of the outlaw motorcycle gang is of particular significance to law enforcement as it illustrates the sociopathic nature of the organization. "Fuck the World" (FTW) is the motto and attitude of outlaw motorcycle members, and the phrase is frequently embroidered on patches or even tattooed on the members themselves. They choose not to live as normal citizens and delight in sporting their own dress code, which is one that many people would consider filthy and repulsive. Acts typically considered outrageous and shocking only serve to enhance the biker's image within his own environment.

With the obvious exception of minority or ethnically dominated gangs, most outlaw motorcycle gangs embrace racist beliefs that closely parallel those of the Ku Klux Klan and the neo-Nazis. This "white supremacist" philosophy is evidenced by the wearing of Nazi swastikas, white-power fists, and other symbols of white supremacy.

Figure 8.2 SIMILARITIES OF ORGANIZATIONAL STRUCTURE

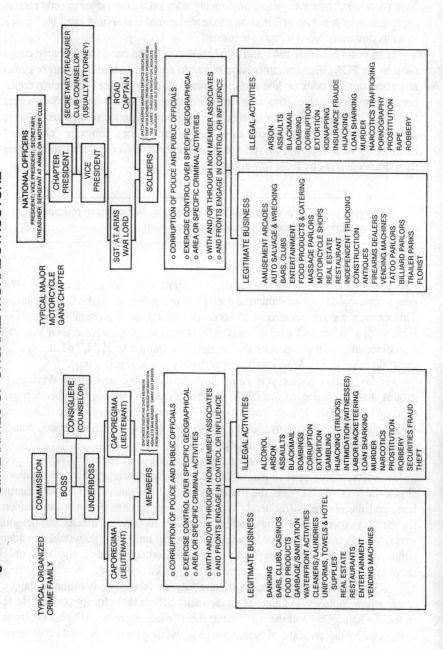

TYPICAL MAJOR MOTORCYCLE GANG CHAPTER

NATIONAL OFFICERS
PRESIDENT; VICE PRESIDENT; SECRETARY;
TREASURER; SERGENT AT ARMS; OR MOTHER CLUB

CHAPTER PRESIDENT

SECRETARY/TREASURER
CLUB COUNSELOR
(USUALLY ATTORNEY)

VICE PRESIDENT

SGT. AT ARMS
WAR LORD

ROAD CAPTAIN

SOLDIERS
{ (PATCH WEARING MEMBERS ENFORCE DISCIPLINE
OVER NON MEMBERS; PROBATIONARY MEMBERS AND
"OLE LADIES" THROUGH INTIMIDATION ASSAULTS
AND MURDER. CARRY OUT ORDERS FROM LEADERSHIP) }

o CORRUPTION OF POLICE AND PUBLIC OFFICIALS

o EXERCISE CONTROL OVER SPECIFIC GEOGRAPHICAL

o AREA OR SPECIFIC CRIMINAL ACTIVITIES

o WITH AND/OR THROUGH NON MEMBER ASSOCIATES

o AND FRONTS ENGAGE IN CONTROL OR INFLUENCE

LEGITIMATE BUSINESS

AMUSEMENT ARCADES
AUTO SALVAGE & WRECKING
BARS, CLUBS
ENTERTAINMENT
FOOD PRODUCTS & CATERING
MASSAGE PARLORS
MOTORCYCLE SHOPS
REAL ESTATE
RESTAURANT
INDEPENDENT TRUCKING
CONSTRUCTION
ANTIQUES
FIREARMS DEALERS
VENDING MACHINES
TATOO PARLORS
BILLIARD PARLORS
TRAILER PARKS
FLORIST

ILLEGAL ACTIVITIES

ARSON
ASSAULTS
BLACKMAIL
BOMBING
CORRUPTION
EXTORTION
KIDNAPPING
INSURANCE FRAUDS
HIJACKING
LOAN SHARKING
MURDER
NARCOTICS TRAFFICKING
PORNOGRAPHY
PROSTITUTION
RAPE
ROBBERY

TYPICAL ORGANIZED CRIME FAMILY

COMMISSION

BOSS

CONSIGLIERE
(COUNSELOR)

UNDERBOSS

CAPOREGIMA
(LIEUTENANT)

CAPOREGIMA
(LIEUTENANT)

MEMBERS
{ (ENFORCES DISCIPLINE OVER MEMBERS
AND NON MEMBERS THROUGH INTIMIDATION,
ASSAULTS AND MURDER. CARRY OUT ORDERS
FROM LEADERSHIP) }

o CORRUPTION OF POLICE AND PUBLIC OFFICIALS

o EXERCISE CONTROL OVER SPECIFIC GEOGRAPHICAL

o AREA OR SPECIFIC CRIMINAL ACTIVITIES

o WITH AND/OR THROUGH NON MEMBER ASSOCIATES

o AND FRONTS ENGAGE IN CONTROL OR INFLUENCE

LEGITIMATE BUSINESS

BANKING
BARS, CLUBS, CASINOS
FOOD PRODUCTS
GARBAGE/SANITATION
WATERFRONT ACTIVITIES
CLEANERS/LAUNDRIES
UNIFORMS, TOWELS & HOTEL
SUPPLIES
REAL ESTATE
RESTAURANTS
ENTERTAINMENT
VENDING MACHINES

ILLEGAL ACTIVITIES

ALCOHOL
ARSON
ASSAULTS
BLACKMAIL
BOMBINGS
CORRUPTION
EXTORTION
GAMBLING
HIJACKING (TRUCKS)
INTIMIDATION (WITNESSES)
LABOR RACKETEERING
LOAN SHARKING
MURDER
NARCOTICS
PROSTITUTION
ROBBERY
SECURITIES FRAUD
THEFT

In addition to their racist values, bikers also practice a chauvinistic attitude toward female associates of the organization. In fact, in most clubs females fall into one of two categories: mamas/sheep or old ladies. Because females are not permitted to be "members" of the gang, their roles in the organization are limited. For example, the mamas are considered "property" of the gang at large and must consent to the sexual desires of anyone at any time. In addition, they also perform menial tasks around the clubhouse. Old Ladies, on the other hand, are wives or steady girlfriends of members and therefore belong to only one member of the club. Old ladies proudly wear colors similar to those of male members, with the difference being the words "property of...," which are displayed on the bottom "rocker" of the club patch.

As indicated, outlaw motorcycle gang members place a great deal of importance on respect for the club's colors, which are basically the uniform of the gang. A gang's colors are typically a sleeveless denim or leather jacket with the club name and claimed territory affixed to the back. The colors consist of a top rocker with the name of the gang and a bottom rocker that usually claims territory, states, or cities occupied by the gang. The gang colors are the proudest possession of a biker and members are expected to protect their colors at all costs.

The biker's motorcycle also plays a major role in his life. So esteemed is the motorcycle that its destruction or loss to a rival gang member not only results in loss of face but also could be grounds for expulsion from the club. The motorcycle is not just a means of transportation for the biker but a requirement for club membership and a status symbol in its own right. The motorcycle, along with the dress of the gang members, perpetuates the image of a disciplined and paramilitary organization and has a certain "shock" value in dealing with members of the general public or other gangs.

There are two prerequisites for motorcycles that outlaw motorcycle gangs frequently enforce: they must be a certain size (usually a 900 cc minimum), and they must be American made. Bikers will commonly spend more time with their motorcycles than with anything else, and it is not uncommon for a biker to park his motorcycle inside his home.

Finally, the club's bylaws or charter, which most clubs enforce, are of particular importance in the role that bikers play. The charter outlines accepted standards of conduct for gang members and administrative procedures for the gang's operations. Charter rules include:

- no member will strike another member

- all members must attend funerals of fellow bikers in the same chapter

- chapters must have one organized meeting per week

- chapter meetings may be attended by chapter members only

- respect your colors

- a club prospect must be sponsored by one member that has known the prospect for at least a year.

As mentioned, hundreds of outlaw motorcycle gangs operate in the United States today, but four of them have emerged as the largest and most criminally sophisticated. These are the Hell's Angels, the Outlaws, the Pagans, and the Bandidos.

OUTLAW MOTORCYCLE GANG ORGANIZATIONAL STRUCTURE

National President. The national president is often the founder of the club. He will usually be located at or near the national headquarters. In many cases, he will be surrounded by a select group of individuals that answer only to him and that serve as bodyguards and organizational enforcers. Quite often, the national president will possess the authority to make final decisions by membership vote.

Territorial or Regional Representative. The individual in this position is also called the vice president and is charge of whatever region or district to which he is assigned. His duties usually include decision making on all problems that the local chapters are unable to solve. Any problems that involve the club as a whole will usually be dealt with through the national headquarters.

National Secretary-Treasurer. The responsibility for handling the club's money, including collecting dues from local chapters, is that of the national secretary-treasurer. He makes changes in existing club bylaws and drafts new ones. He records the minutes and maintains the records on all headquarters or regional office meetings.

National Enforcer. The national enforcer answers directly to the national president. He ensures that the president's orders are carried out. He may act as the president's bodyguard, and he may also handle all special situations, such as retrieving the colors from a member that has left the club. He has also been known to locate ex-members and remove club tattoos from them.

Chapter President. Usually the chapter president, through a combination of personal strength, leadership, personality, and skills, has either claimed the position or has been voted in. He has final authority over all chapter business and members. Usually his word is law within that chapter.

Vice President. Second in command and "right hand" of the chapter president is the vice president. He presides over club affairs in the absence of the president. Normally, he is hand-picked by the president and is heir apparent to the club's leadership.

Secretary-Treasurer. Usually the chapter member possessing the best writing skills serves as secretary-treasurer. He will keep the chapter roster and maintain a crude accounting system. He records the minutes at all chapter meetings and collects the dues and/or fines. He is responsible for paying the chapter's bills.

Sergeant at Arms. Due to the unruly and violent nature of outlaw motorcycle gangs, each chapter has an individual whose principal duty is to maintain order at club meetings and functions. The sergeant at arms is normally the strongest member physically and is completely loyal to the president. He may administer beatings to fellow members for violation of club rules and is the club enforcer for that chapter.

Road Captain. The road captain fulfills the role of gang logistician and security chief for the club-sponsored "runs." The road captain maps out routes to be taken during runs and arranges for refueling, food, and maintenance stops. He will also carry the club's funds and use them for bail if necessary.

Members. The rank-and-file, dues-paying members of the gang are the individuals that carry out the decisions of the club's leadership. This affords the president greater control over the affairs of the gang. At the same time, limited membership helps to ensure that the gang's criminal efforts are not compromised to law enforcement. When a gang becomes too large, there is a tendency to divide the membership into various chapters, based on geographic location.

Probate or Prospective Members. These are the club hopefuls that spend from one month to one year in probationary status and that must prove during that time that they are worthy of becoming members. Many clubs require the probate to commit a felony with fellow members observing, so as to weed out weak individuals and infiltration by law enforcement. Probates must be nominated by a regular member and receive a unanimous vote for acceptance. They carry out all menial jobs at the clubhouse and for other members. They are known to carry weapons for other club members and stand guard during club parties. The probates will not wear the club's colors; instead, they wear jackets with the bottom rocker of the club patch showing the location from which he comes. Until he is voted in, completes his initiation, and is awarded his colors, he has no voting rights.

Associate or Honorary Members. An individual that has proved his value to the gang is known as an associate or honorary member. The associate may be a professional that has, in a manner commensurate to his profession, been supportive of the gang, or he may be a proven criminal with whom the gang has had a profitable, illicit relationship (see Chapter 7). Some of the more noted associates are attorneys, bail bondsmen, motorcycle shop owners, and auto wrecking yard owners. These individuals are allowed to party with the gang, either in town or on runs; they do not, however, have voting status, attend club meetings, or wear club colors.

Source: United States Marshal's Service, U.S. Department of Justice, 1986.

The Hell's Angels

In 1950, the POBOB'S leader Otto Friedli formed a new gang, the Hell's Angels, named after a World War II bomber. The Angels' "mother chapter" was originally established in San Bernardino, California, where it remained until the mid-1960s. During that time, Ralph Hubert (Sonny) Barger, then president of the Oakland chapter, became National President and moved the mother chapter to Oakland, where it currently remains.

The Hell's Angels (HA) are distinctive because they are considered the most professional and the wealthiest of the outlaw motorcycle gangs. They are also an international organization that, according to the U.S. Drug Enforcement Administration, has 33 U.S. chapters, 18 foreign chapters, and an estimated 900 members (450 to 600 are active members). Because of its lengthy and colorful history, the HA have evolved into a model gang that other gangs, both large and small, have continually emulated.

The FBI reports that, during the mid-1960s, the HA began drug trafficking in the San Francisco area with LSD as the main commodity. Later, their inventory expanded to cocaine, PCP, marijuana, and methamphetamines. Today, they are still active in methamphetamine manufacturing and trafficking, and it is estimated that most of the methamphetamine trafficked in California is directly or indirectly tied to the HA organization.

Figure 8.3
Location of Hell's Angels chapters in the continental United States

Figure 8.4
Location of Outlaws chapters in the
continental United States

The Outlaws

The Outlaws motorcycle gang was founded in 1959 by John Davis in *largest* Chicago, Illinois. The Outlaws quickly expanded across the country and, with the absorption of the Canadian "Satan's Choice" gang, became an international organization. Under the current leadership of Harry Joseph Bowman, the Outlaws are considered the largest motorcycle gang in the United States, with an estimated membership between 1200 and 1500 members located in 25 U.S. cities and six Canadian chapters.

The Outlaws are engaged in trafficking of cocaine as well as Valium tablets manufactured by Canadian laboratories and distributed from Chicago to locations throughout the United States.

The Pagans

The Pagans originated in Prince George's County, Maryland, under the presidency of Lou Dolkin. The Pagans are concentrated on the east coast and differ from the other major four gangs because they do not have a geographically fixed "mother chapter." It is, therefore, directed by a "mother club," which is made up of 13 to 18 members that head up other chapters.

Figure 8.5

**Location of Pagans chapters in the
continental United States**

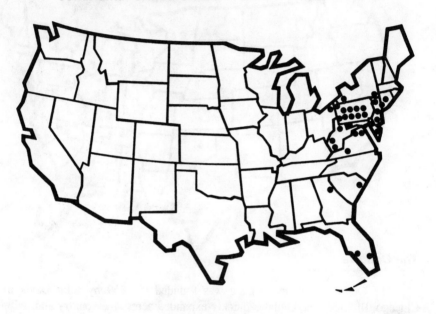

most Ruthless

The Pagans, currently headed by Kirby Keller, have a particular presence in
the Philadelphia area. Between New York and Florida, there are 44 chapters,
with an estimated 700 to 900 members. The Pagans have earned the reputation
of being one of the most ruthless and organized motorcycle gangs. The Pagans
have also become commonly associated with the LCN and have been used as
contract killers and enforcers for certain Mafia families. In addition, the Pagans
play a major role in the illicit sex industry, as they have considerable business
interests in massage parlors and other prostitution outlets and often work closely
with local pornography syndicates to provide protection, models, and the like.

Figure 8.6
Location of Bandidos chapters in the
continental United States

The Bandidos

The Bandidos were formed in 1966 by Donald Chambers in Houston, Texas, but are currently headquartered in Corpus Christi. It is estimated that the Bandidos have 26 chapters with an estimated 500 members. They concentrate in both the southern and northern regions of the country and are generally considered less sophisticated than the three outlaw motorcycle gangs previously discussed.*

The Bandidos are heavily involved in manufacturing and distributing of methamphetamines.

---

*   The term "outlaw motorcycle gang" refers to criminal organizations whose members are required to own motorcycles. One should not infer from this term that all who possess or ride motorcycles are involved in criminal activity.

California Youth Gangs

Reports of violent youth gang activity is not merely media hype but often an actual social phenomenon in many U.S. communities. The youth gang violence, inspired by the drug trade, poses real problems for certain neighborhoods. In many cases, residents are either fearful of leaving their homes or afraid to let their children play in the public parks taken over by gangs. Neighborhood businesses suffer economically because residents are hesitant to leave their homes to shop. The cost of dealing with gangs via community efforts, law enforcement efforts, and the court system is escalating.

A powerful mystique has evolved around gang activity over the years. It is difficult to estimate exactly how many gangs exist in the United States. One reason for this is the secrecy and the ever-changing nature of most juvenile gangs. A major problem in the study of youth gangs is the lack of consensus as to what defines a youth gang.

Defining the Youth Gang

Is it correct to refer to any congregation of youths as a gang? Many law enforcement agencies use the term narrowly to refer to a group of delinquents that hold and defend self-claimed territory or "turf." Frederick Thrasher is a sociologist who, in a pioneering study, attempted to define a youth gang:

> A gang is an interstitial group originally formed spontaneously and then integrated through conflict. It is characterized by the following types of behavior: meeting face to face, milling, movement through space as a unit, conflict and planning. The result of this collective behavior is the development of tradition, unreflective internal structure, esprit de corps, solidarity, morale, group awareness, and attachment to local territory (p. 57).

This definition, first appearing in 1927, still seems to capture the essence of group cohesiveness that remains the prevailing view of many gangs. Yet another behavioral scientist, Malcolm Klein, offered a more recent description of a youth gang, which includes the element of danger:

> Any denotable group of youngsters who (a) are generally perceived as a distinct aggregation by others in their neighborhood; (b) recognize themselves as a denoteable group (almost invariably with a group name): and (c) have been involved in a sufficient number of delin-

quent incidents to call forth a consistent negative response from neighborhood residents and/or law enforcement agencies (p. 13).

Sociologist Lewis Yablonsky made an important contribution to the understanding of the youth gang with his definition of a "near group." According to Yablonsky, human collectives tend to range from highly cohesive, tight-knit organizations to mobs with anonymous members that are motivated by their emotions and led by disturbed membership (p. 109). Teenage gangs fall somewhere in between and are therefore categorized as near groups. Near groups have the following traits:

1. Diffuse role definition
2. Limited cohesion
3. Impermanence
4. Minimal consensus norms
5. Shifting membership
6. Disturbed leadership
7. Limited definition of membership expectations

Youth gangs of many ethnic origins have been somewhat of a perennial nuisance throughout American history. In fact, Benjamin Franklin lamented the trouble caused by youth gangs in pre-Revolutionary War Philadelphia. However, only since the early- to mid-1980s have youth gangs become violent and well established in most major American cities. Perhaps the most threatening development of gangs in the late 1980s was the expansion of two black California-based youth gangs, the Crips and the Bloods.

Black youth gangs in California have roots tracing back to the early 1920s when they first organized as loose-knit, opportunistic street gangs in the south-central Los Angeles area. The early gangs consisted primarily of family members and close friends that generated income from small-time criminal activity while perpetuating a "tough-guy" street image.

By 1965, police authorities in the Los Angeles and Compton areas observed a comparatively higher number of gangs with an increasing degree of criminal sophistication. Gangs would form as protection organizations from rival gangs in other neighborhoods. Examples of gangs during the 1960s include:

- Farmers
- 135s
- Slausons
- Roman 20s
- Huns
- Pueblos
- Businessmen
- Swamps
- Sir Valiants
- Treetops
- Gladiators
- Valiants

Origins of Modern-Day Street Gangs

The Crips were first organized around 1969 or 1970. Some theories about the origin of their enigmatic name are as follows:

• the name Crips might stand for "Central Revolution In Progress" reflecting the antiestablishment atmosphere of the era

• the name Crips may have evolved from the title of a 1950s Vincent Price movie *Tales from the Crypt*

• the name Crips might have been derived from the street gang called the Cribs, which was reportedly one of the largest street gangs in the L.A. area during the early 1960s

• one theory is that the original members of the Crips were crippled and they were called "crips" because of their handicap. It is also maintained that most early Crips carried walking canes as a means of identification

• the term Crips may have evolved from a desire, on the part of gang members, to find a gang name that represented the toughest, strongest thing in existence, and that substance was "kryptonite," the only substance that could kill Superman

Crips gang activity originated on the campus of Washington High School in Los Angeles, where the color blue was adopted as the gang color. It was from here that the reputation of the Crips spread rapidly as a violent street gang committing robberies, assaults, and extortion. Crips members would travel to other neighborhoods to prey on unsuspecting youths there. Other youths also formed gangs to protect themselves from the violence of the Crips, and the perpetuation of the youth gang phenomenon was well under way.

One of the gangs formed in response to the Crips is the "*Compton Pirus*," originating on Piru Street in Compton, California. It was the Compton Pirus that evolved into the first *Bloods* gang in the Los Angeles area. As of the preparation of this text, Compton-based gangs, adopting red as their gang color, are referred to as "Pirus," while gangs from other areas of Los Angeles also using red as a gang color are called Bloods. Although membership numbers are difficult to ascertain for the Crips and Bloods, it is estimated that the Crips outnumber the Bloods three to one, with a total national membership estimated at 70,000.

...the most violent and active members are those between 14 and 18; many of them "wannabees" that want to prove themselves in order to be accepted by other gang members...

As the Los Angeles-based youth gangs evolved, drugs became the chosen money maker for them, and gang rivalries and accompanying warfare became more and more intense. Fully automatic firearms are now used with more frequency than ever before, and since the mid-1980s, the "drive-by shooting" is a common retaliatory gang tactic used in the Los Angeles area.

According to the Los Angeles Police Department, in 1988, Los Angeles-based youth gangs consisted of as many as 192 Crips gangs and an estimated 65 Bloods gangs, and each was composed of numerous smaller gangs or "sets" within the organization. Each set is comprised of several members numbering up to thirty, forty, or even fifty individuals. The age group of each set will generally range from 12 to 14 years of age (called gang-bangers or "gangsters"), but some members may be as old as the mid- to late-twenties (called "OGs" or "original gangsters").

Figure 8.7

Location of CRIPS and Bloods in the continental United States

It is clear that crack cocaine and PCP (Chapter 2) have become the biggest money-generating commodities for the black youth gangs originating in Los Angeles. Older gang members commonly use younger members as street dealers, and it is these members that may realize as much as $400 per day. Much of these drug profits are usually kept within the gang.

Because the price of cocaine in the Los Angeles area has declined so dramatically since the mid-1980s (from $100 to approximately $20 to $30 per gram), gang members are finding that great profits can be realized by purchasing the drug in Los Angeles and smuggling it to other cities in the United States, where it can be converted to crack and sold for exorbitant profits ranging from $100 to $150 per gram.

Of the many unique characteristics of the black Los Angeles gangs is the use of graffiti on public buildings and structures to identify claimed turf. The use of graffiti sends a message to rival gangs that the particular area around the graffiti has been claimed as territory for drug sales and that other gangs should not interfere.

Controlling the Gangs

Although many strategies are being considered in dealing with the youth gang problem, the consensus still focuses on two fundamental goals: reform the juvenile justice system so that it holds juveniles more accountable for their actions and intensify efforts to keep youths from joining gangs.

CRIPS GANG CHARACTERISTICS

- Crips gang members identify with the color blue
- Crips gang members address each other using the name "cuz," short for cousin
- Gang members use graffiti in which they identify themselves as B/K or "Blood Killer"
- All Crips are mortal enemies of the Bloods youth gang
- There are about 192 Crips gangs in the city of Los Angeles
- Crips gang members outnumber Bloods gang members on a ratio of approximately seven to one
- Crips gangs (called "sets") commonly fight each other
- The word "Crip" is commonly found in the gang name, such as "Hoover Crips" or "4-Tray Crips."

Source: Los Angeles Police Department, 1988.

In September 1988, experts on juvenile justice met in Washington, D.C. and made the following statements and recommendations to the Coordinating Council on Juvenile Justice and Delinquency Prevention:

• Juveniles are becoming more active in gangs largely because of the lucrative drug trade.

• Because the juvenile justice system has few available sanctions to use against juveniles, adult gangs employ them in their sale of illegal drugs.

• The juvenile justice system must be reformed to hold youths accountable for their behavior by imposing predictable and consistent sanctions.

• The highly profitable drug trade has brought about an alarming increase in the use of deadly military weapons.

• Many of the victims of gang-related violence are innocent bystanders caught up in the violence.

• Intensive prevention programs, including increased job opportunities, are necessary to keep at-risk youths from joining gangs, and drug education programs are vital to reduce the demand for drugs and begin to eliminate the gang-related drug trade.

• The entire juvenile and criminal justice system, federal, state, and local governments, and businesses and communities must work together to eliminate gang violence.

BLOODS GANG CHARACTERISTICS

• Bloods identify with the color red

• Bloods gang members address each other as "blood" and use the word in the same manner as the Crips use the word "cuz"

• Bloods gang graffiti can be identified by the terms "Blood," "Bloodstone," or C/K, which stands for "Crip Killer"

• There are approximately 65 Bloods gangs in the city of Los Angeles

• Because Bloods gangs were first formed to combat Crips gangs, most Bloods are allied and treat anyone wearing red in their neighborhoods with respect

• The word "Blood" is not usually found in their gang name. "Outlaws" and "Bounty Hunters" are two Bloods gangs.

Source: Los Angeles Police Department, 1988.

The Jamaican Posses

Jamaican organized crime gangs, known as posses, emerged in the United States during the mid-1980s. The approximately 40 posses operating in the United States, Canada, Great Britain, and the Caribbean are conservatively estimated to have 10,000 members. The majority of them are convicted felons or illegal aliens. Almost all posses have connections in Miami and New York, which have large Jamaican populations.

The volatile political history of Jamaica was discussed in detail in Chapter 4 and explains the basis for the creation of dangerous politically motivated gangs. Because of the political segregation of neighborhoods in Jamaica, posses were formed to rally support for their chosen political party. Many posses have chosen to name themselves after the neighborhoods from which they hail (as do many youth gangs).

In the mid-1970s, two large and violent groups emerged in Jamaica: the Reatown Boys and the Dunkirk Boys. The Reatown Boys consisted of members from the Reatown area of Jamaica and were loyalists to the Peoples National Party (PNP). They soon became known by the community as the "*untouchables*" because of the number of murders perpetrated by PNP members. Today they have evolved into the *Shower Posse*. The Dunkirk Boys became known as the *Magentas* and aligned themselves with the Jamaican Labor Party (JLP). They have now evolved into the *Spangler Posse*. Both the Shower and the Spangler Posses are considered the largest of the Jamaican organized crime groups.

JAMAICAN POSSE CHARACTERISTICS

• Posse members are usually well armed and use fully automatic weapons

• Posse members are fearful of police officials and will frequently engage in confrontations with them

• Members use extensive counter-surveillance measures

• Members usually display a total disregard for innocent bystanders caught in crossfire

• Posse members use aliases and false dates of birth

• Members have the ability to adapt to law enforcement methods

• Members use female associates to transport drugs and weapons

---
Source: United States Marshals Service, Threat Analysis Division, September, 1988.

...Jamaican posse members have not hesitated to issue "contracts" on the lives of police and federal agents...

Drug wars between the Spanglers and rival gangs were responsible for an estimated 350 to 500 murders between 1985 and 1987. The Spanglers operate primarily in larger cities and because of their large size, assess a "tax" on drug sales by other smaller groups. It is this tax that is the basis for much of the in-tergang violence in many American cities.

The posses have distinctive operating methods. Compared to the Colom-bians, they are more vertically integrated, as they are involved as importers, wholesalers, distributors, and even retailers. The posses normally purchase co-caine from Colombians or Cubans in Jamaica, the Bahamas, southern Califor-nia, and South Florida in small quantities (usually 4 to 5 kilograms). By ex-cluding the middleman, the posses can substantially raise the profit margins to the point where, for example, one posse controlling 50 crack houses realized $9 million per month.

Figure 8.8

Location of Jamaican Posses in the continental United States

JAMAICAN POSSES AND AREAS OF OPERATION

Blackbush Posse:	New York
Banton Posse:	Miami, Washington, D.C., Baltimore
Bibour Posse:	New York
Black Organization:	Miami
Bushmouth Posse:	New York, Miami, St. Louis
Brown Posse:	Houston
Cuban Posse:	New York, Miami, Philadelphia, Kansas City
Dog Posse:	Boston
Dunkirk Boys Posse:	Dallas, Miami
East Nineties Posse:	New York
Exodus Posse:	Washington, D.C., Baltimore, Miami
Flethees Land Posse:	New York
Gold Star Posse:	Chicago
Jungle Posse:	New York, Boston, Miami, Dallas, Los Angeles
Marvaly Posse:	New York
Montego Bay Posse:	New York, Boston, Washington, D.C., Miami, Houston, Philadelphia, Pittsburgh, Seattle, Cleveland, Atlanta
Nanyville Posse:	New York
Nineties Posse:	Dallas, Miami
Okra Slime Posse:	Los Angeles
Paneland Posse:	New York
Ranker Posse:	New York
Reema Posse:	New York, Boston, Philadelphia, Atlanta, Pittsburgh, Houston, Los Angeles
Red Bandana Posse:	Houston
Riverton City Posse:	New York, Miami, Boston, Washington D.C., Kansas City
Salamander Posse:	Anchorage

Samacon Posse:	New York, Miami, St. Louis
Shower Posse:	Miami, New York, Philadelphia, Dallas, Pittsburgh, Chicago, Boston, Cleveland, Washington D.C., Los Angeles, Seattle, Buffalo, Denver, Kansas City, Atlanta, Detroit, Rochester
Solid Gold Posse:	Chicago, Cleveland, Hartford, Dallas
Southie Posse:	Los Angeles
Spangler Posse:	New York, Boston, Washington D.C., Philadelphia, Pittsburgh, Seattle, Atlanta, Miami, Houston, Dallas, Cleveland, Los Angeles
Spanishtown Posse:	New York, Boston, Washington, D.C., Atlanta, Philadelphia, Houston
Super Posse:	Washington D.C.
Superstar Posse:	Kansas City
Tel Aviv Posse:	Los Angeles, Boston
Tivoli Gardens Posse:	New York, Boston, Atlanta, Miami, Los Angeles
Towerhill Posse:	New York, Miami
Trinidadian Posse:	New York
Untouchable Posse:	Alaska, Washington D.C., New York, Miami
Waterhouse Posse:	New York, Washington D.C., Atlanta, Miami, Boston, Philadelphia, Cleveland, St. Louis, Kansas City, Houston, Los Angeles
Williams Organization:	Detroit

Source: United States Marshal's Service, Threat Analysis Division, September, 1988.

Posse Violence

The Jamaican posse has clearly demonstrated a proclivity for violence sel-
dom displayed by other organized crime groups. For example, in 1988, the Justice Department stated that Jamaican posses have been directly responsible for
over 1000 murders and cited their increasing level of violence throughout the
country as a major public safety threat.

As previously mentioned, most of the violence perpetrated by the posses is
attributed to the crack cocaine "glut" in many urban areas of the United States.
This deluge has caused a decrease in the retail price of the cocaine market nationwide and has created territorial feuds between crack house operators. The
violence used by Jamaican posses is therefore one of their most notable characteristics.

The violence committed by the posses frequently includes torture. Cases in
Washington D.C. and New York have involved victims being shot in the ankles,
knees, and hips prior to being shot in the head. In addition, some cases have
documented victims being tortured in bathtubs through the use of scalding hot
water.

The potential violence and arrogance of the posses are also illustrated by
their willingness to issue contracts on police and federal agents that the posses
feel are disrupting their operation. In one Virginia case, a $25,000 reward was
offered to anyone that killed a police officer. Some Jamaican criminals have
even attempted to entrap police by identifying their telephone and beeper numbers and then luring them to prearranged shootouts.

THE CASE OF LESTER LLOYD COKE

The case of Jim Brown, who became the "top ranking gunman" of
Tivoli Gardens, is an example of Jamaican gang operations. In October, 1984, Brown came to Miami on a visitor's visa in the name of
Lester Lloyd Coke (ironically enough). Ten months later, when Coke
was arrested for marijuana trafficking, his true identity was learned,
which revealed that he was wanted for at least twelve murders in Jamaica. In spite of repeated attempts to extradite Coke to Jamaica, Jamaican government officials refused to accept Coke back or to initiate
extradition proceedings. Coke wasn't returned to Jamaica until March
1986, after being deported after an investigation of Jamaican gangs revealed that he was the leader of Miami's Shower Posse. Coke (or
Brown) ultimately was released from custody in Kingston after being
acquitted of one of the twelve murders. He also has been hailed as a
hero in Jamaica after thousands of supporters paraded in Kingston
following his release.

Source: Ronald A. Pincomb, New Mexico State University. Published in the *International
Association for the Study of Organized Crime Newsletter*, 1989, volume 4, number 2.

Violence by the posses is directed at virtually anyone that creates problems for them in their crack cocaine business, including members of their own posse and rival posses alike. The strategic use of violence against posse enemies is performed to intimidate others that may pose a threat to the organization; the violence is directed to both civilians and law enforcement officials.

Investigations have revealed that posse members have been caught with dangerous explosives such as MK-II grenades, which were once seized from a posse in a 1987 incident. In addition, the following explosives have also been recovered from posse residences: 1/4 pound of TNT, numerous cans of smokeless powder, hundreds of firearms, and clandestine publications on how to produce plastic explosives.

A treaty ratified by the Jamaican Parliament in December 1987 broadened the category of those wanted in the United States and apprehended in Jamaica that could be returned to the United States. Under the terms of the treaty, Jamaica must extradite fugitives wanted in the United States for any crime that would be an offense in Jamaica. The treaty also covers fugitives wanted in the United States for conspiring to traffic narcotics, a charge that was not extraditable before the treaty was ratified. The new treaty and related legislation also permit the extradition of offenders wanted in the United States for the unlawful possession or use of firearms, which is another crime that was not previously covered.

Figure 8.9

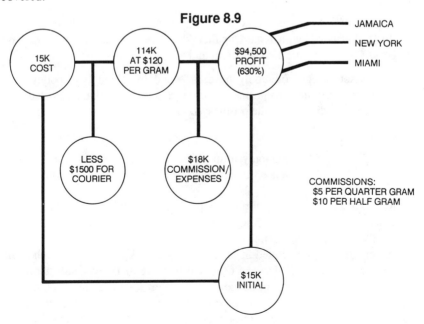

CRACK PROFIT MARGIN

As of the preparation of this book, Jamaican posse activity in America has abated. This is largely attributable to the completion of the 1989 elections there, where Michael Manley was once again elected into office. However, if history is to serve as a predictor for posse violence, then perhaps yet another wave of violent gang activity can be anticipated in American streets, as elections draw near in Jamaica.

Prison Gangs

When studying the evolution of many major organized crime groups, it becomes clear that inmate associations in both state and federal prisons often help sow the seeds of criminal activity. The existence of prison gangs is nothing new, as the Italian Camorra had its beginnings in the Spanish prisons of Naples back in the 1860s.

Indeed, a similar criminal phenomenon has taken place in the United States and has produced many violence-prone criminal organizations. In 1987, the U.S. Bureau of Prisons estimated that 114 prison gangs operated in state and federal prisons across the country. Of these, five have emerged as the largest, most violent, and most sophisticated. These are the Mexican Mafia (EME), the Nuestra Familia (NF), the Aryan Brotherhood (AB), the Texas Syndicate (E Ts E), and the Black Guerrilla Family (BGF).

The more sophisticated of the prison gangs share similar traits, as we have previously discussed, with regard to their dedication to the organization and members. Other traits are also prevalent and are as follows:

- prison gangs commonly have a "blood in, blood out" policy, which requires prospective members to injure or kill a designated target individual in the prison system

- prison gangs operate both inside and outside the prison walls

- prison gangs commonly form alliances within the prisons in order to build presence, strength, and clout within the prison walls

Most gangs are typically formed as protection organizations for members, but once accepted, the recruit enjoys the power, prestige, influence, and protection that the organization offers.

Prison gangs in the United States became widely known in 1957, when the EME first organized at the Deuel Vocational Institute in Tracy, California. The gang originally formed as a protection organization for gang members, but the membership grew rapidly. After gaining considerable size and influence in the prison system, they acquired control over such activities as homosexual prostitution, drug trafficking, debt collection (extortion), and gambling. The group, now numbering an estimated 600 members, focused most of its aggression against white and black inmates, while leaving Mexican inmates alone. ·

The EME established a goal for itself to control drug trafficking in all areas where it had become established. The gang gained a reputation for violence after the 1967 stabbing death of a suspected police informer operating within the ranks of the gang. As violence grew, even some members of the gang felt uneasy. It was the same year that a group of EME members formed its own gang, called Nuestra Familia (NF), meaning "our family." The NF waged war with the EME and over the years has caused numerous deaths.

Because of the ongoing war with the EME, the NF has formed an alliance with the Black Guerrilla Family as well as other ethnic prison gangs. The NF has surpassed the EME in organizational capabilities, and its size, now estimated at around 700 to 800 strong, makes the NF one of the largest prison gangs in the United States.

Another prison gang that has achieved considerable notoriety is the Nazi-oriented Aryan Brotherhood. A characteristic of particular significance is the association between outlaw motorcycle gang members and the AB. Frequently, when members of outlaw motorcycle gangs are convicted and sent to prison, they no longer have the protection of their gang. The AB, being a white-supremacist organization, has commonly accepted bikers into the gang because of this philosophy.

The hierarchy of the AB consists of a commission and a governing council. Members are promoted through the ranks based on individual acts of violence committed on behalf of the gang's organizational goals.

The Black Guerrilla Family (BGF) was founded in 1966 by the late George Jackson in San Quentin Prison. The BGF is a politically motivated organization following a Maoist philosophy and operates on a command structure that incorporates a Supreme Commander, Central Committee, Field Generals, and Captains of Security.

As with the adoption of bikers by the Aryan Brotherhood, the BGF recruits members of black street gangs in prison. Members of the Crips and Bloods have been known to become instant members of the BGF once they are in the prison system.

The last of the five major prison gangs is the Texas Syndicate (E Ts E), which organized in Folsom Prison in 1974. Although considered the smallest gang in membership (an estimated 175 strong), the Texas Syndicate is also considered the most violent of the five major gangs. The gang consists of Mexican-American inmates that originally hailed from the areas of El Paso and San Antonio, Texas. One particular characteristic of Mexican-oriented prison gangs is an intense loyalty between members, which contributes to their reputation for violence. The gang is active in assaults and extortion and has targeted drug trafficking as its primary criminal enterprise both inside and outside the prison.

CASE STUDY: RAY RAY AND THE BGF

The Black Guerrilla Family is a close-knit gang that originated in the 1970s in California prisons. BGF members and affiliates are engaged in many types of crime and are best characterized as "simply prone to violence."

This OCDETF case involved an investigation by a Task Force team consisting of the DEA, IRS, ATF, Los Angeles Sheriff's Office, California Department of Justice, and local police officers from four jurisdictions. Their goal was to uncover and prosecute the narcotics, strong-arming, and homicide activities of the Elrader "Ray Ray" Browning organization. After two years of investigation, working undercover, and using informants, six months of intensive surveillance, and three months of wiretaps on residences, automobiles, and portable phones, 28 defendants were indicted on a variety of cocaine, heroin, and firearms charges. Browning's drug couriers, whose consignment of cocaine was seized by the DEA in Detroit, were also indicted.

Browning was released from prison in 1979 after serving part of a state term for a murder that he committed as a juvenile. In August of that year, a man identified as Browning walked into a cafe and shot to death two men. The attack was to avenge a drug robbery of James "Doc" Holiday, Ray Ray Browning's associate. Ray Ray's conviction was overturned when a California Supreme Court decision rendered inadmissible the testimony of a witness that had been hypnotized in an attempt to refresh her memory.

In 1983, Browning was found guilty of firebombing and shooting into a Pasadena home in an incident related to drug territories. Again, his conviction was overturned, and he was released in September 1985. Browning then began organizing his major drug ring.

Like a corporation's chief executive officer, Ray Ray headed a broad narcotics empire with senior executives in at least four cities. Gross sales were estimated at $1 million to $3 million per month! Profits were funneled into a pricey lifestyle for Browning, his girlfriend and second-in-command, Nei Marie Wells, and a very small group of top confederates such as "Doc" Holiday. The rest were mainly small-time drug dealers ordered by Ray Ray to work for him or close up shop.

At home in Pasadena, everyone knew Ray Ray. Seeing him being driven in his white limousine or smiling behind the wheel of his Rolls-Royce, young boys watched in reverence and adults spoke in hushed tones. To those that knew him, Browning always seemed to beat the system. Folklore produced a man larger than life. Tales of drug rivalries, intimidation, and murder abounded.

The turning point was an incident in Detroit. Big John Milan, a Browning operative, arrived by bus with 18 kilos of cocaine in two suitcases. Observing two men and a dog examining his luggage, Big John refused to claim it. The agents had been alerted to his arrival by their Los Angeles counterparts, who were tapping Ray Ray's phone. They later testified that they did not detain Milan in order to protect the integrity of the wiretap.

Milan called Nei Wells to ask permission to abandon the bags but was told that he might as well get arrested because Ray Ray wouldn't believe his story. He then approached the baggage clerk, who gratuitously told Milan not to claim the bags because the police had discovered the "bricks" inside. At that, John departed without the bags and checked into a Detroit hotel that the gang customarily used. Within a few hours, he changed hotels at Ray Ray's direction. The next evening, two men fired several .45 caliber slugs into Big John's room, wounding him seriously. At that point, Big John decided to cooperate with authorities in order to save his life. Nei's to-the-point comment registered on tape was: "We never heard of dogs sniffing buses before."

John Milan would make a zealous witness but not a particularly well-informed or reputable one. Nei Marie Wells, however, was all of these things. Nei functioned at the center of the web and knew more of the details than anyone but Ray Ray himself. Facing CCE charges and sentencing possibilities of up to 80 years, Nei decided to cooperate, provided she and her children could be protected from Ray Ray's wrath. Nei Wells became "the most diligent, conscientious, cooperating witness" that the prosecutor had ever seen. She is presently out on bond awaiting sentencing, and she and her family are secure in the U.S. Marshal's Witness Security Program.

The raid that closed down the Ray Ray Browning operation involved several hundred officers and agents, who went to 17 locations simultaneously and seized 15 pounds of cocaine, $300,000 in cash, four homes, an apartment building, and 10 cars. They arrested 21 persons, and seven more were later detained on additional federal warrants. The Browning case and several immediate spin-offs resulted in seizures totaling almost a million dollars in cash and several million dollars worth of real estate, jewelry, and vehicles.

Twenty of the 28 charged defendants were prosecuted in federal court. Of those 20, 18 pled guilty and received sentences of up to 20 years in prison without parole; the only defendants to go on trial in federal court were Browning and Holiday. After a three-week trial in which they chose to handle their own defense, both were convicted. While awaiting sentencing, Browning tried to escape from Terminal Island Federal Prison by posing as an attorney, complete with wig, mustache, briefcase, and law book, but was foiled by an alert guard that recognized Ray Ray's "swagger."

Ray Ray is presently serving two life sentences plus 120 years in Leavenworth. He was among the nation's first defendants to be prosecuted under the 1986 statute mandating a life term for a conviction as the chief of a continuing criminal enterprise involving drugs. He was ordered to pay $2 million in fines (just in case anything should be left after forfeitures and the collection of unpaid taxes on the drug income). "Doc" Holiday was sentenced to life without possibility of parole.

The judge remarked at sentencing on August 29, 1988, "When Congress passed the [statute] it had a certain individual in mind. Well, Mr. Browning, you are it." Under the newest drug law, which took effect November 21, 1988, a defendant in Browning's position that is proven to have committed or ordered a drug-related murder faces the death penalty. Perhaps Ray Ray lucked out once again.

Source: Organized Crime Drug Enforcement Task Force, 1988

Ancillary Trafficking Organizations

Other than those organizations already discussed, there are many other smaller organizations operating throughout the United States. These organizations operate in both urban and rural settings and account for a significant segment of the domestic drug trafficking picture.

The urban trafficking organizations make up a significant category of drug dealers. These organizations are frequently well organized, highly structured, and are usually composed of extremely violent career criminals. In many cases, these organizations consist of younger criminals that, as they age, assume a leadership role. Many are later convicted and sent to prison, or they are killed. This places the urban trafficking organizations in a constant state of metamorphoses.

Urban drug gangs exist throughout the country but have been particularly active in such cities as Chicago, Detroit, St. Louis, and East St. Louis, Illinois. It is common for members to be heavily armed with fully automatic weapons and to be especially violence-prone. Violence by these organizations frequently occurs because of rivalries between trafficking groups over "turf," but the violence may manifest itself as aggression toward police, prosecutors, and witnesses in drug prosecutions.

As discussed earlier in this text, most drug sources are either Mexican or Latin American nationals. Females are also commonly used as couriers from the source city to the ultimate destination, and profits for drugs acquired are usually considerably high. For example, a kilogram of cocaine purchased in a source city may cost $12,000 to $15,000 but can be resold for $30,000. Because of this enormous profit margin, control of the industry is a primary goal of the urban trafficking organization.

There are also other "small-time" trafficking organizations operating in rural America. In some cases, drug trafficking may be a variation of another type of criminal activity that has been going on for some time. For example, in some parts of the southeast, rural people that once produced moonshine have discovered that marijuana is more profitable. The isolation of many rural areas enables traffickers to conduct operations such as marijuana farming and clandestine laboratories and, in doing so, remain relatively free of detection from law enforcement authorities. In many cases, such locations are also good areas for use as "drop zones" or secluded landing strips for smuggling pilots.

Summary

Because of the profit potential for drug trafficking, criminal organizations with both foreign and domestic origins compete for the market share. This chapter deals with domestic drug trafficking organizations; many of these have their roots in foreign countries or are relatively new to the illegal drug trade.

The term traditional organized crime is most commonly associated with Italian criminal groups or La Cosa Nostra (LCN or Mafia). The LCN originated in Italy and Sicily during the 1800s and is now considered the premier criminal group in Italy and a major criminal phenomenon in the United States. The origin of Italian organized crime in prisons parallels that of many domestic prison gangs in the United States.

The first Mafioso arrived in the United States in the late 1800s and gained a foothold in such cities as New York and New Orleans. Prohibition (1920-1933) was conducive to Mafiosi criminal activities, which spread to other large cities throughout the United States. Today there are an estimated 25 LCN families, and according to the FBI, 19 of those are involved, in one way or another, with drug trafficking.

Outlaw motorcycle gangs represent yet another domestic criminal group actively involved in the drug trade. Originating in the late 1940s, gangs with names like the Hell's Angels, the Pagans, Bandidos, and the Outlaws have now cornered much of the methamphetamine market and frequently dwell in cities outside the continental United States. Such gangs have also gained a reputation for violence and on many occasions have worked in collusion with other criminal groups such as LCN. The DEA estimates that approximately 850 outlaw motorcycle gangs currently operate in the United States. Some of these organizations have demonstrated considerable sophistication and pose a very real threat to many major U.S. cities.

In the early 1970s, California youth gangs such as the Crips and Bloods organized in the east Los Angeles area. Today, they have grown to about 60,000 to 70,000 strong and occupy an estimated 30 American cities. Youth gangs have concentrated on the crack/cocaine trade and, like outlaw motorcycle gangs, are vertically integrated so that they produce and distribute drugs on both the wholesale and retail level.

Youth gang members are customarily a very young age (between 14 and 18 years old) and have become very willing to engage in violent turf battles with other gangs. This type of criminal group has made it necessary to consider the restructuring of laws dealing with juvenile offenders, to make youthful offenders more accountable for their actions.

Other groups have also recently emerged that parallel the organizations of the youth gangs. Political unrest in the late 1970s and early 1980s created one such violent gang in the area of the Caribbean basin, the Jamaican Posses. The posses began their drug dealing ventures with the smuggling of marijuana (ganja) but have now also identified the crack/cocaine trade as their primary source of revenue. It is thought that posses have formed alliances with other criminal organizations such as the Colombian cartels.

Jamaican posses may account for an estimated 10,000 members with connections to Jamaican neighborhoods in both New York and Miami. In addition to dealing drugs, the posses are very active in firearms trafficking from the United States to Jamaica, where weapons are used to gain unlawful political influence in the Jamaican society.

Prison gangs also represent a unique domestic brand of organized crime. Of the estimated 114 prison gangs operating in the United States, five have emerged as the most sophisticated: the Mexican Mafia, Nuestra Familia, Aryan Brotherhood, Black Guerilla Family and the Texas Syndicate. All of these organizations possess a particularly violent nature, and they have all identified drug trafficking as a primary criminal goal.

DISCUSSION QUESTIONS

1. Discuss the hierarchical structure of the La Cosa Nostra, and compare it to that of the Los Angeles-based youth gangs, the Bloods and the Crips.

2. Review some of the reasons why some researchers perceive La Cosa Nostra as a fragmented group of semi-organized criminals.

3. List those domestic criminal organizations most actively involved in cocaine/crack trafficking.

4. Discuss the historical origins of the Mafia or LCN in both the United States and Sicily.

5. What is the relationship between the American and the Sicilian Mafia in the illicit drug trade?

6. Name and discuss the structure and other similarities of the four major outlaw motorcycle gangs that operate in the United States.

7. Discuss the evolution of outlaw motorcycle gangs and their relationship to the illicit drug trade.

8. List some changes that might be considered in reforming the juvenile justice system as it deals with the problem of youth gangs.

9. Discuss the proliferation of black California street gangs and their role in drug trafficking and the criminal justice system.

10. To what extent do Jamaican posses play a role in international drug trafficking, and in what other illicit operations are the posses involved?

11. Discuss the organizational structure of the Jamaican posses and compare it to that of traditional organized crime.

12. List and compare the various domestic organized crime groups considered the most active in the illicit drug business.

13. If prison gangs in fact operate within the walls of prisons, then do they pose a threat to public safety? Defend your answer.

14. List the five major prison gangs in the United States, and discuss their role in drug trafficking.

15. Explain why urban and rural traffickers play such a significant role in domestic drug trafficking.

CHAPTER 9

FOREIGN
DRUG TRAFFICKING ORGANIZATIONS

Clearly, the realization that the United States is a major user-country has created an incentive for escalating foreign involvement in the drug trade with North America. In June 1988, *Fortune Magazine* stated that "the global drug trade may run up to $500 billion a year, more than twice the value of all U.S. currency in circulation." The degree to which various criminal organizations involve themselves depends greatly on factors such as the type of drug trafficked, the source country's proximity to the United States, established trafficking routes, and the ability to move money and personnel into and out of the country.

Colombian Organized Crime

The term "cartel" has been associated with many Colombian organized crime groups since the mid-1980s. Before we discuss the role and operations of the Colombian cartels, let us first attempt to demarcate the significance of the term cartel. Perhaps we could begin by comparing the function of a cartel to that of a "legitimate" group of business entrepreneurs. One such group, for example, is O.P.E.C. (the Organization of Petroleum Exporting Countries). The O.P.E.C. countries practice political and social manipulation in attempts to coordinate and control the production of oil for maximum economic gain. The Colombian cartel, when used in parlance with organized crime, is similar in that it attempts to control cocaine traffic through illegal means with profit as its principal goal.

The current power of the drug cartels over the Colombian society demonstrates the terrorizing impact of a criminal organization when it becomes a state within a state. One characteristic of these powerful cartels is their willingness (and even brazenness) to display their power and wealth. They have evolved in a country, Colombia, that by one estimate is home to 140 right-wing paramilitary squads and six Marxist guerrilla groups. According to the State Department, the murder rate in Colombia is two-and-one-half times that of New York City.

As of 1989, four principle Colombian cartels have emerged as the most active in cocaine trafficking: *the Medellin, the Cali, the Bogotá* and *the North Atlantic Coast* cartels. All originated about the same time—the late 1970s, and in spite of their differences, they have all worked with one another on occasion.

The term "cartel" is somewhat misleading because it suggests a greater degree of cohesion than exists among major drug trafficking countries. More accurately, they are communities with shared interests of greater or lesser duration; they are groups that pool their drug shipments, share methods of transportation, or exchange certain types of information vital to each organization's drug trafficking operations.

In one sense, however, the Colombian cartels do function like traditional cartels: they attempt to set prices and eliminate any competition through violence and collusion. The cartels have been successful in effectively setting prices for cocaine on both the wholesale and retail levels. They have accumulated the funds necessary to purchase the consent of major forces in the Colombian society, e.g., the police, the judiciary, journalists that influence public opinion. The cartels also initiate threats, acts of violence, and intimidation against those that are not subject to the inducements of bribery.

No society can tolerate a criminal element without corrupting itself in the process...

Of the four major cartels, the two largest are the Medellin and Cali Cartels, which control an estimated 70 percent of the raw cocaine transported from Bolivia, Ecuador, and Peru for processing in Colombia. The Cali and Medellin cartels worked together up until 1987, pooled funds to defend their members, and even worked with the Basque ETA organization, which is noted for its expertise in the use of car bombs. The cartels also have typically staked out territory for drug trafficking. New York, for example, was assigned to the Cali group because it had become well established in its operations there. Other areas, however, such as Miami are considered "open" territories for the cartels.

The membership and organizational structure of the Colombian cartels has remained consistently fluid. That is, leadership varies with drug trends and power plays within the organization. In addition, numerous smaller organizations constantly strive for power and pose competition for the major organizations. As of the preparation of this text, the Medellin and Cali Cartels are at war with one another, and an estimated 100 lives have been lost to this conflict. Because of the high visibility of the Medellin Cartel, this chapter will offer a closer examination of the organization.

The Cali Cartel

Because law enforcement agencies have a tendency to focus their efforts on the best-known of the cartels, the Medellin Cartel, other cartels such as the Cali have more freedom in which to operate. The Cali organization, lead by Gilberto Rodriguez Orejuela, operates primarily out of Cali and Buenaventura, and is closely tied to another organization in the town of Pereira. The Cali organization has demonstrated an ability to expand its operations through the use of alliances with other groups, such as the North Atlantic Coast Cartel. One of the major reasons for the success of the Cali Cartel is its high degree of integration into the Colombian economy. Unlike the larger Medellin Cartel, the Cali Cartel has been careful to cultivate popular support and strong economic, political, and social ties, and to conduct its operations in a discreet, businesslike manner.

While other drug trafficking organizations have engaged in disruptive acts of violence and have attained a high degree of notoriety, the Cali Cartel has been careful to be as unobtrusive as possible, thereby avoiding the crackdown directed against the Medellin Cartel. Because of this, it is rapidly expanding its base of operation in the United States from cities such as Miami, New York, and Los Angeles to other American markets.

The Bogotá Cartel

Although little is known about the Bogotá Cartel, its evolution parallels that of many of the other Colombian groups. Specifically, the Bogotá Cartel began as a smuggling group dealing with contraband emeralds, and later, marijuana. It was through close association with American criminal contacts that trafficking networks were established for cocaine. Among these contacts were Miami and Caribbean associates of the late Meyer Lansky and his associates. Once the group gained access to Colombian political power, cocaine processing and later, trafficking, became its primary focus due to the high profit margin of the drug. According to a 1989 DEA intelligence report, the Bogotá organization has possibly purchased more police and governmental protection than the other cartels.

The North Atlantic Coast Cartel

Generally considered the least cohesive of the four major cartels, the North Atlantic Coast Cartel occupies the cities of Cartagena, Barranquilla, Santa Marta, and Rio Hacha. It is thought that this organization is made up of a loosely knit set of transient associations that formed a short-term arrangement for operating with each other. The North Atlantic Coast Cartel is less vertically integrated than the other three cartels and also began as a smuggling (service-type) operation for the other cartels. As with the other cartels, the North Atlantic Coast Cartel began in the marijuana business and graduated to the cocaine trade on which it now concentrates. Federal sources report that, in one case, the North Atlantic Coast group accepted a proposition from the Medellin and Bogotá cartels to smuggle large amounts of cocaine to prearranged points off the American coasts for a fee. To oversee this operation, the cartel established members on the east coast in Florida cities of Miami, Jacksonville, and Gainesville as well as Atlanta, New York, and Boston. In the west, Los Angeles and San Diego were operational centers for the operation.

CLOSE-UP: CARTEL GUNS SEIZED

In July 1989, drug agents seized an arsenal of heavy machine guns, high explosives, and automatic weapons intended for the assassination of the Medellin drug cartel's top trafficker. Two men allegedly connected with the Cali cartel, a rival Colombian cocaine-smuggling operation, were arrested in West Palm Beach in connection with the seizure.

The plot included the planned purchase of a small drone aircraft to be flown over Medellin cartel leader Pablo Escobar Gaviria's hideout and then exploded, federal drug agents claim. Escobar's Medellin cartel is responsible for up to 80 percent of United States cocaine imports. The weapons were being purchased by the Cali cartel and shipped to Colombia in what federal agents considered a last-ditch effort to assassinate Pablo Escobar. Agents commented that the cartel had shot down Escobar's helicopter, had him cornered, and wanted to finish him off. The weapons were intercepted on Florida's Turnpike as the two suspects were to pick them up from illegal arms dealers.

Customs and Bureau of Alcohol, Tobacco, and Firearms agents confiscated five fully automatic M-60 machine guns, 100 pounds of C-04 explosives, 25 MAC-11 machine guns, 20 AR-15 assault rifles, and $104,00 in cash, along with a plan and a van. Agents said that the M-60 machine guns were to be mounted on helicopters for an attack on Escobar's hideout.

Source: The Kansas City Star, July 21, 1989.

Figure 9.1

Typical Colombian Cocaine Organization

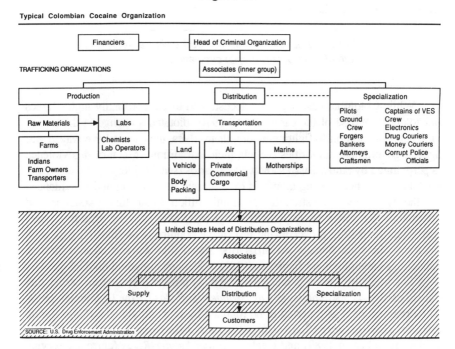

SOURCE: U.S. Drug Enforcement Administration

The Medellin Cartel

In 1988, the U.S. State Department publicly announced that Americans should stay away from the Colombian city of Medellin, the capital of Antioquia and headquarters of the infamous criminal organization known as the Medellin Cartel. The announcement was based on the fact that the Medellin Cartel, Colombia's most organized and vicious drug trafficking organization, claim this city as its international base of operation.

The Medellin Cartel alone is reputed to earn $2 billion to $4 billion a year and to rival many Fortune 500 companies in terms of global reach. "Including the entire spectrum of drug exports, probably $2.5-3 billion a year in profits are attributed to Colombia; drugs now rank above coffee ($2-2.5 billion) as the country's principal foreign exchange earner." (Bagley, 70).

Medellin, Colombia's industrial center, is a city of an estimated 1.5 million people sequestered in the Andes mountains. Although the cartel exerts great influence over the cocaine trade there, it is, as mentioned, rivaled by a smaller but powerful trafficking organization known as the Cali Cartel. These groups repre-

sent two of an estimated 20 organizations that are thought to control most of the
world's lucrative cocaine trade.

---

*...the global drug trade may run up to $500 billion a year, more than
twice the value of all U.S. currency in circulation...*

While Colombia has long been accustomed to extraordinally high degrees
of violence, the rise of the cartels in the 1970s dictated a change in the tide of
violence. In addition to fighting among themselves, the cartels have waged war
against government authorities seeking their extradition. Much of this violence
is perpetrated by paid assassins known as sicarios (see Chapter 4).

The existence of drug money is ever-present in Medellin and is evidenced
by the widespread construction of multi-million-dollar luxury condos and
apartments that tower above the city's skyline. Other than the drug traffickers
that flaunt their drug proceeds, the rest of the country is not blessed with such
luxuries. In 1988 Senator Alvaro Uribe stated that without cocaine profits,
Medellin's unemployment figure, currently at 25 percent, would double.

The Medellin Cartel, perceived as the most powerful of the four earlier-dis-
cussed cartels, is also known as *Los Grandes Mafiosos* by the Colombian press.
The organization was reported to be founded by four individuals: *Pablo Emilio
Escobar Gaviria, Jorge Luis Ochoa Vasques, Jose Gonzalo Rodriguez-Gacha*
(killed by police in 1989) and *Carlos Enrique Lehder-Rivas* (currently serving
time in prison in the United States). As of the preparation of this text, the cartel
is supposedly controlled by Pablo Emilio Escobar-Gaviria, his cousin and business partner, Gustavo de Jesus Gaviria-Rivero, and Jorge Luis Ochoa-Vasquez.

Jose Gonzalo Rodriguez-Gacha, a key player in the cartel, and one of the
12 most wanted traffickers by the U.S. Department of Justice, had earned the
reputation as one of the most vicious of the cartel members. He lived an opulent
life of extravagance and was constantly surrounded by bodyguards and beautiful
women. One of his mansions was a mission-style ranch equipped with a gym
and its own disco. His trademark was to inscribe his initials on his bullets.

---

*The army major was flabbergasted at the offer, delivered by an emis-
sary of Jose Gonzalo Rodriguez-Gacha: in return for destroying confiscated documents and computer disks that provided a detailed blueprint
of Gacha's cocaine empire, the officer, whose monthly salary is $300,
would receive $1.2 million. Cash. If he refused, the drug mafia would
hunt him down and slaughter him.*

Source: Moody, J. (1989). "Nobel Battle, Terrible Toll," *Time* (December 18):33.

In December 1989, an extensive manhunt, consisting of over 1000 police and government troops supported by seven helicopters, was undertaken to locate Gacha through information given by farmers in the area. Ultimately, he was tracked to a farm owned by Escobar. The farm, located about 360 miles from Bogotá, is where Gacha, at age 42, was ultimately shot and killed during an exchange of gunfire with government troops. The manhunt resulted from a national government crackdown on drug traffickers, initiated shortly after presidential contender Luis Carlos Galan was assassinated by unknown gunmen in August of that year.

In recent years, Gacha had achieved prominence by organizing military squads made up of landowners to wage a campaign against the FARC (discussed later in this chapter). The FARC had repeatedly tried to take control of the coca growing fields from the farmers in Colombia.

As mentioned, of all of the cartels, the Medellin Cartel is considered the most sophisticated, with managers that are dispatched to the United States for "tours of duty" as business representatives. Additionally, its headquarters receives fax transmissions from operatives and has links to legitimate business interests. Each controls a separate organization within the cartel, but each works in harmony with the other. By not being in competition with each other, these traffickers have learned that they can both maximize their profits and share resources at the same time.

The Medellin Cartel was reportedly founded during the mid-1970s by Escobar, who was, until then, a known car thief. After realizing the greater financial certainty for profit in the drug trade, Escobar converted his long-established stolen-car trafficking routes to drug trafficking routes. In the late 1970s he convinced Fabio Ochoa, then a smuggler of Scotch whiskey and television sets, to work with him in the cocaine trade. Fabio, now a wealthy rancher, has never been charged with drug trafficking.

One event that gave rise to the violence of the cartel occurred in 1981 when leftist guerrillas kidnapped Fabio Ochoa's 28-year-old daughter Marta and held her for ransom to help finance their movement. A meeting of some 223 cocaine traffickers was then held in Medellin. From this meeting an organization calling itself "Death to Kidnappers" was formed. The group then began systematically to assassinate members of the leftist group regardless of the victims' involvement in the abduction of Fabio's daughter. Marta was soon released, and the cartel surfaced as a powerfully influential criminal organization.

Another significant event contributing to the violence-prone reputation of the cartel goes back to 1984, when Jorge Luis Ochoa was taken into custody in Spain. The DEA, at the time, told him that it would arrange for his release if he would implicate the Sandinistas in drug-smuggling operations. Ochoa refused, claiming that they were not involved. Several months later, Spain refused to extradite Ochoa to the United States because of the political nature of the request and sent him back to Colombia to face drug charges there. Once in Colombia, Ochoa was "mistakenly" released from custody.

NOTABLE DATES IN CARTEL HISTORY

1960s   Cocaine returns to United States drug abuse scene

Late 1970s Cocaine demand begins to explode in United States and is considered a drug of the rich. Cartel activity begins to become more active in South Florida

The Colombian "Cocaine Cowboys" wage cocaine war against competition in Dade County, Florida, where over 250 murders were documented

Colombian cartel activity was first documented in southern California

Roberto Suarez, Sr. and ex-Nazi Klaus Barbie organized a 1,500-man army in Bolivia

1980   Suarez organizes 189th coup of Bolivian government and takes control of the country for one year

1981   As smuggling efforts spread through western United States, M-19 leftist guerrillas terrorize citizens in Colombia

Jorge Ochoa's daughter kidnapped by the M-19

In response to the Ochoa kidnapping, the traffickers formed a massive meeting of all traffickers at the International Hotel, which paralleled the 1957 meeting of Mafia Chiefs at Appalachia

First assassination of a judge by a cartel

1982   Suarez offers to pay off $3 billion Bolivian foreign debt in exchange for immunity from prosecution

1983   Tranquilandia cocaine laboratory discovered: fourteen labs, 80-bed dormitory, air strip, 7,000 pounds of cocaine per month production

1984   Justice Minister Rodrigo Lara Bonilla machine-gunned to death as extradition proceedings progress

Escobar, Ochoa, and Gacha accused of masterminding Lara Bonilla murder

First extradition order signed for Carlos Lehder

Ochoa arrested in Spain on outstanding U.S. warrant

1985 Judge in Lara Bonilla case murdered

First Colombian cartel members extradited to U.S.

Cartel joins forces with former enemies M-19 to attack the Palace of Justice—Extradition files destroyed and 11 Supreme Court Justices killed

1986 U.S. government informant Barry Seal is machine-gunned to death in Louisiana by cartel hit-squad

Seventeen thousand peasants riot in Bolivia in protest government interdiction in coca harvesting

During this year alone over 1,700 people are killed in the city of Medellin, Colombia as a result of cocaine-related violence

Spain extradites Ochoa to Colombia, where he is released and returns to control his cocaine empire

Former Chief of Anti-Narcotics Operation, Colonel Jamie Ramirez Gomez, is murdered

Editor Guillermo Cano of the El Espectador Newspaper is murdered because of his antidrug editorials

1987 Enrique Parejo-Gonzalez, former Justice Minister, is located by cartel hit-squad in Budapest, Hungary and assassinated

Carlos Lehder is extradited to the United States

Colombian Supreme Court voids United States-Colombian extradition treaty after extreme pressure from cartel

1988 Attorney General Carlos Mauro Hoyos is kidnapped and murdered

Pablo Escobar and Panamanian Dictator Manuel Noriega indicted in the United States

Pablo Escobar and Fabio Ochoa indicted by U.S. for murder of Justice Minister Lara Bonilla, murder of Barry Seal, and for a 15-year conspiracy to import cocaine into the U.S. through the Bahamas

1989 Senator Luis Carlos Galan, a leading presidential candidate, is assassinated by five unknown gunmen during a campaign speech

President Barco enacts "summary extradition" and declares an all-out war against the traffickers after Galan's murder

Jose Gonzalo Rodriguez Gacha, former Medellin Cartel boss, is killed in a shoot-out with government troops

Source: Post, M. (1990). "Colombian Crime and Cocaine Trafficking." *The Narc Officer*, (December):11. Reprinted by permission of the International Narcotics Enforcement Officers Association.

Figure 9.2

A COCAINE COLLABORATION: THE OCHOA/ESCOBAR JOINT VENTURE

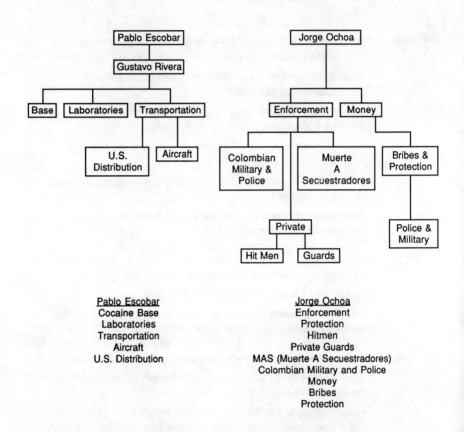

SOURCE: PCOC, 1986

The organizational structure of the cartel insures several distinct advantages for the organization. These are: control over the price and the quality of Colombian cocaine, greater access to smuggling and processing equipment, and mastery of a wide variety of methods to avoid detection by law enforcement.

A chart detailing a temporary cooperative venture based in Medellin, between the Pablo Escobar organization and the Jorge Ochoa organization was confiscated from a mid-level trafficker involved in the operation and was provided by the DEA to the President's Commission on Organized Crime in 1986. As diagrammed, the Escobar and Ochoa organizations combined and divided the trafficking responsibilities typically completed by a single organization. The same component parts, such as labor, processing, transportation, finance, and enforcement, were carried over from the individual organizations, with the Escobar group taking responsibility for production activities and the Ochoa group handling enforcement and finances (PCOC, 1986).

The Medellin Cartel is thought by the DEA to be one of the world's best-organized criminal organizations and thus fits many of the criteria of an "organized crime" unit. The financial division, for example, is not only responsible for collection of revenues and making investments but also for money laundering (see Chapter 6). Their enforcement division is charged with corruption in the form of bribes as well as hiring guards and assassins. Ironically, the cartel seems to employ a decentralized type of management structure, where certain decisions are made on an individual basis by individual family members.

The Medellin Cartel's operating procedure basically involves the financing of coca plant cultivation done by peasants in Peru and Bolivia. The cartel oversees the process of refining the leaves into cocaine paste (or pasta) by mixing dried leaves in special solvents creating a thick pasty substance. This base is then flown by cartel pilots to hidden airstrips in Colombia's vast forest regions. In makeshift labs, the paste is then processed into hydrochloride (powder) by mixing it with ether and acetone. The powdered cocaine is then packed into one kilogram (2.2 pounds) plastic bags and eventually smuggled into the United States.

With each stop along the smuggling route, the cocaine is diluted and its price soars. It is estimated that each shipment contains cocaine from different cartel members, so, in the event that a load is lost through seizure by law enforcement, no one cartel family is financially devastated. The cocaine is then distributed to various independent operators in the United States for street cocaine sales and crack distribution.

According to the DEA, the cartel recruits American pilots whose planes are equipped with some of the most sophisticated electronic navigational equipment money can buy; these pilots are paid about $5,000 per kilo. The enormous profit realized by these players is illustrated by the fact that each shipment averages about 300 kilograms, making the average total take for the cartel pilot about $1.5 million per trip.

Because of the media's attention to the cartels and pressure from the United States and Colombian governments, the Medellin Cartel, its leader Pablo Emilio Escobar-Gaviria, and other top leaders must continue to maintain low profiles. In 1988, the DEA reported that the necessity of keeping this low profile has forced cartel leaders to delegate management responsibilities to other individuals in the organization.

THE MEDELLIN CARTEL/M-19 CONNECTION

The drug-running Medellin Cartel has bought the services of Colombia's most infamous guerrilla group to do the cartel's dirty work. According to highly classified U.S. intelligence reports, the revolutionary group called the "April 19 Movement" or "M-19" has acted as a hired gun for the multi-billion-dollar cartel.

The M-19 and the Medellin Cartel have not always been so tight. M-19 was formed in 1970 and was named after the date that year when a populist ex-president favored by the rebels lost an allegedly fraudulent election. At its greatest strength, M-19 numbered approximately 8,000 guerrillas, but today, it may have fewer than 1,000.

In 1979, M-19 tunneled into an army arsenal in Bogotá and made off with 5,000 guns. In 1980, M-19 stormed the embassy of the Dominion Republic in Bogotá and took 52 hostages, including 15 ambassadors. The American Ambassador, Diego Asencio, was one of those held for 61 days, after which the hostages were freed as the guerrillas escaped into Cuba. M-19 took over the embassy to call attention to human rights violations in Colombia and to guarantee fair treatment of guerrillas that were in jail in Colombia. The M-19's normal method of operation was to pay its way by kidnapping members of wealthy families and collecting ransoms.

In late 1981, the M-19 kidnapped the wrong person. They snatched the daughter of Colombia's alleged first family of cocaine, the Fabio Ochoa family of Medellin. The Ochoas reasoned that they or anyone that was prospering in the drug trade would be safe from kidnappings. The Ochoas banded together with over 200 other narcotics traffickers to form the Medellin Cartel. Its original purpose was to wage war against the M-19.

M-19 released Ochoa's daughter after the cartel murdered dozens of guerrillas. It was the beginning of a strange friendship. M-19 began a hands-off policy toward the cartel and the cartel put M-19 on the payroll. On November 6, 1985, M-19 took over the five-story, marble Colombian Palace of Justice in downtown Bogotá. It was just one block from the Colombian Congress and two blocks from the presidential mansion. Colombian soldiers besieged the building for 27 hours, then stormed it with grenades and gunfire. All 35 rebels died, along with 12 of the 24 supreme court justices.

The sum paid to M-19 for its services, $5 million, was pocket change for the cartel, which makes as much as $7 billion a year supplying the United States and Europe with cocaine. The cartel still hires M-19 for other assassinations of government officials, judges, policy officers, and journalists. Some "sicarios" as the hit-men are called, will kill for as little as $50.

The cartel may be cozying up to one leftist group, but evidence indicates that it also has been killing other leftists by the hundreds, particularly the supporters of Colombian Revolutionary Armed Forces (FARC). FARC was the oldest and largest leftist guerrilla group in Colombia until it struck a deal with the Colombian government in 1984 and became a legitimate political party, the Patrioc Union. Since then, FARC has become the most successful leftist party in Colombian history. It is believed that the Medellin Cartel leaders, who have used their drug profits to become the largest landholders in Colombia, fear that the growing power of the leftist party will lead to land reform. They don't want to see their valuable land holdings divided up among the peasants.

Source: Anderson, J. and D. Van Atta (1988). "The Medellin Cartel/M-19 Gang." *The Washington Post* (August 28):87.

THE CONVERSION PROCESS

When coca leaves are steeped in kerosene, sulfuric acid, and an alkali, coca base is formed. This is a rather crude conglomerate of coca alkaloids and oils and has a cocaine content of 70 to 85 percent. Addition of hydrochloric acid will provide the salt, cocaine hydrochloride, with a purity of 90 to 100 percent depending on the sophistication of the extraction process. It looks like fine white flakes or rocks and feels powdery when crushed.

It is either crude paste or cocaine hydrochloride that is brought from Peru and Bolivia to Colombia for transshipment to Miami and other large American cities by air and sea. From the point of entry the cocaine product is redistributed through a dealer network that is generally separate from the heroin distribution system. Before arriving at the ultimate consumer, it is ordinarily cut (diluted) four to eight times, so that pure cocaine is essentially unknown at present and is not available except to major distributors that have access to it. In fact, some "cocaine" sold on the street turns out to have no cocaine at all in the product.

Note: 500 kilograms of coca leaves are required to produce one kilogram of cocaine paste.

Source: DEA, Fall 1986.

Figure 9.3

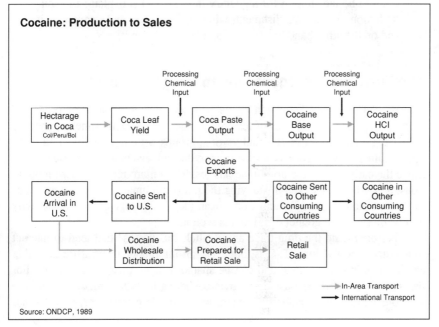

Cocaine: Production to Sales

Source: ONDCP, 1989

It should be noted here that in many areas of South America, the cartels have achieved a degree of popularity. Many poor Latin Americans view themselves as likely candidates for someday becoming cartel members. In other cases, the wealth of the cartels has actually reshaped the Colombian economy, and many citizens on both ends of the financial spectrum enjoy certain short-term financial benefits. For example, Colombia has recently enjoyed one of the highest economic growth rates in South America. This phenomenon is attributed to the presence of illicit drug revenues. Additionally, Pablo Escobar has financed the building of 500 houses for Medellin's poor, thus giving the impression that he is a "Robin Hood-type" protector of the poor. In reality, the poor in Colombia have been devastated by the illegal drug trade primarily because of an exceedingly high rate of addiction there.

Some prominent Colombians have even openly defended the presence of drug traffickers. For example, in an interview published in the January 8, 1989 *Washington Post*, a Colombian attorney named Mario Arango claimed that narcotics trafficking has led to an egalitarian "social revolution." Arango further stated,

> [W]ith narcotics, the mestizos, mulattoes, and blacks...have had the opportunities to enter consumer society and gain substantial wealth. The best vehicles that are driven in the city of Medellin are in the hands of people who have black or dark skins....I consider the drug trade to be the support for a country in crisis. This explains the contradictions in the establishment, which on the one hand denounces it and on the other hand lives with it and benefits from it.

The Terrorist/Insurgent Link to Drug Trafficking

By definition, a distinction exists between the motivations of organized crime groups and the motives of terrorist groups. Organized crime is generally associated with a profit motive and terrorist groups with more political motives, but certain financial gain is necessary for the achievement of political ends. Since the early 1970s, the drug trade has fostered a marriage of the two motivations, as we have observed in studying the political climate in such countries as Jamaica, Colombia, and Burma. Some examples of this type of criminal activity will be discussed in greater detail in this section.

Terrorism and the drug trade are parallel "businesses" that tend to interact in a synergistic fashion. That is, both rely on international infrastructures that extend largely underground and can be shared to achieve mutual benefit. For the terrorist, the drug business provides the cash with which to purchase weapons and finance clandestine operations. The drug trafficker, on the other hand, uses terrorist methods to protect sources of supply and the internal discipline and integrity of his organization. In either case, the result is the disruption of an organized and lawful society through methods of violence that are used outside the norms of international diplomacy and war.

In the 1970s, many terrorist groups began, either directly or indirectly, to generate funds through drug-related activities. This trend is especially prevalent in drug source countries (see Chapter 4). As of the preparation of this text, however, no domestic drug/terrorist groups have been identified.

The Colombia/Panama/Cuba Connection

The use of terrorist tactics in the drug trade is becoming more and more evident in Colombia. In an attempt to halt the extradition of traffickers, many Colombian traffickers have resorted to threats against the government of Colombia and the presence of the DEA there. Many of these threats come from members of the Medellin Cartel, who produce most of the world's cocaine. Cartel member Carlos Lehder, now imprisoned in the United States, stated in 1985 that if the extradition of Colombians were not stopped, he would have 500 Americans killed. Lehder boasted of his contacts with the M-19 as well as elements of the police and army. In addition, Lehder has long-standing connections with international right-wing and neo-Nazi terrorist organizations.

Traffickers have not hesitated to follow up on their threats with violence. In November of 1984, a car bomb exploded outside the fence of the American Embassy in Bogotá, killing one Colombian woman. In January of 1985, a bomb exploded at the Meyer Institute, a language school in Bogotá, owned by a U.S. citizen; three Colombians were injured.

Other examples include: on March 16, 1985, six men traveling in a jeep fired on the Spanish Chancery in Bogotá. This was reportedly in retaliation for the incarceration in Spain of major Colombian cocaine violators whom the United States was seeking to extradite. In late April 1985, an influential Colombian judge was gunned down, the eighth killed that year. As of January 1988, the total had grown to 57 judges and two cabinet members that had been assassinated by suspected drug traffickers in Colombia (DEA, 1985).

To illustrate the magnitude of the terrorist situation in Central and South America, there have been revealing examples of terrorist links to the drug trade in countries such as Colombia, Cuba, Panama, and Burma. As a case in point, Jose Blandon Castillo, a former intelligence aide to Panama's now-deposed dictator Manuel Noriega, provided testimony before the U.S. Senate Foreign Relations Subcommittee in January, 1988. This testimony enabled U.S. prosecutors in Miami to indict Noriega for his involvement in the drug trade (see Chapter 6). In addition, Blandon's testimony also shed light on previous evidence of Cuba's role in the trafficking of drugs to the United States.

Specifically, Blandon had testified that Fidel Castro had orchestrated a system where drugs and arms were trafficked between Central/South America and the United States. His testimony asserted that Castro had a theory, which was: "If you want to have influence in Colombia's political world, then you need influence in the drug trafficking world, too."

Blandon's testimony further described the joint ventures of Noriega, Castro, the Colombian M-19 (discussed next), and the notorious Medellin Cartel in overseeing drug shipments from Colombia to Cuba and on to the United States, as well as the laundering of drug money in Panama and the provision of arms to Marxist-Leninist rebels in Central America. This scheme, according to Blandon, also included participation by Nicaraguan rebels that were supposedly paid in cash for their role in the drug trafficking scheme.

CASE STUDY: LOS DIAMANTES

This Houston, Texas OCDETF investigation offers a quick glimpse of the "Colombian invasion"—following cartel cocaine, cartel employees move into U.S. assignments as wholesalers, money launderers, and street dealers. This conspiracy came to the attention of federal authorities when two Special Agents of an IRS Money Laundering Task Force observed Mario Restrepo in an area frequented by known traffickers and money launderers. The agents followed Restrepo and discovered two residences in southwest Houston that were the hub of a great deal of vehicular and pedestrian activity. The agents stopped an approaching trash truck and arranged with the driver to pick up the garbage outside the houses and give it to them. They quickly set up a 24-hour surveillance and headed for the office with the trash.

In the bags was perfect evidence of a large-scale cocaine distribution and money laundering operation: money wrappers and rubber bands, a duffel bag, and ledger pages recording multi-kilo cocaine transactions. A "drug detection dog" from U.S. Customs responded positively to cocaine residue on the papers. Over the next few days, the surveillance identified additional suspects. By the end of the week, based on the "garbage," search warrants were obtained for the two homes and for four other locations. The searches produced more than $1.3 million in United States currency, 55 kilograms of cocaine, cellular phones and digital pagers, and the current books and records of the drug distribution/money laundering operation. Seven persons were arrested, including Carlos Mancado-Rua, who was wanted by Houston police on a murder charge. A federal grand jury originally indicted seven persons for these offenses; all but one were Colombian citizens. Two teenage boys were later dismissed from the indictment as required by law, and federal juvenile proceedings were commenced against them. Ultimately, the boys were adjudicated delinquents and deported to Colombia. Four of the five remaining defendants entered guilty pleas to drug or money laundering offenses.

A jury trial was conducted for the remaining defendant, Mario Restrepo. During the course of the trial, one cooperating defendant testified for the government and gave the jury a rare insight into that portion of the Pablo Escobar cocaine cartel operating on American soil. The defendant testified how large quantities of cocaine are stored in local stash houses for eventual distribution in Houston as well as New York. He explained that certain members of the conspiracy would actually distribute cocaine, while others were responsible for the receipt of cash and maintaining the accounts receivable books.

It was testified that the local boss of this operation was a Colombian named Samuel Posada Rios Lemonada, or, familiarly, "Lemonada." Lemonada returned to Colombia in August 1988, when his picture appeared on Houston television in the context of a murder investigation. In Lemonada's absence, a 400-kilogram load of cocaine was delivered by a group of traffickers formerly employed by him. The group consisted of the five indicted adults and the 15- and the 17-year-old juveniles.

Between August 9 and September 9, 1988, the group distributed 260 kilograms of cocaine around Houston and drove 140 kilos to New York City. Each and every kilo package bore the name "DIAMANTE," the trademark pf Pablo Escobar of Medellin, Colombia. During the same time period, the group collected more than a million dollars in payment for the cocaine.

In the course of this brief investigation, OCDETF mobilized agents of Customs, INS, DEA, and the Houston Police Department, in addition to the originating IRS team.

An FBI expert in illicit business records and documents testified that the drug records seized from the conspirators evidenced over $5 million in cocaine transactions; $1.5 million was still owed for parts of the last 400-kilo consignment. In addition to more than $1.3 million in cash, two houses, six vehicles, and a submachine gun were seized.

The jury convicted Mario Restrepo on all counts. All defendants forfeited their interest in the houses, cars, money, and electronic communications equipment. Restrepo and his four co-conspirators will be sentenced on April 14, 1989. From his safe retreat in Medellin, Lemonada presumably continues to command markets in Houston through Colombian contacts living there.

Source: Organized Crime Drug Enforcement Task Force, 1988

...terrorism and the drug trade are parallel "businesses" that tend to interact in a synergistic fashion...

Colombia, with one of the most skewed patterns of income distribution in Latin America, has been plagued for decades by increasingly violent guerrilla warfare. All in all, there are some 12,000 to 15,000 guerrilla combatants currently active in Colombia. Two such guerrilla groups most commonly associated with the cocaine and marijuana trade in Colombia during the last 15 years are the *Revolutionary Armed Forces of Colombia*, commonly known as the *FARC*, and the *19th of April Movement*, which is also known as the *M-19* (named after the date on which they were formed). The FARC, the oldest Marxist guerrilla organization in the hemisphere, is also the largest and best-equipped insurgent group in Colombia, and is the armed wing of the Colombian communist party. The Drug Enforcement Administration estimated in 1985 that the FARC operated through approximately 25 fronts, most of which are in coca- and cannabis-growing regions in Colombia. The FARC has some involvement in the cultivation of the coca leaf but primarily acts as a protection organization guarding hidden airstrips and growing areas for drug traffickers.

> In March of 1984, Colombian authorities raided a group of cocaine laboratories in the Tranquilandia area and seized 10 tons of cocaine base. While landing at the clandestine airstrip, the authorities engaged in a firefight with approximately 30 people in fatigue-type uniforms. These people are believed to be members of the FARC. Source: DEA, 1985

According to an article published in the Miami Herald in 1983, the Drug Enforcement Administration had documented Castro's regime as using a Colombian drug ring to funnel arms and funds to the non-Marxist M-19 guerrillas since 1980. The drug ring referred to in the report was allegedly led by a Colombian, Jamie Guillot Lara. He subsequently disappeared and was reported killed in an airplane crash in 1983.

> The M-19 has gained a reputation for extorting money from drug growers and traffickers in cultivation areas. Investigations have revealed that the M-19 has been the recipient of arms from Cuba through the smuggling network of Colombian trafficker Jamie Guillot-Lara.

Guillot had an arrangement with several high-level officials of the Cuban government. The Cubans provided a safe haven for Guillot's drug smuggling vessels from Colombia destined for the United States. In return, Guillot agreed to pay the Cubans for this facilitation.

Guillot also assisted the Cubans by using his ships to smuggle arms to the M-19 in Colombia. In November of 1981, a large quantity of weapons was offloaded from one of Guillot's ships, the Karina, onto another Guillot ship, the Monarca. Shortly thereafter, the Colombian navy sank the Karina; the ship went down down with an estimated 100 tons of weapons on board. Ten days later, Colombian authorities seized the Monarca after it had successfully delivered its weapons cargo to the M-19 (DEA, 1985).

Figure 9.4

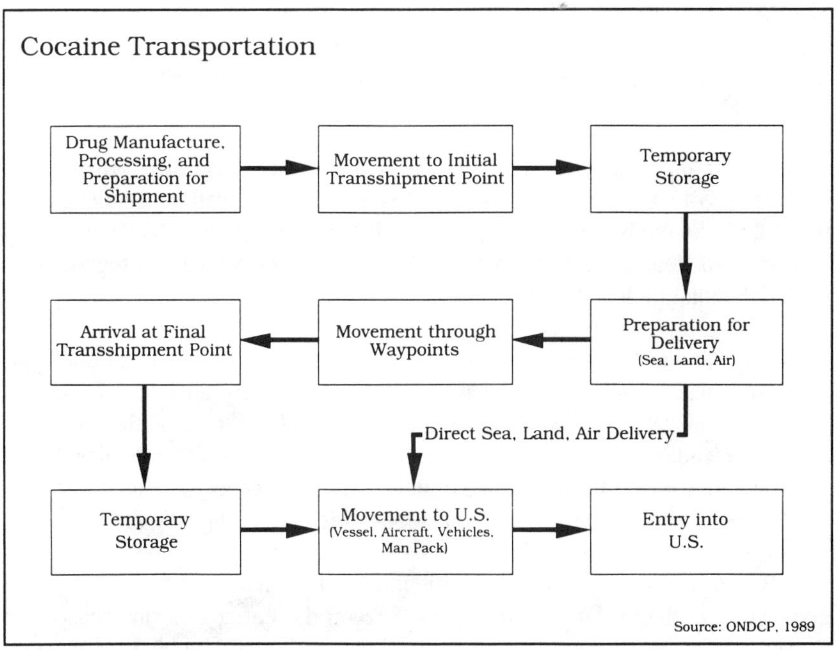

Cocaine Transportation

Drug Manufacture, Processing, and Preparation for Shipment → Movement to Initial Transshipment Point → Temporary Storage

Arrival at Final Transshipment Point ← Movement through Waypoints ← Preparation for Delivery (Sea, Land, Air)

Direct Sea, Land, Air Delivery

Temporary Storage → Movement to U.S. (Vessel, Aircraft, Vehicles, Man Pack) → Entry into U.S.

Source: ONDCP, 1989

The Nicaraguan Connection

According to the Justice Department, there is abundant evidence which indicates that Castro lost little time after the consolidation of the Sandinista regime in Managua to harness his Nicaraguan allies to drug trafficking operations. Antonio Farach, a former minister in the post-revolution Nicaraguan government, testified that he first learned of Nicaragua's involvement in the illicit drug trade during a visit by Raul Castro to Managua in 1981. According to Farach, the purpose for the Cuban Defense Minister's visit was to establish a narcotics infrastructure "for the Nicaraguan revolution" with Cuba's help. When questioned about this, Farach was told by Nicaraguan officials of two moral and political justifications for their state-sponsored drug trafficking:

> In the first place, drugs did not remain in Nicaragua; the drugs were destined for the United States. Our youth would not be harmed, but rather the youth of our enemies. Therefore, the drugs were used as a political weapon, because in that way we were delivering a blow to our principal enemy. In addition to a political weapon against the United States, the drug trafficking produced a very good economic benefit, which we needed for our revolution. We wanted to provide food to our people with the suffering and death of the youth of the United States.

Farach also testified to the personal involvement in the drug offensive of Humberto Ortega, President Daniel Ortega's brother, as well as Tomas Borge, the veteran Sandinista and Minister of the Interior. On March 16, 1986, President Ronald Reagan, in his televised accusation of the Sandinista regime, displayed a photograph and asserted:

> The Sandinistas have been involved themselves in the international drug trade. This picture, secretly taken at a military airfield outside Managua, shows Frederico Vaughn, a top aide to one of the nine commandantes that rule Nicaragua, leaving an aircraft with illegal narcotics bound for the United States. No, there seems to be no crime to which the Sandinistas will not stoop—this is an outlaw regime.

But once again, we can clearly see the confused nature of the politics/drug connection in the president's statement. Several days after Reagan accused the Sandinistas of involvement in cocaine trafficking, the DEA publicly repudiated the charge, stating that no such evidence existed. This led to an embarrassing expose of an attempt by White House operatives to portray the Nicaraguan government of criminal involvement through the activities of well- known drug smuggler Barry Seal. Seale, as discussed in Chapter 10, had been arrested for drug trafficking and had negotiated a plea bargain with the Justice Department. As part of the deal, Seal was to contract for a load of cocaine in Colombia, and then, while transshipping it to the United States, land in Nicaragua under the guise of having engine trouble, photograph the cocaine offloaded and subsequently reloaded on to his plane in Managua, and thereby provide "proof" of a Sandinista-Colombia connection. Unfortunately, the camera provided to Seal by the CIA failed to work and the photographs he subsequently took, which were hand-exposed, were of such a poor quality as to be virtually useless.

The Barry Seal incident was one of several events that led to congressional inquires into the role of the United States-backed contras, with the assistance of United States intelligence agencies and the National Security Council, in cocaine trafficking. Subsequent testimony indicated that both the contras and their intelligence community handlers were heavily involved in cocaine trafficking. For example:

- Several major cocaine seizures were made that directly tied the contras to cocaine smuggling, inc 'iding the infamous "Frogman Case" in San Francisco (the largest west coast cocaine bust up to that time).

- Colombian cocaine traffickers routinely used contra bases in Costa Rica for the refueling of planes and the transshipment of cocaine to the United States.

- Several pilots testified that they regularly flew loads of cocaine to the United States on behalf of the contras in a drugs-for-guns scheme.

- A U.S. Senate inquiry uncovered evidence of regular payoffs to the contras from Medellin Cartel members through El Salvador.

- Direct U.S. government payments to drug traffickers through the State Department's Nicaraguan Humanitarian Aid Organization were uncovered during congressional investigations.

Other Terrorist/Insurgent Groups

The cocaine industry in Peru has produced a large and extremely influential drug trafficking terrorist group called "*Sendero Luminoso*," or the "*Shining Path*." The organization allegedly controls the upper Huallaga Valley, a region that produces over 60 percent of the world's coca.

The group was founded around 1970 by Abimael Guzm'an (known by followers as "Presidente Gonzalo"), a professor of Marxist philosophy at the University of Huamanga in Ayacucho who embraced Maoism during several visits to China. "Guzm'an today is known to his followers as the Fourth Sword of International Communism. The ideology of the Shining Path is `Marxism-Leninism-Maoism, Gonzalo Thought.' The comma is important as it says that Gonzalo's ideas are still in formation and that they are also the fullest, most scientific, most modern development of Communist ideology." (Robbins, 1989).
According to the President's Commission on Organized Crime:

The Shining Path seeks a rural-based revolution to rid the predominantly peasant population of the "imperialistic" influences of the United States and other foreign governments. While existing evidence is insufficient to link the Shining Path to the drug trade, the group has incited peasants, many of whom make their living from coca cultivation, to rebel against anti-coca projects in major growing areas. During 1984, several anti-coca projects, including a United States-supported crop substitution program, were attacked by armed mobs, resulting in many injuries.

Shining Path tactics include converging on a town for the purpose of driving out or murdering local officials and imposing a puritanical new order. This is accomplished by holding "people's trials" and by redistributing livestock and land. Although many believe that Sendero's activities seem unorganized and random, many assert that they are systematically tearing down the structures of authority by removing influential and wealthy citizens from communities.
One of the authors has spoken with DEA officials, who have suggested that the Shining Path is also responsible for numerous violent murders of police officers and high-ranking government officials in Peru in an effort to deter government interference in drug trafficking operations. A case in point is the January 1990 assassination of Peru's former Defense Minister Enrique Lopez Albujar, which was attributed to the Shining Path. According to DEA sources, the methods of operation used by the Shining Path parallel the guerrilla tactics used by the North Vietnamese during the Vietnam conflict. Experts that have studied the Shining Path fear that their level of violence and number of victims will soar greatly in the near future.
Halfway around the world in Burma, the Burmese Communist Party (BCP) has been attempting to exert its control over the Shan state since 1948, when Burma became independent from the British. The Shan state is the primary opium poppy cultivation area in the Golden Triangle, adjoining Laos and Thailand. For years the BCP was involved, to some degree, in extorting tax money from opium farmers in the region. After expanding its operations in the late

1970s, the BCP now controls its own heroin refineries and controls most of the opium grown in the Northern Shan state.

In the 1960s and 1970s, the Shan United Army (SUA) was an insurgent group fighting for the independence of the Shan state. The SUA now focuses on manufacturing heroin, heroin base, and morphine base, and from the smuggling of heroin generate profits to finance its insurgency. To illustrate the volatility of the SUA, members have threatened to kidnap three DEA agents and hold them for $3 million in ransom. Because of the immense profit potential of the heroin trade, the SUA represents a clear example of an insurgent group that has traded its political zeal for the allure of drug profits.

The head of the SUA is Khun Sa, originally named Chang Chi-fu after his Chinese father. He was born in 1933 and, although he never progressed beyond elementary school, he formed his own army out of the remnants of a local militia originally organized by the Burmese government to fight communist insurgents. It is estimated that Khun Sa now commands an army exceeding some 15,000 soldiers whose primary mission is to protect the drug trafficking operations of Khun Sa.

Illustrating the arrogance of Khun Sa is his standing offer to the United States government to phase himself out of the heroin business in exchange for $300 million annually over a period of eight years. Washington has been rejecting this offer since it originated in 1977, not just because drug enforcement officials are understandably skeptical about Khun Sa's sincerity, but because of obvious moral and ethical grounds.

Cuban Drug Traffickers

Since 1959, over one million Cuban refugees have arrived in the United States. Although many have come seeking political freedom, a significant percentage of Cuban immigrants have been documented as having close involvement in drug trafficking operations. There have been three periods of mass Cuban immigration to the United States. These are as follows:

1. before and after the fall of the Batista regime until Fidel Castro halted emigration in 1959,

2. between 1965 and 1972, during the Camarioca boatlift "freedom flotilla," prompting the family reunification program under which more than 250,000 Cubans migrated to the United States,

3. between April 21 and November 10, 1980, during a boatlift from Mariel Harbor, bringing nearly 125,000 new Cuban refugees to the United States

Unquestionably, the greatest concentration of criminals was in the Mariel
Harbor exodus, with nearly 2 percent of those arriving in the United States having been classified as prostitutes, criminals, drug addicts, or vagrants. The minority of these Cuban immigrants was soon given the name "marielito," meaning criminal or undesirable.

The Mariel boatlift had its genesis on April 1, 1980, when a small band
of Cubans in a city bus attempted to gain political asylum by crashing
the gates of the Peruvian Embassy. One Cuban guard at the gate ac-
cidently killed another guard while trying to stop the bus. Fidel Castro
was enraged and publicly announced the removal of all guards from
the gates. Within days over 10,000 people had crowded into the embassy grounds, requesting political asylum. Eventually Castro allowed
them to be flown out of the country. This group and the majority of
those that followed later included primarily decent and working-class
people that genuinely sought liberty. Castro, however, proclaimed the
refugees to be the scum of Cuban society. When the exodus continued, he tried to prove his description by forcibly including convicts,
hard-core criminals, prostitutes, and the mentally ill among those that
left by boat from Mariel.

Source: PCOC, April, 1986

The sophistication and organizational structure of the criminals that immi-
grated during the first two boatlifts was greater than those that came over on the
Mariel boatlift. In particular, many of the earlier Cuban immigrants had ties
with more traditional and well-established criminal organizations in the United
States, particularly gambling and drug operations associated with Meyer Lansky
and Santo Trafficante, Jr. In addition, many of the early Cuban refugees partici-
pated in United States government-supported paramilitary and intelligence operations directed against the Castro government. As a result, they were given considerable training in intelligence techniques (including smuggling) by the C.I.A.,
and, provided with considerable financial and logistical support. When United
States support for these activities ended in the 1960s, many of these immigrants
had no lawful trade to fall back on and initiated organized crime activities to
support themselves. The Marielitos, on the other hand, demonstrated a great
propensity for violence.

During the 1960s, two major Cuban groups became well established in the
United States: *La Compañía*, a well-known drug trafficking organization concentrating primarily on cocaine trafficking, and *The Corporation*, headed by

Jose Miguel Battle. This group is also well established but concentrates primarily on gambling operations.

The Marielitos have been documented as joining established crime organizations such as La Compañía working as collectors and enforcers. They have also been associated with Colombian cartels in the same capacity. Although there is some debate over the exact number of Marielitos that were part of the Mariel boatlift, there have been widespread reports of violent Marielito activity in such cities as Miami, New York, Las Vegas, and Los Angeles.

Asian Organized Crime

Yet another type of organized crime emerging in the drug trade is Asian gangs. Chinese gangs in particular have demonstrated considerable growth in drug trafficking activities. From 1970 to 1980, for example, the number of Chinese in the United States escalated from 435,062 to 806,027. This increase in population might also reflect the fact that Chinese traffickers are becoming more proficient in their smuggling of southeast Asian heroin to the United States. In 1988, DEA reported that in New York, heroin from southeast Asia rose from 3 percent to 40 percent of the total supply in that city.

Chinese organized crime (COC) primarily involves two well-established organizations, the *Tongs* and the *Triads*. Although criminal activity by these two groups marks a relatively new presence in the United States, it represents a degeneration of several much older and secret societies in China.

The Triads, predominantly based in Hong Kong, began in the seventeenth century as an opposing force to China's ruling Manchu government. The Tongs, on the other hand, originated in the nineteenth century as legitimate mutual aid societies that were in the United States to assist immigrant Chinese railroad workers.

Triads and Tongs are both characterized by devotion to members of the organization and by acts of violent retribution against those that reveal its secrets to outsiders. This can be compared to the code of silence believed to be practiced by other groups such as La Cosa Nostra. Since the mid-1960s, three incidents have had particular impact on the growth of Asian organized crime in America:

1. the liberalization of quotas of Asian immigrants in 1965...

2. the ending of the Vietnam conflict...

3. the agreement between the United Kingdom and the People's Republic of China which determined that Hong Kong will revert to the Chinese in 1997, after more than 150 years of colonial rule by the British.

The third event listed above may very well be the cause of Chinese organized crime groups moving to the United States in great numbers. It is estimated that there are as many as 100,000 Triad members belonging to more than 50 Triads in Hong Kong. The primary Triads are organized into five groups, of which the Wo group and the 14K are the largest. In Taiwan, the United Bamboo Gang claims 1,200 members, and the Four Seasons Gang has 3,000 members. Among the Triads known to have active U.S. connections are the Sun Yee On, 14K, Wo Hop To, Wo On Lok, and Leun Kung Lok.

A much greater threat than that of the Triads is represented by the highly structured, Asian street gangs. The Wah Ching is the most sophisticated Chinese criminal organization that operates on the west coast. It boasts some 600 to 700 members. Like the Triads, there is also a highly organized command structure. In New York, Chinese street gangs are affiliated with the Tongs and incorporate the positions of co-presidents, executive officers, and staff.

Drug trafficking by COC does not yet parallel that of the cartels but the scope of their influence is noteworthy, nonetheless. Working with Asian nationals, Chinese-American criminals are the largest importers of southeast Asian heroin, which originates in the Golden Triangle. This was evidenced by a 1989 seizure of more than 800 pounds of processed heroin in New York's Chinatown.

...a much greater threat than that of the Triads is represented by the highly structured Asian street gangs...

Most Golden Triangle heroin is shipped to the west coast of the United States via Hong Kong and through secondary transit points such as Singapore, Seoul, Tokyo, and Taipei. Chinese criminal organizations operate mainly as shippers and wholesalers, that is, they are active in buying the raw product, processing it, arranging for its transshipment, and finally, turning it over to retailers.

Summary

Illicit drugs in the United States finance drug trafficking organizations with both domestic and foreign origin. The Colombian cartels, one of the more visible modern-day drug trafficking organizations, have achieved a certain notoriety for their role in the cocaine business. Of the four major cartels discussed, the Medellin Cartel has emerged as one of the most powerful and influential in the drug trade. It is not considered to be as vertically integrated as other United

States criminal groups because its members do not deal in drugs on the retail level, but it is known to control most of the world's cocaine manufacturing and wholesale business. The Colombian cartels have also gained a reputation for violence and are known for their ability to corrupt political and governmental authorities in pursuit of their goals.

Drugs have also attracted the participation of terrorist and insurgent groups in the cocaine trade, such as the Colombia's M-19 and the Sendero Luminoso organization of Peru. Such groups have been documented as operating in Latin American countries and exerting influence over significant portions of the drug trade. The existence of such groups is fueled by unstable governments and economies of many source countries. The influence of these types of terrorist organizations reach other Latin American countries as well, such as Bolivia, Panama, and Cuba.

Similarly motivated groups exist in southeast and southwest Asian drug-producing countries. For example, in Burma, the Shan United Army (SUA) exerts influence through terrorist activities and is able to control a significant portion of the heroin trade in the Golden Triangle. The SUA is headed by Khun Sa and reportedly has over 15,000 soldiers that are charged with protecting the trafficking operations of the organization.

Other Asian criminal organizations such as the Chinese Triads and Tongs operate both in the United States and Hong Kong and also are very active in the illicit drug trade. With the increase in Asian nationals in the United States, the ranks of the Chinese Tongs are growing in cities such as Los Angeles and New York, to name only a few.

DISCUSSION QUESTIONS

1. List the various foreign organized crime groups that are considered the greatest contributors to the U.S. drug abuse problem. Specify the dangerous drugs with which each organization is most likely to be involved.

2. What role does the Medellin Cartel play in the illicit global drug trade?

3. Why has the Medellin Cartel gained distinction over other cocaine trafficking groups?

4. Describe the cocaine manufacturing process, including the various steps necessary to distribute the drug in the United States.

5. Discuss the four main Colombian cartels and their relationship to each other.

6. Which foreign criminal organizations are the most active in the trafficking of marijuana to the United States?

7. Identify and discuss the link between the FARC and the M-19 (insurgent groups in Colombia) and drug traffickers.

8. Some claim that there is a link between the United States government and certain drug trafficking organizations. What are their concerns?

9. Discuss the interplay between drug trafficking and insurgent terrorists.

10. What is Nicaragua's suspected involvement in the international drug trade?

11. Discuss the roles that former Panamanian leader Manuel Noriega and Cuba's Fidel Castro allegedly played in international drug trafficking.

12. What relationship do the Medellin Cartel and M-19 share?

13. Discuss the insurgent organization known as the FARC, and define its role in the Colombian political arena.

14. Peru's Shining Path is another terrorist-related drug trafficking organization. Discuss its connection with the cocaine trade and global drug trafficking.

15. Historically, what three events played the most significant roles in Cuban immigration into the United States?

16. Discuss the extent to which the Shan United Army (SUA) participates in illicit opium and heroin production in southeast Asia?

17. Explain the expanding role of the Chinese Triads and Tongs in the illicit drug trade.

PART III

FIGHTING BACK

Experts in drug control are constantly considering new ways to control drug abuse and crime. To this end, questions are sometimes raised: do the police have enough enforcement authority to adequately deal with the drug problem? Do they have too much? Is the government spending enough on the drug war? If law enforcement efforts are failing, what should be considered as an alternative?

The remaining five chapters of this book will attempt to deal with these questions and more, by addressing both the government's and the public's responses to the nation's drug abuse dilemma.

CHAPTER 10

THE DRUG CONTROL INITIATIVE

Many controversial and vital issues must be considered when designing drug control strategies. A paradox of sorts becomes evident when we see, for instance: one interest group demanding that law enforcement be given more police authority with which to perform their drug control duties, while at the same time, others protest that expanding the roles of government authority decreases the constitutional and personal freedoms of individuals.

Controlling dangerous drugs involves a profusion of tasks that are sometimes contradictory; these include reducing the overall demand for drugs, reducing both the international and domestic supply of drugs, controlling organized crime, minimizing the spreading of dangerous diseases (such as AIDS) through intravenous drug use, using nontraditional drug enforcement tactics such as reverse stings and criminal profiling, and minimizing the use of dangerous drugs in professional and amateur sports. These issues will be discussed later in this section, but let us first examine the role of the federal government in illicit drug suppression.

A virtual alphabet soup of federal law enforcement agencies are charged, in one fashion or another, with the task of domestic and/or international drug enforcement. The agencies charged with drug enforcement responsibilities include the Drug Enforcement Administration (DEA), the Federal Bureau of Investigation (FBI), the Customs Service, the Coast Guard, and the Immigration and Naturalization Service (the Border Patrol). In addition, a wide variety of other federal agencies, totaling 32, have been organized to coordinate certain aspects of drug enforcement activities.

Because of the bureaucratic fragmentation of federal law enforcement agencies charged with drug enforcement, the exchange of information as well as coordination and cooperation between agencies is often problematic and difficult to achieve. Discussed next is a broad characterization of the primary drug enforcement agencies and the specific roles that they play in the overall federal drug-control strategy.

The History of Federal Drug Enforcement

Alcohol prohibition marked the first legal recognition of problems emanating from substance abuse. The enforcement mechanism for the National Prohibition Act was placed under the Commissioner of Internal Revenue. "Because it seemed logical to place responsibility for enforcement of the Harrison Act within this prohibition unit, a narcotics unit was created" (PCOC). The narcotics unit originally employed 170 agents and had an appropriation of one-quarter million dollars. The Narcotics Unit operated between 1919 and 1927. By 1927, all powers of drug enforcement were transferred to the Secretary of the Treasury.

During the years of the Narcotics Unit's operation, the general public associated narcotics enforcement with the none-too-popular liquor enforcement efforts of the era. Additionally, scandals tarnished the image of narcotics agents when some agents were found to be falsifying arrest records and accepting payoffs from drug dealers. In response, Congress moved the responsibility of narcotics enforcement to the newly created *Federal Bureau of Narcotics (FBN)* in 1930. It was after the creation of the FBN that the term "narcotics agent" was generally adopted to refer to FBN drug enforcement personnel.

For the next 35 years, the mission of federal drug enforcement remained somewhat consistent. Through the mid-1960s, the federal government's drug suppression efforts were primarily directed toward the illegal importation of drugs into the country. The authority of the FBN was expanded in 1956 with the passing of the Narcotics Control Act, which, among other things, authorized narcotics agents to carry firearms and granted them authority to serve both search and arrest warrants.

In 1965, the Drug Abuse Control Amendments (to the 1956 NCA) were passed. These addressed the problem of drugs in the depressant and stimulant category being diverted from legal channels. In 1966, another agency was created to enforce the Amendments the *Bureau of Drug Abuse Control (BDAC)* within the Health, Education and Welfare Department's Food and Drug Administration (FDA).

Another advance in drug enforcement occurred during 1966: a study conducted by the Katzenbach Commission. The study concluded with the following recommendations to reduce both the supply and demand of drugs:

1.   Substantially increase the enforcement staffs of FBN and the Bureau of Customs;

2.   Permit courts and correctional authorities to deal flexibly with violators of the drug laws;

3. Undertake research to develop a sound and effective framework of regulatory and criminal laws relating to dangerous drugs;
4. Develop within the National Institute of Mental Health a core of educational and informational materials relating to drugs.

In 1968, for the first time in history, the Department of Justice was given authority for the enforcement of federal drug laws. With this authority, the FBN and the BDAC were abolished and enforcement responsibility was passed to the newly created *Bureau of Narcotics and Dangerous Drugs (BNDD)*. This was done to eliminate friction between enforcement agencies and to minimize bureaucratic fragmentation within the federal government's drug enforcement effort.

To assist state and local drug enforcement agencies, the *Office for Drug Abuse and Law Enforcement (ODALE)* was established in 1972. Several months after ODALE was created, the *Office of National Narcotic Intelligence (ONNI)* was created. This was to serve as a clearinghouse for any information considered useful in the Administration's antidrug initiative. ONNI was also charged with disseminating information to state and local law enforcement agencies for which there was a demonstrated "legitimate official need."

In 1973, President Richard Nixon implemented a drug enforcement reorganization plan that addressed the supply side of drug abuse as well as the demand component of the problem. One of the most important directives of the plan was the creation of the *Drug Enforcement Administration (DEA)* within the Department of Justice. Under the plan, the Administrator of the DEA would report directly to the Attorney General and would assume all manpower and budgets of the BNDD, ODALE, and ONNI.

As of the writing of this text, the drug enforcement agencies discussed below are those agencies responsible for drug control on the national level.

The Drug Enforcement Administration (DEA)

As previously mentioned, the DEA, established in 1973, was declared the lead agency in the federal government's efforts to suppress the illicit drug trade. Acting under the Justice Department, the DEA is the only federal law enforcement agency that has drug enforcement as its only responsibility. The DEA has primary responsibility for investigating drug-related events and operations for collecting and disseminating drug-related intelligence information and for securing cooperation and coordination between federal, state, and local law enforcement agencies also involved in the drug suppression effort.

Figure 10.1
A Genealogy of DEA's Predecessor Organizations

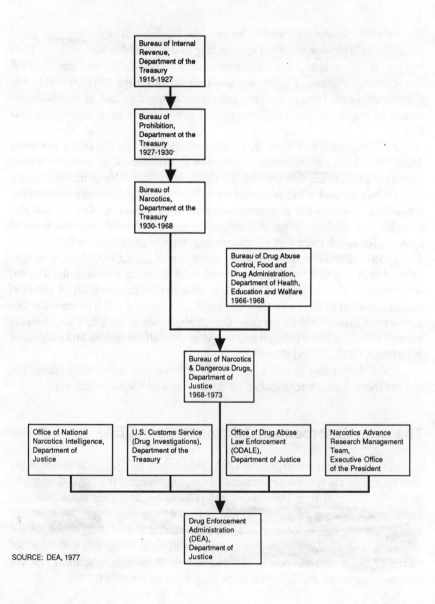

Bureau of Internal
Revenue,
Department of the
Treasury
1915-1927

Bureau of
Prohibition,
Department ot the
Treasury
1927-1930

Bureau of
Narcotics,
Department ot the
Treasury
1930-1968

Bureau of Drug Abuse
Control, Food and
Drug Administration,
Department of Health,
Education and Welfare
1966-1968

Bureau of Narcotics
& Dangerous Drugs,
Department of
Justice
1968-1973

Office of National
Narcotics Intelligence,
Department of
Justice

U.S. Customs Service
(Drug Investigations),
Department of the
Treasury

Office of Drug Abuse
Law Enforcement
(ODALE),
Department of Justice

Narcotics Advance
Research Management
Team,
Executive Office
of the President

Drug Enforcement
Administration
(DEA),
Department of
Justice

SOURCE: DEA, 1977

The dominant philosophy of the DEA is to eliminate drugs as close as possible to their source and to disrupt the drug trafficking system by identifying, arresting, and prosecuting traffickers. In furtherance of this philosophy, drug shipments are sometimes permitted to enter the United States while under close surveillance by agents. Once the shipment is delivered, agents can arrest traffickers and, hopefully, leaders of the drug smuggling organizations. The DEA philosophy, focusing on investigation and conviction, conflicts with the mission of other agencies, such as the U.S. Customs Service, that are charged with interdiction of drugs as soon as they enter the United States. Interagency rivalries are therefore created that tend to hamper the overall effectiveness of the federal drug enforcement initiative.

DEA's mission is both domestic and foreign with a total of over 2,400 special agents and intelligence analysts located throughout the United States and in 42 other countries. Agents stationed in foreign countries possess no arrest powers and act primarily as liaisons with the host law enforcement agencies.

DEA agents and analysts provide information about general trends in drug trafficking as well as specific information regarding the actions of drug criminals. The information collection process begins in drug source countries and includes analysis of drug production (illicit farming operations and laboratories) and transportation methods (smuggling) used by traffickers.

Intelligence collected by DEA is a major source of information about drugs in transit and is also shared with other law enforcement agencies. Through the DEA's intelligence center, the El Paso Intelligence Center (EPIC), intelligence is collected, analyzed, and disseminated from all enforcement agencies.

During recent years, DEA's budget and work force have burgeoned. For example, in 1982 DEA employed 1,849 agents with a budget of $242 million. In 1990, the number of agent personnel ascended to 2,958 with an increased budget of $549 million. As of the preparation of this book, a request has been made for the year 1991 for 500 additional agents with an increased budget totaling $700 million. Although supporters of the federal drug enforcement initiative claim that the greater numbers of agent personnel account for the rising number of arrests and seizures, detractors of federal drug policy claim that this is not the way to proceed.

In 1990, for example, John Lawn resigned his post as DEA administrator and conceded that "the DEA has been unable to keep pace with the major drug trafficking organizations in operations today" (Witkin, 1990). Consequently, many analysts assert that the best way to confront the drug problem is to analyze systematically every aspect of how major drug trafficking organizations operate and then attack the choke points, as opposed to mounting an all-out effort on "every front." In short, the suggestion is to make better use of analysis and linking of raw intelligence information.

CLOSE-UP:
NARCS RISK THEIR LIVES DAILY TO BATTLE DRUG SCOURGE

Washington - In a land crippled by drugs and terrorized by dealers, U.S. citizens have only the police standing between them and armed street punks. Narcotics officers risk their lives daily in Beirut-like neighborhoods where crack is the biggest cash product and human life is the down payment. The enemy is without compassion. It is no exaggeration to say that many would just as soon kill a person as swat a fly.

Some of the drug fighters operate undercover and must remain nameless due to the constant danger of discovery. Many have been killed in action, and their stories can be told by only their survivors. A few can be recognized openly, like officer Robert Yzquierdo.

Because the drug scourge has spread from the inner cities to the smaller towns of this country, Yzquierdo went underground in Redlands, California. He grew his disguise—long black hair with a moustache and beard to match. He even pierced his ears for the right hint of recklessness.

Yzquierdo left his wife and two young sons safely in Texas while he posed 24 hours a day as a drug-dealing outlaw biker on the prowl in and around the redlands. He took on the look, the lingo, and the swagger of the biker.

A methamphetamine dealer high on his own product aimed a rifle at Yzquierdo and threatened to pull the trigger during a drug buy in a Yucaipa motel. Everyone in the room scrambled for safety except the target, Yzquierdo, who stood his ground and coolly talked the addict into putting the gun down.

Another time, Yzquierdo was riding with a dangerous drug dealer in a desolate area outside Mentone when the wary dealer drew a .38 revolver and accused Yzquierdo of being a narc. Again the officer talked his way out of a fix.

A heroin dealer tried to make Yzquierdo inject drugs as proof that he wasn't a cop. The officer put on another convincing performance and satisfied the dealer without injecting the drug. In his undercover role, Yzquierdo put his life on the line without the usual support of backup officers. Only ten people knew his true identity, and he was repeatedly rousted by the police.

All told, Yzquierdo spent nine harrowing months living by his wits before he cropped his long hair, shaved his beard and put on a police uniform. He had made more than 200 narcotics buys, which led to the arrest of 75 dealers. His experience was typical of the thousands of anonymous drugbusters that are fighting a guerrilla war against drug gangs.

They are quick to identify their number one enemy—not the street dealer with a gun, but the drug user whose money finances the killing. The drug-busters have another enemy—bureaucrats that squander the money that Congress has appropriated to combat drugs. That money is desperately needed by the combatants, who are short of people and firepower to battle the multi-billion-dollar cocaine cartels. But the bureaucrats keep much of the money to "study" the drug problem. Ask the officers on the street; they will tell you that they do not need another survey. They need weapons and numbers to match the dealers.

Source: Anderson, J. (1989). "Narcs Risk their Lives Daily to Battle Drug Scourge." *Columbia Daily Tribune* (May 23):6.

DEA's MIXED SUCCESSES

Although arrests and seizures have increased, the street purity has also risen, and prices have either gone down or stabilized. This signifies that the supply of drugs on American streets has gotten more plentiful.

Good news	1985	1989
Total arrests	15,709	25,618
Drug seizures	24,654.9 kg.	81,762.1 kg.

Bad news		
Retail purity (gm.)	50%-60%	65%
Wholesale price	$30,000	$11,000
(per kilogram)	$50,000	$35,000
Retail price (gm.)	$100	$35-$125

Note: Total arrests include those jailed for all illegal drug violations. Seizures, purity, and prices refer to cocaine only.
1 kilogram = 2.2046 lbs.; 1 gram = 1/28 oz.

Sources: Drug Enforcement Administration, National Narcotics Consumers Committee, 1990.

As with all statistical data, change is always possible. For example, as of July 1990, certain American cities have reported a considerable increase in retail prices of cocaine. For instance, in Los Angeles, the retail price of one kilogram of cocaine was $14,000 in June of 1989 compared to $30,000 in 1990. In New York, cocaine prices begin at $35,000 per kilogram in 1990 compared to $23,000 in 1989 (DEA, L.A. County Sheriff's Office, 1990). Data such as these affirm the notion that supplies of drugs are down and that, at least as of this writing, interdiction efforts are showing a certain degree of success.

The Federal Bureau of Investigation (FBI)

The FBI is the chief law enforcement arm of the federal government and a division of the Justice Department. In 1982, Attorney General William French Smith delegated to the FBI concurrent jurisdiction with DEA for the overall drug law enforcement effort. This was a major change in the FBI's normal jurisdiction, which had traditionally included all federal laws not specifically assigned to other enforcement agencies.

Since assuming these new drug enforcement responsibilities, the FBI has assigned over 1000 Special Agents to drug investigations. The primary impetus of the FBI's role in drug enforcement is the investigation of organized crime activity in the drug trade. These investigations include the investigation of specific trafficking organizations and individuals, as well as investigating illegal financial transactions pertaining to drug trafficking.

Both the DEA and FBI are responsible for enforcement of the Controlled Substances Act of 1970. The FBI, however, is more concerned with drug-related violations of such laws as the *Continuing Criminal Enterprise (CCE)* statute and the *Racketeer-Influenced and Corrupt Organizations (RICO)* law. Although the participation of the FBI in domestic drug enforcement benefits the overall goals and objectives of the federal effort, some degree of conflict, overlapping responsibilities, and confusion about jurisdiction between the DEA and FBI exists.

As an offshoot of the FBI's involvement in drug enforcement, the OCDETF task force concept was adopted in 1983. Through this joint law enforcement initiative, many high-level cases have been culminated (see section on OCDETF).

Interdiction Efforts

The process of interdicting drug smugglers is one of the primary focuses of United States drug control policy. Basically, it consists of five rather broad categories of activity: intelligence, command and control, surveillance, pursuit, and capture. The interdiction process addresses areas off the shore and within the 12-mile "Customs search" radius surrounding the United States, as well as all ports of entry.

The term interdiction *refers to efforts to intercept or to deter the shipment of illegal drugs (chiefly marijuana, heroin and cocaine) from foreign countries to the United States.*

In April 1990, the U.S. Air Force introduced a new long-range radar system that was originally designed to provide early warning of a Soviet attack. Its new application is to detect airborne drug smugglers. The system, located in Maine, consists of two gigantic antennas, each spreading more than two thirds of a mile and forming the first "over-the-horizon" capable of seeing 10 times farther than conventional systems—up to 1,800 miles.

The system is operated by bouncing signals off of the ionosphere, and a series of computer screens maps every plane flying over a 4-million-square-mile area of the Atlantic from Iceland to South America. In theory, the system will match the aircraft against known flight plans and air-traffic-control information, identifying suspected drug flights and scrambling U.S. Customs or Coast Guard pursuit planes. It is envisioned that additional pieces of the radar system will be constructed in California, Oregon, Idaho, and North Dakota by 1994.

Figure 10.2

Roles of Drug Interdiction Agencies

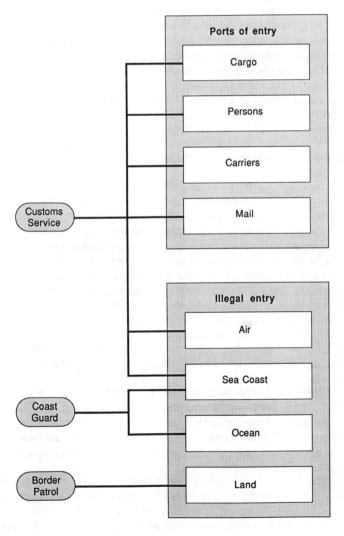

SOURCE: Office of Technology Assessment, 1987.

CASE STUDY: DEVOE AIRLINES

Devoe Airlines was a scheduled commuter air service operating between Miami and smaller Florida cities during the early 1980s. Owned by Miami pilot Jack Devoe, the business was essentially a front for a Colombian drug trafficking operation, which included regular, large-quantity marijuana and cocaine smuggling. In total, 8 to 10 contract pilots employed by Devoe were involved in more than 100 trafficking flights over a five-year period and carried roughly 7,000 pounds of cocaine from South America to the United States. Jack Devoe estimates that his flying organization grossed millions of dollars each month during peak smuggling periods.

Devoe's trafficking pilots initially travelled nonstop routes between the United States and Colombia, but in the 1980s, they developed a transshipment point on Little Darby Island in the Bahamas for purposes of "security and police protection." Devoe hired six to eight employees to work as needed at the island base to unload and repackage drug shipments. There was no interference from Bahamian law enforcement at the Little Darby Island "as long as payments [to officials] were on time."

Typically operating mid-size turbo-prop aircraft, Devoe pilots departed for Colombia either from the base at Little Darby Island or from Florida airports. Their route generally took them through the Windward Passage (see Chapter 4) to Colombian locations about 60 miles south of the equator. In the early stages of the operation, landings were made at official Colombian airports including the airfields at Santa Marta and Riohacha. In at least one instance, cocaine was openly loaded onto the smuggling aircraft at Riohacha airport. In the early 1980s, Devoe shifted landings to clandestine jungle airstrips maintained by the organization's cocaine supplier, Pepe Cabrera. This system streamlined the trafficking process by eliminating transport of the cocaine to an airport. The cocaine shipment was loaded directly onto the aircraft near the strip while the plane was simultaneously prepared for the return flight.

Generally, Devoe pilots returned to the United States within one day. Their preferred return route extended along the Colombia/Venezuela border, over Haiti, and to the Bahamian base on Little Darby Island. There, cocaine was sealed into the wing fuel tanks of a small aircraft and flown directly into South Florida for delivery to the cartel's representative there.

The Devoe organization's methods for avoiding interdiction between South America and the United States were relatively simple and typical of such smuggling operations. A Devoe pilot learned the frequencies of DEA surveillance aircraft on one occasion by "acting like a helicopter buff" inspecting a DEA Cobra pursuit helicopter parked near the Devoe hangar. Inside the helicopter the pilot copied the frequencies from a clipboard hanging in the instrument panel. As the pilot explained to the President's Commission on Organized Crime:

By [subsequently] using our scanner and our knowledge of the frequencies in use, we could monitor the activities of DEA planes. . . . we could learn not only the activities of the planes, but also go up and check the plane out. By learning what types of aircraft DEA was using we could plan our own strategy more effectively....

Devoe also regularly sent "cover-flight" aircraft ahead of the smuggling planes along the trafficking route to monitor DEA and Customs Service surveillance patrols by radio. These planes, which carried no drug cargo, were also used to decoy pursuit aircraft. Once in the United States, Devoe's strategy for clearing Customs was to:

...act normally and file a flight plan, come in and land, and let them inspect the airplane...Customs inspectors were far less interested in a lengthy examination of my plane if I came in on a Sunday afternoon in the middle of the televised football game. If the Dolphins were playing, that was even better.

Using these tactics, Devoe Airlines was able to complete over 100 trafficking flights from Colombia without interference from law enforcement authorities.

Source: PCOC, 1986

The Coast Guard

The Coast Guard focuses on identification and interdiction of maritime smuggling, principally by private, seagoing vessels. The Coast Guard concentrates on larger cases in the open ocean, although it also conducts patrols and makes seizures in near-shore areas, where it has concurrent jurisdiction with the U.S. Customs Service. Primarily, the Coast Guard concentrates on the areas in and around the Gulf of Mexico, the Caribbean, and around south Florida.

Coast Guard seizures are of three distinct types:

1. *Incidental seizures.* These occur while carrying out other more standard missions. Many incidental seizures occur when conducting search and rescue missions where the vessel in trouble turns out to be involved in smuggling activity.

2. *Intelligence-based seizures.* The second most common type of Coast Guard seizure is the seizure that results from hard criminal intelligence. Such intelligence pinpoints the specific location and

time of the smuggling operation. This type accounts for a large
percentage of seizures conducted by the Coast Guard.

3.   *Interdiction patrol operations.* The third and *predominant* type
     of seizure results from drug interdiction patrol operations. Coast
     Guard cutters, usually accompanied by Coast Guard interdiction
     aircraft, search for, identify, visually inspect, and board suspect
     target vessels.

Designated "choke points" are heavily patrolled by Coast Guard cutters in
four Caribbean and Gulf of Mexico areas. The primary goal of this operation is
to identify, through a system of profiling, "mother ships," which meet contact
boats near the coast that deliver drugs into the United States.

The ability of the Coast Guard to interdict illicit drug shipments is restricted by several constraints. These are as follows:

•   Although the Coast Guard will focus on choke points, these areas
     frequently are expanses of ocean 100 miles wide and patrolled by
     a single cutter.

•   The quantity of vessels through the choke points is large, and
     only a small number of the vessels traveling through them can be
     searched.

•   The Coast Guard can only conduct choke point coverage part of
     the time because:

     1.   it has limited equipment and personnel resources

     2.   a cutter must escort seized vessels to a port that could
          tie up the cutter for several days at a time and leave the
          choke point unpatrolled

     3.   the mission of the Coast Guard, interdiction and search
          and rescue, will always take precedence over a smug-
          gling operation

The U.S. Customs Service

The Customs Service has primary interdiction responsibilities for drugs
smuggled through official ports of entry as well as concurrent jurisdiction with
Coast Guard vessels in coastal waters of the United States up to 12 miles offshore (the *"Customs Zone"*). As of late 1986, the Customs Service had about
4,200 full-time inspectors (500 of which were assigned to special contraband enforcement teams), located at 290 ports of entry. It is their responsibility to process all individuals that enter the United States, totaling close to 300 million
persons annually.

CASE STUDY: BARRY SEAL

Adler Barriman Seal, a former TWA 747 Captain, flew cocaine from Colombia to the United States for over seven years during the late 1970s and early 1980s. Seal was recruited as a trafficking pilot by a personal friend who worked for the Colombian cocaine trafficking organization headed by Jorge Ochoa. Seal eventually worked directly with that organization's leadership.

Initially, Seal flew direct trafficking flights between Louisiana and Colombia. He piloted a number of different smuggling aircraft, the largest of which was a Vietnam-vintage C-123 capable of holding tons of packaged cocaine. Seal always departed and returned to his Louisiana base late at night to reduce chances of interdiction. His typical route took him over the Yucatan Peninsula (not over the more heavily patrolled Yucatan channel) and directly over Central America to the eastern tip of Honduras, then south to any one of a number of airstrips and airports in north Colombia.

According to Seal, the Ochoa organization paid Colombian officials bribes of $10,000 to $25,000 per flight for a "window," i.e., a specific time, position, and altitude designated for the smuggling flight's penetration of Colombian airspace. If this payment was not made, the aircraft was susceptible to interception by Colombian authorities. Seal generally arrived in Colombia at dawn. His aircraft was loaded with cocaine and refueled within an hour, sometimes within fifteen minutes, and he returned immediately to the United States.

Seal used two fairly simple techniques to avoid interdiction on his return trip to the United States; both were effective because of the heavy helicopter traffic running between the gulf coast states and the hundreds of oil rigs located offshore. First, when he reached the middle of the Gulf on his return trip, Seal slowed his aircraft to 110 to 120 knots, which caused monitoring to mistake it for a helicopter. Secondly, at a distance of about 50 miles off the United States coast, he dropped the aircraft to an altitude of 500 to 1000 feet in order to commingle with helicopter traffic and thereby arouse even less suspicion.

Once in United States airspace, Seal proceeded to prearranged points 40 to 50 miles inland. The points were mapped out in advance with Loran C, a long-range navigational instrument. Further inland, he was generally joined by a helicopter. The two aircraft continued to a drop zone, where the helicopter hovered close to the ground. Seal then dropped the load of cocaine from the airplane on a parachute; the helicopter picked up the load from the drop zone and delivered it to waiting automobiles, which eventually moved the cocaine to Miami. Seal then landed his drug-free aircraft at any nearby airport.

Seal was paid well for his services. He claims his top fee for smuggling a kilogram of cocaine was $5,000; an average load was 300 kilograms. His most profitable single load netted him $1.5 million. He was never apprehended in connection with this operation.

Author's note: Subsequent to testifying before the President's Commission on Organized Crime, Seal was gunned down and killed in Miami, Florida by gunmen believed to be contracted by the Medellin Cartel.

Source: PCOC, 1986.

Figure 10.3

Interdiction Functions

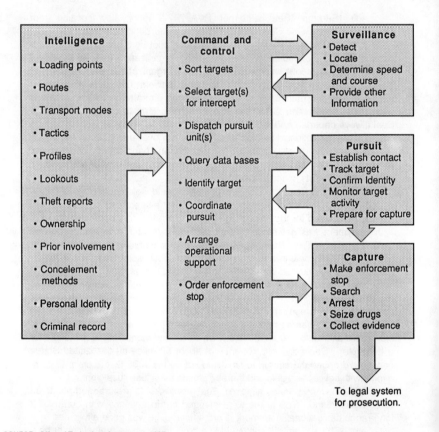

Intelligence	Command and control	Surveillance
• Loading points	• Sort targets	• Detect
• Routes	• Select target(s) for intercept	• Locate
• Transport modes		• Determine speed and course
• Tactics	• Dispatch pursuit unit(s)	• Provide other Information
• Profiles	• Query data bases	
• Lookouts	• Identify target	
• Theft reports	• Coordinate pursuit	
• Ownership		
• Prior involvement	• Arrange operational support	
• Concelement methods		
• Personal Identity	• Order enforcement stop	
• Criminal record		

Surveillance
• Detect
• Locate
• Determine speed and course
• Provide other Information

Pursuit
• Establish contact
• Track target
• Confirm Identity
• Monitor target activity
• Prepare for capture

Capture
• Make enforcement stop
• Search
• Arrest
• Seize drugs
• Collect evidence

To legal system
for prosecution.

SOURCE: Office of Technology Assessment, 1987.

It is also the responsibility of the Customs inspectors to inspect all international cargo, all vessels entering sea ports from foreign countries, all aircraft entering the United States from foreign countries (including general and commercial aircraft), all land vehicles such as trucks, automobiles, trains, and busses, and all international mail.

The Service's interdiction strategy at ports of entry has several components:

- It operates most effectively when it has prior reliable intelligence. Intelligence sources include informants, private citizens, transportation companies, and intelligence agencies.

- Profiles of people, vehicles, and cargo are used to initiate searches. Profiles include data such as the origin of the individual or cargo, and the sex, age or citizenship of the individual (see Chapter 11).

- Inspectors conduct periodic blitz-type inspections of passengers and cargo.

- Officials use drug detection dogs to sniff out hidden drugs as well as metal detection devices and a variety of support and detection technologies to track suspect aircraft.

One primary responsibility of the Customs Service is to interdict drugs in the nation's near-shore waters. This initiative utilizes the Marine Branch of the Service, which uses a system of stopping and searching incoming vessels that behave suspiciously (especially small boats referred to as "go-fast" boats).

A SMUGGLER's VIEW

Well, it used to be easy. However, now it has become a little less attractive for some of the younger pilots. Some of the older pilots, as myself, have been indicted.

We've been cognizant of law enforcement techniques and the improvements in it; and the younger pilots are seeing the newspaper reports of the older pilots and the amount of time they are being convicted on and serving, and it's not as attractive a proposition as it used to be.

I think that the more flights that are interdicted, the word gets around. For instance, I have absolutely—or had in my capacity—no desire whatsoever to go into and would do anything to stay out of the south Florida area simply due to the fact that is where the concentrated interdiction efforts are being made due to the Vice Presidential Task Force, which has been highly publicized and which has taken its toll on the paranoia of the drug smuggler.

Source: PCOC, 1986 (testimony from Barry Seal, drug smuggler).

The best-developed marine interdiction capabilities appear to be in the Miami, area where the Blue Lightning Operations Center (BLOC) operates. This initiative was implemented in February 1986, and is a joint operation between Customs and the Coast Guard designed to collect and coordinate information from air and marine centers. The BLOC tracks suspicious vessels, plots the course and speed of the suspect target, and directs intercepters toward it.

The Customs Air Branch is responsible for interdicting airborne drug smuggling. In 1985, general aviation aircraft were suspected in being responsible for over 50 percent of the cocaine and 10 percent of the marijuana entering the United States. Drug smugglers prefer light, twin-engine general aviation aircraft and will usually fly at a low altitude, placing them under the line-of-sight coverage of coastal scanners. These smugglers will typically operate at night to minimize their chance of detection by law enforcement.

Once suspicious aircraft have been sighted, they are normally tracked both by cutters and/or by high-speed chase planes. The interdiction process will usually involve Customs strike teams that are transported to the landing site by helicopters.

A TYPICAL INTERDICTION SCENARIO

Following a plane from Colombia to a landing site in Tennessee, for example, may involve not only a team of aircraft and helicopters but coordination with the FAA, the North American Air Defense Command (NORAD), and a variety of federal, state, and local police organizations. The problem is made more difficult because smugglers may not have the drugs on board when they land the airplane. In some instances smugglers fly in, air drop, or land their cargo at prearranged sites and then fly on to landing sites elsewhere in the United States.

As will be discussed further in Chapter 11, a 1988 study by the RAND Corporation revealed some disturbing conclusions regarding the ability of the military to successfully affect drug demand through interdiction. The study, commissioned by the Defense Department and directed by Peter Reuter, concluded that it was more costly for the government to attempt to interdict drugs than it was for traffickers to replace seized shipments.

In the study, Reuter found that the assets of the drug traffickers are so vast that the losses caused by interdiction go unnoticed. Dealers have to spend more on transporting shipments than police can on stopping them. He claims that this is because raw materials and highly skilled labor are surprisingly cheap in the markets utilized by drug traffickers.

To facilitate the study, Reuter developed a computer model called SOAR to estimate more exactly how smugglers would adapt if interdiction efforts were increased. In an all-out drug war, assuming that the interdiction rate on 10 of 11 routes could be more than doubled, SOAR estimated that the cost of smuggling would increase 70 percent, but the retail price of drugs would increase only 10 percent. The increase would therefore only affect the street crack user by $2 per purchase.

The Border Patrol

The federal agency most actively involved in interdiction on land between ports-of-entry is the Border Patrol. The Border Patrol operates under the Department of Immigration and Naturalization Service, which is within the Department of Justice. The Border Patrol, as of late 1986, employed approximately 3,700 officers, most of which were stationed along the United States-Mexico border.

The primary function of the Border Patrol is the enforcing of laws related to admission, exclusion, and expulsion of aliens, but while performing this function, Border Patrol agents frequently interdict drugs. This is because some drug smugglers enter the United States through the same routes used by illegal aliens, and some individuals that smuggle aliens also smuggle drugs.

As is typical with many drug interdiction law enforcement agencies, the Border Patrol is grossly lacking in resources—particularly manpower. For example, a recent interdiction problem is the smugglers' use of commercial containers on cargo ships and in trucks. Cocaine has been found in such containers in shipments of cement mix, honey, fruit pulp, caustic lye, and pumpkins. Due to manpower constraints, agents can only inspect 4 percent of the estimated eight million containers arriving yearly.

Interdiction Support Agencies

In addition to the interdiction efforts by the Coast Guard and the Customs Service, there are other support agencies that share certain responsibilities. Such support services include sharing intelligence, equipment, and other resources. The primary support groups used in the interdiction effort are the Department of Defense, the Federal Aviation Administration (FAA), and various state and local law enforcement agencies.

The Department of Defense (DOD). The historical separation of powers between the police and the military is defined under a law known as the Posse Comitatus Act. It was refined in 1981, resulting in a relaxation of the provisions for using military equipment and personnel for domestic law enforcement. While DOD personnel cannot make arrests, the new provisions of the law allow sharing of intelligence equipment and assisting in certain operations that lead to arrests.

The Federal Aviation Administration (FAA). The FAA supports the drug interdiction effort with its flight information systems. The FAA requires all flights by private aircraft that originate in foreign countries to file flight plans 24 hours in advance and to land at the airport nearest to its point of entry that has a customs officer. Those aircraft crossing the border without having filed a flight plan are automatically considered suspicious and are subsequently investigated.

Other agencies sharing certain drug enforcement responsibilities include the Internal Revenue Service (IRS), the United States Marshal's Service and the Bureau of Alcohol, Tobacco, and Firearms. Most of this cooperation is done on a case-by-case basis.

Coordination Organizations

Several agencies offer services to the primary drug enforcement agencies in the federal and state governments. These agencies will be discussed next.

The National Drug Policy Board

The National Narcotics Drug Policy Board (NDPB) was created by the 1984 National Narcotics Act. The Board originated as a Cabinet-level agency consisting of the Attorney General as chairman and the Secretaries of State, Treasury, Defense, Transportation, and Health and Human Services, as well as the Directors of Central Intelligence and the Office of Management and Budget as members.

Despite the diversity of federal agencies involved, it was the Board's objective to coordinate and focus strategies in the fight against drug abuse. Specifically, the statutory language outlining the mission of the National Drug Policy Board was as follows:

1. Maintain a national and international effort against illegal drugs;

2. Coordinate fully the activities of the federal agencies involved; and

3. Charge a single, competent, and responsible high-level Board of the United States Government, chaired by the Attorney General, with responsibility for coordinating United States policy with respect to national and international drug law enforcement.

In 1988, the NDPB was dissolved to make way for the Office of National Drug Control Policy.

Office of National Drug Control Policy (ONDCP)

In 1988, the Office of National Drug Control Policy (ONDCP) was created to assume control of the federal drug policy effort and was to be directed by a high-level "*Drug Czar.*" Director William Bennett, the former U.S. Secretary of Education, assumed this office in 1989 and was charged with formulating a workable plan for drug control on a nationwide basis.

As of the preparation of this book, the ONDCP has released two reports detailing the national drug control strategy. Each of the reports specifies goals and objectives of both domestic and foreign drug control initiatives.

I will not say that we will prevail. It's essential that we win, but it's not inevitable.

Former Director of the Office of National Drug Control Policy
William Bennett

The Regional Information Sharing System (RISS)

The Regional Information Sharing System program is an innovative, federally-funded program that was created to support law enforcement efforts, to combat organized crime activity, drug trafficking, and white-collar crime. The RISS project began with funding by the LEAA (Law Enforcement Assistance Administration) discretionary grant program. Since 1980, the U.S. Congress has made a yearly appropriation of funds to the RISS projects as a line item in the Department of Justice budget.

The primary impetus of the projects is to augment existing law enforcement agencies with intelligence information on criminal activities in their jurisdictions. Additionally, the RISS project provides services to member agencies regarding assistance in asset seizures, funds for covert operations, analysis of investigative data on organized criminals, loans of investigative equipment, and training in the use of such equipment in criminal investigations.

The RISS program operates within seven Regional Information Sharing Projects:

1. Mid-State Organized Crime Information Center (MOCIC). Missouri, Kansas, Illinois, Iowa, Nebraska, South Dakota, North Dakota, Minnesota, and Wisconsin.

2. Western States Information Network (WSIN). California, Oregon, Washington, Hawaii, and Alaska.

3. Rocky Mountain Information Network (RMIN). Colorado, New Mexico, Arizona, Nevada, Wyoming, Idaho, and Montana.

4. Regional Organized Crime Information Center (ROCIC). Texas, Oklahoma, Arkansas, Louisiana, Tennessee, Mississippi, Alabama, Georgia, Florida, Kentucky, South Carolina, North Carolina, Virginia, and West Virginia.

5. Middle Atlantic Great Lakes Organized Crime Law Enforcement Network (MAGLOCLEN). Indiana, Ohio, Pennsylvania, New York, Michigan, Rhode Island, New Jersey, Maryland, and Delaware.

6. New England State Police Information Network (NESPIN). Massachusetts, Maine, Vermont, Connecticut, New Hampshire, and Rhode Island.

7. LEVITICUS. Alabama, Georgia, Indiana, Kentucky, New York, Pennsylvania, and Virginia. The LEVITICUS Project provides coordination to agencies investigating crimes related to the coal, oil, and natural gas industries.

The National Narcotics Border Interdiction System (NNBIS)

The NNBIS system was created to provide guidance for interdiction systems and is under the chairmanship of the Vice President. Regional NNBIS units are established at six locations throughout the country. These regional components are chaired by the heads of various regional enforcement agencies that have responsibility for that particular geographical area. For example, three of these regional directors are admirals in the Coast Guard.

The Organized Crime Drug Enforcement Task Force (OCDETF)

In 1981, the effects of drug trafficking and drug abuse in South Florida had so greatly affected the quality of life there that several particularly vocal public groups demanded immediate attention be given to the problem. In 1982, President Reagan then established a cabinet-level South Florida Task Force known as *"Operation Florida"* to address the problem. The primary focus of Operation Florida was interdiction, arrest, and prosecution of drug smugglers. The task force was staffed with officers from federal agencies such as the DEA, FBI, Customs, ATF, the Marshals Service, the DOD, and the Coast Guard.

The success of the Operation Florida task force prompted the creation of the Organized Crime Drug Enforcement Task Force (OCDETF) in 1983. The objectives of OCDETF are, however, quite different. While the primary focus of the South Florida program is interdiction, the focus of the OCDETF program is the detection and prosecution of leaders of large criminal organizations that control illicit drug importation and distribution. As of the preparation of this text, the OCDETF has proven to be one of the most effective enforcement initiatives in the nation's drug control effort. The participating federal agencies include: the United States Attorney's office, DEA, FBI, Customs, ATF, IRS, Marshal's Service, and the Coast Guard.

Figure 10.4

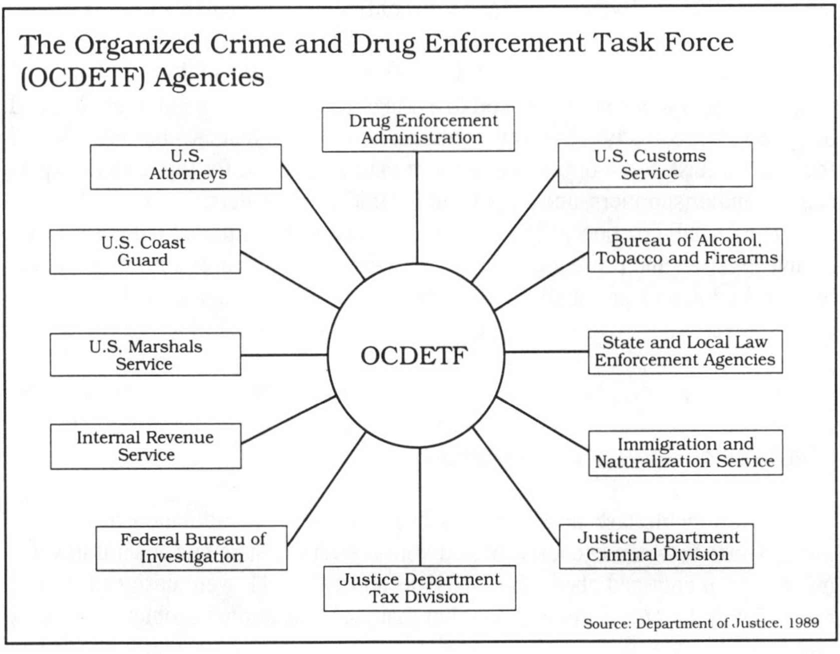

The Organized Crime and Drug Enforcement Task Force (OCDETF) Agencies

Source: Department of Justice, 1989

Particularly supportive of the OCDETF program is the sustained use of the investigative grand jury (see Chapter 11). Prosecutors have employed the grand jury as an investigative technique in over 60 percent of all task force cases. Additionally, investigators are making extensive use of undercover techniques in the development of cases that result in indictments. This technique is particularly suited to the OCDETF mission in which there is a need for a long-term, complicated investigation that requires agents to follow all leads in pursuit of major dealers, be they manufacturers, suppliers, or money launderers.

We are going to take back the streets by taking criminals off the street. It's an attack on all four fronts —new laws to punish them, new agents to arrest them, new prosecutors to convict them, and new prisons to hold them.

President George Bush, 1989

The success of the OCDETF program is evidenced in part by the statistics on net prison terms. In 1988, for example, the percentage of defendants sentenced to terms of five or more years of confinement increased to 54.2 percent, compared to the six-year cumulative rate of 50.9 percent. Of greater significance is the fact that in fiscal year (FY) 1988, top leaders, major suppliers, and mid-level suppliers were sentenced to average prison sentences of 16.4, 7.0, and 8.3 years, respectively. This represents an increase in years sentenced, over all the years of task force operation, of more than 20 percent for top leaders, 6 percent for major suppliers, and 27 percent for mid-level leaders.

The OCDETF concept has evolved to become the principal federal weapon in investigation and prosecution of drug traffickers and their organizations. This has resulted in a clear benefit to not only federal but state and local drug control efforts alike.

The Task of Agency Coordination

A formidable task in the nation's drug war is the coordination of enforcement efforts between agencies located within both the state and federal governments. As mentioned above, both NNBIS and OCDETF were designed to pool resources in the enforcement effort, but many organizational problems still prevail.

Figure 10.5

ORGANIZED CRIME DRUG ENFORCEMENT TASK FORCES

Source: Organized Crime Drug Enforcement Task Force Program Annual Report

On the federal level, "turf" wars and inner-agency bickering often result in a reluctance to share information or coordinate enforcement efforts. For example, confusion often results when many different departments play some role in the drug suppression effort. The U.S. Department of Agriculture, for example, handles crop eradication, Customs is responsible for interdiction yet the armed services also monitor the military's role in interdiction, and the FBI and DEA have similar roles in investigating federal violations of the Controlled Substances Act.

The primary responsibility for coordination on the federal level rests with the Director of the Office of National Drug Control Policy. Former Director William Bennett, appointed by President George Bush in 1989, assumed a hard-line attitude on this problem and stated: "If they're not in line we'll get them in line."

To partially illustrate the problem, examples are given below:

* The Drug Enforcement Administration (DEA), Federal Bureau of Investigation (FBI), the U.S. Customs Service, the State Department, the Central Intelligence Agency (CIA), and the Defense Department all gather intelligence information separately.

- Customs and DEA have been involved in feuds over who keeps assets and money seized during drug investigations.

- An FBI-DEA National Intelligence Center, proposed in William Bennett's 1989 National Drug Strategy, was rejected after certain officials at the Justice Department claimed that it would infringe upon Attorney General William Thornburgh's power.

FEDERAL DRUG CONTROL AGENCIES

The Justice Department
Drug Enforcement Admin.
Federal Bureau of Invest.
Criminal Division
Tax Division
U.S. Attorney's Offices
U.S. Marshal's Service
Federal Prisons
Immigration and Naturalization Service
Office of Justice Programs
Interpol
Inspector General

The Department of Treasury
U.S. Customs Service
Internal Revenue Service

Bureau of Alcohol, Tobacco,
and Firearms

Transportation Department
U.S. Coast Guard
Federal Aviation Admin.
National Highway Traffic
Safety Administration

U.S. Information Agency

The State Department
International Narcotics Matters

Department of Agriculture
Agriculture Research Service
U.S. Forest Service

Department of Interior
Bureau of Land Management
National Park Service
Bureau of Indian Affairs
Fish and Wildlife Service

Health and Human Services
Alcohol, Drug Abuse, and
  Mental Health Administration
Indian Health Service
Food and Drug Administration

Department of Defense
Department of Labor
Department of Education
Veterans Affairs
**Agency for International
Development**

Strategies for Street Level Enforcement

Although the problem of foreign drug traffickers smuggling dangerous drugs into the country is a high priority of the federal government, the coexisting problem of controlling local street-level dealers prevails. Adopting a policy that effectively deals with the street-level dealer is a major priority. Primary responsibility for this task has typically rested with the local law enforcement agency and has been associated with two distinct illegal street markets: discreet and nondiscreet markets.

Discreet drug markets. The discreet retail drug market is one in which the drug seller and the drug buyer are well acquainted. Drug transactions taking place under these circumstances typically involve exchanges of drugs for money in the work place or within a social environment such as a bar or nightclub. Such operations are frequently difficult to discover by police because of the private nature of the transactions and may therefore go undetected for long periods of time.

Nondiscreet drug markets. the nondiscreet drug trade, however, differs from the discreet drug trade in that the drug seller is rarely acquainted with the drug buyer. The nondiscreet market accounts for the so-called *open-air* trade that flourishes in public places. This type of drug market is attractive for the drug dealer because it will generate greater profits because of a greater number of customers available to the dealer. The nondiscreet market is also an easy target for police intervention and control, as its whereabouts are easily learned through police surveillance operations and informants.

One original approach by many municipalities in dealing with offenders caught with small amounts of marijuana is the issuing of citations by uniformed patrol officers. For example, when a small amount of marijuana is seized as a result of a vehicle stop, in lieu of taking the violator into custody, a citation is written and signed by the violator. This process basically works like a traffic citation, as it requires the offender to appear in court on a later date.

This procedure has generally been considered a successful street-level enforcement tactic because it reduces the commitments of time and money by the police, the prosecutor, and the courts through streamlining the adjudicatory process. At the same time, the practice enables law enforcement to identify and convict drug users in the community that might otherwise escape detection by the criminal justice system.

It is clear that law enforcement initiatives alone are not successful in adequately containing the existing problem of street drug trafficking. Modern-day strategies must include tactics such as the enlistment of the support of community groups, seizing assets of both sellers and users, and cracking down on all street sales operations.

Drug dealing, a fragmented and broadly generalized term, addresses all levels of illicit drug distribution and many different types of drugs. Although different types of drugs such as marijuana, methamphetamine, heroin, etc., are prevalent in different geographical areas of the country, the problem of crack cocaine sales has been identified by many larger departments as an enforcement priority. The popularity of crack cocaine among dealers is closely related to its popularity by the drug-using public; that is, crack is a highly addictive drug that consequently creates much repeat business for the seller and generates a correspondingly high profit margin.

CLOSE-UP: THE CANCER OF CRACK HOUSES

She watched as her building and others on Benton Boulevard were practically taken over by crack dealers. "All of a sudden, I looked around me and there were these young guys everywhere," said the woman that asked not to be identified for fear of retribution. "I had folks living in the hallway. They had taken over the building. But it wasn't just my building. They were in the building next door to me. They were in the building on the corner. It had happened in less than six months. That's how quickly a neighborhood can be consumed with that activity."

Source: *The Washington Post*, June 12, 1990.

Street sales of crack cocaine and powdered (HCl) cocaine seem to follow two distinct patterns: the use of the *crack house* and the *nondiscreet market*.

The crack house is the most common means of street distribution of crack cocaine by dealers. Frequently, the crack house is an abandoned house that has been commandeered by street dealers for use as a base of operation. These houses are structurally fortified with steel bars on windows and metal door jambs to prevent easy access by police. The crack house may operate in an "open" fashion, which enables the drug buyer or user to enter the house, purchase the crack, and ingest it on the premises.

Street corner sales have also contributed greatly to the proliferation of the crack cocaine problem. Although primarily an inner-city phenomenon, this nondiscreet method for retail crack sales has, in some cases, created vehicular traffic congestion because of dealers that literally approach any passing automobile and inquire of the driver if he or she is interested in purchasing any crack. This system of illicit drug trafficking illustrates the arrogance and lackadaisical attitude that many street dealers share with regard to the criminal justice system.

Specific tactics used to reduce street sales largely depend on the scope of the problem in each community. The task force concept (previously discussed) is one such tactic and has proven to be one of the more effective enforcement tools in the fight against street trafficking and for use in interdiction. Other traditional strategies to tackle the problem include the use of the "buy-bust," where undercover police officers posing as drug buyers target the street dealer.

New, nontraditional strategies of street enforcement are being considered by many law enforcement agencies. One such tactic is the use of the "reverse-sting." This innovative approach to controlling street drug sales involves undercover police officers that pose as drug "dealers" rather than buyers. The focus of the strategy is to arrest those that purchase crack or attempt to engage in an illicit drug transaction. The reverse-sting concept has three primary advantages: the ability to identify and seize personal assets of the drug dealer (discussed later in this chapter), the ability to arrest large numbers of street dealers and thus deter criminal activity, and the ability to generate positive media coverage of police department activities.

A common problem for police crackdowns on street-level drug operations is *displacement*. For decades, traditional vice units have dealt with the problem of displacement of offenders in attempting to control such operations as prostitution. Typically, once a strong police presence is detected by potential violators, alternative markets for the criminal activity are identified and pursued.

Displacement in retail drug enforcement operations is a common problem. If law enforcement efforts are not as concentrated in outlying areas as in the area of the crackdown, then drug dealers will almost assuredly set up their operations in these outlying areas (also see Chapter 8).

RENO SCORES A VICTORY IN WAR ON DRUGS:
COP — PLUS TARGETS OPEN DEALING

When Capt. Tom Robinson of the Reno (NV) Police Department first tried to organize a Neighborhood Advisory Group in his North-Stead area, he held open meetings in Pat Baker Park in the heart of the black community. The park, nicknamed "Instant Park" because it had literally been put in over a weekend, had been the site of disturbing clashes between local residents and drug dealers, particularly the crack dealers that began to appear in ever larger numbers about two years ago. At one of the first meetings, the officers put up 75 chairs, but only 25 people actually sat in them—an equal number of young toughs stood behind, looking ominous. "One brave resident stood up at that meeting and told us that if we got rid of the drug dealers and troublemakers, they would fill all the chairs," says Chief Robert V. Bradshaw.

Inspired by that challenge, the department put together a plan to drive the dealers from the park, using a Community Policing approach. In addition to traditional undercover operations, the COP-Plus approach included high-visibility patrols, deploying officers in walking beats, and developing liaisons with the area's black ministers.

Within a two-month period, the police made 40 arrests for drug law violations—and all of the arrestees were black. "In the past, whenever we tried to deal with the problems in the park, the headlines in the local paper talked about how the police were the problem," said Bradshaw. Traditional police action often triggered mini-riots—people threw bottles and rocks at the police.

"This time, we held a news conference at the end of the 60-day period, with the involvement of the black ministers, and we didn't have a single complaint about race," says Bradshaw. Bradshaw says that their COP-Plus approach has improved race relations, regardless of the race of the officer.

"Just recently, when we arrested a drug dealer in the park, the people stood up and cheered," said Robinson. He attributes the change to their Community Policing focus. COP-Plus has succeeded in generating information about drug dealing beyond what dangerous and expensive undercover operations produced. "People call their officer and then the officer shares the information with narcotics," says Bradshaw. "We now get calls every day and, within two sunsets, we get them (the dealers)."

Drug Gangs and Gang Violence

Though Reno is typically conservative and low-key, two years ago, an influx of drug gang members from California threatened to rip the city wide open. Notorious gangs, including California's Crips and Bloods, appeared in Reno seeking recruits for their burgeoning crack franchise.

"At that time, we were averaging two drive-by shootings a week," says Bradshaw. One of the most unnerving incidents involved two Los Angeles Crips and three locals that they had recruited into their gang. "Their basic plan was simple—rob someone and then rape someone," says Bradshaw.

First, the quintet stole a vehicle and sprayed it with graffiti, then they robbed and severely beat a college student. Next they snatched a 13-year-old girl from her bicycle and gang-raped her. The police succeeded in catching the perpetrators, and two were sentenced to prison for life.

"We have a Gang Task Force, but it's really been the COP-Plus focus that has driven most of the gangs away," says Bradshaw. He says that the community cohesion fostered by a Community Policing approach persuaded the gangs that there are other places that are more hospitable than Reno for them to ply their trade.

Bradshaw doesn't claim that Reno is drug-free—no city is. But gangs are now a minor problem, and places like Pat Baker Park are no longer plagued by open dealing. He says that communication is what shut the drug gangs down, and that COP-Plus was the catalyst. "And I can't really remember when we had our last call about a drive-by shooting," he says.

"The difference is that people used to stand up and bash the police at meetings and now they go on TV telling everyone what a great job we're doing," says Bradshaw. "Now they want to know why everyone in city government isn't doing as well as the police."

Under this plan, suspects may be arrested on the spot or during a larger scale "round-up" occurring at a later time. This strategy, however, is not as common as others because of certain legal and operational considerations (with regard to officer safety) that are inherent in the operation.

Source: *Footprints — The Community Newsletter*, Spring 1990.

Problem-Oriented Policing ✳ Read

The concept of Problem-Oriented Policing, or "POP" originated in Newport News, Virginia, in 1986. This approach requires police to collect and analyze data on individuals, incidents, and police responses to crimes as a first step to formulating a prevention or enforcement strategy. The data used in this program consists of crime statistics such as arrest statistics and citizen surveys.

The program further reveals that many drug-related problems are not the responsibility of the police but of some other department of the local government. For example, abandoned houses used for crack sales may be the initial responsibility of the building code inspectors.

The POP approach has been used in many cities where crack houses operate, and special tactical squads have been developed for rapid entry into fortified residences. In those areas where street sales are considered to be the biggest problem, concentrated or "saturated" police patrols have been adopted.

- In New York City, Operation Pressure Point, a vigorous street-level strategy in the Manhattan area, was implemented. During the early phases of the operation, the police department's narcotics enforcement unit was strengthened, and a highly visible patrol was initiated. The program lead to a substantially higher number of drug arrests in the area and a reduction in open-air drug operations was evident.

- In Lynn, Massachusetts, a vigorous attack by police was initiated against heroin dealers in the area. By using undercover operations, surveillance, and information gathered from a drug hot-line, police were able to increase drastically the number of arrests in the designated area. Following this crackdown, heroin consumption seemed to decrease, along with incidents of robberies and burglaries.

Source: NIJ, 1989.

Citizen-Oriented Policing ✳ Read

With more and more neighborhoods besieged with crack houses and crack dealers, the concept of Citizen-Oriented Policing has developed. Basically, this concept focuses on citizens that believe that the police cannot adequately control existing crime in the community and therefore cannot insure an acceptable degree of public safety.

Figure 10.6

Local law enforcement strategies against drugs

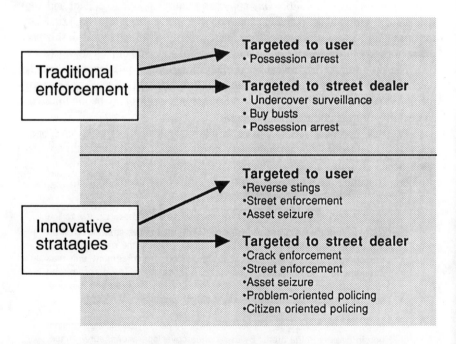

Traditional enforcement	**Targeted to user** • Possession arrest **Targeted to street dealer** • Undercover surveillance • Buy busts • Possession arrest
Innovative stratagies	**Targeted to user** •Reverse stings •Street enforcement •Asset seizure **Targeted to street dealer** •Crack enforcement •Street enforcement •Asset seizure •Problem-oriented policing •Citizen oriented policing

More and more, local law enforcement agencies are diversifying their strategies for combating drugs, variably targeting users and street sellers, and combining traditional techniques with newer approaches.

SOURCE: National Institute of Justice, U.S. Deptartment of Justice, 1989.

These programs do not advocate vigilantism but rather promote a closer working relationship with the police. In Seattle, Washington, for example, citizens banded together to implement a drug hot-line in which information is passed directly to local police authorities. The existence of such a program recognized that citizens of the community can work well with police officials and that the drug problem requires a collective effort between many members and departments of the community.

OPERATION "CLEAN SWEEP" HELPS WIPE OUT DRUGS IN DALLAS

Assistant Chief Sam Gonzales of the Dallas (TX) Police Department is one of 20 people nationwide recently hailed by federal drug czar William Bennett for their efforts "on the true front lines" in the War on Drugs. Gonzales, the only law enforcement official on the list, directs Operation CLEAN (Community and Law Enforcement Against Narcotics), an effort to improve the quality of life in target neighborhoods and to help make them more drug-resistant.

Operation CLEAN depends on strong support and participation from the police, city services, and the community. Target areas are selected because they exhibit a high infestation of drugs, as well as high numbers of offenses and calls for service.

The comprehensive plan involves bringing the immediate crisis under control, with six weeks of high saturation police patrols. At the same time, the community receives a "facelift," as the police and community work with city services on efforts such as cleaning and repairing streets, removing trash, checking for code violations, boarding up unoccupied buildings, and expediting demolition of unsafe, abandoned structures.

To ensure that these short-term remedies have the chance to become long-term gains, the department permanently deploys community officers in the target neighborhoods.

Source: *Footprints — The Community Newsletter*, Spring 1990.

Summary

When one studies the extensive history of United States federal drug control policy, many interesting occurrences can be observed in drug abuse trends, and the formation of public policy relating to drug abuse. Prohibition created the need for enforcement of the federal anti-liquor laws. From the first narcotics unit operating under the Commissioner of Internal Revenue in 1919 to the current Drug Enforcement Administration, which was formed in 1973, many policies and agencies have been implemented. Some of these were more successful than others.

To date, the primary thrust of drug enforcement is carried out by the Drug Enforcement Administration, the Federal Bureau of Investigation, and the U.S. Customs Service. Many other federal agencies also share different degrees of enforcement responsibility in drug control.

A priority of the federal drug enforcement initiative is interdiction, which is the interception of drugs coming into the country. The United States Customs Service, the Border Patrol, and the Coast Guard play major roles in this effort.

Other organizations exist that act as task forces for drug trafficking in the United States. The Office of National Drug Control Policy serves as the coordinating agency for the federal drug control effort. The ONDCP is charged with coordinating efforts with all federal agencies to reduce drug abuse and trafficking.

The Federal Organized Crime Drug Enforcement Task Force (OCDETF) also plays a major role in detecting and prosecuting domestic drug traffickers. The OCDETF is made up of agents representing DEA, FBI, IRS, Customs, ATF, Marshal's Service, and Coast Guard.

On the local level, many different drug enforcement/suppression organizations and strategies exist. Strategies include ways to reduce or eliminate both discreet and non-discreet drug markets operating in communities. This is accomplished by the use of problem- and citizen-oriented policing by the patrol function of local police departments.

DISCUSSION QUESTIONS

1. Explain the evolution of the Drug Enforcement Administration (DEA) and its current role in federal drug control policy.

2. What was considered the first drug enforcement agency that operated in the federal government?

3. When the investigation of drug offenses is considered, name the primary federal drug enforcement agency in the United States, and discuss its emergence.

4. Under what circumstances was OCDETF developed and what purpose does it serve in the overall federal drug suppression effort?

5. Explain why there was so much bureaucracy in the development of so many different drug enforcement agencies during and after Prohibition.

6. Why was the DEA created, and what is its goal?

7. The concept of the Organized Crime Drug Enforcement Task Force (OCDETF) was developed under what set of circumstances? What function does it serve in drug control?

8. Explain the role of the RISS projects in drug enforcement.

9. Describe the concepts of Problem-Oriented and Citizen-Oriented Policing and how these relate to drug control in communities.

10. List some traditional drug enforcement strategies that deal with reducing the supply of illicit drugs.

11. Discuss some new innovative strategies currently being used in drug enforcement to reduce both retail and wholesale illicit drug supplies.

12. Characterize and discuss the differences between discreet and non-discreet illicit drug markets.

13. What is the concept of problem-oriented policing and how does it pertain to the reduction of street-level drug trafficking?

14. Discuss the concept of citizen-oriented policing and what role it plays in reducing street-level drug dealing.

CHAPTER 11

CRITICAL ISSUES IN DRUG CONTROL

Accepting responsibility for the problem is often a first step in problem solving on any scale. Just as an alcoholic must first acknowledge his or her condition to be able to overcome it, the United States must acknowledge the extent to which it provides a market for drugs in order to combat the entire drug menace. This leads to several critical issues facing actors in the war on drugs: Are United States strategies properly balanced? Are United States strategies aimed at both domestic and international criminals? Are United States strategies tackling both ends of the supply/demand cycle? Are United States strategies sufficiently flexible to protect civil liberties for the general public while giving adequate authority to drug enforcement officials? These are just a few of the issues facing drug enforcement policymakers.

In the early 1990s, drug control has expanded its scope and ingenuity to include such tactics as eviction, curfew, random searches, and forfeiture of property. Although many of these techniques have drawn political and social fire from civil libertarians, they have generally been supported by state legislatures, state and federal courts, and the United States Congress. To illustrate the trend toward harsher punitive measures for drug offenders, in October 1989, the Justice Department asked President Bush to consider expanding the application of the death penalty to leaders of drug trafficking organizations.

Commenting on the demand for drugs in the United States was a 1985 remark by Colombian President Belisario Bentancur:

In the world war against narcotics, we need the commitment of the consumer nations to attack the demand with the same vigor we have shown. We can make all the sacrifices possible, but if there is enormous demand, production will never be completely eradicated (*Los Angeles Times*, Dec. 1, 1985).

Many strategies for drug control are controversial. In many cases, conventional methods offer little hope for controlling the problem. As mentioned, unconventional methods will frequently create some controversy because such methods usually rely on expanded police powers. Some citizens therefore fear an erosion of personal freedom. On the other hand, many unconventional methods of drug enforcement have proven more effective than the traditional approaches.

Official Police "Abductions"

One example of unconventional drug control tactics is the controversial practice of kidnapping or abducting drug lords in foreign countries. Such a practice is favored by some, in part, due to the degree of official corruption observed in many foreign countries that commonly protect drug lords from prosecution or extradition.

As a case in point, Dr. Humberto Alvarez Machain was abducted in April, 1990 from his office in Guadalajara, Mexico by a group of Mexican mercenaries working for the DEA. Alvarez was one of 19 persons wanted by the federal government in connection with the 1985 kidnapping/murder of DEA agent Enrique Camarena, which also occurred in Guadalajara (see Chapter 6).

Although this practice usually occurs on foreign soil, many detractors claim that it is an erosion of police authority. Surprisingly, however, the practice of abducting criminal suspects in foreign countries and bringing them to United States soil for trial is more than a century old, and United States courts have found it perfectly legal.

Other official abductions include:

1. The April 1988 abduction of drug kingpin Juan Ramon Matta Ballesteros from Honduras. He was ultimately found guilty of drug trafficking and sentenced to life in prison.

2. Mexican trafficker Rene Verdugo-Urquidez, also accused of involvement in the Camarena murder, was shoved through a border fence by Mexican authorities in 1986. He was ultimately convicted in United States courts.

3. Roberto Suarez Levy, the son of Bolivian trafficker Roberto Suarez Gomez, was arrested in Switzerland in 1980 on drug charges. After nine months of waiting, federal agents arranged with local police to have Suarez smuggled out of the country and to Miami.

The precedents addressing abductions clearly show that judges need not consider how a defendant got into their courtroom. Such morality judgments have generally been left to law enforcement agencies.

As mentioned earlier, the practice of abducting criminals from foreign countries began over a century ago with the abduction of Frederick Ker, an embezzler who absconded to Peru. Ker was hunted down and forcibly abducted. Although his lawyer argued that he was kidnapped, the Supreme Court ruled in 1886 that Ker had no right to due process while abroad and that how he was brought to the courtroom in Chicago had nothing to do with the charges he was facing there.

In another abduction case, however, an exception was delineated by the courts. In 1974, Francisco Toscanino was abducted in Uruguay and transported to the United States. Toscanino's attorney claimed that he was tortured en route to the United States In that case, the court held that it is appropriate for judges to consider the apprehension of defendants if there is a suggestion that the behavior of apprehending officers might "shock the conscience of the court." The Toscanino case also recognized that a United States judge may throw out an arrest if another country objects to the manner in which an arrest was made within its borders.

We will now examine several enforcement alternatives that are currently in effect or under consideration by drug enforcement authorities in the United States.

Drug Courier Profiling

The practice of profiling suspected drug couriers by law enforcement officers is yet another innovative method of apprehending drug traffickers. The technique, originally developed in the 1970s by the DEA for use in detecting drug smugglers in airports, has now been extended to the highways for identifying automobiles driven by drug couriers.

The practice involves trained officers watching vehicles on highways and looking for certain characteristics unique to drug traffickers. The practice gained national attention in 1987 after a segment on *60 Minutes*, a CBS newsmagazine television show, that featured an interview with a Florida state trooper that had achieved a certain reputation for his ability to spot or "profile" such vehicles.

To make the stop, the officer must watch cars on those travel routes that are most likely to be used by smugglers. If the officer identifies any traffic violation, such as speeding, the car can be stopped. The officer then looks for other telltale signs of a typical "drug runner." These include inappropriate dress, a large roll of cash, nervousness around police, the use of a rental car with no car rental papers available for inspection, and the lack of any travel gear such as luggage. Finally, the officer asks the driver for permission (consent) to search the vehicle.

Although drug courier profiling has resulted in numerous drug seizures and arrests, it has been criticized by the American Civil Liberties Union (ACLU), which views it as a violation of a person's personal freedoms and an unfair infringement one's fourth amendment search-and-seizure rights.

The critical issue in drug courier profiling is the constitutionality of the technique and whether it violates one's fourth amendment freedom from unreasonable searches and seizures. Critics of the technique argue that a vague profile is not enough to create "reasonable suspicion" in the officer's minds.

DRUG 'PROFILE' TACTIC UPHELD

The Supreme Court ruled on April 3, 1989 that the Constitution permits the police to stop and question airline passengers that display behavior patterns that may have an innocent explanation but that parallel the actions of drug couriers. While the 7 to 2 decision made little new law, it marked the Court's clearest validation to date of the techniques that the federal Drug Enforcement Administration (DEA) has developed for surveillance and detection of drug traffic through airports and railroad depots.

Over the last 15 years, the agency has what it calls a "drug courier profile," based on patterns of behavior that agent's observations have shown are typical of those individuals that use commercial airline flights to transport drugs. The profile includes paying for tickets with cash, using an alias, boarding a long flight without checking luggage, and staying briefly in distant cities known to be sources of drugs.

Because these actions can be entirely innocent, the profile has long been under attack as an unconstitutional shortcut to establishing the level of suspicion that the Constitution requires before the police can interfere with a person's liberty. Most lower courts have rejected these challenges on the basis of earlier Supreme Court decisions permitting the use of a "totality of the circumstances" approach to brief detentions by the police.

Source: Greenhouse, L. (1989). "High Court Backs Airport Detention Based on 'Profile'." *The New York Times* (April 4):A1.

Lawyers for the DEA's criminal law division claimed in 1989 that agents do not make stops on the basis of profiles. Defense attorneys, on the other hand, maintain that suspicion triggered by a profile will often lead to an arrest on the pretext of a traffic violation. They also assert that "voluntary" questioning and searches by police can, in fact, be highly coercive. Yet another unanswered question is by what standard should one's behavior be analyzed to determine whether it is suspicious? To some officers, the first person getting off a plane may be suspicious, while to other officers, the last person getting off a plane may seem suspicious.

Some previous high court decisions have upheld informal questioning of suspects fitting a suspect profile but have prohibited coercive searches and formal arrests unless the police have additional evidence upon which to base a decision. Until terms such as "coercive," "profile," and "voluntary" have been further defined, the United States Supreme Court may have to fine-tune continually its conclusion as to the constitutionality of this drug enforcement technique.

CASE STUDY: U.S. v. SOKOLOW

On April 3, 1989, a decision written by Chief Justice William H. Rehnquist summarized the overturning of a previous ruling by the United States Court of Appeals for the Ninth Circuit in California. That court had ruled that the brief detention by federal drug agents of a passenger at the Honolulu International Airport was unconstitutional.

The agents detained the man long enough to get a trained dog to sniff his luggage, and then they found several pounds of cocaine in his shoulder bag. When agents stopped the man, they knew little about him except that he had paid $2,100 for tickets from a role of $20 bills, he had just made a round trip flight from Honolulu to Miami, he stayed in Miami less than 48 hours with no checked luggage, he looked nervous, and used a name that did not match the name under which his telephone number was listed.

The man, Andrew Sokolow, was eventually convicted on federal drug charges. The appeals court overturned the conviction on the ground that the agents lacked the "reasonable suspicion" required by the fourth amendment for brief detentions.

While the fourth amendment requires the police to have "probable cause" for a formal arrest, the Supreme Court for the last 20 years has applied a lower standard, "reasonable suspicion," for brief "investigatory stops" that can turn up additional evidence needed for probable cause. The question whenever such a detention is challenged is whether the police had enough evidence for the threshold determination of reasonable suspicion.

In the opinion for the Court, Chief Justice Rehnquist described in some detail the evidence available to the agents in what he described as "a typical attempt to smuggle drugs through one of the nation's airports." He noted Sokolow's attire: a black jumpsuit with gold jewelry. The role of $20 bills "appeared to contain a total of $4000." The Chief Justice said: "While a trip from Honolulu to Miami standing alone, is not a cause for any sort of suspicion, here there was more: Surely few residents of Honolulu travel from that city for 20 hours to spend 48 hours in Miami during the month of July."

He added: "Any one of these factors is not by itself proof of any illegal conduct and is quite consistent with innocent travel. But we think taken together they amount to reasonable suspicion."

The Reverse Drug Sting

The reverse undercover operation is one in which the officer poses as a drug dealer and places buyers under arrest after certain necessary conversations and actions have been documented. Controversy about the appropriateness of the reverse sting as a police tactic centers around the legal question of entrapment. Since the initiation of this covert police tactic, some courts have excluded all but the most compelling evidence obtained in the operation. Other courts, however, have accepted this practice as lawful and appropriate.

Entrapment is *compelling one to commit a criminal act that he or she was not predisposed to commit.*

Other dangers are inherent in this type of operation. For example, an undercover officer working in this capacity must maintain constant contact with street dealers that will soon become familiar with the physical description of the officer and spread the description to other drug dealers.

On the other hand, an advantage of the reverse sting operation is that it requires little funding for "buy money," which is often needed in greater amounts in long-term drug investigations. In many instances, law enforcement agencies may actually generate revenue to help compensate for future drug investigations. In Washington, D.C., for example, undercover officers sold inert substances to would-be drug buyers, who were penalized by the loss of their cash (through forfeiture) rather than by arrest.

The reverse sting usually targets the new drug user rather than one that has been on the street for a while. Experienced users usually patronize a specific dealer, thereby reducing their need to purchase drugs from a stranger on the street corner.

Zero Tolerance

President Reagan's "zero tolerance" enforcement initiative was implemented in March 1988 with the support of Customs Commissioner William von Raab. The policy basically directs the Coast Guard, Customs Service, and other arms of the federal government to enforce existing law to the utmost degree, thereby addressing the demand side of the drug abuse problem. The plan focuses on the seizing of vehicles, boats, and planes if even a tiny amount of any controlled substance is found on board.

Zero tolerance has its roots in the seizure sanctions of federal law where "administrative seizures" are possible without the owner necessarily being convicted of any crime. Police in cities such as New York and Miami have used this method to impound automobiles of drug buyers whose drug purchases themselves would only result in a misdemeanor charge. Customs Commissioner von Raab said in 1988 that the purpose of the zero tolerance program is to "put pressure on drug users who ordinarily are not reached by criminal penalties."

In May of 1988, Customs seized the Atlantis II, an $80 million research vessel once used to explore the wreck of the Titanic, after a routine search netted traces of marijuana and two marijuana pipes in a crew member's shaving kit. The ship was returned but only after its owner, the Woods Hole Oceanographic Institution, agreed to send Customs a letter supporting the antidrug campaign and promising to tighten security.

Controversy about this policy has arisen over the argument that many owners of such vessels and vehicles may risk the loss of their property without personal knowledge of any controlled substance being aboard. Members of the American Civil Liberties Union (ACLU) have stated that this is an unconstitutional practice because of the traditional premise in American jurisprudence that the punishment fit the crime.

Electronic Surveillance and Civil Liberties

The past 25 years have seen a virtual revolution in technology relevant to electronic surveillance. Advances in electronics, semiconductors, computers, imaging, data bases, and related technologies have greatly increased technological options for police surveillance activities. Although the use of electronic surveillance in drug control is nothing new, techniques such as the wiretap have raised renewed concerns over the protection of one's right to privacy.

The major law addressing electronic surveillance, Title III of the Omnibus Crime Control and Safe Streets Act of 1968, that was designed to protect the privacy of wire and oral communications. At the time this act was passed, electronic surveillance was primarily limited to telephone taps and hidden microphones (bugs). Since then, however, basic communications have undergone rapid technological changes with the advent of such technologies as cellular telephones, personal pagers, personal computers, cordless telephones, electronic mail, and electronic bulletin boards. Many of these devices are now commonly used by drug traffickers to assist them in communicating with drug suppliers and customers.

As there are new and increasingly mobile drug gangs evident throughout the country, law enforcement agencies at both the state and federal level are making more frequent use of electronic surveillance technology to combat drug trafficking. Public concerns arise with regard to the circumstances under which these technologies are applied and how they might infringe on first, fourth, and fifth amendment rights. But at the same time, the public is also concerned about crime (especially violent crime) and generally supports the use of electronic technology in criminal investigations. So, the balancing of these concerns remains a critical issue in drug control.

CATEGORIES OF BEHAVIOR
SUBJECT TO ELECTRONIC SURVEILLANCE

1. *Movements.* where someone is. Individuals can be tracked electronically via beepers as well as by monitoring computerized transactional accounts.

2. *Actions.* what someone is doing or has done. Electronic devices to monitor action include: monitoring of keystrokes on computer terminals, monitoring of telephone numbers called with pen registers, cable TV monitoring, monitoring of financial and computerized accounts, and accessing computerized law enforcement or investigatory systems.

3. *Communications.* what someone is saying or writing, and hearing or receiving. Two-way electronic communications can be intercepted (whether the means be analog or digital communication) via wired telephones, cordless or cellular telephones, or digital electronic mail. Two-way nonelectronic communication can be intercepted via a variety of microphone devices and other transmitters.

4. *Actions and communications.* the details of what someone is doing or saying. Electronic visual surveillance, generally accompanied by audio surveillance, can monitor the actions and communications of individuals in both public and private places, and in daylight or darkness.

5. *Emotions.* the psychological and physiological reactions to circumstances. Polygraph testing, voice stress analyzers, and brain wave analyzers attempt to determine an individual's reactions.

Source: U.S. Congress, Office of Technology Assessment, 1985

The primary purpose of electronic surveillance is to monitor the behavior of individuals, including individual movements, actions, communications, emotions, and/or various combinations of these. From a law enforcement and investigative standpoint, the potential benefits offered through new technologies may be substantial: for example, the development of more accurate and complete information on suspects, the possible reduction in time and manpower required for case investigation, and the expansion of the options for preventing and deterring crimes.

From a societal perspective, the possible benefits are also important—including the potential for increasing one's physical security in the home and on the streets, strengthening efforts to prevent drug trafficking, and enhancing the protection of citizens and government officials from terrorist actions.

In general, electronic surveillance is used primarily in gambling and narcotics cases. In 1974 gambling was the most common object of electronic surveillance, and narcotics was second-most common; in 1984 the order was reversed. According to the U.S. Office of Technology Assessment, an average of about 25 percent of intercepted communications in 1984 were incriminating in nature, 2,393 persons were arrested as a result of electronic surveillance, and about 27 percent of those arrested were convicted.

The difficulty in using intrusion as a principle by which to evaluate a "reasonable expectation of privacy" and the appropriateness of using a particular surveillance device is that no criteria have yet been explicitly formulated to determine intrusiveness. Instead, the facts of individual cases seem to determine individual courses of action.

Still, based on court rulings, congressional statutes, and executive orders, it is possible to isolate five dimensions that are important in determining whether the situation warrants violation or protection of ordinary civil liberties. The five dimensions are: the nature of the information, the nature of the area or communication to be placed under surveillance, the scope of the surveillance, the surreptitiousness of the surveillance, and pre-electronic analogy. In evaluating the legitimacy of the government's use of surveillance devices, three dimensions are considered: the purpose of the investigation, the degree of individualized suspicion, and the relative effectiveness of the surveillance.

It is clear that the use of higher technology in surveillance activities by law enforcement agencies will prevail. In particular, with the more frequent use of detection devices and readily available electronic equipment by drug traffickers, the more sophisticated surveillance equipment will be. Implementing such technology will no doubt continue to fall under close scrutiny by courts and public groups in the coming years. Its use, however, is clearly an important factor in the detection and documentation of covert criminal activity in the drug trade.

DIMENSIONS FOR BALANCING CIVIL LIBERTY INTEREST AGAINST GOVERNMENT INVESTIGATIVE INTEREST

Civil liberty interest:

1. Nature of information: The more personal or intimate the information that is to be gathered about a target, the more intrusive the surveillance technique and the greater the intrusion to civil liberties.

2. Nature of the place or communication: The more "private" the area or type of communication to be placed under surveillance, the more intrusive the surveillance and the greater the threat to civil liberties.

3. Scope of the surveillance: The more people and activities that are subject to surveillance, the more intrusive the surveillance and the greater the threat to civil liberties.

4. Surreptitiousness of surveillance: The less likely it is for the individual to be aware of the surveillance and the harder it is for the individual to detect it, the greater is the threat to civil liberties.

5. Pre-electronic analogy: Pre-electronic analogies are often considered in determining intrusiveness, but with widely varying interpretations.

Government's investigative interest:

1. Purpose of investigation: Importance ranked as follows: national security, domestic security, law enforcement, and the proper administration of government programs.

2. Degree of individualized suspicion: The lower that the level of suspicion is, the harder it is to justify the use of surveillance devices.

3. Relative effectiveness: More traditional investigative techniques should be used and proven ineffective before using technologically sophisticated techniques.

Source: U.S. Congress, Office of Technology Assessment, 1985

Drug Testing

Hardly a day goes by without more news detailing the extent of drug abuse in our society. The staggering statistics are clear evidence that something must be done to help curtail the problem. For example, in 1986, the National Institute of Justice (NIJ) reported that 25 percent of all hospital admissions stemmed from drug abuse. In addition, 40 percent of admissions from accidents are drug-related, while cocaine overdose deaths are running at a rate of 25 per week (which is up 25 percent from 1986). Drug addiction of newborn babies is also a growing health concern for the early 1990s. The dollar figure of drug-related accidents is staggering: the national figure has been calculated at $81 billion per year, half of which is attributed to drug abuse.

Testing employees in the work place has been suggested by some as an effective way to identify, treat, and control drug abuse. Despite cries of invasion of privacy and unreasonable search in violation of federal and state constitutions, drug testing in various forms is either legal or in the process of becoming legal.

The Supreme Court has legitimized certain kinds of drug testing. For example, in 1988 the Congress passed the Drug-free Workplace Act. Additionally, federal executive departments and agencies have promulgated drug testing rules. An estimated 20 states and some cities have passed forms of employee drug testing statutes or ordinances.

Because the workplace offers somewhat of a captive pool of subjects, proponents of the drug testing control strategy have advocated that drug testing be accomplished in that forum. Testing for drugs in the work place is generally concerned with the following five areas:

(1) who to test,
(2) when to test,
(3) what procedure to follow,
(4) what to test for, and
(5) what sanctions to impose on employees with positive test results.

Federal and state courts have generally held that an employer may test an applicant for drugs if the applicant is told of the testing beforehand. An employer may, therefore, withhold an employment offer based on a confirmed test result.

The issue of testing employees raises other concerns. Arguments in favor of drug testing for employees generally focus on concerns for employee safety and employer liability. Other pro-testing arguments address issues such as decreased job performance and productivity, rising absenteeism, and rising health care costs. To illustrate this, the scope of the problem is indicated in the tables below:

Most of the controversy over drug testing stems from the arbitrary, random, or unannounced testing of the worker on the job, as mentioned above. Civil libertarians argue that this is a classic invasion of one's privacy and, drug testing in the work place is a violation of one's fourth and fifth amendment rights.

SCOPE OF THE DRUG PROBLEM

*   Estimated 6 million cocaine users
*   Estimated 20 million marijuana users
*   In some populations, 25-45 percent of job applicants showed recent drug use
*   Estimated $60-100 billion annual cost to industry due to alcohol and drug use

PROFILE OF AVERAGE COCAINE/CRACK USER

*   Spends an average $637/week for cocaine/crack
*   25 percent lost jobs
*   25-51 percent lost spouse/friends
*   42 percent lost all money
*   39 percent had automobile accidents
*   25-29 percent stole from work/friends/family
*   51-71 percent preferred cocaine/crack to food and sex

Source: Cocaine Hot-line, Fair Oaks Hospital, Fair Oaks, New Jersey, 1988

In spite of the above assertions, most courts have held that employees may indeed be tested under certain circumstances. Specifically, if the employee is on notice of being tested for drugs, an employer may test upon reasonable suspicion of drug use, after a reportable injury or after a chargeable accident. In addition, legal trends indicate that employee testing as part of a physical examination or random testing if the employee is in a safety sensitive position will become more customary.

The Department of Transportation's extensive drug testing program delineates many specific procedures for administrators to follow. In particular, the program addresses the confidentiality of records and employee identity, specimen tampering, control over the transfer of collected specimen (the chain of custody), certification of laboratories, testing methods (including confirmation of an initial positive test result by MS and GS technology (discussed below)), medical evaluation of test results, and sanctions for confirmed test results of employees.

At the time of this writing, current law does not uniformly identify the drugs for which an employee may be tested. Many companies and agencies have chosen to follow the lead of the Department of Transportation and test only for the NIDA-5 (National Institute on Drug Abuse): marijuana, cocaine, opiates, phencyclidine, and amphetamines.

As mentioned briefly above, most drug testing programs have adopted one of three ways of screening for drugs. These are as follows:

1. *Pre-employment Screening.* This method tests all or selected applicants for employment, usually in conjunction with a pre-employment physical. A positive result will usually be followed up by a second or confirmatory test. In some cases, the applicants are informed ahead of time of the drug test and are questioned about any medication they are on, including reasons for the medication. This is because prescription drugs can be abused as readily as illicit drugs and presence of these drugs should be investigated.

2. *For Cause.* Supervisors or employers can request this test if they suspect that an employee is unfit for work or is impaired by drugs or alcohol. A specimen may be requested to determine if the employee has indeed been under the influence of drugs or alcohol. Typically, this method occurs after an accident or an observable change in behavior of the employee.

3. *Random Urinalysis.* This method involves the selection of an appropriately significant number, as well as a scientifically drawn, random sample of employees for screening. Screening is usually performed several times a year, each time on a different random sample. Basically, this means that all employees in a particular job category are eligible at any time for screening.

CLOSE-UP: RANDOM DRUG TESTING BEGINS FOR TRANSPORTATION WORKERS

On Monday, December 18, 1989, random d-rug testing began for four million transportation workers. Under the new program, workers will face the prospect of being required to give urine samples on short notice. In some cases, computers will select pilots, flight attendants, and other employees to be tested for drugs such as marijuana, cocaine, opiates, amphetamines, and phencyclidine. Transportation Secretary Samuel Skinner is considering the addition of alcohol to the testing list.

Testing rules in the airline industry will take effect first, with maritime, railroad, trucking, transit, and pipeline companies to follow suit by early 1990. Transportation officials eventually expect half of the work force in safety-related jobs to be tested each year.

Department rules require that tests be performed by outside laboratories certified by the Department of Health and Human Services and that companies follow stringent procedures for collecting samples and preventing access to them before testing.

Source: *The Kansas City Star*, Associated Press, December 18, 1989.

As indicated, the testing cycle usually involves the initial screening of a urine, sample followed by a confirmatory test for samples suspected of containing drugs. These procedures are discussed in greater detail below.

Drug Screening. The methods used to screen urine samples are designed to be an accurate and reliable means to distinguish negative specimens from those that may contain drugs or drug metabolites. Drug screening techniques should be precise so that operator technique cannot adversely effect performance. Examples of the major immunoassay technologies are given below.

Abbott-Fluorescence Polarization Immunoassay (FPIA). This system is an extremely sensitive, rapid, precise, and reliable screening technique that is also fully automated. The system functions on an inverse relationship between signal to drug concentration, which provides excellent sensitivity at low drug concentrations. The system also uses a reagent bar-coding technology that virtually eliminates the possibility of operator error.

Roche-Radioimmunoassay (RIA). RIA technology is also an extremely sensitive and reliable screening system. It has even been chosen by the United States Armed Forces as the screening method of choice. Drawbacks to the system are that it requires expensive ancillary equipment for operation and that it uses radioactive reagents to detect the presence of drugs. This requires operators to wear special protective clothing and to be specially trained in handling discarded materials, all of which add to the cost of the testing procedure.

Syva-Enzyme Multiplied Immunoassay Technique (EMIT). The EMIT system functions on a direct relationship between signal to drug concentration; it is less sensitive than FPIA and RIA and less precise at low drug concentrations. The disadvantage of the EMIT system is that there are significant variations in test results between technologies and a high rate of poor performance when challenged by blind testing (EMIT has a 40 percent false negative rate in that it will miss 40 percent of individuals that have smoked marijuana in the previous 48 hours).

Confirmation Tests. As mentioned, when drug tests may affect an individual's personal rights, a positive drug screening must be followed by a secondary or confirmatory test. The second test must be based on different chemical principles with an equal or lower threshold value than the screening test and must specifically identify the drug present in the sample using a different portion of the original sample.

The technology most commonly used for the confirmatory test is Gas-Liquid Chromatography (GC) or Mass Spectrometry (MS). Of these two technologies, the MS is considered the more reliable, but it is also more expensive to purchase and operate. Recently, Hewlett-Packard Corporation has developed a detector, called a mass selective detector (MSD), that is less expensive than a full mass spectrometer and provides the same high quality data.

Chain of Custody. This is the method of documenting which urine sample belongs to which testee, and who handled the sample from the time that it was originally collected. Without strict procedures for establishing the chain of custody of the urine sample, even the most technologically advanced drug testing method will be of no value.

The issue of chain of custody plays a role in several critical phases of the testing procedure. These are as follows:

- Collecting the sample
- Labeling the sample
- Limiting the number of individuals that handle the sample
- Ensuring that samples are stored properly
- Limiting access to information about test results to individuals with a legitimate need to know

Other important issues that should be considered in drug testing are:

(1) the passive inhalation of marijuana when an individual is present in a room where it is being smoked;

(2) the ingestion of certain foods that may result in false positive drug readings (poppy seed bagels may test positive for opiates, for instance);

(3) the lack of standards directing drug testing laboratories to operate under the same set of criteria;

(4) the cause-and-effect relationship between the presence of drugs and one's behavior, which is usually an issue in "probable cause" testing;

(5) the distinction between the different drug testing arenas, such as
     hospitals, treatment centers, sports testing (discussed later in this
     chapter), the military, schools, probation and parole programs,
     etc.; and

(6) the adulterations of specimens, such as when urine substitution or
     dilution take place.

If it is true that a substantial group of drug users use drugs only on week-
ends, at parties, and for purposes of relaxation and diversion, drug testing may
alter drug use patterns. For example, marijuana users will test positive for drug
use for a far longer period of time than cocaine users. A user that wants to get
high on a Friday night is relatively safe from a positive drug test on Monday
morning if he or she uses cocaine, but the same person almost certain of a positive test if he or she uses marijuana. The same relationship occurs with regard
to amphetamines. As a result, some theorize that for those drug users that are
hell-bent on getting high, drug testing may cause many of them to switch to
harder drugs, which last a shorter period of time in their systems.

CLOSE-UP: THE DRUG USER's ROLE

If we could just take the enormous profits out of drug sales....but
how? By confiscating the property bought with the proceeds of drugs?
It already happens. By legalizing drugs? That risks drawing more
young people into drug abuse.
The financial lifeblood of the drug traffic is the drug user, including
the casual user that may think he's doing nothing wrong. Everybody
that buys drugs contributes to the profits and the killings that turn cities
into war zones.

As technology progresses, drug testing may someday be done by the analysis of human hair follicles. A 1987 study by Dr. Gideon Koren of the Hospital
for Sick Children in Toronto compared urine and hair samples for evidence of
drug abuse. Dr. Koren contended that once traces of drugs enter the hair, they
are permanently registered there. Testing hair follicles, he asserted, would
eliminate the problem of employees avoiding detection of drug use by abstain-
ing from drug use just prior to being tested by employers.
In 1990, however, the American Medical Association reported on Koren's
findings and argued that although there is some credence to the testing of hair
follicles for drugs, urine provides the most reliable data to date. According to
the AMA, dyeing or bleaching hair, in addition to exposure to other substances
such as automobile exhaust fumes, can contaminate test results.

These issues and others pose important questions and considerations that must be addressed in this critical area of drug control. Because existing technology is generally considered reliable by professionals in the area, the ironing-out of other ancillary issues may result in effective alternatives to traditional drug control methods.

Needle Exchange Programs

To date, the problem of AIDS (Acquired Immune Deficiency Syndrome) dominates much of the medical profession's public health and policy concerns. Although the transmission of the disease is often accomplished through deviate sexual activity by homosexuals and prostitutes, an estimated 20 percent of AIDS cases were reported to have been transmitted through the sharing of needles by intravenous drug users.

Needle-sharing has become a major problem in inner cities, where heroin addiction prevails. The heroin addict, for example, typically injects himself with the drug several times a day. Because sterile needles are not always available, the sharing of needles between one person and another sometimes occurs. According to testimony before the U.S. House of Representatives in April, 1989, one HIV-infected drug user can conceivably expose up to 100 other users over the course of a few months. (Other communicable diseases such as hepatitis are also transmitted in this fashion.)

In an effort to curb the spread of the disease, both researchers and medical professionals have considered the controversial idea of exchanging dirty needles belonging to drug addicts for clean needles. Most needle exchange programs consist of three basic functions:

1.   To dispense sterile needles to current IV (intravenous) users.

2.   To promote and accept returns of used needles to control how needles are discarded.

3.   To change the behavior of IV drug users through health education and counseling.

Controversy exists with this program because many feel that such a program encourages drug use, that needles will not be used, and that the program will only create more drug addicts and, accordingly, more AIDS carriers. The assertion that the needles will not be used is based on the view that needle sharing is a ritualistic practice, deeply embedded into the subculture of IV drug users.

Another argument against the exchange programs is that giving away needles is illegal. The question of legality may be a valid one, at least in certain jurisdictions, and is constantly being addressed at the state and local government levels.

EXCHANGING NEEDLES IN NEW YORK CITY

After operating seven months, new York City's program to give intravenous drug addicts new hypodermic needles to help them stem the spread of AIDS has finally begun to attract more participants, but remains under attack.

On one hand, city health officials running the program are saying drug addicts are learning to clean needles after using them, but on the other hand, it is difficult to determine whether addicts have actually stopped sharing needles. Health officials are having trouble attracting participants for the year-long experiment—160 have enrolled in a program intended for 400. And detractors, calling it a failure, are demanding that it be ended soon.

Reynaldo H., with a small bible and a pack of Kool cigarettes stuffed in the breast pocket of his Hawaiian-style shirt, said he never imagined being part of the experiment, in which intravenous drug users are given clean needles in exchange for their used ones. But a year ago, the 32-year-old heroin addict and dealer was stricken with AIDS-related infections. "I was sick," he said, describing the open lesions in his scalp and mouth that kept him from eating for days. "The program took me in, got me in a clinic, got my health back and put me in drug treatment."

More than half of the city's estimated 200,000 intravenous drug users are believed to be infected with the deadly virus that causes acquired immune deficiency syndrome, according to the City Health Department, which operates the program. The purpose of the program is to learn whether intravenous drug users can change their behavior and not share hypodermic syringes when injecting illegal drugs. The program, which is to cost $230,000 for a year, also counsels addicts and tests them for AIDS and other diseases.

Source: Marriott, M. (1989). "Drug Needle Exchange is Gaining but Still Under Fire." *The New York Times* (June 7):B1.

When considering the appropriateness of such a program, perhaps we should consider the success or failure of similar programs in places such as England, the Netherlands, Sweden, and Australia, where needle sharing programs have been operational since 1984. The results are extremely consistent. In Amsterdam, for example, researchers noted that 80 percent of needle-exchange users in the program stopped sharing equipment, as compared to 50 percent of non-exchangers. In considering the question of rising addiction among

IV drug users, 71 percent of Amsterdam's exchangers reported a decrease or no change in the rate of IV drug users.

In addition to the previously listed countries, Switzerland has also attempted to deal with its addiction problem through the use of a needle exchange program. In Zurich, community leaders created a ghetto of sorts known as "needle park," where addicts can use heroin or cocaine without fear of arrest from police. Addicts in needle park are estimated to require an average of $400 to $500 daily to support their habits. Many of these addicts consequently turn to stealing, drug dealing, or prostitution as a means of income. The government in Zurich exchanges an estimated 7,000 clean needles daily for used ones in the needle park are where the growing incidence of AIDS ranks only second to the United States.

Forfeiture of Attorney's Fees in Drug Cases

It is logical to assume that, considering the enormous cash flow of many drug traffickers, much of the money earned through illicit drug transactions ends up in the bank accounts of lawyers that represent drug traffickers. Through the use of carefully sculpted laws such as the 1984 Federal Comprehensive Forfeiture Act (CFA), the instances of lawyers knowingly accepting "dirty" money or assets for legal fees have greatly decreased. The most conspicuous legal precedents addressing the issue were handed down by the Supreme Court in 1989 in *United States v. Monsanto, Caplin* and *Drysdale*, and *Chartered v. United States*. These decisions basically held that the government's ability to enforce forfeiture extends to drug assets needed to pay attorney's fees.

In reviewing these cases, the Monsanto decision involved a defendant that was facing charges under the federal CCE statute of creating a continuing criminal enterprise. The indictment asserted that the defendant had acquired an apartment, a home, and a sum of $35,000 in cash as a result of drug trafficking activities. The government subsequently sought to freeze all assets of the defendant until the trial was over. In response to this, the defendant claimed that those assets were necessary to retain a competent lawyer for his defense. His claim was rejected by the district court.

As the trial progressed, an appellate court reviewed the district court's ruling and found that the frozen assets should, indeed, be used to pay attorney's fees. The defendant, however, declined because of the advanced stage of the trial, and he was ultimately convicted of the trafficking charges and was required to forfeit his assets.

The United States Supreme Court has ruled that the government's ability to forfeit extends to drug assets needed to pay attorney's fees

At a later stage in the appeals process, the Supreme Court agreed to hear the case involving forfeiture of attorney's fees. The Supreme Court ruled that the sale or transfer of potentially forfeitable assets is forbidden.

The issue of lawyers accepting drug assets in lieu of payment for services rendered raises several legal and ethical questions. Such legal questions include whether one's fifth or sixth amendment rights are violated through the use of such a tactic. Those opposed to the forfeiture practice point out that the sixth amendment provides the accused the right to counsel and the fifth amendment protects the right to due process under law. On both issues, however, the Supreme Court has upheld forfeiture sanctions against attorney's fees.

The ethical concerns of the forfeiture question have centered around three issues that should be considered. First, in the two cases above, opponents to forfeiture argued that the CFA actually encouraged attorneys to be less than thorough in investigating a client's case so that any fees they might have received would be protected from forfeiture. Additionally, some argue that when faced with losing legal fees under the CFA, an attorney may compromise his client's position during plea bargaining of a longer prison sentence were suggested in lieu of forfeiture of legal fees. In a third scenario, an attorney may be tempted to manipulate the justice system by representing a client on a contingency basis. Although the practice is considered unethical by the American Bar Association, the attorney could conceivably make an agreement with his client that only after *acquittal* of the client would the attorney be paid his designated fee. Thus, the unscrupulous attorney could avoid losing his fee under the CFA.

On the same day that the government argued its case in *Monsanto*, the Supreme Court heard oral arguments in the *Caplin* case. In this case, illicit-drug importer Christopher Reckmeyer paid the law firm of Caplin and Drysdale $25,000 for preindictment legal services. Before the case could go to trial, Reckmeyer pled guilty to the charges, and virtually all of his assets were declared forfeitable by the court—including fees paid to the law firm. After an extended legal process whereby the law firm attempted to secure a release of the fees already paid to them, the Supreme Court ultimately ruled that the forfeiture was lawful and that there are no statutory, ethical, or constitutional impediments to the forfeiture of attorney's fees under the Federal Comprehensive Forfeiture Act.

Drug Control and Sports

Perhaps no segment of society has received more glaring publicity for its use of illicit drugs than America's athletes. The use of drugs by competing athletes dates back over 100 years. During that time, caffeine and alcohol were the drugs predominantly abused. Drug abuse by athletes today has developed to the point where an array of dangerous drugs are commonly used, including amphetamines, steroids, and cocaine. The drug abuse problem among athletes is not limited to professional athletes, but extends to amateur sports at both the college and high school levels.

Drug abuse awareness in sports was heightened in 1985 with the untimely deaths of athletes Len Bias and Don Rogers, both of whom died from cocaine overdoses. With regard to drug use in the NFL, former St. Louis Cardinal Carl Birdsong states, "I don't think drug abuse in the NFL is any greater than in any other segment of society. I think the media has sensationalized drug abuse in the NFL....I'd say 90 percent to 95 percent of them [the players] don't use drugs; they're productive and hard working, devoting a good deal of their time to charities" (p. 43).

Reports, however, of athletes possessing, using, and distributing illicit drugs have now become commonplace in newspapers, magazines, and on television. One popular illicit drug, cocaine, is used both for recreation and to enhance the performance of many athletes. In addition, the nonmedical use of steroids is becoming more commonplace among athletes and nonathletes as well.

The high visibility of many athletes, especially the successful ones, seems to make their drug problems more newsworthy than those of the average citizen. Most of the media accounts of drug abuse involving athletes report the use of illicit recreational drugs. Such activities have created a public outcry for control and have prompted athletic organizations to initiate antidrug programs. What is it that attracts athletes to drug abuse? Three different reasons can be identified to help explain their involvement with illicit drugs:

1. Drugs taken at the time of competition immediately enhance performance.

2. Drugs taken during training or well before competition enhance performance.

3. Recreational or street drugs are often used for the same reasons that nonathletes use them.

Steroids and Athletes

Athletes began using steroids over 30 years ago, after east European and Soviet athletes dominated an international sporting event. It was later discovered that these athletes had used testosterone to strengthen themselves. The American Pharmacy Journal reports: "[H]ad the medical profession been honest with athletes 20 years ago in answering their question, 'what do these drugs do?', and said 'we don't know what they do but they probably work,' we would not have lost face with the athletes" (1986, p. 41).

The allure of steroids to the athlete is one of promise for a stronger body in a shorter period of time. Gabe Mirkin states, "Since the stress of prolonged exercise results in tissue damage, quicker healing means quicker recovery time and ultimately more time for training and muscle building, anabolic steroids have a reputation for this" (1978, p. 89).

Defining Steroids

Anabolic steroids, originally developed in the 1930s to help maintain strength in aging males, are synthetic forms of the male sex hormone testosterone. The many functions of testosterone include stimulating the development of bone, muscle, skin, and hair growth as well as lowering the voice and emotional responses. Because women produce so little testosterone, they develop masculine characteristics when they take anabolic steroids.

When an excess of testosterone is produced in the body, the skeletal growth mechanisms may literally shut down. If this happens, the result can be stunted growth, shriveled testicles, lowered sperm counts, and balding.

Because steroids are a controlled substance in the United States, a prescription is necessary to acquire them. Consequently, physicians have been inundated over the years with requests for prescriptions from athletes in all disciplines; these athletes are all hoping to improve their performance.

A 1986 study of steroid use conducted by Dr. Robert Voy, Chief Medical Officer for the U.S. Olympic team, found that up to 40 percent of the steroids being used by athletes were obtained by prescriptions from physicians. The rest were thought to be diverted from legal distribution channels or manufactured clandestinely.

As mentioned, athletic organizations, especially amateur ones, are concerned with this type of drug activity and may restrict such drugs in an effort to maintain a degree of competitive fairness. Let us now examine the drug control programs.

Drug Control in Amateur Sports

The two major governing bodies for amateur athletics in the United States are the United States Olympic Committee (USOC) and the National Collegiate Athletic Association (NCAA). Each organization bans the use of certain substances by competitors.

USOC. The USOC has developed a list of banned drugs. The list consists of five categories of drugs, including psychomotor stimulants, sympathomimetic amines, narcotic analgesics, anabolic steroids, and miscellaneous central nervous system stimulants. Drugs in these categories are banned to discourage use of them to improve an athlete's performance during competition.

Drug testing is conducted by one of numerous methods for testing urine. The USOC tests athletes in events such as the Olympic and Pan American trials and games. Athletes are disqualified if they test positive for drugs or refuse to be tested. In the event that an athlete withdraws from a competition, no penalty is imposed.

NCAA. During the 1986 NCAA convention in New Orleans, drug testing legislation was passed. The list of banned drugs is similar to that of the IOC but includes substances banned for specific sports, diuretics, and street drugs. Unfortunately, the NCAA does not include narcotic analgesics, which are on the IOC list.

Drug testing is done at 73 NCAA championships and football postseason bowl games. Drug testing during the regular season remains the responsibility of each school. If any player tests positive for any of the banned drugs, the NCAA can render the player ineligible for that particular postseason competition as well as for postseason play for a minimum of 90 days after the test date.

Drug Control in Professional Sports

The trend to pursue drug testing for professional athletes has fallen somewhat behind that of amateur sports events. Many opponents of drug testing in professional sports claim violations of privacy and civil liberties. Resulting from the problem of drugs in professional sports, a variety of programs have been developed and are briefly discussed below:

Tennis. In 1985, the Men's International Professional Tennis Council approved mandatory drug testing, which had been endorsed by the Association of Tennis Professionals. This was the first (and only) professional player's association to sponsor mandatory testing. Random testing for street drugs is also conducted at two of the top five tournaments each year (Australian Open, French Open, Wimbledon, U.S. Open, and Lipton International Players Championship).

Baseball. Peter Ueberroth, former Major League Baseball (MLB) Commissioner, placed emphasis on the removal of substance abuse from professional baseball. As a result, mandatory testing of all baseball management personnel was introduced in May 1985. Although the MLB was hopeful that the MLB Players Association would follow its lead, proposals for drug testing were met with opposition from the association, which warned that any drug testing would be challenged in court. Currently, drug testing is the responsibility of each individual team, and any team player that is convicted of a criminal drug charge is subject to disciplinary action by the commissioner.

Basketball. In September 1983, the National Basketball Association (NBA), along with the NBA Players Association (NBAPA), instituted an antidrug program. Under the program, the NBA is permitted to administer drug tests that consist of four tests in a six-week period without prior notice. The program provides that any player found guilty of criminal charges involving drugs be immediately dismissed from the league. Ousted players may seek reinstatement after a two-year period, but such action requires approval of both the commissioner and the NBAPA. If reinstated and later convicted of a second drug offense, the player is permanently dismissed from the league.

The NBA program is unique in that it focuses on drug education. This is accomplished through a series of seminars on drugs, with emphasis placed on helping rookies adapt to a new lifestyle.

Football. In 1986, National Football League (NFL) Commissioner Pete Rozelle announced a drug-testing program that included mandatory drug testing. Under the program, two unscheduled drug tests during the regular season would be required of each player. The program also requires that any player convicted of a criminal drug violation or requiring hospitalization for substance abuse be removed from the team's roster for 30 days and receive only 50 percent of his pay during that time. A second such infraction would result in another 30-day suspension, but this time the player would not be paid. A third violation would ban the player permanently from the league but would still provide a means for reinstatement after one year.

Other Public Policy Issues

Reduce Aid to Source Countries

Hardliners that advocate reducing aid to foreign countries usually argue that the only way to disrupt drug trafficking is to eliminate the source of supply. One possible means to use leverage against source countries is to cease trade practices and/or eliminate aid to them. The prevailing theory is that if drugs are made less available, the price of them will rise, and will reduce the number of users. This theory may not be a valid one, however, because past increases in drug prices have proven to have little effect on the demand for drugs.

Opponents of this measure argue that it is not the supply but the demand that fuels the drug business and that cutting off one source will just force traffickers to find another. Additionally, many feel that forcing source countries to eradicate crops and extradite their citizens would jeopardize already fragile economies and create political instability. Both of these possibilities would, of course, damage relations with the United States.

Increase Aid to Source Countries

Many feel that, instead, a concerted effort to revive economies and promote economic development in source countries is necessary to persuade these countries to stop trafficking drugs. Under this strategy, all countries affected by drug abuse would contribute some form of aid. The opposition to this proposal contends that such an action would, in effect, reward the drug traffickers and would encourage other countries to participate in the drug trade in order to qualify for aid.

Expand the Role of the Military

While some drug enforcement strategists debate the merits of economic strategies, still others have considered the use of force. The Reagan Administration declared that drug trafficking poses a threat to national security. It has been suggested, therefore, that the United States military is better equipped to deal with such a threat than are civilian law enforcement agencies. This is supported by arguments that the military has at its disposal advanced intelligence capabilities, training, equipment, and other resources to launch a successful, full-scale drug control initiative.

CASE STUDY: BUDDIES

Alan Greenwald began life as the privileged youngest son of a prominent Hagerstown, Maryland family. By age 29, however, he had become the fugitive former ringleader of the state's largest and longest-standing cocaine smuggling ring. Having had casual customer contact with local drug dealers, young Greenwald and his hometown buddy Marshall Jones, a physician's son, reached the fateful decision that made them rich but notorious—to become narcotics kingpins. The two moved to Miami, and on Collins Avenue quickly found a major Colombian supplier, Jorge Torres. With Torres' help, they proceeded to supply Maryland with an estimated $100 million worth of dope over a period of 10 years.

Of course, there were glitches. First, an effort to sell 700 pounds of marijuana in Florida failed. The customers were state drug agents. The buddies were to be locked up for a year, but Jones found a great work-release program, Silver Touch Talent Consultants, which put him right to work—dealing drugs. During their "imprisonment," a boat that they had hired to move marijuana from Jamaica strayed into Cuban waters, its cargo was confiscated, and its three-man crew was imprisoned, requiring congressional intervention to get them freed. By the time of their release, the two buddies had acquired a staff: Steven Silver (of Silver Touch), who served as a money launderer, and the other two Jones brothers, Nathan and Frank, who, along with one Carl Martin, handled the Hagerstown end of things and also worked as couriers.

On his first trip on AMTRAK, young Frank Jones chickened out and threw two kilos of cocaine off the train in Georgia. Both the Maryland and Florida ends of the conspiracy rushed to Savannah and walked the track for days, but to no avail. The package was never found. Other Greenwald/Jones couriers were arrested with cocaine from time to time, such as Dale Blevins at O'Hare Airport and Charles "Billy" Hoffman in Florida, but the organization bought them good defenses. Blevins was acquitted based on an illegal luggage search; Hoffman served a few months. More recently, Jeffrey Sollenberg, a Maryland friend whom Greenwald asked to store money in a basement safe, gave information to Washington County, Maryland detectives, resulting in invaluable evidence against the partners.

Notwithstanding these setbacks, the enterprise was profitable for almost 10 years and, although a full accounting can never be made, some evidence of its level of cash flow is provided by the following:

• During his prison stay, Marshall Jones received $200,000 from Silver and a known $200,000 to $250,000 from Maryland dealers. Jones later invested $325,000 in Silver Touch, and when arrested he was relieved of $136,000 and his $61,000 Maserati.

• Silver is known to have purchased $1.8 million worth of cashier's checks.

• More than $100,000 passed through Sollenberg's safe, including $18,000 seized by the arresting officers.

- In 1986, Guy Varron, a Hagerstown distributor, stored $100,000 for Greenwald and Jones.

- By 1987, federal authorities had seized $1.9 million of the ring's assets, including Silver's Miami recording studio, several houses, a racing boat, three luxury cars, and $135,000 in cash.

- Federal prosecutors confidently estimated that more than 1,600 pounds of cocaine flowed through just the avenues known to be controlled by Greenwald and Jones at purchase prices from $12,000 to $25,000 per pound.

Early on, Jones became the marketing expert, building teams of distributors in Virginia and West Virginia, as well as Maryland, that would sell all the drugs that Greenwald could buy. Raymond Carnahan was Jones' distributor in Alexandria, Virginia. An OCDETF team there, composed of IRS and DEA agents, made undercover purchases from Carnahan and eventually arrested him with a pound of cocaine.

At about the same time, "Billy" Hoffman again was arrested, this time by narcotics detectives in Florida, with a kilo of cocaine and a one-way ticket to Baltimore. After five more months in jail, Hoffman pled to a reduced charge and began to cooperate with authorities. An Assistant State's Attorney in Hagerstown made the connection between Hoffman and Greenwald, and through Hoffman's information, a Washington County, Maryland grand jury returned an indictment against Greenwald. The case and the county prosecutor moved to Maryland's U.S. Attorney's office as the evidence grew. Washington County and Maryland state police investigators worked alongside the DEA, IRS, ATF, and others to expose the organization's tentacles. The long series of investigations that retrospectively uncovered the Greenwald, Jones, and Silver partnership provides a fine example of coordinated enforcement effort by local, state and federal agencies.

To date, more than 125 persons having criminal culpability have been identified in the investigation, and more than 40 have been convicted in Maryland, Virginia, and Florida. Several million dollars worth of drugs have been seized in the three states. Silver and Martin were sentenced to 35 years each; Torres, the supplier, 25. Nate Jones was sentenced to 10 years, and his younger brother, Frank, of AMTRAK fame, awaits sentencing.

Greenwald was the first to fall, and Marshall Jones was the last. Faced with indictments in Hagerstown, Greenwald made arrangements to surrender but instead disappeared. He left behind several thousand dollars, his Mercedes, and his wife, Deborah, eight months pregnant (who was later convicted on state drug charges). In December 1988, Greenwald was indicted in Baltimore for operating a continuing criminal enterprise. Marshall Jones decided to cooperate with federal prosecutors and has continued to do so throughout the many trials. Nonetheless, in January 1989, he was sentenced to 18 years in federal prison, forever closing Maryland's biggest narco-business.

Source: Organized Crime Drug Enforcement Task Force, 1988.

Some jurisdictions have implemented the use of the National Guard to assist drug control officers in raids. The primary use of National Guardsmen is to augment staff in nonthreatening functions in certain operations. These duties include transporting and booking prisoners, facilitating certain paperwork, etc.

Predictably, this school of thought has its critics, who hold that drug trafficking is not a military problem and to empower the military with civilian police powers opposes the country's foundation of democracy, which is based, in part, on the separation of powers. Recent studies have even cast doubts on the ability of the military to make an impact on drug consumption through interdiction.

In 1988, the Pentagon sponsored a study directed by Peter Reuter of the RAND Corporation. The report dealt with the suggestion that the military become more involved with drug interdiction and protecting national borders. The study, reflecting some bias on the part of the sponsor, examined the presumption that the armed forces would be able to construct an impenetrable electronic net around the country through the use of advanced surveillance aircraft.

Reuter devised a mathematical model to estimate the impact that increased spending on interdiction would have on domestic drug consumption. He concluded that a key factor in the issue is that at least 75 percent of the money spent to buy cocaine goes to the bottom level of the market—the street dealers. Only 10 percent of the final price allegedly goes to the production and smuggling sector. The study cited the Coast Guard, an able player at the job of interdiction, which found drugs on only one out of every eight boats that it boarded in 1986, even when acting on intelligence information. Therefore, doubling the number of patrols by adding Navy vessels will not double the success rate, unless intelligence is vastly improved.

Reuter concluded with the assertion that seizures of big shipments have little impact on buyers and little to no impact on demand. At best, according to the results of the study, the use of the military would only reduce cocaine shipments from 120 metric tons to 90 metric tons per year.

Legalize Drugs

While the previous strategies are aimed at reducing drug trafficking, another strategy is based on the assumption that drug abuse will never be eliminated. The strategy that accepts drug abuse calls for legalization of drugs and is aimed instead at reducing the control that criminals have over the drug trade.

The prospect of legalizing drugs has attracted considerable attention from the media, civil libertarians, some public officials, and certain members of Congress. The arguments for and against the legalization of illicit drugs are many and should be carefully weighed with such considerations as public safety and personal freedoms. In addition, other considerations include the rights of the people as a free society versus the rights of innocent victims of the drug trade (see Chapter 12).

Increase Spending for Drug Education Programs

A final strategy focuses on the demand side of the drug cycle. One traditional school of thought is for the government to continue to spend more and more on public education and treatment programs, although it is conceded that this strategy will take many years to be considered successful. In theory, once demand was under control, the supply would soon dry up. Of course, the response to this argument is that to stop drug trafficking, sources must be cut off at the supply side, not the demand side.

Summary

Controversy is nothing new in considering the fate of the drug abuse problem in the United States. Much of the controversy in drug control stems from the tactics that are adopted by law enforcement officials. On one hand, many traditional police tactics have proven less than effective, but on the other hand, the use of more unconventional enforcement techniques, such as the forfeiting of ill-gotten attorney's fees and needle exchange programs, raise concerns for civil liberties and expanded police authority.

One controversial technique that has proven effective in identifying drug traffickers is the criminal profile. Although police tend to shy away from the word "profile," the use of this tactic has resulted in many major seizures. The profiling procedure focuses on drug couriers in transit. The 1989 *United States v. Sokolow* decision has given legitimacy to this procedure, which basically enables agents to stop and question individuals that look or act like a typical drug dealer. The court in this decision has recognized that certain traits are unique to drug dealers and typically are not practiced by the general population.

The reverse sting is another enforcement technique that has proven effective in identifying drug buyers (or users) rather than sellers. This technique requires the undercover officer to pose as a drug seller. The officer is authorized to sell a quantity of drugs to a prospective buyer, but the buyer is immediately arrested and the drugs are seized as evidence. Those that criticize this technique claim that an atmosphere of entrapment prevails and that police are enticing people to commit crimes. The proper use of this technique, however, requires police to show a defendant's "criminal intent" and his or her predisposition to purchase the drugs.

With so many different enforcement techniques, the practice of surveillance is common. Because covert observation by the police has always generated a certain degree of skepticism by the public, the police must take great care in initiating certain surveillance operations. Officers must be careful that the activities for which the suspect is under investigation are authorized (for investigation) under federal guidelines. In addition, the concerns of both the government and civil libertarians must be observed throughout the operation.

Drug testing is not a new concern for drug control strategists, but the issue is far from being resolved. Most of the concern revolves around the questions of who should be tested, where, and under what set of circumstances. Drug testing of federal transportation and law enforcement employees has been authorized, but what about drug testing in the general work place? Some claim that the examination of a blood or urine sample violates one's fourth and fifth amendment rights.

The subject of drug testing leads us into the discussion of the problem of drugs and sports. This issue deals with several aspects, including nonaddictive and recreational drug use, and the use of drugs such as steroids, which are designed to aid the athlete in their particular sport. Regulatory agencies governing drug use in sports have resulted in punitive provisions for those that use dangerous drugs. Such provisions may include: fines, suspension or expulsion from professional athletics, and even criminal prosecution.

DISCUSSION QUESTIONS

1. Discuss why it is important to monitor closely the use of electronic surveillance by law enforcement agencies.

2. List the different ways that criminal activity can be documented through the use of electronic surveillance.

3. Discuss some of the more valid concerns in the practice of "officially" abducting drug traffickers wanted in the United States.

4. List some possible options that the United States government should consider to eliminate international drug trafficking.

5. What fears do civil libertarians have regarding the practice of drug courier profiling by police?

6. Discuss how the "drug courier profile" can aid investigators in interdiction efforts.

7. The reverse sting poses some unique concerns for drug control strategists. List some of the pros and cons of this controversial drug control technique.

8. What is meant by the term "zero tolerance," and why has the term become so controversial?

9. What are some of the legal and moral ramifications of the practice of seizing attorney fees that have been earned from illegal drug enterprises?

10. Discuss why needle exchange programs are controversial throughout the world.

11. List and discuss the three purposes of most needle exchange programs.

12. Discuss the two main cases in which the forfeiture of legal fees was addressed by the Supreme Court. What are some of the pros and cons of this legal precedent?

13. Discuss the different circumstances under which one may be tested for drugs in the workplace. What are the pros and cons of drug testing in such a manner?

14. Discuss how reliability of a drug test can best be insured by an employer.

15. Why is drug testing in the workplace considered by some to be an invasion of personal freedom?

16. Discuss some of the unique problems encountered when considering implementation of a drug testing program.

17. What are the three ways urinalysis screening for drugs is used in private industry?

18. List and discuss the three main reasons why athletes choose to take illicit drugs.

19. Discuss the physiological effects of steroids on the human body.

20. Discuss how the drug control programs of amateur athletics differ from those of professional athletics?

21. Discuss the pros and cons of discontinuing foreign aid to countries that are considered to be source countries.

22. Should the military be considered for the drug enforcement effort? Explain your answer.

23. How does the 1988 study by the RAND Corporation address consideration of increased use of the military in drug interdiction?

CLASS PROJECTS

1. Study the controversies surrounding drug control in your community, and discuss both their strong and weak attributes.

CHAPTER 12

THE ISSUE OF LEGALIZING DRUGS

[I]s dissent necessary? You're damned right. We have a country that could be heaven on earth, but instead it has unnecessary poverty, discrimination against the black and the poor, and the continuous possibility of nuclear warfare....Everything that is wrong about the world is caused by a lack of moral conviction and moral initiative. For the moralist there is always evil in the universe to be combated.

Benjamin Spock, M.D.

As an alternative to the growing problem of drug abuse in America, some politicians and social behaviorists have suggested that the laws governing drug control be repealed or at least modified ("decriminalized"). Glaring questions about the social responsibility of such a policy surface when such a radical shift in public policy is considered. Such questions include: how will legalization affect the crime rate, and how will legalization affect public health? This chapter will attempt to examine these and other related issues.

In April 1988, at he United States Conference of Mayors, Baltimore Mayor Kurt Schmoke, one of several political figures favoring legalization, publicly proclaimed that legalization of illicit substances should be considered by lawmakers. Existing drug control laws, according to Schmoke, were ineffective and failed to serve as a deterrent to crime. His statement created a tidal wave of loosely organized "pro-reformers," who hopped on the legalization bandwagon, claiming that antinarcotics laws create evils worse than the drugs themselves: violent and organized crime, political and law enforcement corruption, and discriminatory enforcement of the law.

Some reformers argue that drug use is a personal moral decision and that it is not the responsibility of government to police social morality. Additionally, many of those that want to legalize drugs claim that crime rates soar as high as they do because drugs are treated as a criminal problem rather than a medical problem. Opponents of legalization argue that, while regulation of public morality may conflict with some personal freedoms, the government has a legitimate responsibility to insure order and public safety in our society.

As of the preparation of this text, the Bush administration rejects the notion of drug legalization. In addition, this view is shared by Congress and most all American opinion surveys to date. With regard to the latter, the National Opinion Research Center, through its studies, has concluded that the public rejects the idea of legalization by five to one. Additionally, five sixths of those surveyed said marijuana should not be legalized. Some argue, however, that such statements of public and political opinion are subject to rapid change as more information becomes available or as social conditions change. Perhaps one should consider how at one time, public opinions also strongly supported segregation, the Vietnam War, and slavery in America.

The fragmented numbers of pro-legalizers include some high-visibility supporters, such as former Secretary of State George Shultz. Shultz has stated that Americans should be at least willing to debate the legalization issue. Conservative political leaders such as economist Milton Friedman and William F. Buckley have also spoken out in favor of legalization. Others that support legalization include academics such as American University Professor Arnold Trebach, who is also the president of the Drug Policy Foundation in Washington. Trebach has publicly supported legalization and has stated that "keeping the drugs within the control of an absolute criminal prohibition makes the situation worse." (Corcoran, A15).

Perhaps most surprisingly, the legalization issue has been raised by some law enforcement officials, such as organized crime expert Ralph Salerno, former New York City Police Commissioner Patrick Murphy, now head of the Police Foundation, and Metro-Dade's Wesley C. Pomeroy. Still other police executives, such as Joseph MacNamera, Police Chief of San Jose, and former Minneapolis Police Chief Anthony Bouza, have raised questions about the damage resulting from law enforcement efforts to suppress drug use.

Much research has addressed the various issues of drug control. The research trend, however, seems to focus on the issue of legalization rather than the more pressing problem of drug abuse suppression, and on how existing drug control policy can be enhanced.

In December 1989, former Drug Control Policy Director William J. Bennett remarked in a speech at Harvard University that, generally, academics have not been supportive of drug control initiatives. Bennett added, "[I]n the great public policy debate over drugs, the academic and intellectual communities have, by and large, had little to contribute, and little of that has been genuinely useful or for that matter mentally distinguished." (Jaschik). In his speech,

Bennett urged academics to focus their research into the improving of drug control methods rather than trying to discredit them.

American Intellectuals may oppose the drug war because of their general hostility to law enforcement and criminal justice.
William Bennett
Director of National Drug Control Policy, 1989

Bennett has publicly claimed that many academics have attempted to identify the root of drug abuse in society not as the drugs themselves, but as poverty, racism, or "some equally large and intractable social phenomenon." Supportive of Bennett's stance on the issue is Harvard Professor Mark Moore, who stated: "[W]e in academe have been ill-prepared to offer help, because the problem has changed so quickly that researchers have not been able to accumulate experience-based knowledge fast enough to keep up with the need to take action" (Moore, 1989). Let us now consider both sides of the legalization argument.

The Pros: Arguments for Legalization

Many of those that advocate the legalization of drugs base their arguments on assertions of the historical practice of the policing of "victimless" crimes. In particular, the experience of Prohibition is singled out. Reformers allege that the passage of the 1920 Volstead Act outlawing the production, possession, and use of alcohol created more problems than it resolved, and that the end of Prohibition in 1933 saw the gangsters, along with their violence and corruption, fade away. This argument is now put forth to support legalization as a means of disbanding modern-day drug gangs in the same fashion.

Many scholars that are supportive of legalization assert, however, that Prohibition was responsible for the transformation of organized crime from small, isolated vice peddlers serving urban political machines to major crime syndicates. This occurred as a result of the profits realized from Prohibition, the political and law enforcement contacts that they made, the respectability that came from serving the drinking public, and the logistical and structural reorganization of organized crime that bootlegging required.

Proponents of drug legalization base their argument on a number of points. One such point is the traditionally conservative libertarian argument stating that a free society allows its people to do as they wish so long as they harm no one. The state, therefore, should be very reluctant to use the criminal law to constrict personal freedoms.

In addition, drug reformers argue that drug laws fail to impact the availability of illicit drugs and may even make the situation worse. For example, a study of the Marijuana Interdiction Program by Mark A.R. Kleiman of Harvard's Kennedy School of Government concluded that the interdiction campaign stimulated domestic production, increased the supply of marijuana in the United States and raised the potency of marijuana available from 1 percent to 18 percent.

A similar study of marijuana eradication campaigns in Kentucky also concluded that the result of the campaigns was increased supply, increased potency, introduction of new dangerous drugs to the market, and the creation of marijuana syndicates in place of the usually small, disorganized growers that had dominated the market prior to the eradication effort.

Of course, skeptics question the specific correlations between the eradication program and the advances in the marijuana production trade. For example, since the late 1960s, trends toward the rising potency of marijuana and trends toward indoor hydroponics growing methods had been well documented prior to the implementation of the eradication program. Additionally, research has concluded that one fundamental reason why traditional organized crime (La Cosa Nostra) has been unable to dominate the domestic marijuana trade is because it represents an easy-entry market for entrepreneurs. According to a 1985 DEA Special Intelligence Report on Domestic Marijuana Trafficking, "efforts to organize certain dispersed [marijuana trafficking] elements of society would prove futile and too costly." This illustrates how difficult and impractical (if not impossible) it would be for the government to attempt to control and tax the marijuana market after legalization.

Reformers also point to the connection between illegal drugs and crime, arguing that addicts are lured to other crimes such as prostitution, burglary, and robbery as ways to help finance their expensive habits. In addition, it is argued that the illegality of drugs forces consumers to enter a criminal underworld to purchase drugs, thereby having contact with criminal actors with whom they would ordinarily never be in contact, creating conditions for both victimization and subsequent criminality.

Proponents of drug legalization argue that those crimes traditionally associated with drug dealing would be greatly reduced if the context of drug control were changed from a law enforcement to a medical model. In addition, the organized crime groups formed around the drug trade would find the illicit market constricted under a medical model and would leave the black market in drugs for other criminal opportunities. Lastly, legalization opponents argue that law enforcement and political corruption associated with drug trafficking, abuse of due process and procedural rights sometimes associated with drug enforcement, and the problem of selective drug enforcement would also be mitigated under a medical model.

According to remarks by Mayor Schmoke in 1988:

If you take the profit out of drug trafficking, you won't have young children selling drugs on behalf of pushers for $100 a night or wearing beepers to school because it makes more sense to run drugs for someone than to take some of the jobs that are available. I don't know any kid who is making money by running booze.

The bottom line for those favoring legalization is that the drug-related crimes are more dangerous than the damage caused by the drugs themselves, and that the war on drugs cannot be won.

Let's now take a closer look at some of the most commonly advanced arguments for the legalization of drugs:

The Tax Revenue. Another common argument in favor of legalization is that it would save billions of tax dollars currently spent on law enforcement efforts. This includes the $8 billion spent on law enforcement and other monies spent on prison facilities to house drug violators every year. In addition, some drug-law reformers envision taxing legalized drugs such as marijuana and generating additional revenues. Of course, these savings may be illusory in that the adoption of a legalization model would require a massive additional investment in drug education programs and drug rehabilitation facilities.

The Futility of Enforcement. As we mentioned above, drug law enforcement has also come under considerable critical scrutiny. Some researchers claim that there has been no reduction in supply from enforcement efforts and have also pointed to an alarming fall in the retail price of drugs and an increase in their potency. Contrasting this view is the federally-funded study of intensive street-level drug enforcement in Lynn, Massachusetts, which pointed to "temporary" and "transitory" successes. This is considered by some to indicate not much more than a marginal success.

In addition, it is argued that fully suppressing the demand for drugs would require the jailing of a large proportion of the nation's population. Fully 70 million Americans admit to having used drugs. Federal studies estimate that, despite constantly escalating numbers of drug arrests, we are still reaching less than 1 percent of users with law enforcement efforts. This is particularly disturbing in view of the notion that the United States ranks number one in the world in the percentage of its population presently behind bars (Associated Press, January 5, 1991).

Restriction of the Drug Market. Reformers also argue that legalization of some drugs, particularly the so-called recreational drugs or "drugs of choice," would serve to restrict the drug market. In view of the fact that most drug experts agree that marijuana, cocaine, and heroin are the preferred substances for most drug users, their availability might reduce demand for more dangerous substances such as Ice and Angel Dust. This would reduce the economic incentive for the production and distribution of these more dangerous substances.

The Hypocrisy of Drug Laws. It is also argued that it is hypocritical to ban drugs when our society has already legalized two exceedingly dangerous drugs, tobacco and alcohol. The argument is that a much larger percentage of the population is threatened through health risks, automobile collisions, assaults, and associated family problems attributed to these drugs than from many of the drugs presently proscribed by law. One should recognize, however, that such a comparison is difficult to make because legalized recreational drugs are not a reality and there is no existing scientific or empirical data to support this assertion.

International Relations. Some drug reformers have also pointed to problems created by drug enforcement efforts, specifically, our strained relationships with certain foreign countries. These reformers argue that foreign relations with countries such as Mexico, Peru, and Colombia are being hampered by the intensity of enforcement efforts and the political rhetoric attached to the drug war.

More compellingly, some critics argue that foreign policy considerations have resulted in a double standard in drug enforcement in the United States. These critics point to the lack of intense criticism (or even, as was the case in Panama military action) directed to United States allies such as the Bahamas (a major transshipment site for cocaine made safe by massive political corruption), Chile (where the DINA, Chile's secret police, has been actively engaged in cocaine trafficking for over two decades), Thailand (a major heroin refining center), and Taiwan (source of much of the financial backing and logistical support for the southeast Asian heroin trade). Critics are also disturbed by the relations between United States intelligence agencies and drug traffickers: the CIA's role in Australia's drug-money-laundering Nugan-Hand bank and in Caribbean drug-money-laundering enterprises; support for fundamentalist Moslem Afghan groups actively engaged in heroin trafficking; and the National Security Council's alleged relationships with General Manuel Noriega and certain members of the Medellin Cartel in support of the Contra's war against Nicaragua.

Personal Freedoms. To some critics of present drug enforcement policies, the possibility of severe threats to personal freedoms posed by tougher drug laws creates concern. New and expanded search-and-seizure powers granted to law enforcement officers, random drug testing by employers, and the use of the military in domestic law enforcement raise major concerns about potential due process abuses, further erosion of constitutional protections, and the potential for serious systematic corruption.

The Crime Rate. As mentioned above, reformers also claim that legalization would cut down on street crimes because addicts could acquire their drugs inexpensively rather than by committing street crimes such as burglary, robbery, and murder for money. Drug reformers also argue that legalization would reduce the drug turf wars that have driven urban homicide rates to record levels in recent years.

Public Health. Proponents of drug legalization argue that the drug laws themselves create many of the severe health problems normally associated with drug use. Obviously, the spread of AIDS, closely associated with the sharing of needles by intravenous drug users, is one such concern. Reformers also point to the problem of pregnant drug addicts, who, out of fear of legal repercussions, may not seek prenatal care.

Finally, some have argued, at least in the case of heroin, that illegality of heroin means that there is no control over the quality of the drug being purchased. Heroin and other drugs are commonly adulterated with dangerous substances by retail dealers, and users are unsure of the potency or quality of the drugs they have purchased. From a pharmacological point of view, it is argued, unadulterated heroin causes little physical damage to the human body (this of course excludes such health threats as AIDS and brutal physical addiction). It is the uncontrolled nature of street heroin that causes poisoning and overdose.

In spite of these arguments for the legalization of drugs, drug reformers have yet to come up with a comprehensive plan that delineates any practical program for legalization. Some reformers have complained that they have not had equal access to federal research monies with which to formulate their approach. Those monies have been exclusively reserved for research on drug abuse pathologies and drug repression strategies.

In 1988, Democratic Congressman Charles Rangle, who represents the drug-infested Harlem district in New York City, and who strongly opposes legalization, posed questions that drug policy reformers will have to answer in coming years:

1. Which drugs should be legalized—marijuana or the harder drugs such as heroin and cocaine?

2. How would the legalized drugs be sold—by prescription, over-the-counter, by hospitals or pharmacies?

3. Would there be an age limit and, if so, how would it be enforced?

4. As addictions and dependencies developed, would there be any limit on the amount of drugs that users could purchase?

5. Who would manufacture the drugs? Private companies? The federal government?

6. Would the drugs be provided to the public at cost? If not, how much profit margin would be allowed? Would they be taxed?

7. Who would assume the responsibility of allowing a drug user to take so much of a particular drug? The government? A physician?

8. Should recreational use of drugs be authorized or just drug use for treatment?

9. Would the legalization of drugs help spread the AIDS virus to a broader percentage of the United States population?

In response to these questions, some reformers have offered the argument that drugs could be sold in the same fashion as alcohol. That is, the substances would be sold to only licensed dealers, who would be taxed and held under close government scrutiny. Regulations would include prohibiting the sale of drugs to anyone under 21 years of age.

Another proposed antidote to the problem is a lesser form of legalization called decriminalization. This vague concept generally calls for the reduction of criminal penalties for drug use or possession while retaining a degree of social disapproval.

Regardless of which approach seems most popular, it seems increasingly clear, at least to some, that a serious fault does exist in the current public policy that addresses drug control. The fault is that current policy has failed to cut drastically the supply of drugs through the use of police action alone.

ARGUMENTS FOR REFORM

- It is not the responsibility of government to regulate the private morality of its citizens.

- Legalization of drugs would provide new revenue to be used in drug education and rehabilitation efforts.

- Drug laws are unenforceable and result in selective and discriminatory enforcement practices.

- Drug laws are hypocritical.

- Drug laws create criminals out of otherwise law-abiding citizens.

- Drug laws strengthen and expand organized crime.

- Drug laws create an environment where police officials are tempted to use unscrupulous enforcement tactics, and they increase the danger of corruption.

GET YOUR HEADS OUT OF THE SAND

I recently asked the U.S. Conference of Mayors to call on Congress to hold hearings on the question of whether to decriminalize narcotics. Many oppose decriminalization, arguing that it would be viewed as an open invitation to use drugs. But the mere fact that there are many legitimate arguments against decriminalization is no reason to hide our heads in the sand and refuse to debate the issue.

As during Prohibition, our drug laws make it illegal to possess a commodity that is in very high demand. As a result, the price of that commodity escalates far beyond its true cost of manufacture. It is the enormous profits available from illegal drugs that have for years made drug trafficking the criminal enterprise of choice.

I learned that working as an assistant U.S. Attorney and as a state's attorney for Baltimore; I prosecuted and won thousands of convictions for drug-related crimes—including murders of police officers and civilians.

But drug traffickers care very little about the sanctions of the criminal justice system. Going to jail is just part of the cost of doing business. It's a nuisance, not a deterrent. The only language the drug underground understands is money.

Decriminalization would take the profit out of drugs and greatly reduce, if not eliminate, the drug-related violence currently plaguing our streets. If there were no money to be made from drugs, drug lords would no longer be willing to risk incarceration selling them.

It's time to consider treating drugs as a health problem, not a crime problem. Instead of spending the money necessary to educate our young people to the detrimental effects of drugs and to treat those that are addicted, we spend billions in a wildly expensive cat-and-mouse game that the mouse is winning 90 percent of the time.

Decriminalization would allow us to redirect billions of dollars now used for interdiction and enforcement toward prevention and treatment. In the meantime, millions of people continue to use drugs, and millions more have lost all confidence that they can live securely in their neighborhoods.

It takes great maturity and will power for a society to step back from a policy that seems noble and justified but, in reality, has only compounded the problem it is attempting to solve. On the subject of drugs, such maturity and will power may now be in order. At the very least, we need a sober national debate on the subject.

Source: Schmoke, K.L. (1988). "Get Your Heads Out of the Sand." USA Today (May).

The Cons: Arguments Against Legalization

The prevailing opposition against drug legalization is voiced by many politicians, law enforcement officials, and concerned citizens alike. Opponents of legalization contend that the problems created by Prohibition were minuscule compared to today's situation. Specifically, children of the 1920s were not the victims of alcohol consumption, at least in an addictive sense.

Additionally, users would possibly face a greater risk of debilitating dependencies from cocaine and narcotics if those drugs were legalized. Today, over a half of a century after the repeal of Prohibition, alcoholism is considered, more so now than ever, one of America's most lethal killers. Indeed, the legalization of drugs would very likely provide drug lords, both foreign and domestic, the vehicle to success that they have been waiting for: the conversion of the black market to an open market.

A primary concern about the reform of drug laws is the erosion of the public morals. Specifically, many feel that the simple act of legalizing drugs would send a public message about society's lack of social responsibility and its unwillingness to deal with such a major health and public safety issue: a kind of surrender to the drug dealers of the world. Opponents, therefore, predict that adoption of such a public policy would increase drug abuse enormously and would multiply the ancillary problems of poor health, violence, and disjoined families.

Drugs are not bad because they are illegal, they are illegal because they are bad.

John Lawn, Former Administrator
Drug Enforcement Administration, 1988

Certainly, legalization would serve as a "quick fix." How responsible is it, some might argue, to take a crime against society and legalize it for the sole purpose of eliminating it as a criminal problem and as a threat to public safety? This is a complex question that has been raised with regard to the legalization of prostitution, gambling, abortion, and pornography, as well as drugs. In the case of violent crimes and property crimes, of course, the answer is obvious. It is not always as clear with morality crimes.

According to some treatment officials, the rate of addiction to alcohol is only 10 percent of those that use it. The addiction rate of crack cocaine, however, would probably exceed 75 percent of those that use it; these are statistics that reformers strategically avoid.

The Alcohol Argument. Opponents to drug reform turn around the alcohol argument by acknowledging alcohol as a dangerous and addictive drug, but the fact that it is so harmful to society is the very reason that additional dangerous substances of abuse should not be added to the list of legal drugs. The toll of alcohol consumption is well documented in broken homes, violence, ruined careers, accidents, and loss of productivity on the job and in the schools. So the question is whether legalized alcohol and drugs would create a worse situation than has legalized alcohol alone.

The Crime Rate. Although proponents of reform argue that legalized drugs would cause a decrease in the crime rate, opponents claim just the opposite—that is, although certain drug-type crimes would be reduced (i.e., smuggling), there would always be a black market. This is particularly significant in considering that many addicts would be unable to hold down jobs because of their addictions to even the cheapest of "government-made" drugs.

New Revenues. In response to those that claim that legalizing drugs would save the public billions in taxes, opponents are convinced that the black market would actually be broadened because of the lack of taxes on illicit drugs. After all, cigarette bootlegging is still one of organized crime's varied enterprises because of high tax-rate differentials.   Additionally, it can be argued that stepped-up enforcement in conjunction with powerful forfeiture laws that provide for government seizure of drug money, property, and assets, would substantially reduce the costs of drug enforcement. In addition, it is maintained that what the government might save in law enforcement costs would be spent many times over in traffic deaths, lost productivity, and medical costs. In fact, a 1983 study found that drug abuse costs the nation $60 billion in one year in these areas.

The Addicts. Another opposing view of reform is the argument that money would still be required even in the event of legalized drugs. Specifically, it is believed that many addicts would not hold regular jobs and therefore would continue to commit ancillary crimes such as robbery, prostitution, and theft in order to acquire money. Even though some studies have indicated that heroin addicts are able to lead fairly normal lives if their drug needs are met, there is no evidence to convince us that all addicts would choose to leave the drug-crimes subculture. Additionally, drug-related crimes that result from intoxicated drug users would no doubt be on the rise, including assault, spouse/child abuse, and drug-related traffic accidents.

Yale University professor Herbert D. Kleber has commented about the idea of legalizing cocaine: "If it were legalized, I think you would see a five- to six-fold increase above the present level of use."

Additionally, perhaps society should remember that when pornography was legalized de facto by the Supreme Court, it did not just go away as some anticipated. In fact, it gradually became more obscene because of public boredom with the product. For example, *Playboy* magazine was superseded by *Penthouse*, which was then outdone by *Hustler*. Then came the sadistic "snuff" films which depicted gang rapes, sadism, and ultimately murder.

Organized Crime. The legalization of drugs would have three profound effects with regard to the black market: (1) it would give drugs a social sanction, creating a broader use of drugs (as was the case with legalized gambling, which created more gamblers rather than reducing the influence of organized crime in the market); (2) it would make drugs available without risk of arrest and prosecution; and (3) if the legal price of drugs did not undercut the price on the illicit market, users would continue to purchase drugs from drug dealers on the street and organized crime would continue to reap its drug-related profits.

After all, as was pointed out above, legal lotteries have not dismantled the illegal numbers racket. Also, the end of Prohibition did not devastate organized crime—it merely led to diversification and new areas of criminal enterprise.

Personal Freedoms. As mentioned earlier, proponents of legalization contend that drug laws increasingly deprive the people of their personal freedoms and that drug users should be permitted to consume drugs in their own home if they desire. While this argument entails a rather lofty debate over political philosophy, it should be pointed out that an equally strong argument can be made that whenever one person's personal freedoms are safeguarded, someone else's may be restricted. In a nation with over 210 million people, carte blanche cannot be given to everyone desiring to live his or her own way without regard to rights and privileges of others.

The Cost of Legalization. While legalization proponents argue that taxes from legal drugs and reduced expenditures related to drug enforcement would result in reductions in government spending, that argument fails to provide for the unacceptable and surmountable social costs of such a program. For instance, a 1983 study by the Research Triangle Institute found that drug abuse costs the American economy over $60 billion annually. The specific costs identified by the study are discussed below:

> $24 billion of the total figure was from drug-related crimes, the police, the courts, the jails, victims, etc.

> $36 billion of the total was the cost of lost productivity, injuries, and other harm caused by heavy drug users.

We spend less than $500 million on treatment and education, and that is nowhere near what needs to be spent.

Rudolph Guiliani,
Former U.S. Attorney
New York, New York, 1988

Given the fact that over half of this enormous figure was attributed to work-related accidents and lost productivity, is it not logical to assume that legalized drugs, selling for a fraction of the price of illicit drugs and therefore being more widely used, would increase that cost figure by five, six, seven times, or even higher? Many experts in the field believe so.

ARGUMENTS AGAINST LEGALIZATION

- Legalization of drugs would allow organized crime groups to continue in the drug trade but on a legal basis, using established drug distribution networks.

- The governing of morality through enforcing "victimless" crimes upholds the moral viability of our nation.

- Legalizing only segments of crimes such as drugs use will not abolish organized crime.

- Just because a law seems unenforceable is no reason to abolish it. For example, laws against murder or robbery have not eliminated such criminal acts.

- Legalizing drugs would create much regulation and licensing and would therefore create many new opportunities for official corruption.

- Just because the criminal justice system seems to be overburdened, laws should not be eliminated. The answer is to dedicate more resources to the system, thus making it a more effective one.

THE PLEA TO LEGALIZE DRUGS IS A SIREN CALL TO SURRENDER

Since I took command of the war on drugs, I have learned from former Secretary of State George Shultz that our concept of fighting drugs is "flawed." The only thing to do, he says, is to "make it possible for addicts to buy drugs at some regulated place." Conservative commentator William F. Buckley, Jr. suggests that I should be "fatalistic" about the flood of cocaine from South America and simply "let it in." Syndicated columnist Mike Royko contends that it would be easier to sweep junkies out of the gutters "than to fight a hopeless war" against the narcotics that send them there. Labeling our efforts "bankrupt," federal judge Robert W. Sweet opts for legalization, saying, "If our society can learn to stop using butter, it should be able to cut down on cocaine." Flawed, fatalistic, hopeless, bankrupt! I never realized surrender was so fashionable until I assumed this post.

Though most Americans are overwhelmingly determined to go toe-to-toe with the foreign drug lords and neighborhood pushers, a small minority believe that enforcing drug laws imposes greater costs on society than do drugs themselves. Like addicts seeking immediate euphoria, the legalizers want peace at any price, even though it means the inevitable proliferation of a practice that degrades, impoverishes, and kills.

I am acutely aware of the burdens that drug enforcement places upon us. It consumes economic resources that we would like to use elsewhere. It is sometimes frustrating, thankless, and often dangerous. But the consequences of not enforcing drug laws would be far more costly. Those consequences involve the intrinsically destructive nature of drugs and the toll that they exact from our society in hundreds of thousands of lost and broken lives....human potential never realized....time stolen from families and jobs...precious spiritual and economic resources squandered.

That is precisely why virtually every civilized society has found it necessary to exert some form of control over mind-altering substances and why this war is so important. Americans feel up to their hips in drugs now. They would be up to their necks under legalization.

Even limited experiments in drug legalization have shown that when the drugs are more widely available, addiction skyrockets. In 1975, Italy liberalized its drug laws and now has one of the highest heroin-related death rates in western Europe. In Alaska, where marijuana was decriminalized in 1975, the easy atmosphere has increased usage of the drug, particularly among children. Nor does it stop there. Some Alaskan schoolchildren now tout "coca puffs," marijuana cigarettes laced with cocaine.

Many legalizers concede that drug legalization might increase use, but they shrug off the matter. "It may well be that there would be more addicts, and I would regret that result," says Nobel laureate economist Milton Friedman. The late Harvard Medical School psychiatry professor Norman Zinberg, a longtime proponent of "responsible" drug use, admitted that "use of now illicit drugs would certainly increase. Also, casualties probably would increase."

In fact, Dr. Herbert D. Kleber of Yale University, my deputy in charge of demand reduction, predicts legalization might cause "a five- to six-fold increase" in cocaine use. But legalizers regard this as a necessary price for the "benefits" of legalization. What benefits?

1. Legalization will take the profit out of drugs. The result supposedly will be the end of criminal drug pushers and the big foreign drug wholesalers, who will turn to other enterprises because nobody will need to make furtive and dangerous trips to his local pusher.

But what, exactly, would the brave new world of legalized drugs look like? Buckley stresses that "adults get to buy the stuff at carefully regulated stores." (Would you want one in your neighborhood?) Others, like Friedman, suggest that we sell the drugs at "ordinary retail outlets."

Former City University of New York sociologist Georgette Bennett assures us that "brand-name competition will be prohibited" and that strict quality control and proper labeling will be overseen by the Food and Drug Administration. In a touching egalitarian note, she adds that "free drugs will be provided at government clinics" for addicts too poor to buy them.

Almost all the legalizers point out that the price of drugs will fall, even though the drugs will be heavily taxed. Buckley, for example, argues that somehow federal drugstores will keep the price "low enough to discourage a black market but high enough to accumulate a surplus to be used for drug education."

Supposedly, drug sales will generate huge amounts of revenue, which will then be used to tell the public not to use drugs and to treat those that do not listen.

In reality, this tax would only allow government to share the drug profits now garnered by criminals. Legalizers would have to tax drugs heavily in order to pay for drug education and treatment programs. Criminals could undercut the official price and still make huge profits. What alternative would the government have? Cut the price until it was within the lunch-money budget of the average sixth-grade student?

2. Legalization will eliminate the black market. Wrong. And not just because the regulated prices could be undercut. Many legalizers admit that drugs such as crack and PCP are simply too dangerous to allow the shelter of the law. Thus, criminals will provide what the government will not. "As long as drugs that people very much want remain illegal, a black market will exist," says legalization advocate David Boaz of the Liberation Cato Institute.

Look at crack. In powdered form, cocaine was an expensive indulgence. But street chemists found that a better and far less expensive—and far more dangerous—high could be achieved by mixing cocaine with baking soda and heating it. Crack was born, and "cheap" coke invaded low-income communities with furious speed.

An ounce of powdered cocaine might sell on the street for $1200. That same ounce can produce 370 vials of crack at $10 each. Ten bucks seems like a cheap hit, but crack's intense ten- to 15-minute high is followed by an unbearable depression. The user wants more crack, thus starting a rapid and costly descent into addiction.

If government drugstores do not stock crack, addicts will find it in the clandestine market or simply bake it themselves from their legally purchased cocaine.

Currently crack is being laced with insecticides and animal tranquilizers to heighten its effect. Emergency rooms are now warned to expect victims of "sandwiches" and "moon rocks," life- threatening smokable mixtures of heroin

Part III: Fighting Back

and crack. Unless the government is prepared to sell these deadly variations of dangerous drugs, it will perpetuate a criminal black market by default. And what about children and teen-agers? They would obviously be barred from drug purchases, just as they are prohibited from buying beer and liquor. But pushers will continue to cater to these young customers with the old, favorite come-on—a couple of free fixes to get them hooked. And what good will antidrug education be when these youngsters observe their older brothers and sisters, parents, and friends lighting up and shooting up with government permission? Legalization will give us the worst of both worlds: millions of new drug users and a thriving criminal black market.

3. Legalization will dramatically reduce crime. "It is the high price of drugs that leads addicts to robbery, murder, and other crimes," says Ira Glasser, executive director of the American Civil Liberties Union. A study by the Cato Institute concludes: "Most, if not all, 'drug-related murders' are the result of drug prohibitions."

But researchers tell us that many drug-related felonies are committed by people that were involved in crime before they started taking drugs. The drugs, so routinely available in criminal circles, make the criminals more violent and unpredictable.

Certainly there are some kill-for-a-fix crimes, but does any rational person believe that a cut-rate price for drugs at a government outlet will stop such psychopathic behavior? The fact is that under the influence of drugs, normal people do not act normally, and abnormal people behave in chilling and horrible ways. DEA agents told me about a teen-aged addict in Manhattan that was smoking crack when he sexually abused and caused permanent internal injuries to his one-month-old daughter.

Children are among the most frequent victims of violent, drug-related crimes that have nothing to do with the cost of acquiring the drugs. In Philadelphia in 1987, more than half the child-abuse fatalities involved at least one parent that was a heavy drug user. Seventy-three percent of the child-abuse deaths in New York City in 1987 involved parental drug use.

In my travels to the ramparts of the drug war, I have seen nothing to support the legalizers' argument that lower drug prices would reduce crime. Virtually everywhere I have gone, police and DEA agents have told me that crime rates are highest where crack is cheapest.

4. Drug use should be legal because users only harm themselves. Those that believe this should stand beside the medical examiner as he counts the 36 bullet wounds in the shattered corpse of a three-year-old that happened to get in the way of his mother's drug-crazed boyfriend. They should visit the babies abandoned by cocaine-addicted mothers—infants that already carry the ravages of addiction in their own tiny bodies. They should console the devastated relatives of the nun that worked in a homeless shelter and was stabbed to death by a crack addict enraged that she would not stake him to a fix.

Do drug addicts only harm themselves? Here is a former cocaine addict describing the compulsion that quickly draws even the most "responsible" user into irreversible behavior: "Everything is about getting high, and any means necessary to get there become rational. If it means stealing something from somebody close to you, lying to your family, borrowing money from people you know you can't pay back, writing checks you know you can't cover, you do all those things—things that are totally against everything you have ever believed in."

Society pays for this behavior, and not just in bigger insurance premiums, losses from accidents, and poor job performance. We pay in the loss of a priceless social currency, as families are destroyed, trust between friends is betrayed, and promising careers are never fulfilled. I cannot imagine sanctioning behavior that would increase that toll.

I find no merit in the legalizers' case. The simple fact is that drug use is wrong. And the moral argument, in the end, is the most compelling argument. A citizen in a drug-induced haze, whether on his back-yard deck or on a mattress in a ghetto crack house, is not what the founding fathers meant by the "pursuit of happiness." Despite the legalizers' argument that drug use is a matter of "personal freedom," our nation's notion of liberty is rooted in the ideal of a self-reliant citizenry. Helpless wrecks in treatment centers, men chained by their noses to cocaine—these people are slaves.

Imagine if, in the darkest days of 1940, Winston Churchill had rallied the West by saying, "This war looks hopeless, and besides, it will cost too much. Hitler can't be that bad. Let's surrender and see what happens." That is essentially what we hear from the legalizers.

This war can be won. I am heartened by indications that education and public revulsion are having an effect on drug use. The National Institute on Drug Abuse's latest survey of current users shows a 37 percent decrease in drug consumption since 1985. Cocaine is down 50 percent; marijuana use among young people is at its lowest rate since 1972. In my travels, I've been encouraged by signs that Americans are fighting back.

I am under no illusion that such developments, however hopeful, mean the war is over. We need to involve more citizens in the fight, increase pressure on drug criminals, and build on antidrug programs that have proven to work. This will not be easy. But the moral and social costs of surrender are simply too great to contemplate.

Source: William Bennett, *Reader's Digest*, March, 1990

Drugs In Amsterdam: The "Dutch Way"

Other countries, such as the Netherlands, have legalized drugs as a remedy for their drug problems. Let us now consider Amsterdam and its experience with decriminalizing drugs. Although drugs are not totally legal in Amsterdam, they are, at least, tolerated.

Over the years, Amsterdam, a city of 700,000, has earned the reputation of being a drug mecca in western Europe because of the widespread availability of marijuana. Indeed, marijuana and hashish alike are imported from many different source countries and are sold openly in coffee shops and ice cream parlors. Only a few blocks from Amsterdam's business district, cocaine and heroin dealers operate without fear of being arrested because the government has adopted a strategy in which these dealers are quarantined to this designated area of town called the "red light district."

This selling is tolerated because Dutch police authorities feel that drug trafficking can be more closely monitored if it is confined to a small area, thereby providing controls not only over drug retailing but over all ancillary criminal behaviors. Throughout the rest of town, marijuana and hash are treated much like alcohol and tobacco are treated in America.

The Dutch policy separates marijuana and hashish from the harder drugs. It is generally felt that if young people can purchase their marijuana in coffee shops rather than from criminal drug dealers that also sell harder drugs, it is less likely that the customer will be tempted by the seller to try other more potent and addictive substances.

In addition, the Dutch have adopted a policy that they feel makes drug use "boring" and less glamorous. The ease with which cannabis products can be obtained removes the mystique often attached to acts of rebellion and nonconformity that many young people engage in as part of the maturing process. Marijuana reformers claim that there is much to be said for this argument in that available data indicate strikingly lower patterns of drug use in Amsterdam than in the United States:

- Following the decriminalization of cannabis in the Netherlands, consumption declined significantly. In 1976, prior to decriminalization, 3 percent of 15- and 16-year olds and 10 percent of 17- and 18-year-olds used cannabis occasionally; by 1985, after decriminalization, the percentages had declined to 2 percent and 6 percent respectively.

- Heroin use in Amsterdam is estimated at 0.4 percent, and cocaine use has stabilized at 0.6 percent.

- Only 8 percent of Dutch AIDS patients are intravenous drug users, compared to 26 percent in the United States.

- Drug experimentation among high school students has dropped from 12 percent in 1976, prior to legalization, to 1 percent today.

Source: Trebach, 1989

Ancillary to the liberal law enforcement approach in Amsterdam is a concomitant medical model used to treat addiction and abuse. In Amsterdam, a widespread methadone maintenance program, targeting heroin addicts, makes use of mobile units that travel around the city bringing methadone treatment to addicts. Of course, the methadone program in Amsterdam is beset by many of the same problems as United States experiments with the heroin substitute. In particular, methadone, which is also an addicting drug, has failed to divert users from heroin, so that some addicts have adopted a style of use combining both heroin and methadone.

In 1988, the Amsterdam health department estimated that there were 7,000 addicts in the city, 20 percent of whom were foreigners. Additionally, police estimate that 60 percent of petty crimes are committed by members of the addict population in Amsterdam. It should also be noted, however, that drug-related homicides in Amsterdam are very rare events. Washington, D.C. has 15 times as many drug-related murders than does Amsterdam. On the other hand, it is likely that the Dutch have considerably more control over street crime than we do in the United States.

Unlike many American cities, Amsterdam has a well-funded and a more-than-adequate police department. Amsterdam's police strength is 3,500, of which 2,900 are uniformed officers assigned to street beats. An estimated 400 of these officers, however, are assigned to the diminutive four-block area of the "red light district" to contain the high rate of crime there. In contrast, the same number of officers (400) is adequate to serve the entire city of El Paso, Texas, a city of about 500,000.

Some Dutch police officials are concerned with the overall rise in the crime rate that has occurred since the tolerance policy towards drugs went into effect. This increase in crime cannot blamed entirely on Dutch drug users. As with many countries that experience a flourishing drug abuse problem, blame is conveniently placed on other countries whose stringent drug control policies have succeeded in ridding the country of many drug abusers and related criminals. It makes sense to assume that someone that steals to support a drug habit in Germany would not pass up an opportunity to steal just because he or she is in Amsterdam, where there is greater availability and affordability of drugs.

One unfortunate and unforeseen side effect of the Amsterdam project is the emergence of droves of porno shops and houses of prostitution in the drug district. Dutch officials are quick to admit that the crime rate has dramatically risen since the so-called "Dutch Way" was adopted.

Those that lend support for the Amsterdam experiment, however, claim that the relationship between sexual trafficking and drugs is difficult to establish because of several perceived factors. For example, some of the prostitution and pornography enterprises in Amsterdam precede the legalization of drugs in that country. In addition, such "red light districts" exist in European cities where drug retailing is not tolerated, although history has shown that the sex and drug industries are very closely correlated.

In the United States, one need only travel through Boston's "Combat Zone," San Francisco's "Tenderloin," or Philadelphia's "Arch Street" districts to find evidence of close links between the sex and drug industries.

The British Experiment

Britain passed legal controls regarding dangerous substances at about the same time that the United States passed similar laws; the first such measure was passed in 1916. The early drug control efforts in both countries were aimed at controlling drug addiction and abuse by outlawing cocaine and opium and their derivatives. Much confusion surrounded the application of drug control laws in both Britain and the United States.

A second piece of antidrug legislation, known as the Dangerous Drug Act, was passed by Parliament in 1920. Basically, the law prohibited possession of opiates or cocaine except with a lawful prescription. Paralleling problems with the Harrison Act in the United States, confusion over the specifics of the new British legislation led to difficulty in its interpretation and enforcement.

In 1924, a committee of British physicians was formed to determine whether drug abuse should be approached as a criminal justice or a medical problem. The committee was inclined toward the latter and instituted the so-called "British system," which prevailed well into the late 1960s.

The "British system" gave opiate addicts, most of whom were older persons, legal access to heroin and morphine. The goal of the program was to wean addicts from their addiction to heroin. This was done through medical supervision of addicts by physicians, who would prescribe just enough heroin for the addicts to stay "well" but not enough to get high.

By the late 1950s, the number of heroin addicts began to grow. By the mid-1960s, England became a major market for smokable heroin, similar to the opium traditionally smoked by Chinese addicts. The availability of this type of heroin was thought to contribute to the increasing numbers of addicts. Compounding the problem was the diversion of heroin from legitimate sources (e.g., doctor's offices) to the streets.

The British system of drug maintenance by prescription is still in operation, although several factors have made it a less effective practice than it had been in the past. First, a sizable increase in illegal heroin supplies was noted in the 1970s, offering a realistic alternative to visiting doctor's offices. This was accompanied by a general economic downturn with high unemployment, declining wages, and racial tensions in most large British cities. Some students of the British system suggest that the real crisis came when British economic policies under the former Thatcher government resulted in declining buying power and an increase in the cost of alcohol, thereby making heroin a cheaper high than booze.

No matter which of the many problems actually resulted in the increase in heroin use in Britain, the fact remains that the system is not as effective as it used to be. Nonetheless, it is interesting to note that recent legislation has relaxed some of the restrictions imposed on heroin maintenance by the Thatcher government, making it once again a more viable option, and that some leading physicians and law enforcement officials, such as H.B. Spear, head of Scotland Yard's drug enforcement wing, have been actively campaigning for an expansion of both heroin and cocaine maintenance programs in Britain.

The Alaskan "Pot" Legalization Experience

Although now illegal, possession of marijuana for personal use was considered lawful in Alaska between 1975 and 1990. During that time, Alaska state law allowed people over 19 years of age to possess up to four ounces of marijuana in private without penalty, though it could not be sold or bartered. In addition to other public concerns, the Alaskan law conflicted with federal law prohibiting the drug.

The "legalized pot" experiment has since given researchers and policy makers a model with which to study. In this section we will consider the history and repercussions of their social experiment with this controversial public policy.

Ironically, Alaska's 1975 legalization of marijuana was not a result of a public movement or one anchored by elected representatives of the people. In fact, it resulted from a decision by the Alaska Supreme Court. The landmark decision was *Ravin v. State*, 537 p. 2d 494. *Ravin* was based on Article I, Section 22 of the Alaska Constitution, which stated that "the right of the people to privacy is recognized and shall not be infringed." In deciding this case, the court held that the state had no authority to exert control over the activities of an individual unless their activities affected the public health and safety of others (or the public at large).

A SYNOPSIS OF THE *RAVIN* CASE

Irwin Ravin—a Homer, Alaska lawyer—had deliberately set out to be stopped while driving and had purposely possessed a small amount of marijuana in his pocket. Later, in his defense, Ravin filed a motion to dismiss the criminal complaint in district court. During the court hearings several experts testified, and numerous books and written articles were introduced into evidence. The district court denied the motion to dismiss, so Ravin appealed to the superior court, which also denied the motion.

Finally, the Alaskan Supreme Court agreed to review the case. The court noted at the time that "most marijuana available in the United States contained THC content of less than one percent." After considering both long- and short-term effects of the drug on users, the court overturned the lower courts' decisions and protected an adult's right to possess marijuana in his own home for personal use. In coming to this decision, the court placed more importance on an individual's right to privacy than on the state's responsibility to preserve public health and safety. The court, however, failed to define an "adult," how much marijuana could be "possessed" and what constituted a person's "own home."

As mentioned, the *Ravin* decision was based on two basic premises: 1) that marijuana was a "harmless substance" and 2) that a 1972 state constitutional amendment guaranteeing Alaskans the right to privacy extended to marijuana use in one's home.

Indeed, the court had declared that the effects of marijuana were not serious enough to justify widespread concern..."at least as compared with the far more dangerous effects of alcohol, barbiturates and amphetamines." The court further held that until conclusive evidence was available to show that marijuana is a dangerous drug, the state could not prohibit its possession and use in the home by adults.*

With regard to the use of marijuana by minors, the *Ravin* court also contended that "adolescents may not be equipped with the maturity to handle the experience prudently...." Therefore, it still made it illegal for anyone under 18 years of age in Alaska to use or possess marijuana.

The lack of consistency and the hypocrisy of current law has resulted in a loss of respect for the government. It has hampered the abilities of federal control officials to control international drug trafficking. In short, legalization of marijuana has been a disaster.

Ramona L. Barnes
Majority Leader
Alaska House of Representatives 1984

In spite of the fact that marijuana possession by minors was outlawed, law enforcement officials in Alaska had a difficult time keeping it out of the hands of school-aged children. For example, in 1982, seven years after the *Ravin* decision, the National Institute of Drug Abuse disclosed that approximately 72 percent of high school students in Alaska had used marijuana at least once. The corresponding figure nationwide was 59 percent. Young people are aware of the hypocrisy of a government that restricts the use of a substance by one age group but authorizes its use by persons only two to three years older.

Yet another study of school-aged children was conducted in 1988 by Bernard Segal, a Professor of Health and Sciences at the University of Alaska. Segal reported that marijuana had "become well incorporated into the lifestyle on many adolescents" and for them, could no longer be considered an

---

* Note: As of the 1990 recriminalization of marijuana in Alaska, the average THC content of "commercial" marijuana ranged between 5 and 7 percent, which is considerably higher than the 1 percent cited by the Alaska court in 1975. Additionally, the popular sinsemilla strain typically averages twice the THC content of commercial marijuana.

experimental drug. The study revealed that overall use of marijuana rose between 1983 and 1988 and that its popularity was 16 percentage points above the national average.

Between 1975 and 1990, interest groups opposed to the legalization measure lobbied in the state legislature to re-outlaw the drug. Large oil companies, for example, made substantial contributions in support of a recriminalization proposal while groups such "Alaskans for Privacy" (a citizen group consisting of local professionals) and members of "NORML" (the National Organization for the Reform of Marijuana Laws) maintained their support for decriminalization.

Alaskans had to ask themselves..."which is our biggest fear: drug use, especially among children, or an erosion of personal liberties?"

In 1989, another citizens group, frustrated by inaction in the legislature, began circulating petitions for a recriminalization measure. The result was the required 42,000 signatures that were obtained for the acclaimed "Proposition Two," which was then placed on the ballot.

In examining the former state drug policy of Alaska, three distinct problems should be noted:

Problem #1. Because possession or distribution of marijuana was a violation of federal law in Alaska, any person using the drug in his or her own home was still in violation of the law. So, one could argue that the state of Alaska had basically sanctioned the use of a substance that the federal law prohibits.

Problem #2. While federal agents, through interdiction efforts, were attempting to curb the flow of drugs into the country, a simultaneous signal was also sent to the traffickers in foreign source countries such as Colombia and Mexico. The message was that the United States does not want foreign-made drugs brought into the country yet, at the same time, certain jurisdictions in the United States are condoning drug use.

Problem #3. Although the state of Alaska permitted the personal use of marijuana in the home, it refused to allow the drug to be sold in the state. So, in order to support the marijuana appetite for drug users, a vast illicit pot growing network was created to meet the demands of the consumer. This developed drug manufacturing problems for not just Alaska but for neighboring states such as Washington and Oregon.

In addition, when drug dealers were arrested in Alaska, the moral stigma was removed as they were seen as merely trying to furnish a product that was already legalized by the state government. Additionally, the penalty for an individual over 18 years of age found in possession of marijuana in a public place was a civil fine of only $100.

In summation, after considerable public outcry over the rise of adolescent drug abuse in Alaska, a voter proposition was passed in November 1990 to "recriminalize" possession of any amount of marijuana. As a result, even small quantities of marijuana are punishable by up to 90 days in jail and a $1,000 fine.

A Proposed Solution

Unquestionably, the issue of legalizing drugs should be debated, as should any other strategy for solving the nation's drug woes. It would seem, however, that legalization is an option whose time has not yet come. To date, the best strategies for fighting the "drug war" are through the use of education, prevention, rehabilitation, and innovative law enforcement strategies.

The appropriateness of certain law enforcement tactics remains the topic of a vigorous debate, even among police executives. It is doubtful, however, that interdiction, eradication, and intensive street-level enforcement strategies alone will yield a "quick fix" to the drug problem. It should be remembered that America's perceptions of its drug problem have emerged from over a century of changing attitudes, morals, and standards of living. Because drug use is a complex social problem, we must expect the solutions to be equally complex.

Perhaps when considering a solution to the problem, we should be aware of the strides and successes that have been achieved over the years in reducing tobacco consumption. The positive image of the cigarette smoker has been greatly minimized over the last ten years due to public campaigns deglamorizing tobacco. This began with a government anti-smoking campaign, which was later embraced by Hollywood and segments of the media. For example, in a report from the Surgeon General, the nation's nicotine addiction rate was at 40 percent in 1964; today, it stands at 30 percent. Not a great difference but a significant one and one that is considered by public health officials to be a notable victory.

As parts of a proposed solution, there are several possibilities that opponents of drug legalization are considering as viable, although sometimes contradictory alternatives. Let's look at each of these.

1. *Deglamorizing Drugs.* This might be the single most important component of drug control in the 1990s. As mentioned earlier, the success of deglamorization of tobacco became evident in the decrease in tobacco use and cigarette smoking over a 25-year period. In the deglamorizing process, massive drug education programs in the schools combined with anti-drug advertising in the media should convince would-be drug users to exercise extreme caution in making their choices.

   All available evidence suggests that drug education is the most effective means of drug control. However, such a strategy would require either a massive infusion of new money into educational programs or a major diversion of present funds from other drug control efforts in order to be successful. Present drug education efforts are woefully underfunded.

2. *Drug Rehabilitation and Counseling.* Once again, considerable research points to great successes in drug rehabilitation and drug counseling. The problem is that these programs are simply not available where they are needed (particularly the inner city) nor are they available in sufficient numbers (most drug rehabilitation programs targeted at lower income groups have long waiting lists). To make use of this promising strategy, new revenues would have to be created or present allocations would have to be diverted from other sources.

3. *Target the Drug User.* A plain and simple fact of drug enforcement is that to quell the drug problem, either the supply or demand of the drugs has to be reduced. Obviously, in focusing resources on interdiction of drugs (i.e., reducing the supply, international and political problems are encountered. These pose serious questions regarding the legality and appropriateness of international law enforcement. An alternative is, of course, to focus our law enforcement resources on the drug user here in our own country. This would send the message that even idle drug use is not to be tolerated.

4. *Break Down the Trafficking Infrastructure.* This solution is in precise contradiction to the idea of targeting the user. Experts in organized crime have long argued that criminal organizations cannot be controlled by either a "headhunting" strategy (arresting

as many illicit entrepreneurs as possible) or by attacking consumers. They argue that the way to control organized drug trafficking is to make the business of drugs very difficult to conduct.

Essential to successful criminal organizations are money laundering mechanisms and corruption, as these make up the infrastructure of the drug organizations. It is argued that the United States facilitates organized crime of all types and drug trafficking in particular, in that, unlike almost any other western nation, we exercise little regulatory control over the activities of corporations, banks, holding companies, trusts, and the like. Stepped-up reporting requirements, stiff penalties, and the reallocation of law enforcement resources from users to the business community allies of drug organizations, it is argued, would strangle the cartels in their own money.

In addition, it is axiomatic in the organized crime literature that corruption is necessary for success. Similar targeting of law enforcement and political corruption would make the logistics of drug trafficking very difficult indeed. This strategy would shift the aim of enforcement strategies from users and small-time dealers to their "upperworld" partners, who have much more to lose and are more likely to be easily deterred.

5. *Broaden Forfeiture Sanctions.* The use of forfeiture sanctions against drug offenders has proven to be a valuable asset to law enforcement in the drug war. As an alternative to incarceration, perhaps imposing stricter forfeiture sanctions against dealers would deter some drug crimes and would supply law enforcement with additional financial resources. Additionally, there is a strong argument to be made for the expansion of forfeiture laws to include money laundering activities by legitimate business allies of drug traffickers. An investment house faced with the seizure of its depositors' assets might be less likely to handle dirty money.

6. *Impose Harsh Fines.* This is yet another alternative to incarceration of drug dealers and users. The use of strict and harsh fines might serve as a deterrent to criminal activity and would aid in financing drug education, rehabilitation, and law enforcement efforts.

A Word from the Authors

Debating a controversial public issue such as this and adequately deliberating all important considerations of the issue is not an easy task. Headway in arriving at a viable solution is frequently stifled by fragmented (mis)information promulgated by people that are merely trying to "muddy the waters" or promote their own personal interests. Clearly, drug dealers and consumers represent one such interest group, but so do some government bureaucracies that do not want to give up funding, private hospitals that profit from drug abuse and related problems, and politicians that often seek votes through emotion and fear rather than reason.

Perhaps one can argue that our country has slowly evolved into a tolerant society. That is, both a drug-tolerant society and a violence-tolerant society. The drug problem for many is merely one that is seen on television or read about in the local newspaper. Unfortunately, many people have an "ostrich type" mind set in that just because they are not victims of drug abuse or because they do not personally know a victim, the drug problem is somebody else's concern.

Additionally, drug users frequently consider themselves victims of governmental and societal repression rather than victims of drug abuse. Accordingly, many people view a "victim" of drug abuse as one that suffers an overdose or experiences some negative physical manifestation created by the use of a particular substance. When this occurs, little consideration is given to the drug user's employer and coworkers that are affected by the user's inability to function on the job, the taxpayer that foots the bill for drug enforcement, and the costs of expensive and often lengthy drug trials, incarceration, and treatment programs for drug dependent people.

In addition, there are the unsuspecting victims of drug crimes, such as those in fatal accidents, assaults, or robberies. Certainly, murder is such a crime. In cases of drive-by shootings the murderers are often intoxicated, under the influence of drugs, or consciously operating on behalf of drug-dealing groups.

For others, the drug problem is one that needs a "quick fix" and therefore should be easily remedied through either ill-conceived legalization policies or, on the other extreme, the introduction of repressive law enforcement measures. Our country's drug problems are the product of over 100 years of social change and evolution, touch-and-go drug control policy, and a myriad of other factors such as the media and the entertainment industry. Additionally, a passive reluctance seems to exist, on the part of our present-day society, to learn from past historical experience in dealing with drug abuse.

It is clear that solutions, whatever they are, will be time consuming and will no doubt require equal yet positive participation on the part of law enforcement, schools, colleges, universities, researchers, and social treatment programs. In addition, an effective drug control policy must include unified participation from a general public that is both willing, informed, and ready to make constructive choices about controlling drug use and related criminal activity.

DISCUSSION QUESTIONS

1. What are the arguments for the legalization of drugs, and how realistic are those arguments?

2. Discuss the possible consequences of drug legalization with regard to public health.

3. List the arguments for not legalizing drugs.

4. If drugs are never legalized in the United States, then what other measures could be considered to insure public safety and health?

5. What would be the possible effects of drug legalization on drug gangs and organized crime groups?

6. How would legalizing drugs in the United States affect international relations or efforts to control "black market" drugs entering the country from foreign sources?

7. What are the social consequences of Amsterdam's drug policies?

8. How would legalizing drugs affect domestic production of "black market" drugs in the United States?

9. Discuss the 1975 Alaska *Ravin* case and how it has affected issues such as personal freedom, public safety, and public health in Alaska.

10. Discuss Britain's experiment with legalizing heroin.

11. Discuss your interpretation of the social changes over the last twenty years that have affected public attitudes either for, or against, legalization of drugs.

CLASS PROJECTS

1. In considering the question of legalization of drugs, what patterns of criminality or addiction do you feel would evolve if drugs were legalized?

2. Survey classmates or friends to see what their position is on the legalization issue. Take note of the reasons given to support their position; are these realistic or rational?

CHAPTER 13

FEDERAL DRUG CONTROL
POLICY AND LAW*

As discussed earlier in this book, many countries, such as China and Babylonia, were early victims of drug use. They also may have been the first to recognize a fundamental correlation between drug use and crime. Lawmakers during that period recognized that a large percentage of people were unable to make judgments about their own ability to safely use mind-altering and addicting substances and therefore posed a threat to public order and safety. Furthermore, these early laws characterized the necessity of a government to attempt to control drug-related crime by making it unlawful to use, possess, or traffic in dangerous substances.

In the United States, the federal response to the country's national drug problem is vibrant with an historical tapestry of both success *and* failure. Critics of federal drug policy and proponents of drug legalization often claim that laws designed to control drug use and related activity are a violation of personal freedoms and are too repressive in nature (see Chapter 12).

If the history of global drug use offers any yardstick as to the dangers of drugs and related activity, as many feel it does, then the option of legalization is not a viable one. The remaining alternative is to control drugs, prosecute offenders, and attempt, through numerous public programs and policies, to deter individual involvement with substances that have been recognized as dangerous.

Perhaps the most threatening component to the illicit drug market is its concomitant organized crime. The term "organized crime" means many things to many people, but those organizations that comprise this criminal entity provide a perfect mechanism for the manufacturing, trafficking, and management of criminal drug operations (see Chapter 7). Typically, the policy cycle shows the

---

* Although this chapter discusses federal drug control laws, most states now have legislation that parallels federal antidrug laws. Subtle differences in drug control legislation usually exist from one state to another and therefore will have varying effects on drug enforcement policy and procedure.

government assuming a particular response to deal with drug use and trafficking, and the drug users and traffickers then taking defensive measures to counter it. The government then assumes yet another strategy, the traffickers again take defensive actions, and so on.

This reactive response has been characteristic of the federal drug control strategy since the mid-1960s. As we will see in the upcoming discussion, federal controls of the last 80 years have generally focused on the supply of illicit drugs rather than on attacking the public demand for them. In 1986, the President's Commission on Organized Crime made the following remarks regarding supply and demand:

> Although the supply and demand of drugs have often been considered separate issues, by both the public and private sectors, they are in fact inseparable parts of a single problem. The success of supply efforts are related to commitments made to reduce the demand for drugs through drug abuse education, treatment, research, vigorous enforcement of drug laws, and effective sentencing. Drug supply and demand operate in an interrelated and dynamic manner. The strategies employed to limit each should be similarly connected.

Today, politicians continue to lend support to measures designed to control drug use. There are growing demands for increased use of drug testing in the work force, stricter laws dealing with both drug users and dealers, and renewed attempts by government to curtail drug-related corruption.

On one hand, it may seem that today's public focus on drug control is so intense that faulty drug control initiatives go unchecked, immunized from critical examination. On the other hand, widespread public concern and a proclivity toward making the public more aware of domestic drug policy may provide an adequate check against misuse of governmental power.

The History of Drug Control Policy

As we observed earlier in this chapter, dependence on opium and morphine grew considerably during and subsequent to the Civil War. Five distinct reasons for this have been cited and are as follows:

1. much morphine was indiscriminately used as treatment on battle-fields and in hospitals...

2. the widespread use of the hypodermic syringe to administer morphine contributed to opiate abuse...

3. between the years 1865 and 1914, the practice of opium smoking spread from Chinese immigrants to American citizens...

4. there was an increase in the use of opium-based medications by the American patent medicine industry...

5. the marketing of heroin as a safe, powerful, yet nonaddicting substitute for opium derivatives.

    Source: PCOC, 1986

The first prohibitionist piece of drug legislation in the United States was a 1875 city ordinance in San Francisco, which banned the operation of opium dens in that city. The opium den was a place where opium addicts could retreat to smoke their opium and remain free from detection by local authorities. Within five years, 27 other states had adopted similar laws to regulate the use of opium.

In 1887, the federal government barred Chinese citizens (but not Americans) from importing opium for smoking. This measure included the raising of the tariff (from $6 to $10 per pound) on a type of smoking opium that was a relatively mild form of raw opium. This effort did little, however, to the incidence of opium addiction or importation.

In 1908, the American Opium Commission was established by Congress to examine the opium problem that then affected the nation. In 1909, as a result of the work performed by this commission, a congressional act was passed that was named "An Act to Prohibit the Importation and Use of Opium for Other than Medicinal Purposes." This measure permitted the importation of opium only for medicinal purposes and restricted its introduction into the country to only 12 ports of entry. The measure failed to affect the manufacture or trafficking of opium within the country.

Opium products were still available without a physician's prescription and were being marketed throughout the country through retail outlets and a growing mail order trade. Counter sale of these drugs had been the rule in most states (OCED Report, 1983).

Another unique aspect of the 1909 measure was that Congress had come to realize that the United States could not relieve the opium problem in southeast Asia without first addressing the problem on our own soil. As the drug abuse momentum grew at the turn of the century, it was recognized by 1909 that indeed drugs were a "major medico-social problem."

Just after the turn of the century, the United States initiated the first International Opium Commission, which met in Shanghai and consisted of representatives of 13 countries. This was considered the first international effort to address the problem of opium addiction and to search for solutions. The Shanghai Convention ultimately adopted several resolutions for dealing with the problem, including:

1. Consider the desirability of reviewing each country's system of regulation of the use of opium in light of the discrepancies among the countries' regulatory systems;

2. Adopt measures to prevent the exporting of opium and its derivatives to countries that prohibit the importation of such items, and;

3. Take measures for the gradual suppression of opium smoking in each country's own territories and possessions.

The first major legal assault on illicit drug consumption was the passing of the 1906 *Pure Food and Drug Act*. Up until that time, opium derivatives had been widely used by physicians for an array of illnesses. Cocaine was another drug commonly used in treatment for illnesses such as hay fever, alcohol, and morphine addiction. The Pure Food and Drug Act required medicines to list narcotic (and alcohol) ingredients on their labels.

In 1909, the United States proposed to the other participating countries that an international conference be held to "conventionalize" the resolutions agreed upon at the Shanghai convention. Such a convention, realized in 1911, was held at The Hague and resulted in the signing of the International Opium Convention in January, 1912. As a direct response to the provisions of the International Opium Convention, the Harrison Narcotics Act was enacted on December 17, 1914 and became the hallmark of federal drug control policy for the next 65 years.

The Harrison Narcotics Act (1914)

The Harrison Narcotics Act was originally titled *An Act to Provide for the Registration of, with Collectors of Internal Revenue, and to Impose a Special Tax Upon All Persons Who Produce, Import, Manufacture, Compound, Deal in, Dispense, Sell, Distribute, or Give Away Opium or Coca Leaves, their Salts, Derivatives, or Preparations, and for other Purposes*. As one could guess from the title of this law, it was a comprehensive legal measure designed to deter any involvement in the opium or coca trade (under this act, cocaine was considered to be a narcotic, instead of what it actually is—a stimulant).

Certain individuals viewed the Harrison Act as a rational way to limit addiction and drug abuse through taxation and regulation. It was a regulatory device which, according to the American Opium Commission, "would bring the whole traffic and use of these drugs into the light of day and, therefore, create a public opinion against the use of them that would be more important, perhaps, than the act itself." The act was heralded as a method of drug abuse control and as a public awareness tool. (Source: OCDE Report 1983).

The success of the enforcement of this act was directly attributed to the chosen source of authority and constitutional power to collect taxes. As the Harrison Act was basically a tax revenue measure, the responsibility of enforcement rested with the Department of the Treasury.

PROVISIONS OF THE HARRISON NARCOTICS ACT

Section 1. This section required that any person that was in the business of dealing in the specified drugs pay a special annual tax of one dollar. In 1918, the Revenue Act increased the special annual tax on importers, manufactures, producers, and compounders to $24; on wholesalers to $12; on retailers to $6; and on practitioners to $3.

Section 2. This section prohibited the selling or giving away of any specified drugs except pursuant to the written order of the person to whom the drug was being given or sold. The written order was required to be on a special form issued by the Commissioner of Internal Revenue.

Section 4. It was unlawful for anyone not previously registered to engage in interstate trafficking of the specified drugs.

Section 8. The possession of any of the specified drugs was illegal, with the exception of possession by employees of registrants and patients of physicians.

Section 9. This section provided that the punishment for any violation of the act was to be not more than $2,000, not more than 5 years in prison, or both.

Section 10. This gave the Commissioner of Internal Revenue the responsibility for enforcing the act.

Following the passage of the Harrison Act, numerous Supreme Court decisions were handed down that shaped the direction of enforcement under this law.

THE HISTORY OF DRUG CONTROL

1909   Representatives of 13 nations meet in Shanghai to discuss ways of controlling illicit drug traffic.

1912   *The International Opium Convention*— the first binding international instrument governing the shipment of narcotic drugs (signed at the Hague, Netherlands).

1920   The first Assembly of the League of Nations established an *Advisory Committee on Traffic in Opium and Other Dangerous Drugs.* Under League auspices, three main drug conventions were developed over the next two decades.

1925   *The Second National Opium Convention*— established a system of import certificates and export authorizations for licit international trade in narcotics.

1931   *The Convention for Limiting the Manufacture and Regulating the Distribution of Narcotic Drugs*— introduced a compulsory estimates system aimed at limiting the amounts of drugs manufactured to those needed for medical and scientific needs.

1936   *The Convention for the Suppression of the Illicit Traffic in Dangerous Drugs*— the first international instrument to call for severe punishment for illegal drug traffickers.

1946   Drug control responsibilities formerly carried out by the League of Nations were transferred to the *United Nations. The Division of Narcotic Drugs* was also created to act as the secretariat for the commission and to serve as the central repository of United Nations expertise in drug control.

1961   *The Single Convention on Narcotic Drugs*— codified all existing multilateral treaty laws. Now placed under control was the cultivation of plants grown as raw material for narcotic drugs. Controls were continued on opium and its derivatives, and coca bush and cannabis were placed under international control, obliging governments to limit production of those drugs to amounts needed for scientific and medical use.

1971 *The Convention on Psychotropic Substances*— Until 1971, only narcotic drugs were subject to international control. This convention extended controls to include a broad range of manmade, mood-altering substances that can lead to harmful dependencies. These included: hallucinogens such as LSD and mescaline, stimulants such as amphetamines, and sedative-hypnotics such as barbiturates.

1981 *The International Drug Abuse Control Strategy* was formed and implemented a five-year program. The strategy included: measures for the wider adherence to existing treaties; provisions for coordinating efforts to ensure a balance between supply and demand of drugs for legitimate uses; steps to eradicate the illicit drug supply and to reduce traffic.

1984 In its *Declaration on the Control of Drug Trafficking and Drug Abuse*, the United Nations General Assembly characterized drug traffic and abuse as "an international criminal activity" that constituted "a grave threat to the security and development of many countries and peoples...."

1987 *The International Conference on Drug Abuse and Illicit Trafficking*— focused on developing long-term drug control strategies, policies, and activities to attack drug abuse and trafficking at the national, regional, and international levels.

The Marijuana Tax Act (1937) — patterned after Harrison Act

Marijuana was not included in the 1914 Harrison legislation because, at the time, it was not considered a particularly dangerous drug. In addition, marijuana had some historic commercial use in the manufacture of rope, twine, veterinary medicines, and other products. Due to public concern over its increasing popularity in recreational use during Prohibition, states began passing legislation against its use or possession. By 1931, "all but two states west of the Mississippi and several more in the east had enacted prohibitory legislation against it" (PCOC 1986).

The Federal Bureau of Narcotics, in an effort to avoid assuming additional responsibilities at the federal level, had minimized the dangers of marijuana use and failed to support federal marijuana control measures. Instead, in its 1932 annual report, the Bureau urged the states to adopt a Uniform State Narcotics Law, which transpired in 1932.

Finally, as a result of increasing public pressure, the FBN supported the Federal Marijuana Tax Act, which was passed in 1937. This congressional measure was basically a nominal revenue measure patterned after the Harrison Narcotic Act. At the time of its passing, it was estimated that there were over 10,000 acres of marijuana being cultivated in the United States.

Closely resembling provisions of the Harrison Act, it required that any person whose business related to marijuana pay a special tax. Additionally, the transfer of marijuana had to be pursuant to a written order on a special form issued by the Secretary of the Treasury. The person transferring the marijuana was then required to pay a tax of $1.00 per ounce if registered and $100.00 per ounce if not registered.

The Comprehensive Drug Abuse Prevention and Control Act (1970)

Although legal controls and public drug policy will be discussed in greater detail later in this text, the primary federal law addressing drug control will now be examined. The legal infrastructure of the federal drug control effort is the 1970 Comprehensive Drug Abuse Prevention and Control Act, Title II of which is also known as the *Controlled Substances Act* (*CSA*). This federal measure updated all previously existing drug laws and gave uniformity to federal drug control policy. Generally speaking, there are four provisions of the CSA, which consist of:

1. mechanisms for reducing the availability of dangerous drugs;

2. procedures for bringing a substance under control;

3. the criteria for determining control requirements; and

4. the obligations incurred by international treaty arrangements.

The CSA places all substances that were in some manner regulated under existing federal law into one of five schedules. The criteria for which drugs are placed in these schedules is based on the medical use of the substance, its potential for abuse, and safety or addiction (dependence) liability. These five schedules are:

Schedule I   *— no current medical use*
- The drug or other substance has a high potential for abuse.
- The drug or other substance has no currently accepted medical use in treatment in the United States.
- There is a lack of accepted safety for use of the drug or other substance under medical supervision.   *LSD, Marijuana, heroin*

Schedule II   *— restricted use due to addictiveness of drugs*
- The drug or other substance has a high potential for abuse.
- The drug or other substance has a currently accepted medical use in treatment in the United States or a currently accepted medical use with severe restrictions.
- Abuse of the drug or other substance may lead to severe psychological or physical dependence.   *Cocaine, narcotics,*

Schedule III
- The drug or other substance has a potential for abuse less than the drugs or other substances in Schedules I and II
- The drug or other substance has a currently accepted medical use in treatment in the United States
- Abuse of the drug or other substance may lead to moderate or low physical dependence or high psychological dependence

Schedule IV
- The drug or other substance has a low potential for abuse relative to the drugs or other substances in Schedule III.
- The drug or other substance has a currently accepted medical use in treatment in the United States.
- Abuse of the drug or other substance may lead to limited physical dependence or psychological dependence relative to the drugs or other substances in Schedule III.

Schedule V
- The drug or other substance has a low potential for abuse relative to the drugs or other substances in Schedule IV.
- The drug or other substance has a currently accepted medical use in treatment in the United States.
- Abuse of the drug or other substance may lead to limited physical dependence or psychological dependence relative to the drugs or other substances in Schedule IV.

9 - Control mechanisms

In addition, the law imposes nine control mechanisms on the manufacture, purchase, and distribution of controlled substances. These are as follows:

1. *The Registration of Handlers.* This provision requires the registration of any person that handles or intends to handle controlled substances and also stipulates that this person must obtain a DEA registration number. The DEA number is a unique number assigned to each handler of drugs, importer, exporter, manufacturer, wholesaler, hospital, pharmacy, physician, and researcher.

2. *Record-Keeping Requirements.* The law also requires that, regardless of which schedule the drug is under, full records must be kept of all quantities manufactured, purchased, sold, and inventoried by each handler. Basically, this requirement creates a "paper trail" for investigators in the event that improprieties in the handling of drugs are discovered.

3. *Quotas on Manufacturing.* The DEA limits the quantity of controlled substances listed in Schedules I and II that can be produced during any calendar year. These overall production limits are subdivided into manufacturing quotas, which are granted to the registered manufacturers that desire to produce the controlled substance.

4. *Restrictions on Dispensing.* The term "dispensing" refers to the delivery of the controlled substance to the ultimate user, who may be a patient or research subject. Some drugs such as Schedule I substances are not obtainable via prescription anyway so they can only be used in research situations.

5. *Limitations on Imports and Exports.* This provision pertains to international transactions involving the shipment of controlled substances that require prior approval, such as the filing of a declaration.

6. *Restrictions on Distribution.* When controlled substances are transferred from one manufacturer to another, from one importer to another, or from one wholesaler to another, accurate records are required. Extremely stringent requirements are imposed on those supplying Schedule I and II drugs. Basically, this restriction ensures that only authorized individuals obtain Schedule I and II drugs.

7. *Conditions for the Storage of Drugs.* The DEA establishes the requirements for the storage and security of drugs on the premises that house controlled drugs. Special high-security measures are required of handlers that have Schedule I or II drugs on the premises. For drugs in Schedule III, IV, and V, the requirement of an alarm and security system is imposed.

8. *Reports of Transactions to the Government.* This requirement mandates that periodic reports on certain drugs be submitted to the DEA. A special automated computer system keeps track of those drugs in Schedules I and II (as well as Schedule III narcotics). There is also a requirement mandating that drug inventories be filed once a year.

9. *Criminal, Civil, and Administrative Penalties for Illegal Acts.* It is through the CSA that all legal controls are given their ultimate authority. Such controls have proven to be of a great benefit to federal law enforcement and suppression efforts.

Drug Control in the Reagan Era

In 1980, when Ronald Reagan was elected president, the general consensus within the federal drug control community was positive. Many drug enforcement practitioners "were soon disappointed—Reagan talked a good game, but despite his speeches bemoaning the threat of violent crime, when it came to more money for fighting crime, including drug traffickers, Reagan was as parsimonious as Carter" (Shannon, 1988).

In 1981, Reagan, under the prodding of his legal adviser David Stockman, declared a 12 percent across-the-board cut for all federal agencies except the Pentagon. Drug enforcement was not spared, and certain effects were felt immediately. DEA and Customs airplanes and cars were grounded; money to make undercover drug transactions ran out.

Things changed, however, during the years following the recession of the early 1980s, as the Reagan administration's spending on drug law enforcement more than tripled, from $800 million in fiscal year (FY) 1981 to $2.5 billion for FY 1988. The administration soon emphasized the supply side in its war on drugs: more than 70 percent of 1988 federal antidrug spending was for law enforcement programs such as *crop eradication* in foreign source countries and the *interdiction* of drugs entering the United States from foreign countries (see Chapter 4).

Reagan-era drug control initiatives included the passing of the *Department of Defense Authorization Act of 1982*. This act contained a provision called "Military Cooperation with Civilian Law Enforcement Authorities," which permitted military personnel to operate military equipment that had been loaned to civilian drug law enforcement agencies. The act otherwise broadened the authority of the military in national drug control efforts.

The year 1984 was a prolific one for the 98th Congress and drug control legislation. An example of some of the most important laws passed during this year include:

The Comprehensive Crime Control Act of 1984. This act increased many existing penalties for an array of drug offenses.

The Controlled Substance Registrant Act of 1984. This act made it illegal to steal any quantity of controlled drugs from a registrant.

The Aviation Drug Trafficking Control Act. This act amended the 1958 Federal Aviation Act to require the administrator of the FAA to revoke airman certificates and aircraft registrations of those convicted of violating any federal or state law relating to controlled substances.

The Comprehensive Forfeiture Act of 1984. Extensive revisions of federal, civil, and criminal forfeiture laws were made in the passing of this act. In part, the act streamlined the process in which personal assets could be seized by federal and state officers.

A comprehensive Anti-Drug Act passed in October, 1986 was designed to enhance existing penalties. In November 1988, yet another, more comprehensive drug bill was passed that shifted priorities from the supply to the demand side. In this legislation, a set of strict penalties focused on the recreational drug user rather than the drug dealer. Another controversial provision of the bill permits, but does not require, the death penalty for anyone that kills a policeman during the commission of a drug-related crime and for murderers that have been involved in at least two drug-related crimes.

The U.S. Build-Up in Latin America

Generally speaking, the international thrust of the drug war is led by the State Department's *Bureau of International Narcotics Matters*. The Bureau controls an interregional air wing of more than 50 aircraft, which include fixed-wing, C-123 cargo transports, and Vietnam-era helicopters. The aircraft are used to ferry troops, move supplies, and most important, to spray crops (Massing, 1990). Eradication initiatives by the State Department include the spraying of coca, marijuana, and poppy fields in Colombia, Guatemala, Belize, Jamaica, and Mexico.

While the Bureau monitors the skies, the *Drug Enforcement Administration* (*DEA*) focuses on ground smuggling. Traditionally assigned to domestic drug enforcement, the DEA is strengthening its presence in Latin America. Today, more than 150 agents work in 17 countries. Agency personnel are also more and more involved in paramilitary actions in the coca-growing regions of South America, where, armed with machine guns and jungle knives, they conduct helicopter raids on processing labs and clandestine air strips.

The *Central Intelligence Agency* (*CIA*) has also expanded its presence in Latin America in recent years, with new agents assigned to Colombia, Peru, and Bolivia, just to name a few. At CIA headquarters in Langley, Virginia, a Counter-Narcotics Center of the agency collates the steady stream of data coming from agents, informants, wiretaps, radar, and satellites.

The *Pentagon* is yet another player in United States-Latin American drug control. The U.S. Southern Command in Panama is stepping up activities in Latin America. To this end, the situations in Andean nations are regularly assessed to determine the needs of the local military and police. For example, in 1988, Colombia, Peru, and Bolivia received a total of $3 million in military aid, compared to the estimated 1990 total of $170 million (Massing, 1990).

During the latter part of the 1980s, the *U.S. Customs Service* also extended its services to Latin America to assist drug source countries in sealing off their borders. In addition, the Coast Guard has commissioned mobile training teams to instruct local policemen in river interdiction.

Legal Tools in Drug Control

The use of innovative antidrug laws has proven to be one of the most powerful weapons against drug trafficking. Many of the most effective laws have been in effect for some time, but there are now many new laws that address the many unique aspects of the drug trade and the constantly changing structure of drug organizations. This section will look at some of the most effective drug control tools on the federal level.

RICO — *most powerful tool fout, has in fighting O.C.*

The 1970 Racketeer-Influenced and Corrupt Organizations Act (RICO) is yet another invaluable tool in the fight against organized crime in the drug trade. Successful application of the RICO statute in recent years has resulted in the conviction of top-level La Cosa Nostra members in such cities as Kansas City,

Designed for going after Tops (managers) of O.C.

St. Louis, Philadelphia, and Cleveland. Cases such as these help illustrate to the general public the magnitude of such organizations and the extent to which they operate.

Although the act has been law since 1970, its was not widely used until the early 1980s. Prior to that time, prosecutors tended to apply the RICO statute to criminals that were not members of large crime organizations or that were not management-level OC players.

RICO is a statute that criminalizes a pattern of conduct characteristic of organized crime. It authorizes the seizure of assets and profits of illegal enterprises. Specifically outlined in the RICO statute are the criminal acts that constitute a "pattern of racketeering," two of which must have occurred during the last ten years. Under RICO, racketeering is defined as "any act or threat involving murder, kidnapping, gambling, arson, robbery, bribery, extortion, or trafficking in narcotics or dangerous drugs."

25,000 fine / or 20 years in prison

CLOSE-UP: HOW RICO WORKS

To help illustrate how RICO works, consider the ABC drug cartel, which is a criminal group controlling the "South Shore Bank" through known criminals or their associates that hold key positions. Through this control, the cartel is able to launder money from the sales of illegal drugs conducted throughout the country and in South America.

Assume that 1) a bank president and certain members are criminally prosecuted under RICO and identified as a "criminal enterprise," 2) the RICO predicate acts include drug trafficking, 3) and members of the cartel were shown to receive profits from drug sales and to have acquired personal assets as a result, and that 4) with drug money, the drug cartel assumed legitimate control over other businesses such as the Oasis Restaurant, Oyster Bar, and the Hungry Man Catering Service. At the time of the criminal indictment, all such assets (equivalent to their illicit proceeds) are frozen to prevent liquidation of them prior to seizure. After conviction, these assets are then seized.

At this point, the investigation is not yet over because some members of the drug cartel will no doubt remain in control of the bank. The civil provisions of RICO are now placed into motion, as members of the cartel can be permanently enjoined from controlling the bank. A lesser standard of proof than is required in a criminal case is needed to accomplish this (the criminal case standard is "beyond a reasonable doubt"). The prosecutor must establish the cartel's control over the bank and request "injunctive relief." The bank may then be placed under a government trustee, and cartel members are then prohibited from assuming control over it. From here on out, if the government can demonstrate that a ABC drug cartel member is assuming control, that member will then be held in contempt of the civil order under RICO and prosecuted.

Source: Lyman, 1989

The Continuing Criminal Enterprise Statute (CCE)

The Federal Continuing Criminal Enterprise Statute (Section 848 of Title 21, United States Code), enacted as part of the Comprehensive Drug Abuse Prevention and Control Act of 1970, is one of the strongest statutory weapons against drug trafficking. This statute, like RICO, gives prosecutors the means to reach the organizers, managers, and supervisors of major drug trafficking organizations.

Prosecution under this statute requires proof of five elements in order to sustain prosecution:

1. The defendant's conduct must constitute a felony violation of federal narcotics laws.

2. The conduct must take place as part of a continuing series of violations.

3. The defendant must undertake this activity in concert with at least five other individuals.

4. The defendant must act as the organizer, manager, or supervisor of this criminal enterprise.

5. The defendant must obtain income or resources from this enterprise.

The CCE provides for some of the most severe criminal penalties for illicit drug trafficking. These include: imprisonment for a minimum of ten years with no possibility of parole. In addition, the court may impose a life sentence with no provision for parole, and fines totaling $100,000. Moreover, under CCE, all profits and assets that have afforded the defendant a source of influence over the illegal enterprise are subject to forfeiture.

Conspiracy

The use of conspiracies in drug enforcement has proven to be one of the most beneficial tactics of the last decade. Although conspiracies have existed for quite some time, the use of such laws is now common among federal, state, and local authorities alike.

Although state law in this area may differ from one jurisdiction to another, the basic principles of conspiracy are the same. Conspiracy is defined as an agreement between two or more persons that have the specific intent either to commit a crime or to engage in dishonest, fraudulent, or immoral conduct injurious to public health or morals. In studying this definition, one can easily see the benefits of such a law in the area of drug control.

Figure 13.1 ELEMENTS OF CONSPIRACY

D = Defendant

(1) Agreement between (2) two or more persons (3) who have the specific intent (4) to either (a) commit a crime or (b) engage in dishonest, fraudulent or immoral conduct injurious to public health or morals.

AGREEMENT - there must be a true agreement to promote or facilitate a particular objective.

- **AGREEMENT SUFFICIENT** - at common law, the agreement itself is the only act required to complete the crime; federal and about half of states now require some additional overt act in furtherance of the conspiracy (although the act need not be illegal in itself and only one conspirator need do an act).
- **PROOF** - agreement may be inferred from concert of action (look for mutual adoption of a common purpose).
- **FALSE AGREEMENT** - undercover agent or other "false agreement" situations are not conspiracies - ther must be a true actual intent to carry out unlawful objective by at least two parties. (MPC is contra; party with true intent still liable).
- **UNKNOWN CONSPIRATORS** - D must agree with at least one other person but need not agree with (or even know identity of) all other members of the conspiracy.
- **SINGLE OR MULTIPLE CONSPIRACY** - the agreement is the essence of conspiracy; thus, there is only one conspiracy even if agreement encompasses seperate diverse criminal acts and even if agreement entails a continuous course of criminal conduct.

- **STATUS DEFENSE TO SUBSTANTIVE CRIME** - if D conspires with B, it is no defense to either part that D may not be capable under the legal definition to commit underlying crime himself (e.g., a man cannot rape his own wife).
- **DIPLOMATIC IMMUNITY** - that one party is immune from prosecution is no defense to the other party.
- **DIMINISHED CAPACITY DEFENSE** - if B, the only other conspirator, possesses a diminished capacity defense negating specific intent (e.g., intoxication, infancy, insanity), a few courts preclude conviction of D as well as B; better view including MPC permits convictions of D regardless of B's personal mens rea defenses.
- **ACQUITTAL ON MERITS** - if B, the only other conspirator, is acquitted on the merits (i.e., not because of procedural or personal mens rea defenses), D may not be convicted.
- **HUSBAND-WIFE** - today, D may conspire with a spouse (not so at old common law).

TWO OR MORE PERSONS

WHARTON'S RULE

- **Consent Crimes** - if crime logically requires the voluntary participation of another (e.g., bribery, incest, adultery, gambling), there is no conspiracy unless agreement involves additional person not logically essential.
- **Purely Redefined by Substantive Crime** - if substantive crime requires a number of participants (e.g., 5 or more conducting gambling operations), there can be no conspiracy charge of conspiracy unless agreement involves persons who are not guilty of the substantive crime itself.
- **Model Penal Code** - abandon's Wharton's Rule.

SPECIFIC INTENT - D must have the specific intent with regard to a criminal objective.

- **MENS REA DEFENSES APPLY** - D may assert any mens rea defenses which negate specific intent.
- **PURPOSEFUL AGREEMENT** - it is always sufficient that D enters the agreement with the conscious object of of causing, promoting or facilitating a result which he knows to be criminal.
- **CORRUPT MOTIVE DOCTRINE** - many states require that D actually had a corrupt motive (that he knew that intended conduct was illegal) except where the act is inherently wrong.

- **SUPPLIER CASES** - D's "agreement" consists of providing goods or services which the knows will be used to commit a crime.

More Knowledge - normally not sufficient, but conviction is possible if: (1) goods supplied are highly dangerous (e.g., explosives), or highly regulated (e.g., drugs); (2) the crime is very serious (e.g., homicide, kidnapping); (3) there is continuous involvement, or (4) if D affirmatively encouraged use more of this goods when he had a reason to know that the use was illegal.

Knowledge Plus Stake - D may be convicted if the knows that his goods or services are used for a criminal purpose and he has a "stake" in the success of the criminal objective (e.g., D charges an inflated price).

CONSPIRATORIAL OBJECTIVE

- **CRIME** - it is a conspiracy to agree to commit any crime, including a misdemeanor.
- **PUBLICLY INJURIOUS CRIME** - it is a conspiracy to agree with another to do any at (even if lawful) which is injurious to public health or morals and is accomplished by dishonest, fraudulent, corrupt or immoral means (MPC and some states are contra limiting conspiracies to "crimes").

DEFENSES

- **ABANDONMENT** - once a conspiracy has been formed, it is no offense that D subsequently withdrew, even if done prior to the completion of the underlying crime. (MPC and some states contra, but only if D: (1) completely renounces criminal purpose, and (2) makes substantial efforts to prevent the commission of the underlying crime).
- **IMPOSSIBILITY** - factual impossibility is not a defense though D may prevail if the conspiratorial objective is simply not illegal, regardless of D's contrary belief.

SPECIAL CONSEQUENCES

- **SEPERATE OFFENSE** - conspiracy is a seperate offense, distinct from the underlying crime (i.e., there is no merger).
- **VENUE** - a criminal charge may be brought in any county where some act in furtherance was committed by any of D, X, and Y are interested in the success of each other's agreements with B, there is a "rim" connecting all the "spokes" in one conspiracy.
- **HEARSAY EVIDENCE** - in a trial for conspiracy, otherwise inadmissable hearsay statements of co-conspirators are admissable against D if made in furtherance of the conspiracy.

VICARIOUS LIABILITY

- **General Rule** - in addition to conspiracy and the substantive crime intended, D may be convicted of other crimes committed by members of conspiracy in furtherance of conspiratorial goal (it is no defense that D did not intend nor know of the acts).
- **Chain Conspiracy** - if D is part of a "chain" of known illegal acts (e.g., smuggling-trafficking-retailing of drugs), he is liable for all crimes committed to further the conspiratorial goal (look for "community of interest").
- **Wheel Conspiracy** - if D conspires with B and B enters into similar seperate and unrelated agreements for similar crimes with X and Y, B is the "hub" of a "wheel conspiracy;" if there is a community of interest so that D, X, and Y are interested in the success of each other's agreements with B, there is a "rim" connecting all the "spokes" in one conspiracy and all all parties are liable for the criminal acts of the others. If there is no community of interest, there are 3 seperate conspiracies and only B is liable for the acts of all others (as well as for 3 conspiracies).

ATTEMPTED CONSPIRACY (SOLICITATION) - one who attempts to induce, encourage or command another to commit a crime is guilty of solicitation; if the other person agrees there is a conspiracy. (in many states, D must make some substantial effort to prevent the crime).

Drug trafficking is a criminal endeavor that usually requires more than one player, e.g., a grower sells drugs to a manufacturer that contracts a smuggler for transportation. The smuggler then transports the drugs to a wholesale buyer, who in turn sells them to a retail distributor. The retail distributor then sells the drugs to numerous dealers and users on the street. Given the required documentation by investigators, conspiracy charges can be brought against all such players in a drug operation.

Conspiracy is an agreement between two or more persons that have the specific intent either to commit a crime or engage in dishonest, fraudulent, or immoral conduct injurious to public health or morals.

Because most conspiracy cases involve numerous defendants, a degree of confusion may result. Generally, there are three types of conspiracy cases that are most commonly used in prosecutions of drug traffickers. These are: the chain, the wheel, and the enterprise conspiracy.

The Chain. Chain conspiracies occur when a certain criminal endeavor is dependent on the participation of each member of the criminal organization. Each member represents a "link" in the chain and the success of the criminal goal requires all participants. If one link in the chain is broken (i.e., the member fails to accomplish his or her particular task), the criminal act will be incomplete. To successfully prosecute a chain conspiracy, each member must be shown to be aware of the intended goal of the operation.

The Wheel. Wheel conspiracies are comprised of one member of a criminal organization that is the "hub" or organizer of the criminal plan and members that make up the "spokes." Wheel conspiracies must show that all members that are spokes are aware of each other and agree with each other to achieve a common illegal goal. For this reason, the wheel conspiracy is a difficult one to prosecute, as it is difficult to show a common agreement between the spokes.

The Enterprise. As discussed under the RICO section, a person that has been shown to participate in two or more patterns of racketeering may be prosecuted. The definition of enterprise conspiracy makes it a separate crime to conspire to commit any of the substantive offenses under RICO. Basically, RICO defines the term as an agreement to enter into an enterprise by engaging in a pattern of racketeering. The enterprise conspiracy recognizes that in some criminal organizations not all members have one common goal. Therefore, all that must be shown is a member's willingness to join a criminal organization (an "enterprise") by committing two or more acts of racketeering.

Forfeiture Sanctions in Drug Control

Forfeiture is the ancient legal practice of government seizure of property used in criminal acts. Such an enforcement strategy has proven to be one of the most effective legal tools in the fight against illegal drugs. The federal government's momentum was somewhat slow in the area of forfeiture until recent years. For example, in 1983, more than $100 million in cash and property was seized and forfeited to the government by convicted criminals. The figures in 1989 are more than double that of 1983.

The 1984 Federal Comprehensive Forfeiture Act increased existing forfeiture powers under federal law. This was accomplished in part by lessening the degree of proof necessary for officials to seize property from the traditional "beyond a reasonable doubt" standard to "probable cause." The Act reads:

[A]ny property of a person convicted of a drug felony is subject to forfeiture if the government establishes probable cause that the defendant acquired the property during the period of violation, or within a reasonably short period thereafter, and there was no likely source for the property other than the violation.

The Comprehensive Forfeiture Act, in addition to many state laws addressing forfeiture of assets, enables officers to seize automobiles, aircraft, vessels, bank accounts, securities, as well as real estate holdings and privately owned businesses. In addition, it enhances penalty provisions of the 1970 Controlled Substances Act to include a 20-year prison term and/or fines of up to $250,000.

Basically, the act works in this fashion:

If a drug dealer uses his automobile to drive to a location to sell a quantity of drugs, his car then becomes the conveyance which the dealer used to facilitate the crime. The car therefore, is permitted to be seized under law. Along the same lines, if investigators can show that an automobile was purchased with drug money, it is also allowed to be seized under the law.

Federal law also contains a sharing provision where an equitable transfer of the property can be facilitated. This provision basically divides up property and distributes it among participating law enforcement agencies. Subsequent to the seizure, a determination is made to determine the degree of involvement of each participating agency, and a proportionate distribution of the assets is then made between the agencies.

Grand Juries and Immunity

The use of the grand jury has proven effective in drug suppression efforts because of the broad range of power that it enjoys. The roots of the grand jury go back to the twelfth century, when it served as a safeguard against governmental abuse. The grand jury sought citizen approval for prosecutorial actions. Some of the more powerful rights granted the grand jury are represented by its authority to subpoena persons and documents, to punish, to grant immunity, to issue indictments, and to maintain secrecy of the proceedings.

The grand jury has been successfully used on both the federal and state levels, and in the case of the latter, the authority to call a grand jury may rest with the governor, the state attorney general, or the local prosecutor.

As indicated, the ability of the grand jury to grant immunity broadens the powers of this investigative body. This is particularly useful because many witnesses are criminals that have intimate knowledge of criminal operation.

Most criminals are aware that, under the fifth amendment, they cannot be compelled to give testimony against themselves. When this occurs, prosecutors may pursue one of several options:

1. The prosecutor can compel the testimony by seeking a contempt citation if he can prove that the testimony would not incriminate the witness.

2. The prosecutor can release the witness and continue the proceedings without the benefit of the witness' testimony.

3. A plea bargaining agreement can be sought, where the witness' testimony would be given with the understanding that a lesser charge could be levied against the witness than if he did not give the testimony.

4. Total immunity from prosecution can be given by the prosecutor in exchange for the witness' testimony. In this case, once the witness is given total immunity, he can then be compelled to testify. Refusal, under these circumstances, can result in punishment of the witness.

There are two kinds of immunity that may be granted to witnesses in organized crime prosecutions:

1. *Transactional Immunity.* A witness given transactional immunity for testimony about a certain criminal act is literally immune from ever being prosecuted for that particular crime in the future. Some witnesses have in the past attempted to blurt out additional crimes connected with the primary offense in an attempt to take an "immunity bath" and be free from all responsibility of those crimes. In fact, immunity is not attached when the witness purposely mentions additional crimes. It is extended to other crimes, however, when the prosecutor chooses to mention them during the examination of the witness in court.

2. *Derivative Use Immunity.* When derivative use immunity is granted to a witness, the witness is only immune from having his own testimony later used against him. If evidence of an independent nature is uncovered, however, the witness may be prosecuted on the basis of that evidence.

The Witness Security Program

Prior to the inception of the Federal Witness Protection program, those witnesses that testified on behalf of the government were sometimes brutally tortured or even murdered. Until 1970, the protection of government witnesses was left up to each individual law enforcement agency. Because of limited resources and inconsistent services, the need arose for a single unified federal program.

The Witness Security Program (hereinafter referred to as WITSEC) was implemented in 1971, and since then, more than 5,000 witnesses have entered the program and have been protected, relocated, and given new identities by the Marshal's Service. The program is the first of its kind in the United States and has served as a prototype for similar programs in other countries.

The WITSEC program, operating under the United States Marshal's Service, has now been proven to be one of the most significant prosecution tools in cases involving large-scale organized crime figures. The program is one that basically offers witnesses lifelong protection if they testify against organized crime figures. Such a program is necessary because of criminal conspiracies, secretive and clandestine drug operations, and the general covert nature of organized crime.

There is no more devastating evidence than the first hand testimony of
a trusted confidant exposing and decoding the innermost workings of a
criminal enterprise.

Stanley E. Morris, Director
The Witness Security Program
United States Marshal's Service, 1989

The "WITSEC" program is considered a successful program, as more than eight out of every ten defendants are convicted and receive substantial prison sentences.

CLOSE-UP: THE FEDERAL "WITSEC" WITNESS

Life is closing in on him. He has been an insider to all kinds of criminal activity, such as drug trafficking, money laundering, and bribery. But he's been offered a chance to turn his life around and to start all over again.

This man has been targeted as a potential witness for the case that the government is developing against his criminal associates. If he agrees to testify against others in the organization, the government has offered him protection under the Witness Security Program.

He knows that the information he brings to the witness stand would be devastating to his associates. His testimony would put them in prison for years and destroy a sophisticated criminal network, but he's afraid. These guys believe in retribution—an eye for an eye.

He is told that a lifetime of protection is available to him and his family as long as they follow the established security guidelines of the program. The man agrees to testify, and as he does, he closes the door to his former life. The person that he was no longer exists. He and his family will be given new names and a new place to live, and they will never again publicly refer to their former lives.

Source: *The Pentacle*, 1988 (U.S. Marshal's Service).

Summary

Drug control in the United States dates back to the late 1800s, when opium and its extracts were recognized as dangerous. Momentum on the federal level began in 1906 with the passing of the Pure Food and Drug Act, which required medications containing opium or coca derivatives to say so on their label. In 1914, the Harrison Narcotic Act further controlled opiates by restricting the dispensing of them to medical purposes and pursuant to a written authorization. Ambiguities in the law, however, prevented this act from being fairly enforced.

In 1937, marijuana was controlled under the Marijuana Tax Act in much the same way as opiates were under the Harrison Act. Taxes were imposed for those growing marijuana, in an effort to deter growers from involvement with this plant.

In 1970, the Controlled Substances Act was passed as an effort to update all preexisting federal drug laws. This comprehensive act placed all supposed dangerous drugs in one of five schedules. Each drug was categorized according to danger. The law also set forth new criminal and civil penalties for possession and distribution of drugs.

The year 1970 also marked the enactment of several new and innovative drug control laws that are still being used today. One such law, RICO (Racketeer-Influenced and Corrupt Organizations Act), enables law enforcement to prosecute leaders of large trafficking organizations and to seize assets associated with the organizations. A similar law, the Continuing Criminal Enterprise Act (CCE), also affords authorities special powers in arrest and forfeiture of assets of drug kingpins.

To provide further aid in the drug enforcement initiative, conspiracy and forfeiture legislation have greatly enhanced the ability of law enforcement officers to arrest dealers and associates of dealers. These laws also provide the legal basis to seize assets acquired by drug offenders.

DISCUSSION QUESTIONS

1. Discuss some of the most common historical uses of drugs.

2. Discuss China's role in global drug addiction and how that country attempted to deal with its own opium problem.

3. Discuss the early historical (both medical and recreational) use of cannabis.

4. List the early drug control laws that attempted to regulate dangerous substances in the United States.

5. Discuss the Civil War's unique association with the drug morphine.

6. Compare the drug abuse climate in the United States before and after Prohibition.

7. Discuss the intent of the Harrison Narcotic Act of 1914, and examine any flaws in the drafting of this law.

8. What circumstances led to the passing of the Marijuana Tax Act of 1937?

9. How has the historical use of opium in China affected drug abuse in the United States today?

10. What are some of the most significant provisions of the Controlled Substances Act of 1970?

11. What commercial uses did cannabis have prior to the passing of the Marijuana Tax Act?

12. Discuss the first antidrug law passed in the United States and the circumstances surrounding it.

13. What significance was the passing of the Pure Food and Drug Act of 1906?

14. What major drug control legislation was passed during the Reagan administration?

15. The RICO statute requires that a pattern of racketeering be established. What are the predicate offenses that constitute a pattern of racketeering?

16. How do the CCE and RICO statutes differ?

17. Discuss the elements of a conspiracy.

18. How do the forfeiture sanctions under federal law help in the national drug control effort?

19. Why is the grand jury considered a valuable asset in the prosecution of drug offenders?

20. List and discuss the two types of immunity most commonly used in federal drug prosecutions.

21. Discuss how the Federal Witness Security program (WITSEC) aids in the prosecution of high-level organized crime figures.

CHAPTER 14

CONTROL THROUGH TREATMENT AND PREVENTION

The addict is denied the medical care he urgently needs, open and above-board sources...are closed to him, and he is driven to the underworld where he can get his drug, but of course surreptitiously, and in violation of the law....

American Medicine Magazine, 1915,
after the passage of the Harrison Narcotic Act.

Although drug enforcement efforts are designed to deter drug abuse, there will always be those that develop dependencies on addictive substances or that seek escape through the use of drugs and alcohol. Clearly, there are too many drugs in America and an unacceptable number of people using them. Many of these people simply fail to respond to prevention or education programs, and their lives are literally committed to the acquisition of illegal drugs.

Understanding the Drug User

Many illusions exist about drugs and those that use them. Therefore, this section will attempt to uncloud perceptions of the role of the drug user in society.

Undoubtedly, the drug dependent person presents not only a danger to himself but also to those around him. The user lies to friends and family. He takes advantage of those that attempt to help him. He steals from loved ones to support his habit, and is frequently involved in a lifestyle that includes predatory criminal acts such as robbery, assault, and murder. This is why society's response to the drug problem involves not just the medical and health-care industries, but also the criminal justice system.

Today, society bears most of the burden for offering treatment to those that have fallen victim to drug abuse. Failure to provide a means for addicts to "get well" does not only endanger the lives of the addicts, but also threatens the well-being of those that become victims of drug crimes, communicable diseases such as AIDS, and other related drug abuse problems.

Unfortunately, the tendency to believe that drug treatment is a supple, nurturing, and easy way out of drug dependency is quite far from the truth. Indeed, to the drug addict, the successful drug treatment program is one that imposes stringent physical and emotional demands and is, therefore, an unappealing experience.

It is also a misconception that all drug users develop a dependency and therefore require drug treatment. Indeed, most people that use drugs do not become addicted the first time that they use them. For example, the casual drug user, one that uses drugs no more than once a month, does not really need drug treatment in order to stop using drugs. But a social (including governmental) climate of intolerance of drug use is an important ingredient in building a drug-free community.

The heroin or cocaine user that uses the drug once a week is a different story. This person may be able to ward off dependency alone but is more likely to require a treatment program than those users that fall in the once-a-month category. Still, there are others that are only persuaded by arrest and adjudication through the criminal justice system. Finally, there are those addicts that are physically and psychologically addicted to drugs and that genuinely require a formalized treatment program such as Narcotics Anonymous (NA).

Studies have been conducted over the past 25 years in hopes of identifying biological or personality factors to connect drug use to potential drug users. To date, there is no empirical evidence to show what type of person is the most likely candidate for drug use or addiction nor is there evidence as to which user can control his drug use and which cannot. In reality, many drug users make poor assessments as to their ability to tolerate the effects of drugs. In fact, they are often the last to realize that they are addicted.

The use-to-abuse cycle is one that slowly engulfs the drug user. For example, many addicts experience what could be termed a "honeymoon" of drug use early in their abuse cycle. Typically, this begins with the use of alcohol, cigarettes, and sometimes marijuana at a young age. The use-to-abuse cycle then expands over time to the use of harder, more effective drugs. The honeymoon stage may last several years and is usually a manageable period for the drug user. Once the potency of drugs and the instances of use increase, the honeymoon is over, and the user is well on his or her way to physical dependency.

Addressing the problem of treatment of drug abusers, former drug czar William Bennett stated in his 1989 National Drug Control Strategy:

> If our treatment system is to do the job required of it, the system must
> be expanded and improved. We need more treatment 'slots,' located

where the needs are, in programs designed to meet those needs. We must improve the effectiveness and the efficiency of treatment programs by holding them accountable for their performance. We must find ways to get more drug dependent people into treatment programs, through voluntary and, when necessary, involuntary means. And we need much better information about who is seeking treatment, who is not, and why.

Adding to the list of drug abuse misconceptions is the premise that addicts will eventually come to their senses and seek treatment. Several reasons can be identified as to why the addict avoids treatment. First, the addict by nature is one that has chosen to seek out the euphoric effects of drugs; he can logically be expected to prefer such effects to the demands of a formal treatment setting. Second, drug treatment by its very nature denies the addict his or her only real form of pleasure—drugs. Finally, because drug abuse usually involves ingesting illicit drugs, which are illegal to posses, many addicts fear that confidentiality will not be maintained and that local police may learn their identities.

It is a fact that many of the addicts that begin treatment programs eventually drop out of them and return to their drug abuse lifestyle on the street. Sometimes this is because the addict is lured back into drug abuse circles by associates. Additionally, it is sometimes because he hopes to "stay clean" for a period of time so that his drug tolerance goes down; smaller and cheaper amounts of drugs will then produce better "highs."

According to the Treatment Outcome Prospective Study (TOPS), a 1989 comprehensive study conducted at the Research Triangle Institute, one of every two addicts seeking treatment is doing so because of an encounter with the criminal justice system and not because of his or her personal desire to kick the habit. Ironically, another 1988 TOPS study supports a different notion—that those addicts required to undergo treatment by court order do as well as those that do so under their own volition. Such studies, therefore, support the role of the criminal justice system in drug treatment and control.

As mentioned, the drug addiction cycle is compounded by the common, socially accepted use of addicting drugs such as caffeine, alcohol, and nicotine. Regardless of the type of drug on which one becomes dependent, a treatment program must be identified. The immediate objectives of most treatment and rehabilitation programs can be generally characterized in three ways:

1. To control or eliminate drug abuse.
2. To give the drug user alternatives to his/her (drug-using) lifestyle.
3. To treat medical complications (both physical and psychological) associated with drug use.

Problems of drug abuse and addiction also prevail, in part, because such activity is a covert activity. Accordingly, drug use usually comes to the attention of the family and the community only when it has developed into either a personal or public problem.

Treatment Programs

Drug treatment is diverse, reflecting variations in types and severity of drug use, and in strategies to treat it. Most of the nation's 5,000 drug treatment programs fall under one of five broad categories: 1) detoxification programs, usually inpatient, which have the short-range goal of ending a user's physical addiction to substances; 2) chemical dependency units, primarily private inpatient or residential three-to-four week programs; 3) outpatient clinics, offering counseling and support for those that want to stop using drugs while they continue to work in the community; 4) methadone maintenance programs, which treat addicts by coupling counseling with the administration of methadone, a prescription medicine that blocks the craving for heroin while eliminating the usual pain of withdrawal; and 5) residential therapeutic communities, where users may spend up to 18 months in a highly structured program. To aid in the treatment process, there are support organizations such as Narcotics Anonymous, which will be discussed later in this chapter.

Detoxification

When treatment alternatives are considered, the term "detoxification" is frequently used. Detoxification is usually the first step of the treatment process and is designed to withdraw a patient slowly from his or her dependence on a particular drug. Its aim is to stabilize the heavy drug user until his body is relatively free of drugs. This process generally takes from 21 to 45 days and is best performed on an inpatient basis.

"Detox," in and of itself, is not considered a form of treatment. The distinction is that detoxification helps users get off drugs, while treatment helps them to stay off. Therefore, experts generally agree that the detoxification process does little good unless it is followed up by a sound treatment program.

Subsequent to the detoxification process, the patient is no longer physically addicted to the drug and, theoretically, is able to abstain from future use of the drug. Research suggests that there is no single method of detoxification that is considered effective in the treatment of all drug abusers. Detoxification procedures are therefore individualized to meet the needs of each patient.

A patient's susceptibility to this form of treatment depends on several variables. These include: the type of drug to which the patient is addicted, the degree of tolerance that has developed, and how long the patient has been dependent on the particular drug. Let us now look at some typical detoxification scenarios.

Heroin Detoxification. The detoxification process is often a futile one due to the instances of relapse by many addicts. For example, opiate drug addicts tend to have a high relapse rate because they return to their peer and social groups that are still involved in drug abuse. Methadone maintenance, discussed later in this chapter, is considered one of the more successful ways to accomplish the goal of detoxification.

Self treatment, or the "cold turkey" approach, is fairly common among drug addicts and is usually attempted at the addict's home. In some cases, this approach is undertaken in therapeutic communities or with the support of friends. In almost all cases, this type of detoxification is not successful.

Alcohol and Barbiturates. Detoxification or withdrawal from either alcohol or barbiturates is considered extremely dangerous and should be performed only under medical supervision. In this situation, withdrawal may not occur until several days after the last dose. With these two drugs, detoxification is usually accomplished by a physician administering increasingly smaller doses of the drug to the patient to ward off withdrawal symptoms.

Marijuana and Other Hallucinogens. Because these two categories of drugs are not physically addicting and there are no withdrawal symptoms, detoxification can usually be accomplished with little or no hospitalization.

Cocaine and Amphetamines. Of the two, cocaine poses the greatest challenge in treatment, primarily due to the addict's craving for the drug. So far, there are no proven successful treatment strategies comparable to those that have been developed for heroin addiction. Depression is common in the patient that is experiencing withdrawal from these drugs, and suicide attempts may become prevalent. Treatment for cocaine and amphetamines is not usually life threatening but can cause great discomfort for the patient.

Detoxification is a treatment process in which a patient is slowly with-drawn from dependence upon a particular drug.

Narcotic Antagonists

The term "narcotic antagonists" refers to a category of drugs that were developed as a treatment for heroin addiction but that do not produce physical dependence. These drugs, as the name implies, block or reverse the effects of drugs in the narcotic category.

Naloxone (Narcan), having no morphine-like effects, was removed from the CSA when it was introduced in 1971 as a specific antidote for narcotic poisoning. Nalorphine (Nalline), introduced into clinical medicine in 1951 and now under Schedule III, is termed a narcotic agonist-antagonist. In a drug-free individual, Nalorphine produces morphine-like effects, whereas in an individual under the influence of narcotics, it counteracts these effects. Another agonist-antagonist is pentazocine (Talwin). Introduced as an analgesic in 1967, it was determined to be an abusable drug and was placed under Schedule IV in 1979.

Figure 14.1

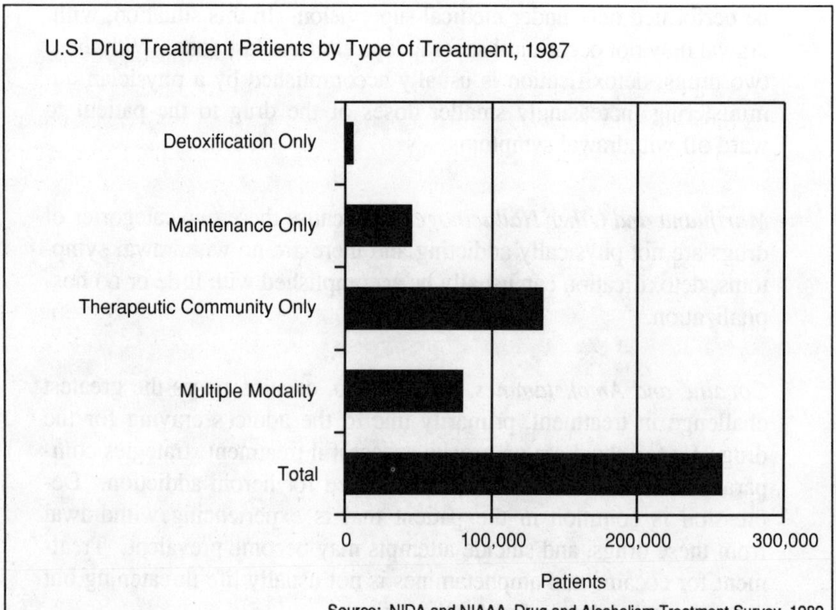

U.S. Drug Treatment Patients by Type of Treatment, 1987

Source: NIDA and NIAAA, Drug and Alcoholism Treatment Survey, 1989.

Maintenance (Substitute Therapy)

The term maintenance refers literally to maintaining a drug abuser on a particular type of drug for the purpose of helping him or her avoid the withdrawal syndrome. Opiate drug addiction, for example, is a common problem for many treatment programs because it is so widespread. Because there is a cross-tolerance and cross-dependence between all opiates, any of them can be used to eliminate withdrawal symptoms and to detoxify the addicted patient.

Methadone maintenance is the most common type of maintenance program. Methadone, a synthetic narcotic analgesic, was first introduced during World War II because of a shortage of morphine. It is an odorless, white crystalline powder that shares many of the same effects as morphine, but the two are structurally dissimilar. Methadone is best known for its use in the controversial methadone maintenance program that was introduced in 1964.

We cannot change the nature of the addict or addiction. We can help to change the old lie 'once an addict, always an addict' by striving to make recovery more available. God, help us remember this difference.

Narcotics Anonymous, 1987

The use of methadone in treatment of persons addicted to opiates has always been a controversial practice. The drug does have one distinct advantage over heroin—methadone is a longer-acting drug, requiring less frequent administering. Time-tested results of methadone maintenance reveal that those addicts that went through the program had much less criminal involvement and were better able to function within their communities.

As mentioned, the effects of methadone closely resemble the effects of morphine and heroin but fail to provide the user the euphoric effects caused by those two drugs. Methadone is also an extremely physically addicting drug—a fact that has created much of the controversy surrounding its use. Additionally, the effects of methadone differ from those of morphine. In particular, methadone has a longer duration of action, lasting up to 24 hours, thereby permitting the administration of the drug once a day as treatment for heroin addiction.

The program is structured so that the patient leaves a urine sample at the clinic, where the urine is tested for signs of morphine (heroin is excreted as morphine) and other drugs. Once the patient has demonstrated that he is responsible and is committed to rehabilitation, he is permitted to take a one-day supply of methadone. Later, the take-home dosage is increased to a three-day supply.

Detoxification is achieved through slowly reducing the amount of methadone mixture administered to the patient. Frequently, however, addicts find that their psychological dependence is more difficult to overcome than their physical dependence, and, therefore many addicts remain in the program for most of their lives.

The Psychological Approach

As with most psychoanalytic types of treatment, a lengthy commitment is generally required on the part of the patient. The role of the psychoanalyst in drug treatment is to try to identify certain repressed feelings in the patient that were experienced early in life and that may contribute to drug abuse. Once the feelings or thoughts are uncovered, they can be dealt with through traditional psychoanalytic methods. Studies have shown that the length of treatment ranges from a few weeks to several years, and that the success rate for recovery is marginal at best.

Group Treatment

Group therapy in drug treatment has demonstrated one of the highest success rates of any type of drug treatment program. Group treatment programs use an approach that creates an environment of personal interaction between peers. In theory, group interaction is more successful than the one-on-one interaction between the psychoanalyst and the patient. This is because the analyst often lacks a basic understanding of the drug abuse process and other variables that contribute to addiction. The analyst, therefore, often acts as a facilitator for the group.

The treatment group may be formed during different phases of addiction and treatment, and may involve not just the patients but their family and friends as well.

The Therapeutic Community

Therapeutic Communities (TCs) are designed to get patients to face the fact that they are addicted to drugs, and to promote change in their personalities so that they can live without drugs. TCs have been established in many communities and were originally modeled after the Maxwell Jones communities for psychiatric patients. The program relies on the equal participation by TC residents in decision making and program organization.

TYPES OF TREATMENT PROGRAMS

Outpatient Programs. Outpatient programs range from completely un-structured drop-in or teen rap centers located in store fronts to highly structured programs offering individual, group, and family therapy. Most outpatient programs provide basic individual counseling and re-quire that patients be self-motivated. Generally, the programs are small in size and serve between 20 and 30 clients.

Inpatient Programs. The inpatient programs for drug abusers are growing but are still relatively small in number. These programs pro-vide more intensive service for patients that require a controlled setting. Unlike some other drug treatment centers, some inpatient programs have lock-up wards, where patients cannot leave. Services provided include: diagnostic testing and evaluation, psychotherapy, group ther-apy, and counseling. The inpatient treatment program is generally the most expensive of the drug treatment plans, and because of this, is usually a shorter program in length.

The Halfway House. This is offered as an alternative for those that need to be housed in a location away from their own homes. Clients attend school or work during the day and return to the halfway house in the afternoon or evening, where they will eat and sleep. The halfway house is frequently used as a transition from a therapeutic community to the outside community or in conjunction with outpatient therapy.

One of the first TCs was founded in California in 1958 and was called Synanon. By the late 1970s, Synanon had become controversial and was no longer regarded as a treatment program. In spite of this, certain components of the original program were thought to be successful, therefore, the Synanon model remains one of the foundations of hundreds of TCs throughout the United States.

TCs, staffed by both former addicts and professionals, range in organiza-tion from the structured to the democratic . Each model usually attracts a par-ticular type of drug abuser. For instance, a person that is suffering from the use of hallucinogens and that is searching for "a new identity" usually desire a more democratic treatment environment. An opiate drug addict, on the other hand, that suffers severe social and personal problems and has an addiction fueled by attempts to avoid depression, usually requires a more structured treatment envi-ronment.

The majority of TCs are structured in a hierarchical manner and closely resemble concepts adopted by Phoenix House or Daytop Village in New York. These types of treatment centers, however, are more easily adapted to the intravenous drug user. The historic success of the TC is evidenced by fewer relapses into drug use, higher rates of abstinence, and a higher incidence of good self-image and job satisfaction.

Each member of the TC is given certain responsibilities and is expected to carry his or her own weight. House rules are imposed and are rigidly enforced. The TC staff uses a reward system, in which good behavior is rewarded through the assigning of more responsible duties at the TC. Bad behavior is dealt with through "learning experiences" such as the suspension of privileges.

The typical length of stay at a TC is anywhere from 6 to 24 months and may cost from $1,200 to $2,500 per month. Because of this, TCs experience an extremely high attrition rate, with 4 out of 5 patients dropping out or being expelled from the program. For those completing the program, however, the success rate is high. Generally, 4 out of 5 of those successfully completing the program remain drug-free for several years after treatment.

Narcotics Anonymous

Narcotics Anonymous (NA) is a drug treatment program that started in California in 1953. Since then NA has spread to all parts of the United States (and some foreign countries) and supports a World Service Office in Los Angeles that unifies its global efforts.

The NA program was adapted from Alcoholics Anonymous (AA), from which NA borrowed its twelve-step program for recovering addicts. The philosophy of NA basically says: if you want what we have to offer, and are willing to make the effort to get it, then you are ready to take certain steps. The NA group operates in a relatively unstructured manner, that is, it has regular meetings at specified places and times. The group members are required to follow the twelve steps and are duly registered with the World Service Office in Los Angeles.

The goal of the organization is to carry the message to the addict as well as to provide group members a chance to express themselves and hear the experiences of others. NA offers two types of meetings: open (to the general public) and closed (for addicts only).

The meetings vary in format from group to group, as some are participation meetings, some are question-and-answer sessions, some are meetings for the discussion of special problems, and some are a combination of some or all of these.

THE TWELVE STEPS OF NARCOTICS ANONYMOUS

1. We admitted that we were powerless over our addiction, that our lives had become unmanageable.

2. We came to believe that power greater than ourselves could restore us to sanity.

3. We made a decision to turn our will and our lives over to the care of God as we understood him.

4. We made a searching and a fearless moral inventory of ourselves.

5. We admitted to God, to ourselves, and to another human being the exact nature of our wrongs.

6. We were entirely ready to have God remove all these defects of character.

7. We humbly asked him to remove our shortcomings.

8. We made a list of all persons we had harmed, and became willing to make amends to them all.

9. We made direct amends to such people wherever possible, except to do so would injure others.

10. We continued to take personal inventory and when we were wrong, promptly admitted it.

11. We sought through prayer and meditation to improve our conscious contact with God as we understood him, praying only for knowledge of his will for us and the power to carry that out.

12. Having had spiritual awakening as a result of these steps, we tried to carry this message to addicts, and to practice these principles in all of our affairs.

Source: Narcotics Anonymous, 1987

Social Reintegration

This is the process whereby the benefits gained from treatment and rehabilitation are sustained and the drug user adapts to a drug-free, productive existence within the community. This can happen in several ways: he can return to his family; he can complete or further his education; he can learn new skills; he can become employed on a full-time or part-time basis; he can continue participation in self-help groups; or he can develop friendships in non-drug-using environments.

Statistics show that most drug addicts lack a formal education. In many cases, they drop out of high school, and when they attempt to get jobs, find themselves at a serious disadvantage. For those that do get jobs, frequently they are fired because of absenteeism due to drug abuse. Unemployment contributes to the drug-using cycle, and social reintegration then becomes difficult and sometimes impossible.

Halfway houses (mentioned above) were developed, in part, to help bridge the transition between drug abuse and reintegration back into the community. In these houses, residents have responsibility for their own lives—preparing food, cleaning their rooms, and managing their own money matters. In the houses, other members as well as therapeutic staff members offer the residents support and assistance in coping with the stress of learning to live independently.

Relapse

Over a period of years, drug misuse may be somewhat cyclical, and many people grow out of their drug dependence over time. Studies have revealed that even during the course of abusing drugs, periods of abstinence occur. It is not uncommon for drug users to drop out of the program prior to its completion. Programs, therefore, must be prepared to readmit patients that have dropped out so that those patients have an opportunity to achieve control over their own drug use.

Research has shown that many drug users experience a temporary relapse at the end of treatment and rehabilitation. In many cases, however, after a period of a few weeks or months, these same users often achieve long-term stability and, eventually, abstinence. This strongly suggests that treatment opportunities offered by rehabilitation and social reintegration can be an important means of reducing the demand for drugs at early stages of abuse.

Problems with Drug Treatment

Factors that complicate the treatment process are attributed to the fact that drug addiction has both psychological and physiological characteristics. This differs from diseases that are considered treatable through conventional medical methods.

One major logistical problem to overcome is the lack of treatment capacity. Many publicly-funded programs, particularly those in large cities, maintain long waiting lists. Obviously, if an addict realizes that he may not get treatment for several months, his drive to seek help may become greatly diminished.

It is an unfortunate fact that many treatment centers are not located in towns, cities, or neighborhoods where the need for treatment is greatest. Because of this, some programs have vacancies and others have waiting lists. Moreover, new drug treatment programs are difficult to begin, as funding is sometimes hard to secure and residents are frequently opposed to treatment centers being located in their neighborhoods.

Another problem in the drug treatment process is the soaring cost of health care. Drug treatment in the United States is a big business and accounts for millions of dollars in private, corporate, and insurance monies. For some employers, for example, costs of inpatient treatment may run as high as $1,000 a day for a 28-day treatment program.

Today, trends indicate that fewer patients are referred to inpatient care in lieu of the readily available, lower-cost outpatient programs. The dilemma becomes manifest when one tries to balance the cost of treatment with the quality of treatment—a frustrating and difficult task. Studies show that many people tend to gravitate toward "brand-name" hospitals or rehabilitation services, regardless of their recovery rate.

When searching for a treatment solution, drug counselors tend to look for variables such as whether the hospital is approved by the Joint Commission on Accreditation of Hospitals, the availability of extended outpatient aftercare, the quality of the staff, and the recovery rate of the institution.

As we have seen, many treatment programs exist for the drug dependent person. The best programs insist on a sound code of conduct, individual responsibility, personal sacrifice, and sanctions for misbehavior. The evidence is mounting to support the notion that when these elements exist, the best results are attained.

The Cost of Drug Treatment

When considering the great need for drug treatment programs, one should first consider that the largest proportion of drug addicts are white males between the ages of 18 and 40. Many such individuals have the financial means or health insurance with which to pay for treatment. At private institutions, where these addicts most commonly seek treatment, it is not uncommon to have vacancy rates of up to 45 percent.

Publicly supported facilities, however, were financially strapped during the 1970s and 1980s, and they were virtually unprepared for the great influx of addicts generated by the crack epidemic. Federal funding was increased in the late 1980s and early 1990s to compensate for this.

Figure 14.2

Counselor's Choice

These treatment centers were recommended by addiction counselors and directors of employee assistance programs at major corporations. The duration of treatment, and hence costs, can vary with the severity of the addiction. Note that some centers do not include the cost of detoxification and aftercare in the basic rate.

Treatment centers	Total beds	Typical stay (days)	Typical cost	Aftercare included in cost?	Seperate women's program?	Out-patient program?	Adoles-cent program?	When opened	Comments
The A.R.T.S. Passic, NJ 201-472-0364	24	28	$6,860[1]	no	no	yes	no	1980	Patients exposed to real-world, urban environment while in treatment.
Ashley Havre de Grace, Md 301-273-6600	60	30	7,500	yes	yes	yes[3]	no	1983	Special program for relapsed addicts.
Betty Ford Center at Eisenhower Rancho Mirage, Calif 800-392-7540 (Calif) 800-854-9211 (out of state)	80	28	5,500[1]	yes	no	yes	no	1982	Trying to play down celebrity image.
Chit Chat Treatment Centers Wernersville, Pa 215-678-2332	181	28	5,460[1]	yes	no	yes	yes[4]	1959	Emphasizes therapeutic approach, with patients helping each other recover.
Edgehill Newport Newport, RI 800-252-6466 (NY,NJ,New Eng) 401-849-5700 (outside NE)	160	30	7,200	no	yes	yes	no	1980	Concentrates on alcoholism but also treats multiple abuse.
Gateway Rehabilitation Center Aliquippa, Pa 800-472-1177 (Pa) 800-472-4488 (out of state)	90+	28	4,900[1]	no	yes	yes	no	1972	Teaches more effective coping techniques.
Goenold on Cape Cod Falmouth, Mass 617-540-6550	70	14	2,310[1]	no	yes	yes	yes	1982	Special program for hearing-impaired addicts; also 3-month inpatient program.
Hazelden Center City, Minn 612-257-4010, x3307 (Minn) 800-262-5010 (out of state)	400+	30	4,300	no	yes	yes	yes	1949	Pioneer of "Minnesota" model, involving individual, group and family therapy.
Koala Centers Nashville, Tenn 615-665-1144	700+	28	8,000	yes	yes	yes	yes	1970	Network of 34 centers in 10 states, mostly east of Mississippi.
Little Hill-Alina Lodge Blairstown, NJ 201-362-6114	60	4-5 mos	75/day[1]	no	yes[2]	no	no	1959	Primarily treats relapsed alcoholics, minimum stay 3-months; bans smoking, reading, phone calls.
Parkside Medical Services Park Ridge, Ill 312-698-4730	1,800	28	6,000-8,000	yes	yes	yes	yes	1959	Network of over 50 centers in 18 states nationwide.
Alcohol & Drug Treatment Center at Stanford Med Center Palo Alto, Calif 415-723-6682	14	13	5,400	no	no	yes	no	1977(o) 1986(i)	Short inpatient program, extensive outpatient care running as long as 1 year.

[1] Excludes detoxification. [2] Men and women follow the same program but are kept separate. [3] For participants in inpatient program only. [4] Outpatient only.
(o) = outpatient. (i) = inpatient

SOURCE: Forbes Magazine, 1987.

If a single variable were identified that most greatly impedes the improvement and expansion of treatment, it would be the lack of trained, qualified personnel. In many cities, salaries are often too low to attract or retain those with proper training. Indeed, many starting salaries for drug treatment counselors begin at or below $14,000 per year, a figure that is unrealistically low for a professional position. Although improvements are slowly being made in this area, it will be some time before the competency and responsibility of treatment meets the needs of most communities.

Drug Prevention

As former federal drug czar William Bennett stated in his National Drug Control Strategy: "[I]n the war against illegal drug use, the real heroes are not those who use drugs and quit; they are those who never use them in the first place." Thus, the goal of prevention is to insure that Americans, especially children, never begin the cycle of drug abuse, even through experimentation.

Unquestionably, drug prevention should begin in the home, with the parents of the potential drug user as the primary facilitators. After parents, school is probably the most effective place for the drug-education process to take place. School is where children spend a majority of their time and where they are subjected to peer groups. Additionally, it is school where first-time drug users frequently acquire their drugs.

Drug prevention strategists have identified two ways to influence whether an individual decides to use drugs. The first is to make him or her not want to use them, and the second is to impose severe penalties to convince would-be users that the consequences of drug abuse outweigh the advantages.

Drug prevention through education is designed to reach those not yet personally affected by drug abuse to inform people about the hazards of drugs, and to reduce curiosity about drugs. Studies have revealed, however, that addicts are more than familiar with the hazards of drug use, but that they minimize their likelihood of experiencing any difficulty. Prevention strategies, therefore, must address the potential first-time user as well as the hard-core addict.

One of the more disturbing trends revealed by surveys on drug abuse is the decline in the average age of first-time substance abusers. In numerous studies, substantial numbers of school-aged children have reported initiating the use of alcohol, tobacco, and marijuana by the time they reach junior high school.

Various prevention programs have been implemented to address this problem. It is widely held that programs in drug prevention should focus on building the self-esteem of young people, their decision-making skills, and their ability to resist peer pressure to use drugs. Two programs that have met with considerable success in this area are the DARE (Drug Abuse Resistance Education) program, which originated in Los Angeles, and the SPECDA (School Program to Educate and Control Drug Abuse) which began in New York City.

> ...The goal of drug prevention is to insure that Americans, in particular children, never begin the cycle of drug abuse, even through experimentation.

Project DARE

Project DARE began as a joint project between the Los Angeles Police Department and the Los Angeles Unified School District. The focus of the program is to equip fifth, sixth, and seventh grade children with the skills and motivation to resist peer pressure to use drugs, alcohol, and tobacco. A particularly innovative aspect of the program is the use of full-time, uniformed police officers as instructors. The officers are selected by DARE's supervisory staff.

The core curriculum consists of a 17-lesson program, each of which consists of a 45- to 60-minute lesson that teaches the children various self-management skills and techniques for resisting peer pressure. The focus of the training rests on the premise that children who feel positive about themselves will be more successful in resisting peer pressure. Other lessons emphasize the physical, mental, and social consequences of drug abuse, and others identify the different methods of coping with stress and having fun.

The scope of the 17-lesson DARE program core curriculum is outlined below:

1. *Practices for Personal Safety.* The students are acquainted with the role of the police officer and with how they can protect themselves from harm. The thrust of the lesson is to explain to the student the need for rules and laws designed to protect people from harm.

    The list of student rights, presented in a notebook provided to the students, is reviewed. These rights include the right to say no to another person that is trying to get you to do something wrong, the right to say no to someone that is trying to touch you in unacceptable ways, etc. Finally, the 911 emergency system is introduced to show the student how to summon help.

2. *Drug Use and Misuse.* This segment explains drugs to the students and discusses the definition of drugs and the positive and negative effects of drugs on the body and mind. A true/false quiz is then taken by each student that tests understanding of the les-

son. The word "consequences" is defined and studied in class, and the consequences of various actions are considered. The students are then asked to consider the consequences of using and not using drugs.

3. *Consequences.* Both negative and positive consequences of using drugs are discussed during this lesson. The students are required to fill out a work sheet that asks them to list positive and negative consequences of using marijuana and alcohol. The officer points out that those who try to persuade others to use drugs will emphasize positive consequences, leaving the many negative consequences unstated.

4. *Resisting Pressure to Use Drugs.* A key component to this lesson is introducing the students to the different types of peer pressure to take drugs that they may face. It teaches them to say no to such offers by considering the negative consequences of drug use. DARE instructors introduce four different sources of influence on people's behavior: personal preferences, family expectations, peer expectations, and the mass media. After defining "peer pressure," the DARE instructor explains different types of pressure that friends use to get others to use alcohol or drugs. These methods include threats and intimidation.

5. *Resistance Techniques: Ways to Say No.* This lesson reinforces the previous lesson by teaching students different ways to respond to peer pressure. Various techniques of resisting pressure are written on the chalkboard and discussed. These include: giving a reason or excuse, changing the subject, walking away, and ignoring the person.

The instructor also stresses that people can consciously avoid such confrontations by choosing to avoid hanging out with drug users. Because long-term consequences for not taking drugs are usually not as effective as citing short-term consequences, an emphasis is placed on explaining short-term consequences such as: "I don't like the taste."

6. *Building Self-Esteem.* In this lesson, DARE instructors discuss that self-esteem is created out of positive and negative feelings and experiences. Students learn to identify their own positive qualities. The students are taught that drug use stems from poor self-esteem and that those with high self-esteem think for them-

selves and have accepted their limitations as human beings. In
short, when people feel good about themselves, they can exert
control over their behavior.

PROJECT DARE: WAYS TO SAY NO

Saying "no thanks"	"Would you like a drink?" *"No thanks."*
Giving a reason or excuse	"Would you like a beer?" *"No thanks, I don't like the taste."*
"Broken record" or saying no as many times as necessary	"Would you like a hit?" *"No thanks."* "Come on." *"No thanks."* "Just try it." *"No thanks."*
Walking away	"Do you want to try some marijuana?" **Say no and walk away while saying it.**
Changing the subject	"Lets smoke some marijuana." *"I hear there is a new video game at the arcade."*
Avoid the situation	**If you know of places where people use drugs, stay away from those places.** **If you pass them on the way home, go the other way.**
Cold shoulder	"Do you want a beer?" **Just ignore the person.**
Strength in numbers	**Hang around with nonusers, especially where drug use is expected.**

---

7. *Assertiveness: A Response Style.* Assertiveness is taught as a
    technique to refuse offers of drugs. The lesson begins with the
    DARE officer asking the class what occurrences happened during
    the previous week to heighten their self-esteem. It is then em-
    phasized that once a person achieves self-esteem, then he can
    more easily think for himself without being pressured to do what
    he believes is wrong.

The word "assertive" is then defined and discussed, and it is stressed that people should learn how to assert their rights confidently without interfering with the rights of others. Role playing is then developed, where each student has a partner and good assertive styles are practiced (good posture, strong voice, eye contact, calm manner, etc.).

8. *Managing Stress Without Taking Drugs.* This step helps students recognize stress in their lives and how to relieve it without taking drugs. The "fight or flight" response to danger is discussed with the students along with the physiological changes that accompany that response. It is noted that modern-day stressors such as taking a test fail to provide the individual with a means to "flee" or "fight," and alternative ways of coping with stress must be learned.

Students then work in groups and devise ways of dealing with two types of stressors (from a class list) in their lives. Strategies are then shared with the rest of the class and are discussed. Many such methods include ways to relax and exercise, talk out problems with a family member or a friend, and so on.

9. *Media Influences on Drug Use.* This lesson focuses on ways to resist media influences to use alcohol and drugs. Various advertising strategies to promote certain products are discussed, and the DARE instructor tries to explain how to see through the strategies. For example, by showing a product being used by people that are enjoying themselves, the advertiser suggests that people that actually use the product will indeed have more fun.

The students then work in groups to create an anti-alcohol or anti-drug commercial while using the techniques employed by professional advertisers. Each group then performs their own commercial before the class.

10. *Decision Making and Risk Taking.* The objective of this lesson is to teach students to apply decision-making skills in evaluating the results of various kinds of risk-taking behavior, including drug use. First, the class generates a list of risk-taking behaviors, including the many everyday types of risks commonly encountered. Although many risks are worth taking (e.g., making new

friends, trying out for a play, etc.), many are not and can result in harm (e.g., swallowing an unknown substance, riding with a drunk driver, etc.)

The students are taught that any assumption of risk involves a choice. The choices that we make are influenced by several factors, including family, friends, the mass media, and personal values. The key to intelligent decision making is to think through the likely outcomes of various alternative actions.

11. *Alternatives to Drug Abuse.* This lesson examines rewarding alternative activities that do not involve taking drugs. Students are asked to remember the reasons why people take drugs and what basic needs people have. They are then reminded that these needs can be met in healthier ways than taking drugs (such as playing games or exercising).

    The students then fill out a work sheet titled: "What I like to do." In this exercise, students write down their favorite activities and explain to the class why these are better than taking drugs.

12. *Role Modeling.* This phase involves older students that have resisted peer pressure to use drugs. These students are brought into the room as role models. The younger students then ask the older students questions that they previously prepared.

13. *Forming a Support System.* Students are shown in this lesson that positive relationships with different people create a support system for the student. In this lesson, two fundamental questions are posed: Why do people need other people? What do other people do for us? The DARE instructor explains that everyone has needs that can only be met through positive relationships with other people.

    The students then complete a work sheet titled "Choosing Friends," which requires them to indicate what qualities they look for in friends (e.g., people that are honest with me, people that won't get me into trouble, etc.). When they are finished, students share their responses and discuss barriers to friendship and how to overcome them.

14. *Ways to Deal with Pressure from Gangs.* In this lesson, students learn how to deal with pressure put on them from gangs and how to evaluate choices available to them. The students begin with naming the social activities that they most enjoy and with whom they like to share these activities. These relationships help satisfy needs for recognition, acceptance, and affection. It is also recognized that people join gangs to satisfy these same needs.

Students are made aware that gangs use strong-arm tactics to get what they want. The students are then taught to cope with bullying and intimidation by first avoiding places where gangs hang out and by leaving money or other valuables at home. Other techniques include keeping busy with constructive activities that meet the needs for friendship and love.

15. *Project DARE Summary.* This lesson is a summary of what the student should have learned through Project DARE. The class is divided into competing teams, and the officer reads a series of questions about DARE, giving each team an opportunity to earn points for each correct answer. Scores are then computed, and a winner is announced. Each student then individually completes a true/false questionnaire titled "What do you know about drugs?" The officer reviews the answers.

16. *Taking a Stand.* As homework, students must complete a work sheet, "Taking a stand," which asks them to articulate how they will (1) keep their body healthy, (2) control their feelings when angry or under stress, (3) decide whether to take a risk, (4) respond when a friend pressures them to use drugs or alcohol, and (5) respond when they see people on television using drugs or alcohol. This document represents the student's DARE Pledge. Then, every student reads their pledge before the class, and whichever student's pledge is voted the best, that student reads his pledge before the class assembly the following week.

17. *DARE Culmination.* The winning DARE pledge is read in front of a school assembly by its author. Each student that completed the DARE curriculum receives a certificate of achievement signed by the Chief of Police and the Superintendent of Schools.

Project SPECDA

Project SPECDA originated in New York and parallels Project DARE in principle. It is a collaborative project by the city's Police Department and Board of Education and offers students a 16-session curriculum, with the units split between fifth and sixth grade. Like DARE, SPECDA makes students aware of the social pressures that cause drug abuse and teaches acceptable methods of resisting peer pressure to experiment with drugs.

The program involves weekly 45-minute classes taught by SPECDA instructional teams, which are composed of a full-time police officer and a drug counselor employed by the schools. SPECDA is described as a two-track program that also includes the participation of the Police Department's Narcotics Division. In the program, detectives within the Narcotics Division intensify efforts to increase drug arrests and concurrently attempt to close "smoke shops" located within a two-block area of each school.

CLOSE-UP: THE SPECDA PROGRAM

Police officer Ronald Cato of New York City's SPECDA unit greets the sixth grade class at Our Lady of Miracles School with a big grin. Cato is a large man, powerfully built, but the students sense immediately that he is warm, accessible, and that he genuinely cares about what happens to them.

The children, a New York mix of black, brown, yellow, and white, are primly dressed in clean school uniforms. The teacher, a middle-aged nun with spectacles, stands in the back, watching approvingly.

"How many of you know someone who uses drugs?" Officer Cato asks the class.

Several students raise their hands.

"And how many of you have been offered drugs?" he continues. He counts the outstretched arms.

Out of 25 students, eight—nearly one-third—say that they already have had to make a choice about whether to use drugs.

No hint of surprise crosses Officer Cato's face. He pauses a moment and then begins his lesson. He wants to reach these children and hopes to arrest the demand for drugs.

Source: The National Institute of Justice, Arresting the Demand for Drugs, November 1987.

A SPECDA pilot program was evaluated in April 1985 by the Criminal Justice Center of the John Jay College of Criminal Justice. Researchers in the study obtained information from classroom observations, interviews, and pre- and post-test questionnaires. The findings of this study include:

1. SPECDA students showed significant gains in factual knowledge about drugs and the nature and scope of drug abuse. Most important, SPECDA students expressed a greater awareness of the risks of drug use, including one-time or occasional use, and of the role that peer pressure plays in drug abuse.

2. At the conclusion of the pilot program, SPECDA students showed strong positive attitudes toward SPECDA police officers and drug counselors, though not toward police officers in general.

3. On both the pre- and post-test questionnaires, students asserted that they were unlikely to use drugs within the next year. A majority of the students that were interviewed volunteered that SPECDA had strengthened their resolve to become or remain drug-free.

Prevention programs such as DARE and SPECDA have clearly demonstrated the need for drug abuse education in the early years of a child's development. As of the preparation of this text, educators are constructing programs in which children at all levels of schooling will experience drug sensitivity education that is being developed for all levels of pre- and post-secondary school years.

Summary

There are many ways to deal with drug abuse in our society. Because of the social dangers of drug abuse, more and more attention is being given to this critical issue. The immediate objectives of most treatment programs are to control or eliminate drug abuse, give the drug user alternatives for his or her lifestyle, and treat medical complications associated with drug use.

Treatment programs include detoxification, chemical dependency units, outpatient clinics, methadone maintenance programs, and residential therapeutic communities. After treatment, social reintegration is an important step in making the patient a productive member of the community. The halfway house is often used for this purpose; it permits members to assume certain responsibilities in maintaining the operation of the house.

Drug prevention is another essential component to fighting drug abuse. The two ways to achieve the drug prevention goal are to make potential first-time users not want to use drugs and to impose severe criminal penalties to deter first-time drug abuse. Prevention Project's DARE and SPECDA are both designed to focus on children and teach them certain fundamental basics of individual thinking, decision making, and personal choices when faced with the prospect of using illicit drugs.

DISCUSSION QUESTIONS

1. List the three ways that treatment and rehabilitation programs are generally characterized.

2. List the five categories of drug treatment.

3. Describe the detoxification process and its role in drug treatment.

4. How does the methadone maintenance program serve the treatment of opiate drug addicts?

5. How does the therapeutic community program treat drug addicts?

6. What are some problems with drug treatment in our communities?

7. Discuss some of the factors that drug treatment counselors look for when recommending a treatment facility for an addicted person.

8. List the two goals of drug prevention.

9. Discuss how Project's DARE and SPECDA function and why they are so successful.

DISCUSSION QUESTIONS

1. Give the time when inbreeding should be practiced and when it should be avoided.

2. State four advantages of cross-breeding.

3. Describe the several ways in which heredity relates to disease resistance.

4. How does the immunization program serve the prevention of animal disease?

5. How does the therapeutic immunity program treat animal disease?

6. What are some problems with immunization in our communities?

7. Discuss some of the reasons that must be taken into account for fear when recommending management help for sick animals.

8. What are the two goals of drug prevention.

9. Discuss how Programs DARE and START improve health and why they are successful.

CONCLUSION

Perhaps it can be generalized that the two most perplexing aspects of our drug problem are that it is so widespread and that it affects the lives of so many. Because the problem is so widespread, many people are quick to formulate opinions through "armchair quarterbacking," and pass judgments on how best to solve it. Although a diversified and subjective study of the problem has its virtues, true solutions may only be obtainable through an objective, systematic analysis of relevant facts and circumstances. Hopefully, this text has proffered sufficient information for such an analysis.

In September 1989, when Colombia's President Barco requested military advisers and equipment from the United States to assist in that country's drug war, many people criticized the gesture, claiming that it was an inappropriate use of U.S. military puissance. Indeed, some feared that this might even spark another world war. The action was met with cries that we did not need another war such as Vietnam.

Perhaps we should consider that war is already upon us. Like Pearl Harbor, many of our neighborhoods have already been invaded; mass murders of police, judges, journalists, and citizens closely parallel Nazi Germany's purge of thousands of decent, innocent human beings; and drive-by shootings in growing numbers of cities are reminiscent of military combat on numerous bloody battlefields throughout history.

No, military intervention may not be the answer. Certainly no single solution discussed in this text is the answer. The solution to the drug problem, like seeking a cure for a disease, must begin with an understanding of the problem. It also requires that governments, states, and neighborhoods all work together, not against each other, in furtherance of a resolution. Too much time has already been lost to the chaos, the uncertainty, and the coinciding terror.

There are those who query: what is it then, that I can possibly do to fight a problem that has conquered governments and succeeded in ruining millions of lives? Maybe therein lies the problem. Although none of us has the power to govern international problems, we all have control over our immediate lives and our destiny, that is, control over our own "corner of the world."

Let us hope that someday very soon each of us will realize that this is indeed "our" world—our only world. These are our neighborhoods and our

403

homes. These are our children, our own flesh and blood, and tomorrow's future. Let us look around and find our own corner of the world, wherever it is, however small. Let us fight for, and protect that corner, whether it is our house, our community, our family, or whatever. For if we give up and wave the white flag, these days of suffering and ruined lives will be remembered as the "good old days," because we will then be the conquered and drugs and drug abuse will be the victor.

REFERENCES

Abadinsky, H. (1985). *Organized Crime*, 2d ed. Chicago: Nelson Hall.

_____ (1989). *Drug Abuse: An Introduction*. Chicago: Nelson Hall.

Adler, P.A. (1985). *Wheeling and Dealing: An Ethnography of an Upper Level Drug-Dealing and Smuggling Community*. New York: Columbia University Press.

Albini, J.L. (1971). *The American Mafia: Genesis of a Legend*. New York: Doubleday & Co.

Allen, H. and R. Kaiser (1987). "The Age of Aquarius Grows Up." *The Columbia Daily Tribune* (Nov.): 16.

Alexander, S. (1988). *The Pizza Connection: Lawyers, Money, Drugs and Mafia*. New York: Weidenfeld and Nicolson.

Anderson, J. (1989). "Narcs Risk their Lives Daily to Battle Drug Scourge." *The Columbia Daily Tribune* (May 23): 6.

Anderson, J. and D. Van Atta (1988). "The Medellin Cartel/M-19 Gang." *The Washington Post* (August 28): 87.

Arlachhi, P. (1986). *Mafia Business: The Mafia and the Spirit of Capitalism*. London: Verso.

Ashley, R. (1975). *Cocaine: Its History, Use, and Effects*. New York: St. Martin's Press.

Backer, T.E. (1987). *Planning for Workplace Drug Abuse Programs*. Washington, DC: National Instiutute on Drug Abuse.

Bagley, B.M. (1988). "Colombia and the War on Drugs." *Foreign Affairs* (Fall)..

Bakalar, J.B. and L. Grinspoon (1988). *Drug Control in a Free Society*. Cambridge: Cambridge University Press.

Barrett, R.E. (1987). "Curing the Drug-Law Addiction: The Harmful Side Effects of Legal Prohibition." In R. Hamowy, *Dealing with Drugs: Consequences of Government Control*. Lexington, Massachusetts: D.C. Heath.

Beaty, J. and R. Hornik (1989). "A Torrent of Dirty Dollars." *Time* (December 18):50-56.

Bell, R. (1987). Toward a Drug Free America. *Challenge News Letter*. National Drug Policy Board (March).

Birdsong, C. (1986). "Why Atheletes Use Drugs," *American Pharmacy* NS26, 11 (November).

Bonnie, R.J. (1980). *Marijuana Use and Criminal Sanctions.* Charlottesville, VA: Michie Co.

Bonnie, R.J. and C.H. Whitebread, II (1980). "The Forbidden Fruit and the Tree of Knowledge: An Inquiry into the Legal History of American Marijuana Prohibition." *Virginia Law Review* 56 (Oct.): 971-1203.

Bradley, B. (1988). "Drug Suspicions Follow Officials in High Places." *The Christian Science Monitor* (February 26): 17.

Brecher, E.M. and the Editors of Consumer Reports (1972). *Licit and Illicit Drugs.* Boston, MA: Little, Brown.

Bureau of Justice Assistance (1987). *Report on Drug Control.* Washington, DC: U.S. Department of Justice, Office of Justice Programs.

Bureau of Justice Statistics (1983). *Prisoners and Drugs.* Washington, DC: U.S. Department of Justice.

_____ (1986). *Drug Use and Crime: State Prison Inmate Survey.* Washington, DC: U.S. Department of Justice.

_____ (1987). *Drug Use Forecasting.* Washington, DC: U.S. Department of Justice.

_____ (1987). *Report on Drug Control.* Washington, DC: U.S. Department of Justice.

_____ (1989). *BJS Data Report.* Washington, DC: U.S. Department of Justice.

Byron, W.J. (1989). "There's More Behind Drug Abuse Than Boredom." *The Kansas City Star* (June 4): G6.

Carver, J. (1986). *Drugs and Crime: Controlling Use and Reducing Risk Through Testing.* Washington, DC: National Institute of Justice, U.S. Government Printing Office.

Chambliss, W.J. (1971). "Vice, Corruption, Bureaucracy, and Power." *Wisconsin Law Review* 4.

Cockburn, L. (1987). *Out of Control: The Story of the Reagan Administration's Secret War in Nicaragua, the Illegal Arms Pipeline, and the Contra Drug Connection.* New York: Entrekin/Atlantic Monthly Press.

Corcoran, David (1989). "Legalizing Drugs: Failures Spur Debate." *New York Times* (Novermber 27): A15.

Department of Health and Human Services (1988). "Mandatory Guidelines for Federal Workplace Testing Programs, Final Guidelines Notice." *Federal Register* 53, 69 (April 11).

Drug Enforcement Administration (1984). *Domestic Marijuana Trafficking.* Special Intelligence Report, Office of Intelligence. Washington, DC: U.S. Department of Justice.

_____ (1985). *Drug Enforcement Administration Booklet.* (Summer). Washington, DC: U.S. Department of Justice.

Duster, T. (1970). *The Legislation of Morality: Law, Drugs, and Moral Judgement.* New York: Free Press.

Engelberg, S. (1988). "Nicaraguan Rebels Tell of Drug Deal." *New York Times* (April 8)., L6.

Epstein, E.J. (1977). *Agency of Fear: Opiates and Political Power in America.* New York: Putnam's.

Federal Government Information Technology (1985). *Electronic Surveillance and Civil Liberties.* Washington, DC: Congress of the United States, Office of Technology Assessment.

Fogarty, K. (1986). "Parents Who Use Drugs." *The Columbia Missourian* (October 26): C1.

Gardiner, J.A. (1970). *The Politics of Corruption: Organized Crime in an American City.* New York: Russell Sage Foundation.

Goldstein, P. (1985). "The Drugs/Violence Nexus: A Tripartite Conceptual Framework." *Journal of Drug Issues* 15 (Fall): 493-506.

Goode, E. (1972). *Drugs in American Society.* New York: Knopf.

Greenhouse, L. (1989). "High Court Backs Airport Detention Based on 'Profile.'" *The New York Times* (April 4) A1.

Grimes, C. (1990). "Details Given on Noriega's Surrender." *St. Louis Post Dispatch* (January 5): A14.

Grinspoon, L. (1987). "Cancer Patients Should Get Marijuana." *New York Times* (July 18): 23.

Grinspoon, L. and J.B. Bakalar (1985). *Cocaine: A Drug and Its Social Evolution,* rev. ed. New York: Basic Books.

Grinspoon, L. and J. Laszlo (1988). "Should Cancer Patients Smoke Marijuana to Limit Nausea?" *Physicians Weekly* (June).

Gropper, B. (1985). *Probing the Links Bteween Drugs and Crime.* Washington, DC: National Institute of Justice, U.S. Government Printing Office.

Gugliotta, G. and J. Leen (1989). *Kings of Cocaine.* New York: Simon and Schuster.

Gusfield, J.R. (1963). *Symbolic Crusade: Status Politics and the American Temperance Movement.* Urbana, Illinois: University of Illinois Press.

Hamowy, R., ed. (1987). *Dealing With Drugs: Consequences of Government Control.* Lexington, Massachusetts: D.C. Heath.

Hayslip, D.W., Jr. (1989). *Local-level Drug Enforcement: New Strategies.* Washington, DC: National Institute of Justice.

Helmer, J. (1975). *Drugs and Minority Oppression.* New York: Seabury Press.

Henningfield, J.E. (1989). *Insight Magazine* (May 9): 53.

Ianni, F.A.J. (1972). *A Family Business: Kinship and Social Control in Organized Crime.* New York: Russell Sage Foundation.

_____ (1974). *Black Mafia: Ethnic Succession in Organized Crime.* New York: Simon and Schuster.

Innes, C.A. (1986). *Drug Use and Crime.* Washington, DC: Bureau of Justice Statistics, Department of Justice: U.S. Government Printing Office.

International Association for the Study of Organized Crime (1989). *Criminal Organizations,* 4,2.

Inciardi, J.A. (1986). *The War on Drugs: Heroin, Cocaine, Crime and Public Policy.* Palo Alto, CA: Mayfield Publishing Co.

Isikoff, M. (1988). "'Zero Tolerance' Held in Low Regard." *The Washington Post* (July 13): A18.

Jaschik, S. (1990). "Scholars Are Irked by Bennett Speech Criticizing Their Approaches to Nation's Drug Problems." *Chronicle of Higher Education* (January 3): 1.

Jones, H.B. (1985). *What the Practicing Physician Should Know About Marijuana.* Narcotic Educational Foundation of America. Washington, DC: U.S. Department of Justice/Drug Enforcement Administration.

Kaut, S. (1989). "Addicts Drawn to Life of Crime to Support Drug Habits." *The Kansas City Star* (February 5): A14.

Kleiman, M. (1985). "Drug Enforcement and Organized Crime." In *Politics and Economics of Organized Crime,* Lexington, Massachusetts: D.C. Heath.

Klein, M. (1971). "Violence in American Juvenile Gangs." In D. Mulvihill and M. Tumin with L. Curtis, (eds.) *Crimes of Violence.* National Commission on the Causes and Prevention of Violence, Vol. 13. Washington, DC: U.S. Government Printing Office.

Lamar, J. (1988). "Kids Who Sell Crack." *Time* (May): 20.

Levins, H. (1980). *The Kabul Connection.* Philadelphia (Aug.): 114- 120; 192-203.

Lyman, M.D. (1987). *Narcotics and Crime Control.* Springfield, Illinois: Charles C Thomas Publishing Co.

_____ (1989). *Gangland: Drug Trafficking by Organized Criminals.* Springfield, Illinois: Charles C Thomas Publishing Co.

_____ (1989). *Practical Drug Enforcement: Procedure and Administration.* New York: Elsevier Publishing Co., Inc.

Marriott, M. (1989). "Drug Needle Exchange is Gaining but Still Under Fire." *The New York Times* (June 7): B1.

Marshall, J. (1987). "Drugs and United States Foreign Policy." In R. Hamowy (ed.), *Dealing with Drugs: Consequences of Government Control.* Lexington, Massachusetts: D.C. Heath.

Massing, M. (1990). "U.S. On Full Drug War Footing." *Kansas City Star* (January 28): G3.

Mastrofski, S. and G. Potter (1987). "Controlling Organized Crime: A Critique of Law Enforcement Policy." *Criminal Justice Policy Review* 2, 3: 269-301.

McCoy, A.W. (1972). *The Politics of Heroin in Southeast Asia.* New York: Harper and Row.

Mieczkowski, T. (1986). "Geeking Up and Throwing Down: Heroin Street Life in Detroit." *Criminology* 24 (Nov.): 645-666.

Miller, N. (1988). *Toward a Drug Free America.* The National Drug Policy Board (March).

Mills, J. (1986). *The Underground Empire.* New York: Dell.

Mirkin, G. and M. Hoffman (1978). "Drugs: Is the Prize Worth the Price?" *The Sportsmedicine Book.* Canada: Little, Brown & Co.

Mintz, J. and V. Churchville (1987). "Vice Officers Walk the Line Between Crime and the Law, In Drug World Integrity Easily Eroded." *The Washington Post.*

Moody J. (1989). "Nobel Battle, Terrible Toll." *Time* (December 18): 33.

Musto, D. (1973). *The American Disease: Origins of Narcotic Control.* New Haven: Yale University Press.

Nadelmann, E.A. (1989). "Drug Prohibition in the United States: Cost, Consequences, and Alternatives." *Science* 245 (Sept. 1): 939- 947.

_____ (1988). "U.S. Drug Policy: A Bad Export." *Foreign Policy* 70 (Spring): 83-108.

National Criminal Justice Association Newsletter (1988). Washington, DC: National Criminal Justice Association (January).

National Drug Policy Board (1988). *Toward A Drug Free America.* Washington, DC: U.S. Government Printing Office.

National Institute of Justice (1987). *Drug Testing, Crime File Study Guide.* Washington, DC: National Institute of Justice.

_____ (1987). *Issues and Practices: Arresting the Demand for Drugs: Police and School Partnerships to Prevent Drug Abuse.* Washington, DC: National Institute of Justice.

_____ (1987). *Issues and Practices: Aids and the Law Enforcement Officer: Concerns and Policy Responses.* Washington, DC: U.S. Department of Justice, Office of Communication and Research Utilization.

_____ (1987). *Major Issues in Organized Crime: A Compendium of Papers Presented by Experts in the Field.* Washington, DC: National Institute of Justice.

_____ (1988). *Attorney General Announces NIJ Drug Use Forecasting System.* Washington, DC: U.S. Department of Justice, U.S. Government Printing Office.

National Institute on Drug Abuse (1982). "Drug Taking Among the Elderly." *Treatment Research Report.* Washington, DC: U.S. Department of Health and Human Services.

_____ (1983). "Women and Drugs." *Research Issues* 31. Washington, DC: U.S. Department of Health and Human Services.

_____ (1985). "Effects of Drugs on Driving, Driver Simulator Tests of Secobarital, Diazepam, Marijuana, and Alcohol." *Clinical and Behavioral Pharmacology Research Report.* Washington, DC: U.S. Department of Health and Human Services.

_____ (1985). *Treatment Services for Adolescent Substance Abusers.* Washington, DC: U.S. Department of Health and Human Services.

_____ (1986). *National Trends in Drug Use and Related Factors Among American High School Students and Young Adults, 1975-1986.* Washington, DC: U.S. Department of Health and Human Services.

_____ (1986). *Urine Testing for Drugs of Abuse*, Research 73, Monograph Series. Washington, DC: U.S Department of Health and Human Services.

Nelli, H. (1976). *The Business of Crime: Italian and Syndicate Crime in the United States.* New York: Oxford University Press.

O'Brien, R. and S. Cohen (1984). *The Encyclopedia of Drug Abuse.* Facts on File.

Pennsylvania Crime Commission (1980). *A Decade of Organized Crime, 1980 Report.* St. David's, Pennsylvania: The Commonwealth of Pennsylvania.

Permanent Subcommittee on Investigations, Committee on Governmental Affairs (1983). Crime and Secrecy: The Use of Offshore Banks and Companies. Washington, DC: 98th Congress, 1st Session, U.S. Senate.

Post, M. (1990). "Colombian Crime and Cocaine Trafficking." *The Narc Officer*, (December): 11.

Potter, G., L. Gaines and B. Holbrook (1990). "Blowing Smoke: An Evaluation of Marijuana Eradication in Kentucky." *American Journal of Police* IX, 1: 97-116.

Potter, G. and P. Jenkins (1985). *The City and the Syndicate: Organizing Crime in Philadelphia*. Lexington, Massachusetts: Ginn Press.

President's Commission on Organized Crime (PCOC). (1986). *America's Habit: Drug Abuse, Drug Trafficking and Organized Crime*. Washington, DC: U.S. Government Printing Office.

_____ (1986). *The Edge: Organized Crime, Business and Labor Unions*. Washington, DC: U.S. Government Printing Office.

_____ (1985). *Organized Crime and Heroin Trafficking*. Washington, DC: U.S. Government Printing Office.

_____ (1984). *Organized Crime and Cocaine Trafficking*. Washington, DC: U.S. Government Printing Office.

_____ (1984). *The Cash Connection: Organized Crime, Financial Institutions and Money Laundering*. Washington, DC: U.S. Government Printing Office.

Rangel, C. (1986). *The Crack Cocaine Crisis*. Committee on Narcotics Abuse and Control, 99th Congress, Joint Hearing.

Raspberry, W. (1988). "Living and Dying Like Animals." *The Washington Post* (November 2): A21.

Reuter, P. (1983). *Disorganized Crime: The Economics of the Visible Hand*. Cambridge: MIT Press.

Reuter, P., G. Crawford and J. Cace (1988). *Sealing the Borders: the Effects of Increased Military Participation in Drug Interdiction*. (January) (R-3594-USDP). Santa Monica, California: The RAND Corporation.

Riding, A. (1988). "Intimidated Colombian Courts Yield to Drug Barons." *The New York Times*. (January 11): A3.

Rinehart, R. et al. (1981). *Thailand: A Country Study*. Washington, DC: U.S. Government Printing Office.

Robbins, C.A. (1989). "Bloody Footprints on Peru's Shining Path." *U.S. News and World Report* (September 18): 49.

Schmoke, K.L. (1988). "Get Your Heads Out of the Sand." *USA Today* (May).

Select Committee on Narcotics Abuse and Control (1986). *The Crack Crisis*. Joint Hearing, 99th Congress, Second Edition, July.

Shannon, E. (1989). *Desperados: Latin Drug Lords, U.S. Lawmen, and the War America Can't Win*. New York: Viking Penguin, Inc.

Smith, D.C. Jr. (1975). *The Mafia Mystique*. New York: Basic Books.

Smith, R.N. (1986). "The Plague Among Us." *Newsweek* (June 16): 15.

Stellwagen, L.D. (1985). *Use of Forfeiture Sanctions in Drug Cases.* Washington, DC: National Institute of Justice, U.S. Government Printing Office.

Szasz, T. (1974). *Ceremonial Justice: The Ritual Persecution of Drug Addicts and Pushers.* Garden City, New York: Doubleday.

Toborg, M.A. and M.P. Kirby (1984). Drug Use and Pretrial Crime in the District of Columbia. *Research in Brief.* Washington, DC: National Institute of Justice.

Thrasher, F.M. (1927). *The Gang.* Chicago, IL: University of Chicago Press.

Trebach, A. and E. Englesman (1989). "Why Not Decriminalize?" *New Perspectives Quarterly* 6, 2 (Summer): 40-45.

Trebach, Arnold (1987). *The Great Drug War: Radical Proposals That Could Make America Safe Again.* New York: Macmillan.

_____ (1982). *The Heroin Solution.* New Haven: Yale University Press.

United States Department of Justice (1978). "The Investigation of Nicky Barnes." *Drug Enforcement Magazine* (July).

_____ (1983). Investigation and Prosecution of Illegal Money Laundering. Narcotic and Dangerous Drug Section Monograph, *A Guide to the Bank Secrecy Act*: Washington, DC: U.S. Government Printing Office.

_____ (1986). Black Tar Heroin. *Special Report.* Washington, DC: U.S. Department of Justice, Office of Intelligence.

_____ (1988). *Intelligence Trends Special Report: From the Source to the Street.* Vol. 1. Washington, DC: U.S. Department of Justice.

_____ (1988). *Drugs of Abuse.* Washington, DC: U.S. Department of Justice.

U.S. Department of the Treasury (1987). *Anti-Drug Law Enforcement Efforts and Their Impact.* (August). Washington, DC: U.S. Customs Service.

Wagner, J.C. (1987). "Substance-Abuse Policies and Guidelines in Amateur and Professional Atheltics." *American Journal of Hospital Pharmacy* 44 (February).

White, P.T. (1989). "Coca: An Ancient Indian Herb Turns Deadly." *National Geographic Magazine* 175, 1 (January).

White House, The (1989). *National Drug Control Strategy* (September). Washington, DC: U.S. Government Printing Office.

Wisotsky, S. (1987). *Breaking the Impasse in the War on Drugs.* Westport, Connecticut: Greenwood.

Yablonsky, L. (1966). *The Violent Gang.* Baltimore, MD: Penguin Books.

Zinberg, N.E. (1984). *Drug, Set, and Setting: The Basis for Controlled Intoxicant Use.* New Haven: Yale University Press.

INDEX